No Country for Nonconforming Women
Feminine Conceptions of Lusophone Africa

LEGENDA

LEGENDA is the Modern Humanities Research Association's book imprint for new research in the Humanities. Founded in 1995 by Malcolm Bowie and others within the University of Oxford, Legenda has always been a collaborative publishing enterprise, directly governed by scholars. The Modern Humanities Research Association (MHRA) joined this collaboration in 1998, became half-owner in 2004, in partnership with Maney Publishing and then Routledge, and has since 2016 been sole owner. Titles range from medieval texts to contemporary cinema and form a widely comparative view of the modern humanities, including works on Arabic, Catalan, English, French, German, Greek, Italian, Portuguese, Russian, Spanish, and Yiddish literature. Editorial boards and committees of more than 60 leading academic specialists work in collaboration with bodies such as the Society for French Studies, the British Comparative Literature Association and the Association of Hispanists of Great Britain & Ireland.

The MHRA encourages and promotes advanced study and research in the field of the modern humanities, especially modern European languages and literature, including English, and also cinema. It aims to break down the barriers between scholars working in different disciplines and to maintain the unity of humanistic scholarship. The Association fulfils this purpose through the publication of journals, bibliographies, monographs, critical editions, and the MHRA Style Guide, and by making grants in support of research. Membership is open to all who work in the Humanities, whether independent or in a University post, and the participation of younger colleagues entering the field is especially welcomed.

ALSO PUBLISHED BY THE ASSOCIATION

Critical Texts
Tudor and Stuart Translations • *New Translations* • *European Translations*
MHRA Library of Medieval Welsh Literature

MHRA Bibliographies
Publications of the Modern Humanities Research Association

The Annual Bibliography of English Language & Literature
Austrian Studies
Modern Language Review
Portuguese Studies
The Slavonic and East European Review
Working Papers in the Humanities
The Yearbook of English Studies

www.mhra.org.uk
www.legendabooks.com

STUDIES IN HISPANIC AND LUSOPHONE CULTURES

Studies in Hispanic and Lusophone Cultures are selected and edited by the Association of Hispanists of Great Britain & Ireland. The series seeks to publish the best new research in all areas of the literature, thought, history, culture, film, and languages of Spain, Spanish America, and the Portuguese-speaking world.

The Association of Hispanists of Great Britain & Ireland is a professional association which represents a very diverse discipline, in terms of both geographical coverage and objects of study. Its website showcases new work by members, and publicises jobs, conferences and grants in the field.

www.legendabooks.com/series/shlc

STUDIES IN HISPANIC AND LUSOPHONE CULTURES

1. *Unamuno's Theory of the Novel*, by C. A. Longhurst
2. *Pessoa's Geometry of the Abyss: Modernity and the* Book of Disquiet, by Paulo de Medeiros
3. *Artifice and Invention in the Spanish Golden Age*, edited by Stephen Boyd and Terence O'Reilly
4. *The Latin American Short Story at its Limits: Fragmentation, Hybridity and Intermediality*, by Lucy Bell
5. *Spanish New York Narratives 1898–1936: Modernisation, Otherness and Nation*, by David Miranda-Barreiro
6. *The Art of Ana Clavel: Ghosts, Urinals, Dolls, Shadows and Outlaw Desires*, by Jane Elizabeth Lavery
7. *Alejo Carpentier and the Musical Text*, by Katia Chornik
8. *Britain, Spain and the Treaty of Utrecht 1713-2013*, edited by Trevor J. Dadson and J. H. Elliott
9. *Books and Periodicals in Brazil 1768-1930: A Transatlantic Perspective*, edited by Ana Cláudia Suriani da Silva and Sandra Guardini Vasconcelos
10. *Lisbon Revisited: Urban Masculinities in Twentieth-Century Portuguese Fiction*, by Rhian Atkin
11. *Urban Space, Identity and Postmodernity in 1980s Spain: Rethinking the Movida*, by Maite Usoz de la Fuente
12. *Santería, Vodou and Resistance in Caribbean Literature: Daughters of the Spirits*, by Paul Humphrey
13. *Reprojecting the City: Urban Space and Dissident Sexualities in Recent Latin American Cinema*, by Benedict Hoff
14. *Rethinking Juan Rulfo's Creative World: Prose, Photography, Film*, edited by Dylan Brennan and Nuala Finnegan
15. *The Last Days of Humanism: A Reappraisal of Quevedo's Thought*, by Alfonso Rey
16. *Catalan Narrative 1875-2015*, edited by Jordi Larios and Montserrat Lunati
17. *Islamic Culture in Spain to 1614: Essays and Studies*, by L. P. Harvey
18. *Film Festivals: Cinema and Cultural Exchange*, by Mar Diestro-Dópido
19. *St Teresa of Avila: Her Writings and Life*, edited by Terence O'Reilly, Colin Thompson and Lesley Twomey
20. *(Un)veiling Bodies: A Trajectory of Chilean Post-Dictatorship Documentary*, by Elizabeth Ramírez Soto

No Country for Nonconforming Women

Feminine Conceptions of Lusophone Africa

Maria Tavares

LEGENDA
Studies in Hispanic and Lusophone Cultures 32
Modern Humanities Research Association
2018

Published by Legenda
an imprint of the Modern Humanities Research Association
Salisbury House, Station Road, Cambridge CB1 2LA

ISBN 978-1-78188-533-8 (HB)
ISBN 978-1-78188-534-5 (PB)

First published 2018

Copy-Editor: Richard Correll

CONTENTS

ACKNOWLEDGEMENTS

No Country for Nonconforming Women is a revised version of my PhD thesis, which I completed at the University of Manchester in 2011. This study focuses on the literary creations by female authors Dina Salústio (Cape Verde, 1941–), Paulina Chiziane (Mozambique, 1955–) and Rosária da Silva (Angola, 1959–) and how their work provides a reflection on the condition of Cape Verdean, Mozambican and Angolan women in their dealings with patriarchy over time — from the socialist to the democratic era. I first became interested in Lusophone women's writing and in issues related to gender and postcolonialism in Portuguese-speaking Africa thanks to the inspiring teaching and the ground-breaking work of Hilary Owen. So, firstly, I would like to thank Hilary for all the lively intellectual exchanges, and for all her unconditional support, guidance and patience throughout my personal and professional journey to completing my PhD. Working under her supervision was a pleasure and a privilege; her enthusiasm, dedication, professional rigour and generosity were always an inspiration for me, and I am very grateful to her.

I would also like to thank Par Kumaraswami, Lúcia Sá, João Cézar de Castro Rocha and Ellen Sapega for all the suggestions and valuable intellectual input, and the Fundação para a Ciência e a Tecnologia for sponsoring my postgraduate work. I am also grateful to the Editorial Board of Legenda's 'Studies in Hispanic & Lusophone Cultures' series, and to the editors and anonymous readers of the following journal and edited volume to which I contributed, whose feedback helped me to make this book stronger. In relation to chapter 1 in particular, an earlier version of the article on Dina Salústio's *Mornas Eram as Noites*, entitled 'Resituando as Margens e o Centro: Uma Leitura de *Mornas Eram as Noites*, de Dina Salústio' (2008), was published by *Revista Teia Literária*; and an earlier version of the analysis of *A Louca de Serrano*, entitled 'Das Margens e dos Centros: Uma Leitura d'*A Louca de Serrano* de Dina Salústio' (2014), appeared in a volume which was edited by Fábio Mário da Silva and published by the University of Lisbon. A number of colleagues invited me to present portions of this work at conferences. I therefore wish to thank also Ana Margarida Martins, Carmen Tindó Secco, Carmen Ramos Villar, Denise Saive, Elena Brugioni, Joana Passos, Sheila Khan and Sofia Santos.

In 2008 and 2009, I was able to go to Mozambique and Cape Verde, respectively, to carry out fieldwork thanks to the Fundação Calouste Gulbenkian, which awarded me fieldwork grants. I would like to thank the Universidade Eduardo Mondlane, which hosted me in Maputo, and Nataniel Ngomane, to whom I am particularly grateful for all his help, and above all for his friendship. I am also grateful to my colleague Ana Margarida Martins, with whom I shared this trip and all the wonderful experiences that came with it, and in particular to Paulina Chiziane, who opened the doors of her home to us and gladly agreed to give us an interview which would turn out to become a full day of very stimulating conversation. I have returned to Mozambique in subsequent years and was always received with the same enthusiasm and friendliness in places like the Arquivo Histórico, the Associação de Escritores Moçambicanos and more recently the Fundação Fernando Leite Couto; and for this I am truly grateful. In Cape Verde, it was thanks to my good friends Fernando Gonçalves and Josina Fortes that I was able to have a very successful fieldwork trip. I also want to thank the writer Vera Duarte and especially Dina Salústio for all her time, for the books that she gave me and for the conversations that we had, which enlightened me so much regarding her trajectory as a writer and her work as a whole.

As I was moving towards completion of my book project, I had the support of the (then) School of Modern Languages and especially the Department of Spanish and Portuguese of Queen's University, Belfast, which enabled me to have the time to carry out this task. I am, therefore, indebted to Janice Carruthers and Isabel Torres for their support. Additionally, I was lucky enough to be welcomed as a visiting scholar at the Freiburg Institute for Advanced Studies (FRIAS), where I was given the space and conditions to work on my book. Hence, I would like to thank Britta Küst, Petra Fischer and Nikolaus Binder in particular for enabling me to have the best possible conditions to complete this book and always making me feel so welcome at FRIAS. I am also indebted to Mozambican artist Silvério Salvador Sitoe, who so enthusiastically and generously authorised me to use the image of his 2009 painting entitled 'Xingombela' on the cover of my book. Finally, I would also like to thank Sarah Martin and Richard Correll for their tremendous contribution to this book in terms of editing/proof-reading and copy-editing, respectively.

There are also a number of other very important people who have been standing by my side for quite some time now and have contributed to this project in numerous ways — whether through their support, hospitality or engaging conversations — but always through their friendship. Hence, I would like to thank Carla Castelhano, Felisbela Vieira, Inês Silva, Iris Lui, Jennifer Oliveira, Sunayna Jamnadas and Suzanne Whiteman for their unconditional support and generosity over the years. I also want to thank Denise Saive, Rui Castro and Sofia Santos for their hospitality and all the vibrant intellectual exchanges. Recently I had the good fortune to meet Dan Mc Carthy, Colin Ireland and Honóra Ní Chríogáin, who have become my Dublin family. I want to thank them for their kindness and for always making me feel at home.

I also want to acknowledge my family's extraordinary support — my mother Maria de Fátima Tavares; my father Aquilino Galina Fortes; my siblings, Herbertt, Lauzinda, Sónia and Vera Fortes; my brothers-in-law, Paulo Rui Monteiro, Ricardo Soares and Benvindo Varela; my sister-in-law, Anabela Rodrigues; my grandfather, João dos Santos, and especially my grandmother, Júlia Tavares, who passed away recently and did not get to see this book project come to fruition. My nieces and nephews — Débora, Gabriel, Marcelo, Mariza, Rafael I, Rafael II, Soraia and Victória — have been my greatest source of strength, determination and resilience. Finally, I am profoundly indebted to Immo Warntjes, in whom generosity, intelligence and sense of humour are perfectly combined. I want to thank him for sharing my hopes and my dreams, and for his unfailing support. He helps me to be a better person and a better professional, every single day.

In 2016, Professor Hilary Owen retired from the University of Manchester, after twenty-one years of service and a life dedicated to enhancing and shaping the fields of Portuguese and Lusophone African Studies. This book is dedicated to her and to the memory of Júlia Maria Tavares, my grandmother, and the bravest person that I have ever known.

M.T., Dublin, 16 June 2018

LIST OF ABBREVIATIONS

AEC	Associação de Escritores Cabo Verdianos [Cape Verdean Writers' Association]
AEMO	Associação de Escritores Moçambicanos [Mozambican Writers' Association]
BJLA	Brigada Jovem da Literatura de Angola [Angolan Literary Youth Brigade]
CEDAW	Convenção sobre a Eliminação de Todas as Formas de Discriminação Contra as Mulheres [Convention on the Elimination of All Forms of Discrimination against Women]
CEI	Casa dos Estudantes do Império [House of the Students of the Empire]
FESA	Fundação Eduardo dos Santos [Eduardo dos Santos Foundation]
FNLA	Frente Nacional de Libertação de Angola [National Front for the Liberation of Angola]
FRELIMO/Frelimo (revolutionary movement/party)	Frente de Libertação de Moçambique [Mozambique Liberation Front]
GURN	Governo de Unidade e Reconciliação Nacional [Government of National Unity and Reconciliation]
HCB	Hidroeléctrica de Cahora Bassa [Cahora Bassa Hydroelectric Plant]
ICF	Instituto da Condição Feminina [Institute of Womanhood]
ICIEG	Instituto Cabo-verdiano para Igualdade e Equidade de Género [Cape Verdean Institute for Equality and Gender Equity]
IMF	International Monetary Fund
INALD	Instituto Nacional do Livro e do Disco [National Book and Disc Institute]
LIMA	Liga Independente de Mulheres Angolanas [Independent League of Angolan Women]
MINFAMU	Ministério da Família e Promoção da Mulher [Ministry of Family and the Promotion of Women]
MNR	Mozambican National Resistance
MORABI	Associação de Apoio à Auto-Promoção da Mulher no Desenvolvimento [Association in Support of Women's Self-Promotion in Development]
MpD	Movimento para a Democracia [Movement for Democracy]
MPLA	Movimento Popular de Libertação de Angola [People's Movement for the Liberation of Angola]
NGO	Non-Governmental Organization
OMA	Organização da Mulher Angolana [Angolan Women's Organisation]
OMCV	Organização da Mulher Cabo Verdiana [Cape Verdean Women's Organization]
OMM	Organização da Mulher Moçambicana [Mozambican Women's Organisation]
PAICV	Partido Africano da Independência de Cabo Verde [African Party of Independence of Cape Verde]
PAIGC	Partido Africano da Independência da Guiné e Cabo Verde [African Party for the Independence of Guinea and Cape Verde]

PALOP	Países Africanos de Língua Oficial Portuguesa [Portuguese-speaking African countries]
PIDE	Polícia Internacional e de Defesa do Estado [International and State Defence Police]
RENAMO/Renamo (guerrilla movement/party)	Resistência Nacional Moçambicana [Mozambican National Resistance]
SADC	Southern African Development Community
SEPMD	Secretaria de Estado para a Promoção e Desenvolvimento da Mulher [State Secretariat for the Promotion and Development of Women]
UEA	União de Escritores Angolanos [Angolan Writers Union]
UNITA	União Nacional para a Independência Total de Angola [National Union for the Total Independence of Angola]
UPA	União dos Povos de Angola [Union of the Peoples of Angola]
UPNA	União das Populações do Norte de Angola [Union of the Populations of North Angola]
WB	World Bank

INTRODUCTION

No Country for Nonconforming Women: Feminine Conceptions of Lusophone Africa

> Embora as assunções acerca da realidade das nações e das diferenças entre nações sejam vias socialmente significativas em que categorizamos o mundo em torno de nós e através das quais nos localizamos num sentido colectivo, a forma, o conteúdo e o significado dessas categorias permanecem abertos à interpretação individual e à negociação. Por isso, entendemos que a ênfase não deve ser posta apenas nos que constroem a nação, mas também nos que a (re) constroem, seja pela sua capacidade de retroacção, seja ainda pelo seu labor específico com vista à descoberta de alternativas.
>
> [The assumptions about the reality of nations and the differences between nations are socially significant ways of categorising the world around us, and ways through which we position ourselves in a collective sense. However, the form, content and meaning of those categories remain open to individual interpretation and negotiation. As such, it is our understanding that the emphasis should be placed not solely on those who build the nation, but also on those who (re)build it, either through their capacity to act retroactively or through their specific labour, with the aim of discovering alternatives.][1]
>
> Gabriel Fernandes

This study puts forward a comparative analysis of the literary production of three female authors who write from the particular contexts of their countries of origin in the postcolonial era: the Cape Verdean Dina Salústio, the Mozambican Paulina Chiziane and the Angolan Rosária da Silva. Emerging from three young and very different nation states, the three female authors are themselves very distinct, not only with regard to their generation, but also in biographical and bibliographical terms. They have, however, one very specific aspect in common, which is the fact that all of them were the first female novel writer to publish in the context of their independent countries, thus constituting a major breakthrough in the male-dominated literary canons of their cultural nations. Their works demonstrate the importance of examining nationalism and national identity through gender. At the same time, they highlight the potential of situated gender analyses in the understanding and contestation of the power networks which consolidate the supremacy of hegemonic national narratives, both colonial and postcolonial. As such, this study aims to observe the authors' cultural construction of their complex postcolonial nations from a female-focalised point of view, as well as their representation of the women of these nations and their interaction with the transcultural contexts of each country analysed. The main argument that this study develops, in three distinct chapters (each one devoted to the literary production of each author), is that the building of the post-independence nations under analysis is structured by gender differentiation.

The theoretical framework of this study's main argument is developed according to the work of specific postcolonial theorists, who have devised global theories that analyse and deconstruct hegemonic discourses of identity. This study will engage with and amplify these theories, whilst examining their application to the specific Lusophone works under analysis (Medeiros 2007: 5). Hence, Benedict Anderson's understanding of the nation as an 'imagined political community' (1991) is explored along with Homi Bhabha's theorisation of the dynamics of national discourse (1990), whose instability comes from the friction between its pedagogical and performative dimensions. This emphasis on empowering marginality takes us to Edward Said's reflections on exile (2001a). For Said, the condition of exile represents an irrecoverable displacement of the human being with regard to her/his homeland, a state which she/he will permanently try to revoke. Andrea O'Reilly Herrera (2001) uses the term *insílio* to emphasise the psychological and emotional dimensions of this state, which precedes the actual physical exile. Reflections on the active involvement of the displaced in the renegotiation of the nation are also at the core of Mary Louise Pratt's theorisation of contact zones, autoethnography and transculturation (1991). The emphasis on the disruptive potential of autoethnography is recaptured in Graham Huggan's study of the Post-Colonial Exotic (2001), focusing specifically on the potential of what he called 'celebratory autoethnography'. Considering that these approaches are largely gender blind, this study questions their premises further by incorporating postcolonial feminist theories and feminist theories from sociology. Anne McClintock's (1995) and Nira Yuval-Davis's (1997) important proposals for the analysis of nationalism through the lens of a gender power theory made multiple experiences of the nation accessible. Amina Mama (2001) added to these strong theorisations with her proposal of the analysis of individual and national identity through gender, with a view to understanding and dismantling the power structures in operation within. Considering that the three countries examined had one-party socialist regimes immediately after independence, Catherine Scott's study on gender and development theories also facilitates a situated analysis of gender (1995).

With this in mind, this study aims to add to the existing scholarship on Lusophone literature, from a postcolonial theoretical point of view, by assessing the feasibility and limitation of the application of such theories to gender-related issues in the specific context of postcolonial Lusophone Africa. Informed by an interdisciplinary approach, this comparative study will analyse the works by these African female authors focusing on the Marxist and post-Marxist legacies for women and gender politics. In so doing, it will simultaneously explore the possible existence of common spaces or points of convergence that link these women's experiences of Portuguese colonialism and socialist experiment.

Cape Verde, Mozambique and Angola: The Emergence of a Literary National Consciousness

Located in different regions of the African continent, Cape Verde, Mozambique and Angola are three very young Portuguese-speaking nation states which were Portuguese colonies until 1975, a year after the 25 April Carnation Revolution took place in Portugal, bringing the fascist regime and the state's imperial project to an end. Considering that their autonomy was achieved at the end of a long and complex process of colonisation and anti-colonial struggle, it comes as no surprise that literature acquired a very important role in the intellectual effort to define these nations. Used primarily as a vehicle for the affirmation and diffusion of anti-colonial and pro-nationalist ideals, literature became a privileged place for intellectual reflection on the emergence of an autonomous collective identity.[2] This remained at the core of the cultural discourses of nationhood which followed the birth of the nation states.[3]

The three countries discussed here have strikingly dissimilar historical trajectories, notwithstanding their common Portuguese colonial inheritance (cultural and linguistic), the shared experience of resistance against the coloniser, and even the common alignment with Marxism after independence. This is the outcome of particular pre-colonial, geo-social and cultural characteristics, as well as specific colonial projects, anti-colonial interventions and post-colonial dynamics. Hence, literature as both producer and product of national culture reveals very distinct characteristics in each of these geo-cultural spaces. As the historian Patrick Chabal (1996) reminds us, in order to understand the origins and the impact of these national literatures in the construction of a national identity, it is necessary to take into consideration the contextual characteristics that distinguish these particular Lusophone African countries — not only from other African countries, but also, I would add, from each other. Chabal identifies five crucial historical factors that ultimately determine these distinctions:

> (1) the distinctiveness of the Creole island cultures of Cape Verde and São Tomé and Príncipe; (2) the poor colonial integration, uneven economic development and the complex racial and social mix of Angola and Mozambique; (3) the social and cultural impact of the regime of the Portuguese dictator Salazar (the *Estado Novo*, or New State) on the African colonies; (4) the dynamics of nationalism, the effect of the war of liberation and, for Angola and Mozambique, of the 'civil' wars which followed and (5) the impact of outside cultural, intellectual and literary influences on the development of the literatures of Lusophone Africa. (Chabal 1996: 12–13)

As a result, these specificities have come to condition, in diverse ways, both the emergence of a literary national consciousness prior to the establishment of the nation states, and the consolidation and development of this consciousness throughout the postcolonial era. What is made clear from the outset is the close relationship between literature and nation in these African countries, which leads to literary texts becoming '*textos-memória* da História dos países' [texts that preserve the memory of the History of the countries] (Mata 2006: 17–31).

Hence, various scholars working on Lusophone African literatures in their early stages noted that due to the urgency of anti-colonial cultural affirmation, these literatures had close connections with the ideological and political projects of nationhood which were drafted in the nation states from which they emerged (e.g. Hamilton 1975; Santilli 1985: 7–30; Laranjeira 1992: 19–32; Laranjeira with Mata and Dos Santos 1995; Chabal et al. 1996). However, the advent of independence and the various postcolonial forms that the nations took brought about significant shifts in perspective.[4] Such shifts rearranged the priorities and concerns of these literatures, making them openly question and problematise (in various ways and to varying degrees) the national cultures under construction. As Mata points out, it was no longer the power structures operating within the relationship between the colonised and the coloniser that took precedence. Rather, it was the analysis of the influence of colonial structures on the post-independence generation, and the subsequent sociocultural effects of this, that began to assume greater significance. As Mata puts it:

> Um dos territórios da enunciação pós-colonial é o desvelamento da continuidade da lógica colonial de dominação, agora internalizada, para além dos interrelacionamentos global/local nas relações internas transversais, que cruzam o interior destas sociedades. Este deslocamento do olhar para o interior, para as relações de poder internas torna-se, neste contexto, um dos critérios configuradores da estética pós-colonial. (Mata 2006: 18)
>
> [One of the territories of postcolonial enunciation is the unveiling of the continuity of the colonial logic of domination, which is now internalised, as well as the global/local interrelationships within the internal transversal relationships that intersect at the core of these societies. This shift of the gaze towards the inside and the internal power relations becomes one of the shaping criteria of postcolonial aesthetics in this context.]

In other words, the moment at which the cultural nation, as conceived within a political and ideological project, starts to be questioned by literature signals an attempt to deconstruct hegemonic and univocal discourses of nationhood, as well as opening up possibilities for rethinking national identity.

Literature, Postcoloniality and Female Authorship

Cape Verde, Mozambique and Angola became one-party authoritarian, socialist states after independence, under the aegis of PAIGC (Partido Africano da Independência da Guiné e Cabo Verde [African Party for the Independence of Guinea and Cape Verde]), FRELIMO (Frente de Libertação de Moçambique [Mozambique Liberation Front]) and MPLA (Movimento Popular de Libertação de Angola [People's Movement for the Liberation of Angola]) respectively. With this in mind, it is worth considering literature in postcoloniality as a key weapon for the intellectual subversion of a cultural nationhood constructed by the Marxist-led political elites. Strategies used by these elites to legitimise their entitlement to power after independence include emphasising their participation in the liberation struggle, and reinterpreting history to make the birth of national identity coincide with the origins of the anti-colonial struggle. The men who created the political parties that attained power after independence — namely Amílcar Cabral (PAIGC), Eduardo Mondlane (FRELIMO) and Agostinho Neto (MPLA) — are therefore perceived as the military fathers of the modern nations (Gentili 1999: 278–85; Souto and Cruz e Silva 1999; Cardoso 1974; Laranjeira with Mata and Dos Santos 1995: 88–99; Lopes 2002: 31–59 and 193–218). This in turn would ultimately lead to the validation of a specific, unified and paternalistic Marxist conceptualisation of national identity; one that canonical postcolonial writers such as Pepetela, Mia Couto, Manuel Rui, Paula Tavares, Luandino Vieira, Germano de Almeida, Ungulani Ba Ka Khosa, João Paulo Borges Coelho and José Eduardo Agualusa — to name only a few of the best known and researched — have in very different ways interrogated and reworked. In their creations, these authors propose reinterpretations of the past without allowing the processes of history and memory to be subordinated to political and ideological demands.[5] In doing this, they have opened up possibilities for the recovery of other subaltern spaces and the exploration of marginalised and contentious discourses and experiences which had been left outside the boundaries of the national narrative by the centralising cultural structures of the Marxist nation state.

Bearing in mind the specific historical, geographical, social, political and cultural contexts of the three countries mentioned above, as well as the particular biographical contexts from which the three female authors write, it comes as no surprise that the debates on identity and nationalism that they portray, both fictionally and through a gender perspective, should mirror and problematise the distinct discourses of nationhood built throughout history. This enables them to reveal the complex structures of power in operation, which are based on shifting forms of difference. It becomes clear at this point that by acting both as women and as writers, in their work, the authors are simultaneously subjects and objects. Hence, their reflection on fundamental questions regarding national identity — from a female-focalised point of view, taking the historical, social and economic occurrences that marked the consolidation of their nations as a point of departure — is twofold, as their voicing of the experiences of African women runs parallel to their own experiences as African female writers. It is worth remembering, at this point, the words of Padilha and Mata in the introduction to the 2007 collection of essays entitled *A Mulher em África: Vozes de Uma Margem Sempre Presente*:

> No caso da literatura, vale lembrar que tal exclusão [das mulheres] se repete em todos os sistemas literários nos quais há nitidamente uma predominância de vozes masculinas, pois os textos, como produtos simbólicos e como 'documentos do imaginário', na expressão de Jacques le Goff, submetem-se aos mesmos aparatos de dominação impostos pelas ideologias hegemónicas. (Mata and Padilha 2007b: 13)

> [In the specific case of literature, it is worth remembering that such an exclusion [of women] is repeated in all literary systems, in which there is a clear predominance of male voices. This is because texts as symbolic products and 'documents of the imaginary', in Jacques le Goff's words, are subject to the same domination apparatuses imposed by hegemonic ideologies.]

As mentioned before, they are, indeed, unique in various ways, particularly in the sense that, as female authors who write from their post-independent countries, they have not only succeeded — to varying extents — in disrupting the historical exclusion of female voices from the literary systems of their countries, but they have also conquered a space in the male-dominated sphere of novel writing.

Generally speaking, there are not many female voices in the Cape Verdean, Mozambican and Angolan literary canons, due to women's historically limited access to the public sphere. Nonetheless, there is an emergence of isolated female voices in poetry, in different literary projects ruled by diverse agendas, as demonstrated by an analysis of some of the most important anthologies of Lusophone African literature published to date (Ferreira 1997; M. P. de Andrade 1976, 1979; Almada 1988; Feijoó 1988; Mendonça and Saúte 1989; Manjate 2000; Saúte 2004). Scholars such as Maria Nazareth Fonseca and Padilha have already examined the female presence in some of the most important anthologies and collections of interviews,[6] with a view to observing the place occupied by women in the literary canons and the terms of their admission to those canons. According to Padilha (2002: 151–56), in the anthology by Ferreira (1997), the presence of selected female authors is legitimised by their educational background (closely related with their race in the specific cases of Angolan and Mozambican literature), their involvement in the liberation movements or their relationships with important male writers. Padilha also highlights the fact that Laban's (1991; 1992; 1998) collections of interviews are very much male-dominated as well: out of twenty-five Cape Verdean authors interviewed by Laban, Orlanda Amarílis is the only female writer; out of twenty-six Angolan authors interviewed, Paula Tavares is the only female writer; and out of thirty-one Mozambican authors interviewed, Glória de Sant'Anna, Noémia de Sousa, Lília Momplé and Paulina Chiziane are the only four female writers. The scholar argues that these numbers mirror the marginalisation of female authorship.

Aside from looking at Ferreira's anthology, Fonseca (2007: 489–518) also examines some poetic anthologies that were published after independence. Given the scope of this study, we will mention only three. In Feijoó's (1988) anthology, Paula Tavares, Doriana (Ana Francisca Silva Major) and Ana de Santana are the only female authors included. Almada's (1988) anthology, published in the same year, includes six female authors: Alzira Cabral, Ana Júlia, Arcília Barreto, Dina Salústio, Lara Araújo and Vera Duarte. Finally, the collection compiled by Mendonça and Saúte (1989) in the following year includes only Noémia de Sousa and Clotilde da Silva as representatives of female authorship. According to Fonseca, although the space allocated to the female voice within the literary canons is still very small, in these anthologies the female authors take a much more intimate approach than before, addressing women's experiences and spaces, as well as the female body.

Ultimately, both scholars conclude that, indeed, very few female poets were allowed into the literary canons. They consider the most significant to be those who were actively involved in the anti-colonial struggle through their participation in the bulletin *Mensagem*, published between 1948 and 1964 by the CEI (Casa dos Estudantes do Império [House of the Students of the Empire]) in Lisbon, and whose literary work is considered to be fundamental for the modern literature produced in their countries of origin: Alda Lara and Maria Eugénia Neto (Angola); Noémia de Sousa (Mozambique); Alda do Espírito Santo (S. Tomé e Príncipe); and Vera Duarte (Cape Verde). Despite having a very clear ideological agenda, their works successfully broke the silence that surrounded female subjectivity and women's experience of nationhood, bringing forth a national discourse very much based on motherhood, as opposed to fatherhood (see Owen 2007b: 43–105; Padilha 2002: 157–72). Throughout the anti-colonial struggle, the need to prioritise the fight for independence and the construction of a national identity might have somehow conditioned these female authors' portrayal of the gender question. Nonetheless, the aftermath of independence should theoretically have enabled women's liberation, considering the strong emphasis placed upon it by the three liberation movements throughout the revolutionary struggle, as well as their logic of modernisation, which included refusing all forms of discrimination (be it racial, ethnic, of class or gender).

Revolutionary Movements and the 'Woman Question'

PAIGC, FRELIMO and MPLA, the victorious movements which attained power after independence (in Cape Verde, Mozambique and Angola, respectively) were all socialist, generally speaking. They therefore proceeded to create governmental and societal structures inspired by socialism. Nevertheless, their ideological positionings within socialism differed. For example, in Cape Verde PAIGC (and PAICV (Partido Africano da Independência de Cabo Verde [African Party of Independence of Cape Verde]), after Guinea-Bissau and Cape Verde became two independent states in 1980) took into consideration the historical sociocultural characteristics of the island setting (a Creole community; much more Western than African-oriented, with a long and solid history of emigration) in its adaptation of socialism. Nonetheless, in both Angola and Mozambique (former settler colonies of a very heterogeneous nature), the MPLA and FRELIMO embraced a much more orthodox Marxist-Leninist stance. Notwithstanding the distinctions in terms of orientation between the parties, they turned their respective countries into one-party authoritarian states (Chabal et al. 2002: 1–28; Gentili 1999: 325–36). Gentili defines the one-party ideology as follows:

> A ideologia do partido único que foi elaborada nos primeiros anos e resiste até hoje, com as suas diferenças e morfologias, pode ser resumida nos seguintes pontos: o partido único exprime e concretiza a unidade nacional fundamental, não reconhece nem admite divisões étnicas, tribais, regionais ou de classe; qualquer oposição ao partido único é considerada ilegítima porque dividida e, portanto, referida ao tribalismo que, por sua vez, é fomentado por conspirações obscurantistas objectivamente aliadas e cúmplices das tramas imperialistas; finalmente, o partido único é democrático uma vez que nele está representado todo o povo e é o instrumento para o mobilizar, onde atingir a integração nacional e o desenvolvimento económico. (Gentili 1999: 334).
>
> [The one-party ideology, which was created in the early years and is still

> around today, with its differences and morphologies, can be summarised by the following points: the single party expresses and embodies the fundamental unity of the nation, and it does not recognise or allow ethnic, tribal, regional or class divisions; any opposition to the single party is considered to be illegitimate because it is divided and, therefore, points to tribalism, which, in itself, is fuelled by obscurantist conspiracies that are objectively associated with and complicit in imperialist plots; finally, the single party is democratic, given that it represents the whole population, it is the instrument used to mobilise the population, and it is the place where national integration and economic development come together.]

This definition becomes particularly helpful when we consider the treatment of the woman question inside these socialist states. It is true that their policies did generally contribute to an improvement in women's living conditions (with the democratisation of education and health, as well as the creation of protective legislation for women in terms of access to work and justice, for example) and they did create some space for women's economic liberation and integration into the work force, mostly through work done by women's organisations. Emerging from inside PAICV, FRELIMO and MPLA, respectively, OMCV (Organização da Mulher Cabo Verdiana [Cape Verdean Women's Organization]), OMM (Organização da Mulher Moçambicana [Mozambican Women's Organisation]) and OMA (Organização da Mulher Angolana [Angolan Women's Organisation]) were mass organisations created to encourage the involvement of women in the parties and to create a space for debate over issues that referred specifically to womanhood. However, despite their achievements throughout the anti-colonial struggle (OMM and OMA's; OMCV was not created until 1981) and even in the post-independence era, in the long term they proved to be inefficacious in promoting a real gender struggle. As branches of their respective parties, their actions were limited to PAICV, FRELIMO and MPLA's decisions and negotiations of nationhood (B. Isaacman and Stefhan 1984; OAW 1984; Foy 1988: 66–98; Scott 1995: 105–19; N. C. dos Santos 2000; Sheldon 2002: 115–52; Ducados 2004; Casimiro 2005: 55–84; Pereira 2005; Monteiro 2009: 71–105; Arnfred 2011).

Indeed, the conceptualisation of women's liberation within a socialist framework was contradictory and, ultimately, it often remained discriminatory for them. According to Hilary Owen and Phillip Rothwell (2004: v–xvi), there were two main reasons for this. Firstly, the regimes' emphasis on dismantling the colonial structures operating in social and political spheres located their field of struggle in the public realm only, where both women and men were perceived as equally oppressed by the colonial capitalist economic system. This meant that no other locations of struggle — such as the household within the private sphere — were contemplated or even recognised, which would, in turn, allow gendered power structures to persist. Secondly, given that the private sphere was outside the limits of the modern discourse of the nation, it was immediately associated with traditionalism, obscurantism and backwardness. Hence, due to their historical link with the private sphere, women became the prime targets of modernisation, being called upon to contribute to the modern project of the nation in the male-created revolutionary public sphere, while simultaneously continuing to fulfil their traditional roles in the private sphere — thus being subject to men's authority. Conversely, women were also sometimes forced to abandon precisely those traditional structures that empowered them (Owen and Rothwell 2004: viii–ix). In other words, the regimes' depoliticisation of the private sphere led to the maintenance and reinforcement of patriarchal sociocultural structures which legitimised male authority over women (Urdang 1989; Scott 1995: 105–19; Sheldon 2002: 115–52).

In this context, it is imperative to observe the extent to which the three regimes successfully created and maintained a sense of national unity. In Cape Verde, again due to the specific characteristics of the country, PAIGC/PAICV was more successful in the execution of this project. Yet, in Angola and Mozambique the situation was very different for MPLA and FRELIMO. After independence, both countries were confronted with the reality of heterogeneous and complex states to govern. Despite having been very successful in the first few years after independence, the urban-based, southern-influenced and markedly Changaan Frelimo government started facing discontent in the rural areas, especially as the one party-state became increasingly authoritarian. Subsequently, in the 1980s, it was forced to acknowledge and fight RENAMO (Resistência Nacional Moçambicana [Mozambican National Resistance]), a dissident group mostly sponsored by South Africa and Rhodesia, which caused escalating disruption and destruction of Frelimo's government structures and state. The internal conflict between the two forces was to last for fifteen years, from 1977 until 1992 (Chabal 2002: 98–101; Gentili 1999: 363–69). As for the urban-based, mostly Creole and Kimbundu-influenced MPLA government in Angola, its consolidation of a unitary nation faced even greater difficulties, notwithstanding the fact that the party won the 1975–76 war against FNLA (Frente Nacional de Libertação de Angola [National Front for the Liberation of Angola]) and UNITA (União Nacional para a Independência Total de Angola [National Union for the Total Independence of Angola]). This occurred mainly because its attempt to control the countryside met with armed resistance from UNITA, which turned the MPLA into a primarily urban-based government. Nevertheless, the one-party state, which soon acquired a totalitarian nature, ruled the controlled areas with an iron fist, whilst watching the social inequalities and divisions within the population increase dramatically. The civil war between the MPLA and UNITA was to last for twenty-seven years, from 1975 until 2002 (Chabal 2002: 101–02; Wheeler and Pélissier 2009: 362–75). Although this happened to a lesser extent in Cape Verde, in Mozambique and Angola women played a very important role in the negotiation of internal cultural differences (ethnic, linguistic, regional and tribal), as the male-dominated socialist parties sacrificed gender struggle and women's liberation for the sake of a unified imagined community (Scott 1995: 113). In other words, the maintenance of men's utopias was often achieved at the expense of women's dystopias, something which emerges strongly in the writings of all three female authors under analysis here.

State of the Theories

Along with the post-Utopian writers already mentioned above, these three female authors develop a reflection on the limitations of the socialist concept of nationhood which emerged in their respective countries. In order to achieve this, Salústio, Chiziane and Da Silva focus specifically on the workings of patriarchy in the socialist era, as well as in the democratic era. Another very important aspect that the three authors share is a thematic framework focusing on the condition of Cape Verdean, Mozambican and Angolan women through the recuperation of female memories that traverse and cut across the established histories of the cultural nations. This recuperation then opens up and develops the debate on national identity as it is experienced by diverse groups of women, thus enabling an investigation of gendered social relations. This is achieved through the historicisation of female genealogies; the analysis of how female identities came to be constructed and negotiated by the discourses of community and nationhood; and the exploration of the strategies put forward by women, in different contexts, to deconstruct hegemonic patriarchal conceptions of the world and the consolidation of certain male roles within it. Hence, all three authors demonstrate the potential for rethinking national identity through gender, from a female-focalised point of view, as this discloses the power structures in operation within the dominant ideologies that construct the discourses of cultural community. Ultimately, I will argue that this broadens the discussion on the need to reimagine subjectivities and/in collectivities at national and transnational levels.

The common thematic issues outlined above, and the strategies deployed to explore them, as well as the connection between the national and transnational levels which will be relevant here, all indicate the value of applying a comparative and postcolonial methodology to the study of the literary production of these three authors. If it is true that comparative literature is a discipline that was markedly European and Western oriented in its origins, it is also a matter of fact that the emergence of 'new' literatures promoted the opening up of the field, with a view to providing greater flexibility and adaptability to those contexts that elude a purely Western logic. In other words, the discipline has had to adjust to the needs of other literatures. In turn, this move towards decentralisation not only promotes the value of those literatures in terms of their differences, as they do not conform to a universalising logic, but it also creates space for the adequately contextualised and localised analysis of these emerging literary phenomena (Chevrier 1989: 215–43; Abousema 1990: 263–70; Coutinho 2001: 315–31). Paulo de Medeiros (2006b: 28) claims that since the publication of Said's *Orientalism* in 1978, Postcolonial Studies 'has proceeded to establish itself largely as both a sort of inheritor of the discipline of Comparative Literature and as a contesting discourse'. Having initially emerged from within English literature departments, postcolonial studies would soon be challenged due to the limitations that a clearly Anglophone theorisation (based on the experience of British colonialism) encountered in its application to different historical and sociocultural settings (Medeiros 2007: 1). A. M. Martins (2012: 19–21) reminds us that the first challenges were posed by Francophone postcolonial studies, which refused to accept any such exclusive definition of the postcolonial, thus paving the way to the emergence of other dimensions within the field.

For almost two decades now, scholars working on Lusophone Studies from a postcolonial perspective have been thoroughly developing the discipline by engaging simultaneously with these established theories and the specificities of the various Lusophone texts and contexts (Medeiros 2007: 5) through a process that Manuela Ribeiro Sanches (2007: 129) called 'the "indigenization" of theories and approaches circulating globally'. In this threefold process that scholars like Medeiros, Sanches and Leite have been advocating for the past decade, the reflections on postcoloniality are formulated from locality (cautiously avoiding any essentialisms of a 'Lusophone exceptionalism'); within an interdisciplinary approach (a necessity for any postcolonial approach); and through 'um esforço de tradução das referidas propostas para contextos precisos, assinalando-se a necessidade de considerar as transformações, os limites ou potencialidades das viagens da teoria' [an effort to convey these proposals in specific contexts, emphasising the need to consider the transformations, limits or potential of travelling theory] (Sanches 2006a: 9). Over the years, the debate has been prolific and this critical and revisionist posture has allowed for the emergence of new critical approaches within postcolonial studies (Leite 2015: 140), with more theoretical tools being made available to address the constantly changing realities and challenges of postcoloniality. Examples of this would be the potential arising from the applicability of subaltern studies to the specific context of African literatures (Sanches 2012: 291–310); the plurality of critical postures that move beyond the dichotomy Eurocentrism/Afrocentrism in African criticism, and better account for the work developed by new African writers, with their new visions and challenges (Leite 2015: 129–42); or even the intersection between cultural memory studies and postcolonial studies in the study of a post-imperial Europe, which has seldom been a preoccupation of postcolonial studies (Medeiros 2012).

State of the Art

As women of their time, born between 1941 and 1959, these authors contributed in different ways to the consolidation of the three parties that gained power after independence in their countries of origin. But, most importantly, I would also add, they made use of the spaces created for women by the socialist governments in order to establish their literary voices. Although the first works published by all three of them were poems,[7] clearly echoing the earlier tradition of female poetic intervention in their countries' literary systems, the fact is that they were more or less successful, ultimately, in entering a historically male literary realm: the sphere of novel writing. In doing so, they made an important contribution to the construction of a space for the female literary voice within the openly masculinised literary canons of all three countries, a voice that projects itself at both national and transnational levels, as indicated by the extensive number of critical works on their literary productions published in recent years. An extensive list of studies that reflect the research done so far on the literary works of Salústio, Chiziane and Da Silva can be found in the bibliography. Of these, it is worth mentioning a few for their specific contribution to this study, as outlined below.

I will start by highlighting Chabal's *Vozes Moçambicanas: Literatura e Nacionalidade*, which is divided into two sections, and provides an analysis of the origins and development of Mozambican literature and its impact on the construction of a Mozambican national identity (1994). This historical analysis, which demonstrates the close relationship between literature and history within the Mozambican context, also focuses on Mozambican writers themselves, by presenting a collection of twenty-two interviews in the second section of the study. It is worth mentioning that the only female writers who feature on this list are Noémia de Sousa and Chiziane. Maria Teresa Salgado's 'Um olhar em direcção à narrativa contemporânea moçambicana' focuses solely on Mozambican contemporary fiction and its specificities, looking particularly at the literary works by Mia Couto, Ungulani Ba Ka Khosa, Lília Momplé and Chiziane (2004: 297–308). According to the scholar, the works by these authors demonstrate a commitment to building new models that adjust to their national context and enable the affirmation of their identity, a proposal which is echoed in the study by Ana Mafalda Leite (2003b: 185–99). In 'Em torno de Modelos no Romance Moçambicano' the scholar focuses on some specificities of the Mozambican novel, especially from the mid-80s onwards, to address the authors' proposals of new models and strategies which are more in consonance with the local traditions. In this context, it is worth highlighting Leite's emphasis on the fact that Chiziane, as well as Marcelo Panguana and Ungulani Ba Ka Khosa, make use of an 'escrita oralizada, que tenta recuperar as formas tradicionais da arte de contar' [oralised writing that attempts to recover the traditional forms of the art of storytelling] (2003b: 187), an idea which will be explored further later on in this study (see Chapter 2). Finally, I would highlight the important work by Russell Hamilton, who, along with others, 'laid the necessary literary-historical groundwork and provided a transition to a postcolonial perspective on Lusophone literatures' (Medeiros 2007: 2). Hamilton's analysis, entitled 'A Feminist Dance of Love, Eroticism, and Life: Chiziane's Novelistic Recreation of Tradition and Language in Postcolonial Mozambique', focuses particularly on the form, content and international appeal of Chiziane's literary work *Niketche: Uma História de Poligamia* (2003: 153–67). The scholar puts much emphasis on the novel's portrayal and treatment of traditional issues and institutions (such as, for example, polygamy), but what is particularly relevant in Hamilton's reading is the observation of the *mulata*'s racial and sexual connotations and placement within the 'national family'; this shall be explored in depth in the present study as well (see Chapter 2).

Regarding general research on female authorship, female literary representations, and the recovery of female genealogy from a female-focalised point of view, it is relevant to reference the studies collected in *O Rosto Feminino da Expansão Portuguesa — Actas II*, which were the result of an international conference that took place in Lisbon, in 1994. By focusing on female voices, the studies presented by Inocência Mata (1995: 251–58), Fernanda Cavacas (1995: 267–74) and Simone Caputo Gomes

(1995: 275–84), for example, attempt to rescue women and women writers from a historical place of silence, renegotiating their places in history and within their respective literary canons. It is also worth referring to the work by Fernando Vale (1999) on the conditions under which African women writers of children's and juvenile books write, emphasising the work by Salústio. With regard to specific studies on the literary works by the authors under analysis here, there are many that could be referenced at this point (especially on the work developed by Chiziane, the most widely known of all three authors). As such, and taking into consideration the scope of the present study, I have made a selection according to the literary works which will be analysed and the analytical postures which will be adopted. With regard to Salústio's literary work, it is certainly important to make reference to the work by Simone Caputo Gomes, who has written abundantly on Cape Verdean authorship, and notably on Salústio's creations (1995; 2000a; 2000b; 2003; 2007; 2015). I would reference in particular Gomes's articles entitled 'Mulher Com Paisagem ao Fundo: *Dina Salústio Apresenta Cabo Verde*' (2000a) and 'Echoes of Cape Verdean Identity: Literature and Music in the Archipelago' (2003), in which the scholar focuses on the short story collection *Mornas Eram as Noites*, its emphasis on a female Cape Verdean perspective of national identity, and the parallel between women's experiences and the 'mornas' as a cultural item. In this context, it is important not to forget Jorge Valentim's study on the structure and content of the same literary work, through the lens of Roland Barthes's reflections on music (2007). Fátima Cristina Correia's master's thesis entitled 'Marcas da Insularidade no Romance Cabo-Verdiano *A Louca de Serrano*, de Dina Salústio' adds to this important work developed on Salústio by reflecting on the author's reinterpretation of the question of insularity, a well-rehearsed theme within Cape Verdean literature (2004).

With regard to Chiziane's work, I will start by mentioning Mata's article entitled 'Paulina Chiziane: Uma Colectora de *Memórias Imaginadas*'. This study observes the illusion of an autobiographical identity journey, from a feminine perspective, through the recovery of memories, which Chiziane's main characters seem to engage in in *Balada de Amor ao Vento* and *Ventos do Apocalipse* (2000). Maria Nazareth Fonseca's study entitled 'Campos de Guerra com Mulher ao Fundo no Romance *Ventos do Apocalipse*' focuses on the peculiar structure of the novel and its use of micro-narratives in the recovery of the storytelling ritual 'Karingana Wa Karingana' (2003). In 'Novos Espaços no Feminino: Uma Leitura de *Ventos do Apocalipse*, de Paulina Chiziane', Deolinda Adão explores female identity construction and power relations within gender through the lens of works by theorists such as Judith Butler, Gayattri Spivak, Chela Sandival, Donna Haraway and Trinh T. Minh-ha (2007: 199–207). Considering African women as victims of a double marginalisation (due to their gender and race), Adão notes that although they are actively engaged in the reconstruction of their own identities, their actions are limited by male hegemonic power. Still focusing on the literary work *Ventos do Apocalipse*, Shirlei Campos Victorino's 'A Geografia da Guerra em *Ventos do Apocalipse* de Paulina Chiziane' explores how the novel promotes the problematisation of African women's situation in extreme conditions (2007). In addition, Sheila Khan's study of the same novel highlights Chiziane's portrayal of the identity exile which the Mozambican population experienced throughout the internal conflict, as a result of the post-independence social, ideological and political measures, as well as the war context itself (2008: 119–32). Finally, Sandra Campos proposes a reflection on *Balada de Amor ao Vento, Ventos do Apocalipse, O Sétimo Juramento* and *Niketche: Uma História de Poligamia* which observes the literary representations of the female body and sexuality and their inscription of difference within femininity (2004).

Lourenço do Rosário's article entitled '*Niketche* — O Existencialismo no Feminino' notes the effort made by the author to focus on the experience of women from distinct cultural backgrounds within the Mozambican nation (2007: 115–18). In 'Paulina Chiziane: Romance De Costumes, Histórias Morais', Leite (2003a) also promotes a discussion on Chiziane's *Niketche: Uma História de Poligamia* (as well as on *O Sétimo Juramento*), not only emphasising the novelty of a feminine perspective within the African literary realm, but also celebrating what the scholar called the 'carnavalização dos géneros' [the carnivalisation of literary genres]. Furthermore, Ana Margarida Martins's study entitled 'The Whip of Love: Decolonising the Imposition of Authority in Paulina Chiziane's *Niketche: Uma História de Poligamia*' addresses Homi Bhabha's concepts of the performative and the pedagogical in the narration of the nation as a cultural product. She builds upon these concepts to explore Chiziane's production of a counternarrative of the nation that simultaneously rejects Frelimo's discourse of socialism and exposes the marketing discourses that generate the gender exotic which is consumed by the Portuguese public (2006b). Robson Dutra's reading of the same literary work focuses on the seduction dance named 'Niketche' as a symbol of traditional culture which is subverted by the main female character, Rami (2007). Finally, Patrícia Rainho and Solange Silva's article entitled 'A Escrita no Feminino e a Escrita Feminista em *Balada de Amor ao Vento* e *Niketche, Uma História de Poligamia*' reads both literary works with a view to providing a reflection on the distinction between feminine writing and feminist writing, as well as their manifestations in the above-mentioned novels (2007). Regarding the work by Rosária da Silva, Hamilton (2000) has written one of the few studies produced on it to date. In 'Uma Reconfiguração Pós-Colonial de Realidades e Ficções: *Totonya*, o Primeiro Romance Angolano Escrito por uma Mulher', the scholar proceeds to the presentation of the literary work *Totonya*, exploring its women-related themes, its female perspective and the reinterpretation of national identity as portrayed by Da Silva.

Studies of female-authored literary production within the literary systems of each country under analysis here were also very useful for this study. At this point, it is relevant to underline the works developed by Gomes, Sônia Maria Santos and Hilary Owen. In 'A mulher lê a realidade: escritura feminina em Cabo Verde', Gomes (2000b) explains the research that she had been working on and describes her work methodology. With the aim of mapping the female authored literary prose produced in Cape Verde, she proceeded to the critical reading of the literary works. The reading was carried out within specific theoretical frameworks to explore the cultural construction of gender, the operation of the patriarchal ideology (in society and within the construction of the national literary canon) and the interdisciplinary studies of gender. Gomes also presented the study entitled 'O Texto Literário de Autoria Feminina Escreve e Inscreve a Mulher e(m) Cabo Verde' in which she introduces the Cape Verdean islands, gives a panoramic view of the Cape Verdean female authorship (from Antónia Gertrudes Prisich to Vera Duarte), and provides extracts of literary works by Fátima Bettencourt, Dina Salústio, Vera Duarte, Orlanda Amarílis, Ivone Aída and Maria Margarida Mascarenhas (2007). Furthermore, in her article 'Experiências Femininas no Quotidiano Crioulo', Sônia Maria Santos (2009) also focuses on Cape Verdean female authors, providing a study of the works by Orlanda Amarílis, Dina Salústio and Fátima Bettencourt, from a perspective which emphasises the recovery of the day-to-day female experience and its impact on the process of rewriting national identity. Finally, I must refer to the seminal work by Hilary Owen, who has written extensively on Mozambican female authorship, focusing on Chiziane in particular (2003; 2004; 2007a; 2007b; 2008a; 2008b; 2014a; 2014b), and has helped shape the field of Lusophone African Studies. Owen's study entitled *Mother Africa, Father Marx: Women's Writing of Mozambique, 1948–2002* (2007b), which focuses on nationalism and gender issues, provides an important and up-to-date analysis of the literary works by the Mozambican female authors Noémia de Sousa, Lina Magaia, Lília Momplé and Paulina Chiziane, and their contributions to the construction and continuous debate of national identity. Given the scope of this work, the emphasis was placed on the chapter entitled 'Paulina Chiziane: The Unmanning of Mozambique', which provided a crucial contribution to this study, as it questions the viability and limitations of a multi-ethnic Mozambican society (2007b: 150–99).

Regarding studies of female authored literary production from distinct literary systems, in a comparative perspective, I must underline the works developed by Inocência Mata, Pires Laranjeira, Joana Passos and Ana Margarida Martins. In 'Mulheres de África no Espaço da Escrita: A Inscrição da Mulher na sua Diferença', Mata (2007a) explores literary works by female authors from within the context of Lusophone Africa to assess their impact on the construction of nationalist resistance and transition to the post-colonial era. She starts by focusing on the generation of women who wrote from within the anti-colonialist and anti-fascist resistance (Alda Espírito Santo, Alda Lara, Noémia de Sousa, etc.), and therefore were limited in their approach to female claims. Then, she moves on to focus on the younger generation (Ana Paula Tavares, Chiziane, Salústio, Odete Semedo, Vera Duarte, Conceição Lima, etc.) which triggers an important shift in terms of the themes explored and within the male-dominated literary systems. Regarding Pires Laranjeira's work, in 'O Feminino da Escrita: Espinhoso Marfim' he proposes three critical texts which were adapted to form a whole text (2007). These critical texts are based on Conceição Lima's poetry book entitled *O Útero da Casa*; on Mata's collection of critical essays entitled *Literatura Angolana: Silêncios e Falas de Uma Voz Inquieta*; and on Chiziane's *Niketche: Uma História de Poligamia*. Focusing specifically on the scholar's last text, it is important to highlight Laranjeira's effort to generate a parallel between the works of Chiziane and Mia Couto, in which, by comparison, Chiziane's appears to present flaws. Passos's study entitled *Micro-universes and Situated Critical Theory: Postcolonial and Feminist Dialogues in a Comparative Study of Indo-English and Lusophone Women Writers* (2003) proposes a comparative approach between the works of female authors in which Salústio and Chiziane are included (through the analysis of the literary works *A Louca de Serrano* and *Ventos do Apocalipse*). The scholar compares these works with literature by Anglophone female authors (Nayantara Sahgal, Arundhati Roy, Githa Hariharan) in an Anglicised theoretical framework (Postcolonial and Feminism Studies). As for Martins's work entitled *Magic Stones and Flying Snakes*, it presents a comparative analysis of the works by Chiziane and the Portuguese female writer Lídia Jorge (2012). The scholar focuses particularly on the strategic use of gender and sexual difference to deconstruct structures of exoticism. In terms of interviews with the authors, it is imperative to mention the work by Michel Laban (1998) and Leite et al. (2012b; 2014b). Finally, two important collections of essays are particularly worthy of recognition: the above-mentioned *A Mulher em África: Vozes de Uma Margem Sempre Presente*, edited by Mata and Padilha (2007b), which focuses solely on female authorship in Lusophone Africa; and *Paulina Chiziane: Vozes e Rostos Femininos de Moçambique*, edited by Maria Geralda de Miranda and Carmen Lucia Tindó Secco (2014), which addresses Chiziane's work only, and includes interviews with the author, as well as with other prominent Mozambican authors on Chiziane's literary work.

The present study is, therefore, organised into three different chapters, each of them dedicated to the individual analysis of selected literary works by each of the three authors, as detailed below.

Dina Salústio

The opening chapter analyses the work of Dina Salústio, focusing specifically on the novel *A Louca de Serrano* (1998a) and the short story collection *Mornas Eram as Noites* (1999a). Born on 27 March 1941 on Santo Antão island, in Cape Verde, Bernardina Augusta da Purificação Fortes de Oliveira Loureiro Salústio is the oldest of the three authors. She studied in Angola and Portugal, and has a degree in Social Work. She has been actively engaged in the Cape Verdean sociocultural scene over many years, as she used to work for the Ministry of Foreign Affairs, she is a member of the OMCV, and a founding member of the AEC (Associação de Escritores Cabo Verdianos [Cape Verdean Writers' Association]). As a poetry and fiction writer, she has published widely in some of the most important national and international newspapers and magazines, of which I highlight *Pré-Textos*, *Ponto & Vírgula*, *Revue Noire*, *Tribuna*, *A Semana* and *Mudjer.*[8] Along with the poet Vera Duarte and the short story writer Fátima Bettencourt, Salústio is one of the most dynamic Cape Verdean female authors, as to date she has made two novels available to the public (aside from the aforementioned novel *A Louca*, the author published *Filhas do Vento*, in 2009), and one short story collection (*Mornas*).

According to Salústio, her personal trajectory had a major impact on the choices she made throughout her literary projects. In an interview granted to the present author in November 2009, at Cape Verde's National Library, Salústio revealed that her desire to become a writer emerged early in her childhood (M. Tavares 2009). Given that she did not want to go to school until she was old enough to join the third grade, she spent a lot of her time wandering around the neighbourhood, observing people and listening to their stories. She was particularly impressed by the stories of the *desterrados* [exiles] — those who were punished by being forcefully sent to other islands — and the *contratados* [hired workers] — those who, in an attempt to escape the difficult living conditions on the islands, were hired as a labour force to work in very harsh conditions at the *roças* [plantation farms] in São Tomé e Príncipe. This made her want to write about people in a whole different dimension, one that would not conform to the realist Cape Verdean tradition. Daily contact in São Vicente with the intellectuals Jorge Barbosa and Baltazar Lopes, two of the founding members of the *Claridade* movement who were friends of her father, was also very significant for her. However, the author claims that what really fascinated her from an early age was the world of female experience:

> Mas, as mulheres eram muito altivas, tinham muitas coisas para contar, tinham muitas histórias, tinham muitas brigas. Portanto, elas cercavam-nos, protegiam-nos. Tudo isso veio dar-me um conhecimento razoavelmente maior das mulheres do que dos homens. Mas, os homens estão sempre lá na minha escrita. Não só como a sombra, a motivação, mas como o outro lado da mulher. (M. Tavares 2009)
>
> [But the women were very noble; they had a lot of things to say, many stories to tell, they fought a lot. Therefore, they surrounded us, protected us. All that made me substantially more knowledgeable about women than men. But men are always there in my writing, not just as the shadow, the motivation, but also as the other side of the woman.]

An important step towards becoming a writer was her growing awareness (through Brazilian magazines and newspapers that reached the islands by ship) that women could also be writers and publish. Hence, the advent of independence generated more empowering conditions for women to enter literary circles in the second half of the eighties, as it brought education and prompted women to occupy a space in the public sphere.

As a woman of her time and social sphere, Salústio was mobilised by the PAIGC's representatives on the island who were clandestinely working for liberation. The author recognises the influence of her teacher, Dulce Almada Duarte, one of the first women to join PAIGC's struggle (M. Tavares 2009). On this subject, Lopes (2002: 149) points out that Salústio, as well as Joaquim Salústio, who would later become her husband, was part of a group of youngsters who were mobilised in São Vicente by Manuel Rodrigues. He was one of the first people to go back to Cape Verde undercover, as a PAIGC spokesperson. It is therefore not surprising that after independence, Salústio was so enthusiastic about the party; this is made explicit in the poem 'Um Caso de Amor' [A Love Story] (1990). The poem focuses on the love story between PAICV and Cape Verde, emphasising that by fighting together and for the same purposes, both people and party brought about autonomy from the *outros senhores* [other masters], in a clear reference to the colonial past. It affirms that this relationship paved the way for the development of the country which could already be felt then, in a clear reference to the Cape Verdean post-colonial success story. This brings us to another area of influence on Salústio's literary production: the work that she did and the challenges that she met as a member of the OMCV, the ICF (Instituto da Condição Feminina [Institute of Womanhood]) and later on, the ICIEG (Instituto Cabo-verdiano para Igualdade e Equidade de Género [Cape Verdean Institute for Equality and Gender Equity]). The author published an important sociological study entitled *Violência Contra as Mulheres* [Violence Against Women] (1999b), which was sponsored by the ICF (currently ICIEG, a governmental entity that is responsible for the proposal and implementation of policies promoting gender equality). It is also worth highlighting the author's active public involvement in the promotion of ICIEG's projects; for example, she participated in a campaign which was broadcast on national television.

Salústio claims that the short story collection *Mornas* is the one which reflects most deeply on the living conditions of Cape Verdean women and their complicity with the legitimisation of those conditions. This happened mostly because the short stories were initially written to be published as newspaper articles, so they were up-to-date and very much oriented towards what was happening at the time in society. Although she has had very little international projection as an author, the awards she has won, the inclusion of her literature in important anthologies and the Cape Verdean national educational curricula, and even the tentative national and international academic production (articles and theses) on her writing certainly legitimise and affirm the quality of her work, simultaneously contributing to its dissemination.[9] Nevertheless, Salústio still believes that the Cape Verdean literary scene is very much male-defined and oriented, as well as paternalist towards women writers. Without devaluing her own work, she questions its inclusion in the educational curricula, claiming that it might be a strategy of tokenism, given that there are so few Cape Verdean female authors (M. Tavares 2009).

Through her persistence and dedication, Salústio has managed to not only take advantage of the space created for women within the literary circle of the islands but also to make a clear statement through her work that opposes the historically masculine predominance in the Cape Verdean literary canon. This statement shifts the literary perspective towards the Cape Verdean female experience of nationhood, thus generating a space for reflection on the female dimension, from a female point of view, as well as voicing a historical absence. The chapter of the present study which is dedicated to Salústio's works *A Louca de Serrano* and *Mornas Eram as Noites* focuses on and discusses precisely this recuperation and empowerment of women's micro-histories, which are relegated to the silent margins by the macro-history of the nation. Considering the emphasis that Salústio places on the discussion of Cape Verdean cultural identity and its reading from a female perspective, this study will focus primarily on the novel *A Louca*, by examining the national discourse and its subsequent cultural manifestations. It will do so in order to achieve a better understanding of the historical, social and cultural constructions of identity —

particularly gender identity — within the Cape Verdean nation, and also to evaluate the renegotiation strategies and alternatives proposed by the author.

Following on from a discussion of Benedict Anderson's conception of the nation as an 'imagined community' (1991: 12), this analysis attempts to show how the literary work proceeds to deconstruct and renegotiate Cape Verdean national identity, from a female perspective, thus 'substituting *an* imagined community (Anderson 1991) with diverse fragments of the nation (Chatterjee 1993), restoring a multiplicity of histories that postcolonial studies and subaltern studies have been demanding', as proposed by Sanches (2007: 133). The study is primarily informed by background historical information that observes the inheritance of cultural and racial miscegenation from the colonial period, as well as the extent of Lusotropicalist ideological influence. The particular nature of socialism on the islands is also considered, since it is also responsible for shaping social structures and behaviours and forging subjectivities in the postcolonial setting. Subsequently, the analysis moves to discuss the consequences of this cultural inheritance for the construction of Cape Verdean identity. Following on from Anne McClintock's theory (1995: 360) that national discourse dictates power structures that manifest themselves in terms of gender, class and race, which then become categories that need to be studied together in order to be fully understood, this examination proceeds to observe how daily life demonstrates the intersection of these categories in Salústio's work. Finally, given that, according to the above theory, both women and men are socially constructed by national discourse and, therefore, have different roles and positionings, the current study places emphasis on the author's depiction of gender conceptualisations. Hence, it explores female and male location within the Cape Verdean *national family* by analysing the general development of women's social status and the portrayal of female gender that Salústio proposes. At the same time, it also explores Cape Verdean masculinity and the demystification of the *super-macho* ideal (Yuval-Davis 1997: 4).

Following on from this work, the study moves to examine the short story collection *Mornas*. The thirty-five short stories that constitute this literary work present a kaleidoscope of Cape Verdean reality, focusing, above all, on subjectivities. Given the author's selection and treatment of themes (women's position; the construction of female and male subjectivities in different settings; childhood; emigration; colonial interference pre- and post-independence), my analysis relies on Homi Bhabha's conception of the dynamics of national discourse (1990: 291–322). For Bhabha, the identity of a nation is a narrative construction which often reflects the stories of a dominant group, to the detriment of other narratives by minority groups, as a homogenising experience that all people are meant to identify with. The theorist emphasises the temporal dimension of these discursive strategies in order to oppose historicism's notion of nation as a simultaneous and horizontal experience, which tends to be exclusivist (1990: 292). If on one hand, the pedagogical dimension of national identity arbitrarily defines the nation and its limits, on the other hand the national subjects are continuously reinventing the nation and defying its limits through performativity. In other words, the ambivalent nature of national discourses provokes their incessant displacement through other experiences of nationhood, thus proving the impossibility of a fixed universal discourse and allowing constant renegotiation to take place (1990: 297). In *Mornas*, national discourse is continuously renegotiated, allowing marginality to emerge as a potential site for the formation of counter-narratives and, thus, for the renegotiation of identities. The study will therefore provide a reading of the short story collection through a gender mapping of Bhabha's theorisation of the pedagogical and performative dimensions of national identity. As Sanches (2007: 133) advocates in her readings of Bhabha, 'the aim is not to destroy grand narratives and substitute them with playful intertwining of alternative *petits récits*, but rather reconstitute a diversity that Enlightenment universals are hardly able to cope with'.

Paulina Chiziane

The second chapter of this study provides an analysis of three literary works by Paulina Chiziane, *Ventos do Apocalipse* (1999), *Niketche: Uma História de Poligamia* (2002) and *O Alegre Canto da Perdiz* (2008). Born on 4 June 1955 in Manjacaze, Gaza province, in Mozambique, Paulina Ricardo Chiziane is the best-known of the three authors. Having moved to Lourenço Marques at an early age, Chiziane studied at a Catholic Mission school, despite the fact that her family was Protestant. She studied Linguistics at Eduardo Mondlane University and was a member of the Mozambican Red Cross's staff for many years. She is also a member of the AEMO (Associação de Escritores Moçambicanos [Mozambican Writers' Association]). As a writer, she has been rather active for many years, having published, amongst other things, some pieces with *Tempo* magazine;[10] a testimony in a collection entitled *Eu Mulher em Moçambique* (1994: 12–18); five novels — *Balada de Amor ao Vento* (2003), *Ventos do Apocalipse* (1999), *O Sétimo Juramento* (2000), *Niketche: Uma História de Poligamia* (2002) and *O Alegre Canto da Perdiz* (2008); and the short story collection *As Andorinhas* (2009). In addition, she edited, along with the Angolan writer Dya Kasembe, a collection of testimonies by female Angolan survivors of the civil war, which is called *O Livro da Paz da Mulher Angolana: as Heroínas sem Nome* (Kasembe and Chiziane 2009). Finally, in more recent years Chiziane has co-authored three titles which represent a shift in the author's writing, from a purely fictional paradigm to a more reflexive one that opens up discussions on various traditions and aspects of African thought: *Por Quem Vibram os Tambores do Além?* (Chiziane and Pita 2013a), *Na Mão de Deus* (Chiziane and M. C. da Silva 2013b), and *Ngoma Yethu: O Curandeiro e o Novo Testamento* (Chiziane and M. Martins 2015). Seeing that, compared to the other two authors, Chiziane has produced a notably larger body of literary work to date, only the three novels specified above will be explored here.

According to Chiziane, her desire to write manifested itself very early and, to a certain extent, it was very much a consequence of her upbringing and the environment of that upbringing (Chiziane 1994: 14–15). Born to a very modest Tsonga family in the countryside, she spoke Chope and had a very traditional education, which clearly defined the roles that both women and men were supposed to perform. When her family moved to Lourenço Marques at the beginning of the 1960s, aside from learning Ronga and Portuguese, and entering the Catholic school, she was able to observe the continuities between the two types of education she was then receiving — traditional and Catholic — as regards the predefined roles of women (Chiziane 1994: 14–15). Her close observation of discriminatory social conditions such as these inspired her to start thinking and writing about the human condition, in general, and that of women in particular. Books, especially those by the Portuguese female poet Florbela Espanca, as well as the stories that her grandmother used to tell her around the fire, had a great impact on Chiziane (M. Tavares and A. M. Martins 2008). Therefore, soon after she started producing her own texts, she began to dream about writing a novel — a dream which was postponed when she got married and wanted to become what she had been educated to be, that is, a good wife. Nevertheless, her marriage did not work out and that made her think in greater depth about her own and other women's social conditions, a theme that became her greatest inspiration:

> Olhei para mim e para outras mulheres. Percorri a trajectória do nosso ser, procurando o erro da nossa existência. Não encontrei nenhum. Reencontrei na escrita o preenchimento do vazio e incompreensão que se erguia à minha volta. A condição social da mulher inspirou-me e tornou-se meu tema. Coloquei no papel as aspirações da mulher no campo afectivo para que o mundo as veja, as conheça e reflita sobre elas. Se as próprias mulheres não gritam quando algo lhes dá amargura da forma como pensam e sentem, ninguém o fará da forma como elas desejam. (Chiziane 1994: 15–16)
>
> [I looked at myself and all the other women. I went through the trajectory of our existence looking for our faults. I didn't find any. Through writing, I re-encountered the means to deal with the emptiness and lack of understanding that surrounded me. The social status of women inspired me and became my theme. I put women's aspirations on paper in the emotional realm so that the world could see them, get to know them, and reflect upon them. If women don't speak up for themselves whenever something that they think or feel gives them a bitter taste, no one will do it the way that they want it to be done.]

She was strongly engaged in Frelimo's activism when she was a youngster and this involvement increased her awareness of the limitations of the Marxist-Leninist conceptualisation of nation and of the socialist discourse for women (A. M. Martins 2006; Chabal 1994: 298–99). In addition, her own experience as a black woman struggling to write a novel, get it published and be recognised as an author within the male-dominated AEMO influenced her significantly. Hence, her writing projects frequently offer reflections on these limitations, simultaneously pointing in alternative future directions which recuperate and recycle certain socialist principles. Although she does not like her work to be generally labelled feminist, Chiziane did assert that her first novel to be published, *Balada de Amor ao Vento* (2003), is very much a feminist book in the sense that, in the author's words, 'a minha mensagem é uma espécie de denúncia, é um grito de protesto' [my message is a kind of denunciation, a rallying cry] (Chabal 1994: 298). By the time she published her second novel, *Ventos do Apocalipse* (1999), she was more careful with the characterisation of her work, emphasising a women-centred point of view to the detriment of a feminist stance (Guerreiro 1999). This novel was written in the aftermath of the work Chiziane did with the Red Cross during the internal conflict, which opposed Frelimo and RENAMO forces from 1977 until 1992. A particular story that she heard at a refugee camp, about a woman called Minosse who had lost her pregnant daughter the previous night, stayed with her and prompted her to write a reflection on that war (M. Tavares and A. M. Martins 2008). Again, Chiziane created very important female characters, whose complexity allows the observation not only of predefined gender roles, but also of how their supposed predictability was used in the war context. As Chiziane put it,

> Quis mostrar que as mulheres não são só vítimas. Nesta guerra vi casos concretos. A Renamo tinha um truque muito bom. Quem fazia o trabalho de reconhecimento da aldeia e das zonas que eram atacadas eram as mulheres. A mulher aparecia na aldeia, conversava, ia buscar água e observava, porque sabia de tácticas de guerra. Era depois ela quem dava o sinal às tropas que estavam escondidas. Os estereótipos colados à imagem da mulher funcionaram muito bem nesta guerra, na qual participaram de uma forma muito cruel. E ninguém deu por isso. Quando eu digo que as mulheres são invisíveis, são-no em todos os aspectos. (Guerreiro 1999)
>
> [I wanted to demonstrate that women are not just victims. I've seen concrete cases during this war. Renamo used a really good trick. Women were the ones who would make the reconnaissance of the villages and areas to be attacked. A woman would show up at a village, engage in conversation, fetch water and observe, because she knew military tactics. Later, she was the one who would give the signal to the hiding troops. The stereotypes which are attached to the image of women worked really well during this war and they used them in a very cruel way. And no one noticed. When I say that women are invisible, I mean it in every aspect of the word.]

The novel *Niketche: Uma História de Poligamia* (2002) emerged as a consequence of Chiziane's work in the northern province of Zambézia, where she had the opportunity to become familiar with matrilineal cultural traditions, which were very different from the patrilineal ones she knew. According to the author, the cultural disparities were so significant that she actually felt like a foreigner in her own country (M. Tavares and A. M. Martins 2008). Nevertheless, Chiziane claims that she particularly enjoyed the process of writing this novel, as well as the feedback that she was able to obtain from both ordinary Mozambican readers in informal situations and international readers, who surprised her by demonstrating the universal dimension of the literary work (M. Tavares and A. M. Martins 2008). In *O Alegre Canto da Perdiz* (2008), which also portrays Zambézia, she expresses her astonishment at the *mestiçagem* [miscegenation] and interaction between races in Quelimane. This novel required a great amount of historical research on a theme which has several levels of complexity in a country like Mozambique, which contains such diversity within it. According to the author, although she was aware that the theme might interest other audiences, this was a book that she wrote for her country and, for the first time, with an awareness of that country (M. Tavares and A. M. Martins 2008). In an interview given to Gil Filipe (a reporter from the Mozambican daily newspaper *Jornal de Notícias)*, Chiziane claimed that with this novel she hoped to make use of her own experiences in Zambézia and of all the region's historical specificities, to reopen the debate on the project of the nation and national identity:

> É um povo muito sofrido, sei que outros povos que formam o povo moçambicano também sofreram, mas ali... é na sua terra onde o regime colonial português experimentou as suas grandes teorias de miscegenação [*sic*], falando concretamente das teorias políticas de Gilberto Freyre. É uma coisa que se sente, ou seja a pessoa entra naquela terra e sente que 'aqui houve alguma coisa'. Eu colocava-me questões como 'como foi possível, o que é que aconteceu, como é que se deu este processo?...'. E foi com muita mágoa que eu percebi que a materialização destes grandes princípios políticos e filosóficos foi feita no corpo das mulheres. Portanto, é o sangue delas que, de certa maneira, esteve no prato da balança para a construção deste projecto de nação. (Filipe 2008)

> [Those people have suffered a lot. I know that other people who form the Mozambican population have also suffered, but those people... It was on their land that the Portuguese colonial regime tested their grand theories of miscegenation, referring specifically to the political theories of Gilberto Freyre. It is something that you can feel. When you enter that land, you feel that 'something happened here'. I would ask myself questions such as 'How was this possible? What happened? How did this process take place?' And I was very sad to discover that the materialisation of these great political and philosophical principles was achieved through women's bodies. To a certain extent, it was, therefore, their blood that was sacrificed for the construction of this nation.]

Although, to a certain extent, the amount of published work speaks for itself, there are many other factors that demonstrate Chiziane's acclaim at both national and international levels. Notwithstanding the fact that her first two novels had already been published in Mozambique (the first by AEMO and the second self-published), it was not until she participated in the Frankfurt Book Fair that her work attained visibility. From 1996 onwards, her work began to be published by the Portuguese publishing house Caminho and to date it has been translated into English, French, German, Spanish, Catalan and Italian. In 2003, AEMO and HCB (Hidroeléctrica de Cahora Bassa [Cahora Bassa Hydroelectric Plant]) created the José Craveirinha Literary Prize, which is the most important Mozambican literary prize, and awarded it jointly to Paulina Chiziane (for the literary work *Niketche*) and Mia Couto. Naturally, this prize helped to consolidate Chiziane's work, its acceptance and recognition. Her work has, therefore, been incorporated into the Mozambican educational curricula, included in various important anthologies (Chabal 1996; Laban 1998; Panguana and D'Oliveira 1999; Manjate 2000; Saúte 2000) and widely discussed and disseminated by academic researchers. Despite acknowledging that Mozambican academia still offers significant resistance to her work, Chiziane claims to have conquered her 'space', one which has been legitimised by the recognition of international scholars such as Russell Hamilton and Hilary Owen, as well as by her many anonymous readers in Mozambique. Echoing Dina Salústio, Chiziane affirms that she had to be very persistent over time in order to get her books published and to have them be taken seriously, particularly in Mozambique, where, in her opinion, the literary scene was dominated by a recognised cultural elite (composed of people who had been connected with the liberation struggle in some way or belonged to an important social group). As a black woman from a non-privileged social group, she fought to prove that people from those social circles could also produce interesting, high-quality material. Through her projects, she thus presents alternative ways of thinking about subjectivity and national identity, always assuming a female stance, criticising obsolete patriarchal social structures, recuperating traditional empowering tools for women, and proposing new strategies for building a more gender equal society.

Hence, the second chapter of this study is devoted to the analysis of the three afore-mentioned literary works. In all of her works, Chiziane attempts to portray Mozambican society, in distinct moments of Mozambican history, placing women and the female voice at the core of the discussion and defying the limits of their idealisation within the socialist nation. This analysis will therefore show how Chiziane updates the utopian ideal of the Mozambican nation firstly by revealing its tendency to exile rather than integrate and then by proposing strategies to overcome this propensity for exile. In light of this thematic framework, I will analyse these literary works by drawing on Edward Said's (2001a) reflections on exile and Monserrat Guibernau's (1996) study on Nationalism. According to Said (2001a: 173), exile materialises into a fracture between the human being and her/his own homeland which is beyond repair. It is a 'sense of constant estrangement' in which the absence of a sense of belonging translates into the urgency of re-establishing uninterrupted links to the origins — a restructuring agency that develops in different ways (2001a: 175). Hence, following on from Said's definition of exile, this study will primarily analyse the post-independence nation as an internally exiled community. In research based on various accounts of experiences relating to the Cuban Diaspora in the USA, Andrea O'Reilly Herrera (2011: xvii–xxxiii) uses the term *insílio* to refer to this very particular type of exile. Herrera claims that this 'inner' or 'internal' exile is a state of mind that precedes the physical parting from the homeland and emerges as feelings of denial or frustration towards the official governmental entity itself and the discourse that it sustains (2011: xvii).

In *Ventos* (1999), this exiled community, composed of a group of villagers that become refugees, assumes different shapes and behaviours, according to the different stages of the identity journey that the narration unravels. Hence, my analysis will also focus on Chiziane's renegotiation of the nation. Once again, the limitations of Anderson's 'imagined community' will be discussed, considering Paula de Meneses's assertion that its application to the specific context of Mozambique is problematic due to the cultural diversity of the country (2012: 312). Expanding on Anthony D. Smith's and Anderson's theorisations of the nation, Guibernau affirms that the power of nationalism comes from its ability to create a sense of belonging to a certain community; so that 'national solidarity responds to a need for identity of an eminently symbolic nature, in so far as it provides roots based on culture and a common past, as well as offering a project for the future' (1996: 5). The present study will therefore focus on the proposals advanced by Chiziane, through different moments and within various societal contexts, to recuperate a sense of community. In this process, it addresses the renegotiation of traditions, symbols and rites that speak to the population in a modern, post-independence scenario.

However, the examination of the experience of gender within that of exile will also reveal and problematise its own homogenising tendency, simultaneously demonstrating that gender exile itself is not a single, unified experience. In *Niketche* (2002), women represent the community of the exiled within the patriarchal nation, on account of their marginality. Their behaviour will be observed throughout the various moments of the novel, as they become aware of themselves and their alienation, and gradually generate the conditions to recreate the nation through the voicing of women, the re-appropriation of the female body and the inscription of women's difference. At the same time, my study will deconstruct gender exiles by examining how social categories of race, class, colour and ethnicity interact to bring about distinct experiences of womanhood, within both a patriarchal power structure and a female power structure. To this end, Said's theorisation of exile will be elucidated by Carlos Serra's (2000: 14–166) social study on racial and ethnic representations in Mozambique in the democratic era. According to Serra (2000: 20–21), racism and ethnicism are phenomena that emerge in the intersection of social interaction, the dispute over power resources, and education. Hence, people who are racist or ethnicist make sense of the world by creating power structures in which certain groups are somehow more suitable for accessing power than others (2000: 2–22). The results of the study revealed that Mozambicans do indeed perceive racism and access to power and resources as interconnected realities (2000: 79–83). Although gender was largely absent from Serra's debate, his study generally demonstrates the potential of a cross-disciplinary approach to the subject of gender as it unveils, in this specific context, multiple experiences of gender exile.

This reflection on gender and race is taken up again in *Alegre Canto*, as Chiziane undertakes the construction of a female genealogy through the genderisation of memory. In their introduction to a volume entitled *Gendered Memories*, John Neubauer and Helga Geyer-Ryan (2000) claim that 'we can assume that memory is influenced by the particular social, cultural, and historical conditions in which individuals find themselves. And since men and women generally assume different social and cultural roles, their ways of remembering should also differ' (2000: 6). Through the analysis of the stories of three generations of Zambezian women, Chiziane recuperates micro-memories of the region and the nation, which dialogue with the macro-memory, simultaneously unveiling the act of remembering as a gendered one. In addition, the complex construction of the female characters illuminates the debate on how memories are marked not only by gender, but also by other social conditions, such as race and class. Ultimately, I argue that this reworking of the past from a postcolonial point of view makes way for a better understanding of the postcolonial condition (Sanches 2007: 131).

Rosária da Silva

Finally, the third chapter of this study is devoted to the analysis of the literary work *Totonya* (2005), by the Angolan writer Rosária da Silva. Born on 4 April 1959 in Gulungo Alto, Kwanza Norte province, Rosária Manuel da Silva is, of all three authors, the youngest, the least known and the one who has published the least. Having studied at the Agostinho Neto University, in Luanda, where she obtained a degree in Educational Sciences (specialising in Portuguese Linguistics), she has been very active on the Angolan cultural scene for many years. As a journalist, she has contributed to various newspapers (*Kilamba, O Independente, Jornal de Angola* and *Kilombo Kwanza-Norte Actualidade*) and has written in different genres (essays, short stories, poetry, plays), which were published in different outlets.[11] Considered to be a key point of reference in the Angolan literary generation of the eighties, Da Silva is a founding member of the BJLA, the *Brigada Jovem da Literatura de Angola* [Angolan Literary Youth Brigade], a literary movement that was created in 1981, and also a member of the UEA (União de Escritores Angolanos [Angolan Writers Union]) (Kandjimbo 2001). Although she is the first female novelist in the history of modern Angolan literature, to date she has only made available to the public the novel *Totonya*, which was first published in 1997, and reprinted in 2005, 2014 and 2017.

Despite all efforts to contact Da Silva, I was unable to trace the author and thus unable to interview her to find out more about her biographical trajectory, impressions, projects and proposals. Hence, all the information that I have accessed about her was gleaned from other sources, including the valuable article already referred to which was written by Hamilton (2000), who had the opportunity to meet her personally in December 1997, in Luanda, at the First International Encounter on Angolan Literature. Hamilton (2000: 61) starts by emphasising the fact that Da Silva is the first black, indigenous Angolan female novel writer, a fact which is reinforced in the book itself when the author dedicates it 'à memória dos meus antepassados familiares (família Mbaxi Ya Mukuta)' [to the memory of my ancestors (Mbaxi Ya Mukuta family)], a family of the Mbundu ethnic group (Kimbundu speaking people, who are the second largest ethnolinguistic group of Angola) (R. da Silva 2005: 3). The critic also highlights the innovative nature of *Totonya* in terms of three specific aspects: the author's use of language, the thematic framework chosen and Da Silva's awareness of a foreign readership.

Regarding her use of language, Hamilton claims that the author promotes the dissemination of Bantu languages by deliberately choosing to resort to what she calls the 'ortografia científica' [scientific orthography] of African languages, as opposed to the 'ortografia administrativa' [administrative orthography]. According to the critic,

> A tal 'ortografia administrativa' é a convencional, formulada por missionários e adotada pelas autoridades administrativas nos tempos coloniais para transcrever vocábulos das línguas indígenas. Por outro lado, a 'ortografia científica' deriva do alfabeto fonético internacional e é preferida por linguistas, e também pelos reconfiguradores das realidades sócio-históricas, culturais e pedagógicas em vários países africanos. (2000: 66)

> [The so-called 'administrative orthography' is the conventional one, formulated by missionaries and adopted by the administrative authorities during the colonial era to transcribe the words of the indigenous languages. On the other hand, the 'scientific orthography' is derived from the International Phonetic Alphabet and is favoured by linguists, as well as those who reconfigure the socio-historical, cultural and pedagogical realities in various African countries.]

With reference to the daring thematic framework chosen by Da Silva (a revealing approach to unusual themes such as eroticism, women's sexuality, gender relations and tensions, and domestic violence), Hamilton claims that *Totonya* is a novel which reflects post-independence Angolan literature's tendency of becoming more open and free in social and ideological terms (2000: 64–68). Finally, on the subject of the book's potential readership, Hamilton underlines Da Silva's enthusiasm and her desire to get *Totonya* distributed outside Angola, as part of the dynamic atmosphere that surrounded the emerging BJLA and the Angolan literary generation of the 1980s as a whole. According to Hamilton, although the author is writing in Angola, about Angola and for Angola, the way she cleverly provides a reflection on a localised reality which is also very much a universal one — that of domestic violence and gender struggle in a rapidly changing post-colonial era — reveals her agenda of making the novel travel beyond Angolan frontiers (2000: 68). Indeed, time proved Hamilton right, taking into consideration the fact that the third and fourth editions (2014 and 2017, respectively) of *Totonya* were published in Portugal.

Considering some aspects of Da Silva's biography, there is much to suggest her active engagement with MPLA's ideological conceptualisation of the post-colonial nation, and active involvement at various levels in MPLA's socialist machine over a period of time. Da Silva is of Kimbundu origin, born and raised in Kwanza Norte (hence of an ethnic group that supported the MPLA and in a region which was under the party's control throughout the civil war). Having seen Angola become independent at the age of sixteen, she later moved to Luanda to enrol at university. As mentioned before, she became a founding member of the BJLA at the age of twenty-eight, which clearly indicates that she took advantage of the educational opportunities and the public space opened up for women by the MPLA socialist government. Furthermore, she wrote the lyrics for the OMA congress, which indicates her belief in both the party and the organisation, and suggests an involvement in the promotion of women and defence of their rights within a socialist logic. It is also very relevant to point out that the first edition of *Totonya* was sponsored by three governmental entities — the National Bank of Angola, the Port of Luanda and the Ministry of Fishing — and a private foundation that belongs to José Eduardo dos Santos, MPLA's chairman and Angola's president between 1979 and 2017 — the Eduardo dos Santos Foundation (Fundação Eduardo dos Santos, FESA) (Hamilton 2000: 62). This last fact points most certainly to a hidden agenda on the part of the MPLA, which might have emerged from the fact that Da Silva was the first female novel writer in post-independent Angola, thus revealing the MPLA government's tokenist gesture to publicly affirm their support for women in general, and women writers in particular. This agenda could also have arisen from the fact that *Totonya* focuses on women's emancipation and the renegotiation of female identities, from a female point of view, in a post-independence scenario. Again, this is a project which the governmental entity would most certainly have liked to be linked to, during the period when the World Bank had established the 'woman question' as one of the priorities of the 1990s development plan for African countries that intended to access its funding (Scott 1995: 69–86). Nonetheless, considering the treatment of the 'woman question' in *Totonya* and the scope of the proposed discussion, it is feasible to suggest that Da Silva took advantage of the contextual historical circumstances in order to put forward her own subversive proposal, impose her literary voice, and somehow oppose the male dominance in the Angolan literary circuit.

Despite having been awarded an Honourable Mention in the 1996 literary competition, named after the Angolan poet António Jacinto, the work of Da Silva still remains very much unknown internationally, with the exception of a very few academic works and references (Hamilton 2000; Kandjimbo 2001; Owen 2008b; Gallo 2009; Costa 2012). In an interview given to Mayrant Gallo, when she was asked about which writers are read in Angola, the Angolan writer Isabel Ferreira claimed that Angolan readers generally tend to look for those authors who are circulated and recognised at an international level (Gallo 2009). Ferreira added that besides this established generation of writers who make up the Angolan literary canon there is another good generation who, although they have made great efforts to produce and get published, find themselves ignored and even 'ocultada intencionalmente' [intentionally hidden] (Gallo 2009). In Ferreira's words:

> Existem escritores da nova geração que já vão obtendo algum sucesso em Angola, mas que não são conhecidos no círculo internacional, por falta de divulgação ou por ausência de uma política de distribuição das obras e dos autores, como Jacinto de Lemos, Conceição Cristóvão, Botelho de Vasconcelos... O Ondjaki já vai sendo conhecido a nível internacional, embora jovem... E tem mais! Na literatura feminina, as autoras vêm mostrando um posicionamento aguerrido, desafiando as regras com uma escrita ousada e inquieta. Falo de escritoras como Amélia Dalomba, Elsa Major, Chó do Guri e Ana Branco. Há também a Rosária da Silva, a única romancista angolana cuja obra foi muito bem referenciada no círculo nacional, com o romance *Totonha.* (Gallo 2009)
>
> [There are writers of the new generation who have been successful in Angola, but who are unknown in international circles due to a lack of dissemination or an absence of distribution strategies for their work, as is the case with authors such as Jacinto de Lemos, Conceição Cristóvão, Botelho de Vasconcelos... Ondjaki is already being recognised internationally, despite being young... And there are more! In terms of female literature, the authors have taken a brave stance, defying the rules with their bold and restless writing. I am referring to authors such as Amélia Dalomba, Elsa Major, Chó do Guri and Ana Branco. There is also Rosária da Silva, the only Angolan female novelist whose work has been frequently referenced within the national circle, through the novel *Totonya.*]

Ferreira's statement becomes particularly enlightening when we consider the lack of recognition of Da Silva's work outside Angola, especially if we take into account, for instance, that Salústio's work has been disseminated mostly by international academic researchers and that Chiziane's work only gained projection after the German translation was made available at the Frankfurt Book Fair. Indeed, the consolidation of these two authors' works, their inclusion in their respective national literary canons and the consequent 'guarantee' that they will be given the opportunity to carry on publishing, seems to depend substantially on an international recognition that Da Silva has not yet achieved. This assumption explains her urgent need for *Totonya* to be studied outside Angola, her eagerness to translate it into English, and even perhaps the fact that she is still to publish a new novel, which was supposed to be released in 2005. Nevertheless, *Totonya* is a highly referenced literary work that provides a daring critical reflection on the post-independence socialist conceptualisation of Angolan nationhood from a female point of view, thus defying the patriarchal, male-oriented nature of modernity in those terms and opening a space for the rethinking of female subjectivities.

My third chapter will therefore analyse *Totonya*'s deconstruction of the Marxist-Leninist ideological discourse of nationhood through its exposition of cultural, ethnic and gender marginalisation. In the novel, cultural and ethnic forms of exclusion emerge in the delimitation of two *Angolas* — the twin cities of Luanda and Benguela — that confront each other directly. Gender struggle cuts across this friction, as the examination of gender representations in both settings unveils power structures that entrap women in positions that are subalternate to men. Following on from these premises, and expanding on Phyllis Peres's (1997) research on the works of contemporary Angolan fiction writers, my analysis will provide a reading of *Totonya* through the lens of Mary Louise Pratt's (1991) theorisation of contact zones, autoethnography and transculturation, as well as Graham Huggan's study of the Post-Colonial Exotic (2001: 34–57). In *Transculturation and Resistance in Lusophone African Narrative*, Peres (1997) proposes a reading of literary works by Luandino Vieira, Pepetela, Uanhenga Xitu and Manuel Rui as narratives of resistance that promote a debate on Angolan national identities and communities. In this context, Pratt's understanding of transculturation becomes very useful for Peres's research, as it enables a deeper understanding of how the Angolan authors problematise the construction of an Angolan national identity, by reflecting on the different layers of complexity that make up the acculturation imposed by the dominant Portuguese culture. In turn, these layers also reveal uninterrupted negotiations of sociocultural elements such as race, gender, class, generation, ethnicity, region and tribe (Peres 1997: 10–15).

With a view to exploring the issues concerning sex and gender in greater depth, the present study will also make use of Pratt's theorisation, in order to dismantle *Totonya*'s thematic proposal and intellectual approach. According to Pratt, the term 'contact zone' refers 'to social spaces where cultures meet, clash, and grapple with each other, often in contexts of highly asymmetrical relations of power, such as colonialism, slavery, or their aftermaths as they are lived out in many parts of the world today' (1991: 1). These contact zones, Pratt continues, can be positive or negative, and they always question instituted models of community. In colonial environments, where negative contact zones arise, autoethnographic texts are particularly important tools for dismantling predefined representations, as they 'are representations that the so-defined others construct *in response to* or in dialogue with those [ethnographic] texts' (1991: 2). Thus, this dialogue materialises in the form of transculturation, another phenomenon that occurs in the contact zone and a concept created by the Cuban sociologist Fernando Ortiz, to enunciate the active role of marginal groups in selecting and appropriating certain features of the dominant culture (as well as vice versa) (Pratt 1991: 2). It is therefore an empowering phenomenon, in the sense that it opposes the univocality of the 'imagined community' (Sanches 2007: 133) and forces it to recreate and update itself. *Totonya* will, as a result, be read as a novel that exposes and dismantles the assimilative nature of the official discourse of nationhood through a female strategic autoethnography, which takes us to Huggan's study of the Post-Colonial Exotic. While reflecting on the reception of African literature among Western audiences and its treatment by Western publishers, Huggan concludes that those publishers generally tend to create a masquerade of Africa in order to make it more appealing for Western consumers. Nonetheless, this phenomenon which he describes as 'the anthropological exotic' (2001: 37) is met with 'ethnographic counter-discourse[s]' emerging from contemporary African literary production, which he moves on to explore (2001: 40). In this approach, Huggan considers both phenomena within an oppositional logic that emphasises the confrontational relation between colonised and coloniser, colonial and anti-colonial or postcolonial, thus bypassing other power struggles that transverse these occurrences. Considering the already mentioned characteristics of *Totonya*, my analysis will focus on Huggan's proposed 'celebratory autoethnography', which the critic describes as follows: '[...] turning the language of Western evolutionist anthropology against itself, [it] enables an allegedly "subordinate" culture to regain its dignity; and to reclaim its place, not within the imagined hierarchy of civilization, but as one civilization among others — and a sophisticated one at that' (2001: 43). As such, in *Totonya*, 'celebratory autoethnography' will be understood as a strategy of ethnographic counter-discourse emerging in postcolonial Angola, with a view to dismantling, resisting and renegotiating sex and gender power structures, and giving the debate on nationalism and national identity a whole new dimension.

Conclusion

My concluding remarks will demonstrate how, through their different literary projects, Salústio, Chiziane and Da Silva rethink nationhood and national identity from a non-conforming, female-focalised perspective and thus conceive alternative worlds that emerge from within the specific and localised experiences of their respective countries of origin. My comparative observation of their individual trajectories and projects, within the aforementioned theoretical framework, accommodates a contextualised gender analysis that particularises each of the three contexts studied. At the same time, it brings to light the existence of common spaces or points of convergence that reproduce commonalities in African women's experience, without claiming 'inventar um universo homogéneo — o "pós-colonialismo lusófono"' [to invent a homogeneous universe — the "Lusophone postcolonialism"] (Meneses 2012: 318). In order to think about national and individual identity through gender, the three authors strategically proceed to what Mama calls 'the politicization of personal experience' (2001: 67), i.e. they use the situated micro-histories of women's everyday lives to examine how identity and subjectivities come to be constructed and maintained by hegemonic ideological discourses and national narratives. The authors' analyses of these sociocultural dynamics within modern discourses of nationhood unveil power structures that reflect colonial continuities in post-independence and operate with a view to maintaining univocal, centralised, paternalistic and patriarchal imaginations of community. In their works, the consolidation of these hegemonic identity discourses implies the disempowering and subsequent alienation of *other* collective cultural experiences and projects, a goal which is ultimately achieved through the crystallisation of conventional gender identities. Hence, the authors' literary projects interweave the depictions of these power dynamics and the proposal of subversive challenging identities which question those patriarchal and exclusivist conceptualisations, simultaneously putting forward more democratic ways of experiencing individuality in/and community. From the situated experiences of Cape Verdean, Mozambican and Angolan women, Salústio, Chiziane and Da Silva propose reflections on identities through the lens of gender. As Mama put it,

> The intellectual challenge of identity lies in the exercise of adding gender to the arsenal of analytical tools required to rethink identity, so that we can deepen our understanding of power, and increase our strategic capacity to engage with and challenge its destructive capacity. Being an optimist, I assume that we still have the chance to do so. (Mama 2001: 69)

Considering the quality of the challenging work developed by the three aforementioned authors, this is a view that the present study strongly endorses.

Notes to the Introduction

1. All translations are mine, unless otherwise stated.
2. In accordance with post-Lacanian, Feminist and Postcolonial theorisations, identity is understood here as 'subjectivity'. Ashcroft, Griffiths and Tiffin (1998: 220) assert that 'the concept of subjectivity problematizes the simple relationship between the individual and language, replacing human nature with the concept of the *production* of the human subject through ideology, discourse or language'. For a discussion on the emergence of subjectivity in historical and modern conceptions of community, see, for example, Bhabha (1994) and McClintock (1997).
3. Discourse is henceforth to be understood, according to postcolonial theories, as deriving from Michel Foucault's conceptualisation of the term as a set of practices, beliefs and orientations that are produced by a dominant group and internalised by dominated groups, thus constituting the social existence of a given community. There is, therefore, a structure of power in operation underneath the institutionalisation of these 'discursive practices'. See Ashcroft, Griffiths and Tiffin (1998: 42); Barry (2002: 175–77); Bhabha (1994); McClintock (1997).
4. Taking into consideration the evolution and problematisation of the terms 'Post-Colonialism' and 'Postcolonialism', the hyphenated version will henceforth be used to refer to a geographical

reality, a historical period, and a political and ideological shift. The non-hyphenated version will be used to emphasise the contextualised analysis of cultural products, representing alternative discursive practices and strategies that aim for the decolonisation of the mind and the imagining of new knowledge systems. On this debate, see, for example, Shohat (1992); Ashcroft, Griffiths, and Tiffin (1995; 1998; 2002); McClintock (1995); Leite (2003a: 9–40); Sharp (2009).

5. On the revisionary work proposed by these canonical postcolonial writers, see, for example, Peres (1997); Matusse (1998); Noa (1998); Sepúlveda and Salgado (2000); Leite (2002); Padilha (2002); Rothwell (2003); Chaves and Macêdo (2003); Rothwell (2004); Chaves (2005); Sepúlveda, and Salgado (2006); Mata (2006); Chaves and Macêdo (2006); Chaves, Macêdo, and Vecchia (2007); Padilha and Ribeiro (2008); Ribeiro and Meneses (2008); Gordon (2009); Leite et al. (2012a; 2012b; 2014a; 2014b).
6. The best-known collections of interviews with Lusophone African writers have been published by Laban (1991; 1992; 1998). It is worth mentioning four other works which compile interviews with Mozambican authors: Chabal (1994: 71–349); Saúte (1998); Panguana and D'Oliveira (1999); and, more recently, Leite et al. (2012b; 2014b).
7. See Chiziane (1993); Salústio (1986; 1990; 1991); Almada (1988); R. da Silva (1988a; 1988b).
8. See, for example, Salústio (1986; 1990; 1991; 1993; 2003).
9. In 1994, Salústio was awarded the first prize in a national competition for authors of children's literature. In 2000, she was awarded the third prize in a competition for authors of children's literature within the PALOP (Países Africanos de Língua Oficial Portuguesa [Portuguese-speaking African countries]). Regarding the insertion of her work in anthologies, see, for example, Almada (1988: 151–59) and T. V. da Silva (2002: 161–91).
10. See Chiziane (1990; 1993).
11. See, for example, R. da Silva (1988a; 1988b).

CHAPTER 1

Of Margins and Centre

The Reinvention of the National Narrative in Dina Salústio's *A Louca de Serrano* and *Mornas Eram as Noites*[1]

> What is certain is that 'normality' cannot be separated from the hierarchization of identities. The great hegemonic, rational, political-philosophical mechanisms are precisely what fabricate normality, with the consent of the group concerned.
>
> ETIENNE BALIBAR

Introduction

This chapter will focus on the analysis of two of Dina Salústio's literary works: the short story collection *Mornas Eram as Noites* [Warm Were the Nights] (1999a) and the novel *A Louca de Serrano* [The Madwoman of Serrano] (1998a).[2] It will aim to argue that in these works, Salústio attempts to rescue women from the margins of Cape Verdean history and culture by re-reading both of these aspects from a feminine perspective. By giving centrality to the universe of women — their places within the *national family*, their anxieties, and their struggles — the author portrays and discusses the construction of *Caboverdianidade* [*Cape Verdeanness*; Cape Verdean cultural identity] and the conceptualisation of gender within it. At the same time, Salústio demonstrates the importance of tradition in defining cultural roles and proposes strategies for the renegotiation of these elements that constitute the identity of a specific group.

My examination will focus primarily on the novel *A Louca*, discussing Anderson's conception of the nation as an 'imagined community' (1991: 12). According to the theorist, 'nation-ness' and 'nationalism' are cultural constructions whose contemporary legitimacy is rooted in the historical and contextualised evolution of these concepts. As such, he defines a nation as an 'imagined political community — and imagined as both inherently limited and sovereign' (Anderson 1991: 6). Despite recognising that eighteenth-century nationalism originated in Europe, Anderson defends the view that it was exported by the imperial powers to their colonies and consolidated there mostly through educational systems and print media. It would ultimately enable natives to imagine themselves as members of the nation, he continues. Nevertheless, the intricacies of the colonial nation would end up generating the bilingual intelligentsia who, due to their ability to access more than one conception of nationhood, would become the first creators of alternative paradigms of nation (Anderson 1991: 113–40). The emphasis that Anderson places on the agency of those who are marginal to the homogenising experience of the nation and somehow find ways to subvert it, becomes particularly relevant for the present study. On the one hand, it highlights the flexibility of the conceptualisation of the nation (in the sense that it remains constantly open to renegotiation, regardless of the powerful elites' investment in maintaining it). On the other hand, it accentuates the existence and potential of marginal discourses of nationhood, which problematise and reconstruct the nation by proposing alternatives. In doing so, it forces us to question the limits of the theory when it encounters the local specificities — in this case, the Cape Verdean islands. With reference to the Cape Verdean national identity project, is it possible to talk about *an* 'imagined community', pre- and post-independence?

This discussion will be informed by relevant background historical information which observes the colonial inheritance of cultural and racial miscegenation; the extent of the influence of Lusotropicalist ideology; the impact of the discourses of *Africanisation* throughout the anti-colonial struggle; the post-independence socialist ideological conceptualisation of nationhood; and the post-socialist revitalisation of creolisation in a multiparty democratic context. It will also recall the evolution of women's roles in Cape Verdean society throughout the colonial, anti-colonial and post-colonial periods, with a view to understanding how female identity came to be culturally constructed as subalternate. The study will then move on to discuss the consequences of this cultural inheritance for the construction of Cape Verdean identity — particularly gender identity — by following on from McClintock's (1995) theorisation on gender and nationalism. In their important studies on nationalism and gender, Anne McClintock (1995) and Nira Yuval-Davis (1997) argue that, as discourses that constitute people's subjectivities and collective identities, all constructions of nationhood imply specific conceptualisations of gender which are not fixed and need, therefore, to be understood within their particular historical, geographical and sociocultural contexts. The generation of very clear representations of womanhood and manhood thus becomes central to the imagination of extended unity within communal projects, regardless of their political nature (colonial, anti-colonial or post-colonial). This demonstrates that constructions of nation are effectively rooted in gender difference. Considering that, as Cynthia Enloe (1989: 44) put it, 'nationalism typically has sprung from masculinised memory, masculinised humiliation and masculinised hope', it imposes a power structure based on gender difference which on the one hand, limits women's access to national resources and on the other hand, legitimises men's access to those same resources.

According to Yuval-Davis and Floya Anthias (1989: 7; quoted in McClintock 1995: 355), women have frequently been involved in nationalism in five principal ways: as biological reproducers; as reproducers of the limits of the nation; as producers and disseminators of national culture; as signifiers of national difference; and as active participants in national struggles. This produces women as the 'symbolic bearers of the nation', as McClintock (1995: 354) observes, although they have no real access to national agency. Therefore, the analysis of nationalism alongside a theory of gender power opens up a wide variety of possible debates. At the same time, these debates certainly must be understood within their locality. McClintock (1995: 360) asserts that

> There is no single narrative of the nation [as] different groups (genders, classes, ethnicities, generations and so on) do not experience the myriad national formations in the same way. Nationalisms are invented, performed and consumed in ways that do not follow a universal blueprint.

For McClintock (1995: 360), national discourse dictates power structures that materialise in the construction of sociocultural categories such as gender, class and race. These emerge interwoven, which is why, in her view, they need to be studied together, in their specific context of emergence (1995: 360). As Medeiros (2006a: 344–47) reminds us, most of McClintock's theory is based on the specificities of the South African context, and would certainly have benefited from a reflection on the relationships between gender and race within the Portuguese Empire. This brings us back to my analysis of *A Louca*, the emphasis of which will be placed on two important themes. Firstly, the author's capturing of scenes from daily life so as to depict cultural habits, behaviours, traditions, and gender conceptualisations — especially, the Cape Verdean male and the myth of the *super-machos* [super males] — which are considered to be elemental components of national identity. And, secondly, Salústio's portrayal of female gender, as well as the renegotiation of strategies and alternatives that the author proposes.

Following on from this work, the study will focus on the short story collection *Mornas* with a view to analysing some of the thirty-five short stories in which Salústio puts forward a kaleidoscopic portrayal of Cape Verde, from a female-focalised perspective. Considering the author's emphasis on how identities — especially gender identity — come to be officially constructed by national discourse and the active role people play in the continuous renegotiation of those identities, the analysis will rely on Bhabha's (1990: 291–322) conception of the dynamics of national discourse. Bhabha (1990: 292–97) claims that national identity is ambivalent because it possesses an arbitrary pedagogical dimension that is constantly challenged and renegotiated by national subjects through performativity. This ambivalence is therefore empowering, as it becomes an excellent space for rewriting the nation. As such, this study will provide a reading of *Mornas* through a gender mapping of Bhabha's theorisation of the pedagogical and performative dimensions of national identity so as to observe the collection's attempt to renegotiate national discourse, allowing marginality to emerge as a potential site for the formation of counter-narratives.

Cape Verde: Some Notes on History and Society

At this point we are led to recall some historical facts that concern the Cape Verdean society and the progressive struggle to consolidate a Cape Verdean identity, which might shed light upon this portrayal. Located on the coast of Senegal, Cape Verde is an archipelago composed of ten islands and thirteen uninhabited islets. Since its early occupation in the second half of the fifteenth century, it has been made up of a Creole society, that is, one in which the majority of the population is *mestiça* [mestizo], and its culture derives from a mixture of European and African traditions which have progressively homogenised (M. P. de Andrade 1997: 23). The uniqueness of this society and the geographical and economical specificities of the archipelago led to the particular nature of Portuguese colonisation implemented there. The singularity of Cape Verde was much used by the *Estado Novo* in order to build a discourse that would justify to the world Portugal's maintenance of colonies in the post-Second World War period. Therefore, the regime adopted and adapted Brazilian sociologist Gilberto Freyre's cultural theory of Lusotropicalism. Freyre first created the basis of what would later become the Lusotropicalist theory with the publication of *Casa-Grande e Senzala* [The Masters and the Slaves], in 1933. Focusing on the specificities of the formation of Brazilian society, Freyre (1986: 4) praised the distinctive character of Portuguese colonisation in Brazil, claiming that

> [...] the singular predisposition of the Portuguese to the hybrid, slave-exploiting colonization of the tropics is to be explained in large part by the ethnic or, better, the cultural past of a people existing indeterminately between Europe and Africa and belonging uncompromisingly to neither one nor the other of the two continents.

Emphasising the Portuguese colonists' 'fortunate predispositions of race, misology, and culture', Freyre celebrated the hybridity created by the Portuguese in the colonial societies also through their engagement in miscegenation, against which, the sociologist claims, 'he [the Portuguese colonist] had no racial scruples and but few religious prejudices' (1986: 18).

In the decades that followed the publishing of *Casa-Grande e Senzala*, Freyre proceeded with the development of this theory in numerous publications, which would ultimately acquire its final form with the publishing of *O Luso e o Trópico* [The Portuguese and the Tropics] (1961). This publication, which was sponsored by the *Estado Novo* regime, is profoundly based on defending the distinctive character of Portuguese interactions with the peoples from the tropics, as opposed to those of other European imperial powers. This would, of course, be a very convenient doctrine from the *Estado Novo*'s point of view, at a time in which other colonial powers had already engaged in decolonisation and Portugal refused to contemplate giving autonomy to its overseas territories. According to Cláudia Castelo (1999: 61), in its appropriation of Gilberto Freyre's cultural theory of Lusotropicalism, the dictatorial state used the reality of biological *mestiçagem* [miscegenation] to propagate the myth of the distinctive character of Portuguese colonisation:

> As teses de Gilberto Freyre — o tradicional não racismo dos portugueses, a sua capacidade de adaptação aos trópicos, a unidade de sentimento e de cultura que caracterizaria o 'mundo que o português criou' servem, melhor do que quaisquer outras, os interesses político-ideológicos da política externa portuguesa.
>
> [Gilberto Freyre's theses — focusing on the traditional anti-racism of the Portuguese, their capacity to adapt to the tropics, and the unity of sentiment and culture which characterised the 'world created by the Portuguese' — served the political and ideological interests of the Portuguese foreign policy better than any other.]

Castelo (1999: 83–84) observes that the Lusotropicalist ideology was very well received by Cape Verdean intellectuals in the first half of the twentieth century, who read it as scientific proof of their individuality and turned their attention towards themselves and the archipelago's sociocultural reality (despite their disappointment with Freyre's disapproving comments about Cape Verde). Notwithstanding the impact of this discourse of creolisation on the imagination of a Creole national identity, it is important to observe its evolution throughout the distinct historical moments of the nation state.

In his study of the conditions of the emergence of a Cape Verdean national imagination, Gabriel Fernandes (2006: 243–44), a Cape Verdean expert in Political Sociology, concludes that in Cape Verde there are no elements that support the existence of a nationalism *sensu stricto*, nor of a nationalism that makes culture and politics coincide. For Fernandes (2006: 55–239), this is due to the structural conditions of the Cape Verdean society, among which he highlights creolisation (which made political mobilisation based on ethnicity impossible); education (which provided the indigenous people with the cultural tools to negotiate their social status and circulate within the Portuguese colonial universe, simultaneously facilitating the emergence of a Creole self-awareness); diaspora (which makes the nation extrapolate its geographical limits); and political and ideological constructs (which, on the one hand hampered the emergence of a Creole nationalist subjectivity, and on the other facilitated its transnational trajectory). Nonetheless, Fernandes adds that one cannot deny the existence of a *sui generis* Cape Verdean nation, of which creolisation is the most defining factor (2006: 245). As such, he departs from the interventions of cultural and political Cape Verdean elites to identify three crucial moments of nationalist effort.

The first moment, which he calls 'A era da desconstrução simbólico-cultural' [The era of symbolic and cultural deconstruction], coincides with the one Castelo observed earlier. From the beginning of the twentieth century until the 1950s, Nativist and *Claridade* intellectuals began a symbolic and cultural struggle from within the colonial system in which 'a luta pela superação do quadro de dominação e pela alteração da correlação de forças dentro da nação obedece a uma estratégia de integração, e não de confrontação' [the struggle to overcome the context of domination and change the corresponding power relations within the nation followed a strategy of integration rather than of confrontation] (2006: 248).[3] The second moment, 'A era da confrontação político-militar' [The era of political and military confrontation], incorporates the period of the anti-colonial struggle (i.e. from the mid-1950s until 1974). Replacing the symbolic struggle with a political and military one, this moment prioritised the principle that everyone is entitled to autonomy outside the constraints of colonialism (2006: 248–49). As such, the discourse of *Africanisation* which characterised this struggle implied the refusal of both the Portuguese and Cape Verdean discourses of community: Creole culture was too flexible to suit the intentions of essentialist nationalism (2006: 249). Hence, from 1956 onwards, through the formation of the liberation movement that united Guinea-Bissau and Cape Verde under the leadership of PAIGC (Partido Africano da Independência da Guiné e Cabo Verde [African Party for the Independence of Guinea and Cape Verde]) in the fight for independence, Guinea-Bissau became the symbolic identity reference for Cape Verdean nationalist intents.[4] If on the one hand this struggle made possible the emergence of a politically and culturally independent Cape Verdean nation state, on the other hand it represented the 'suspension' of a national imaginary based on Creole culture (2006: 240–50).

Finally, the third moment identified by Fernandes is 'A era da (re)construção ideológica e discursiva' [The era of ideological and discursive (re)construction], which corresponds to the post-colonial period. This moment observes two distinct directions of the nationalist effort: primarily through the affirmation of Africanism and, subsequently, through the reaffirmation of *Caboverdianidade* (2006: 250). Following the achievement of independence in 1975, PAIGC's political agenda led the party to once again put forward an imagination of the nation based on unity between Cape Verde and Guinea-Bissau, thus emphasising an Africanist cultural orientation, to the detriment of a Creole one. Nevertheless, the political separation between Guinea-Bissau and Cape Verde in November 1980, followed by the creation of PAICV (Partido Africano da Independência de Cabo Verde [African Party of Independence of Cape Verde]), opened up a new stage for the development of national identity, marked by an 'acentuada *desideologização* da cultura' [a significant *de-ideologising* of culture], in which *Caboverdianidade* was galvanised again (2006: 251). It is, however, important to point out that the newly created PAICV reinstated the adoption of a one-party political regime, thus emphasising the notion of a nation based on centralism and unity. Furthermore, its ideology had strong Marxist-Leninist roots, and the party itself had important connections with the socialist bloc (J. V. Lopes 2002: 465–512; Foy 1988). Nonetheless, given the distinctive nature of the Creole archipelago, this party had to be particularly careful in adjusting its socialist policies to the specific Cape Verdean context. This leads Elisa Andrade (2002: 268–69) to state that:

> Though officially socialist, Cape Verde was in practice governed by what Aristides Lima called 'an administrative and paternalist system of power' — that is essentially a pragmatic state in which the government ruled with the consent of the majority of the population — as expressed in one-party legislative elections. He writes: '...the national revolutionary democracy, as it is understood in the constitution, embodies both a political and social dimension. As a national democracy, it aims to consolidate the nation. As a revolutionary democracy, it seeks to establish a society free of exploitation, especially as the hitherto powerless social strata have now been brought into power'.

1990 was the year that marked the end of the one-party regime in Cape Verde. According to Chabal, this change occurred not because of the party itself — since PAICV was generally successful in improving people's living conditions — but because of what it represented: an ideology that was obsolete and thus, 'not flexible and open enough' (2002: 94). Hence, the need for Cape Verdeans to proceed with their nation state's political and social modernisation by implementing the multiparty system, which would allow MpD (Movimento para a Democracia [Movement for Democracy]) to take power in 1991. Humberto Cardoso (1993: 181–230), a commissioner for MpD, is much more implacable in his analysis of Cape Verdean civil society throughout the fifteen years under the one-party regime. Cardoso emphasises the ideological and structural colonial continuities in post-independence. He simultaneously claims that PAIGC/PAICV's authoritarian and monolithic posture — legitimised by an armed struggle which took place outside the geographical limits of the nation state — alienated and ultimately suppressed Cape Verdean civil society. He adds that

> Uma violenta crise de valores instalou-se, criando o espaço para o alcoolismo endémico, o consumo público de drogas e o sexo indiscriminado. As crianças, particularmente, são objecto de assalto, não se lhes deixando espaço para realmente viverem a sua infância sem os constrangimentos de se submeterem ao exercício da vaidade dos pais e ao sexismo adoptado pela sociedade adulta. (1993: 191)
>
> [A violent crisis of values set in, paving the way for endemic alcoholism, public consumption of drugs, and sexual promiscuity. Children were particularly affected by this; they did not have enough space to really live their childhoods, due to the constraints of their parents' pride and the sexism adopted by adult society.]

Indeed, Fernandes (2006: 251–52) observes that the MpD intended to revoke this alienation by allowing Cape Verdeans to find themselves again. Yet, the party's political treatment of this debate led it, once again, to promote an imagination of *Caboverdianidade* not as self-referential, but in relational terms, this time with Africa and Europe as its cultural references. This translocal orientation of Cape Verdean national identity (Fernandes 2006: 255), which is very much conditioned by historical and socioeconomic factors, does not make *Caboverdianidade* non-viable because, as Andrade reminds us, Cape Verdeans have a 'relatively homogeneous Creole culture' (2002: 265). In fact, Fernandes (2006: 263–72) suggests that this translocation might actually be an interesting area for the continuous renegotiation of Cape Verdean identity in the contemporary setting, considering the potential for a cosmopolitan creolisation historically presented by Cape Verdeans. This refusal to conform to univocal perceptions of identity and the urge to evolve are traits that can be recognised in the female characters of the Madwoman and Gremiana, who openly defy the established order in *A Louca*.

In this context, it becomes important to observe the historical evolution of women's roles and places within Cape Verdean society. In a 2010 study on Cape Verdean women's participation in social life, Marisa Carvalho (2010: 66) observes that since early colonisation, African women had a fundamental, though discreet role in this setting. As white women's substitutes (since they rarely travelled into the islands), they were greatly responsible for social and physical reproduction, and were often slaves. After the abolition of slavery, Carvalho continues, the private sphere remained women's realm, as they carried on taking care of the domestic domain, particularly of children, who sometimes never got to know their fathers (2010: 66). At this point, the author observes these facts as marks of a socially accepted unofficial polygamy, which would come to influence future societies dramatically. Considering the calamities that have affected the archipelago over time (such as drought and famine), Cape Verdean women have been forced to face extreme hardship. As the heads of families, they have very often had to deal with this alone, given that men would frequently emigrate in search of better lives (2010: 66–70). PAIGC's pro-liberation struggle would come to refute women's stagnant construction by insisting on their active incorporation in the nationalist effort, in a socialist emancipatory logic that emphasised their liberation, alongside men's, from colonial constraints (Foy 1988: 91–98). In the words of Amílcar Cabral, PAIGC's founder,

> The freedom of our people also means the liberation of women [...] [The party must] defend women's rights, respect and require respect for women... but convince women of our land that their liberation must come about through their own efforts, by their work, dedication to the party, respect for themselves and first and foremost resistance against all affronts to their dignity. (Cabral 1980: 97–98; quoted in Foy 1988: 92)

According to Eurídice Monteiro (2009: 77–84), women's struggle for their rights had a strong impulse during the liberation struggle and it achieved many goals throughout the first fifteen years after independence. The creation of OMCV (Organização da Mulher Cabo Verdiana [Cape Verdean Women's Organization]) in 1981 was one of the high points of this struggle throughout PAIGC's single-party government, as the organisation successfully promoted women, opened the debate on their oppressive sexual construction, and fought to improve their lives (2009: 84–86). From the 1990s on, in a multiparty political context, OMCV became an NGO, and many other interventionist institutions that work towards the emergence of a more equalitarian society were created (2009: 87–89).[5] Notwithstanding these solid advances, Monteiro claims that women's subalternity is still alive in contemporary Cape Verdean society. On the one hand, male practices of physical and psychological abuse towards women within the household are still very common; on the other hand, women are still overloaded, having to work within both the public and the domestic spheres (2009: 101–02; Salústio 1999a). Regarding people's access to education and work, Monteiro asserts that despite the general improvements, the number of illiterate women is still much higher that the number of illiterate men. Furthermore, women carry on sacrificing their careers for their families; they still earn less than men do; many remain economically dependent on their husbands; and jobs in the public sector, as well as in governmental power structures, are still very much male-dominated (2009: 102–05). Finally, Monteiro emphasises the existence of power structures within womanhood, which refute this category's homogeneity:

> Para além de as relações de poder entre os sexos, fundamentadas pelas leis patriarcais, são visíveis as relações de poder entre as próprias mulheres, marcadas sobretudo pelas desigualdades sociais, confirmando assim a ideia de que as mulheres cabo-verdianas não fazem parte de uma categoria social homogénea, mas pertencem a um colectivo social composto por múltiplas identidades. (2009: 105)
>
> [Aside from the power relations between sexes, which are based on patriarchal laws, power relations between women themselves are also visible. These are marked above all by social inequality, thus confirming the idea that Cape Verdean women are not part of a homogeneous social category, but that they instead belong to a social collective composed of multiple identities.]

Again, in her examination of the representation of Cape Verdean women's historical roles at the intersection of social elements such as gender, class and race, Salústio seems to aim to provide a more accurate framework for the context of their interpretation, which takes us back to the analysis of *A Louca*.

A Louca de Serrano

As mentioned before, the effort to retrieve women's voices from the silent margins of the official nation by recapturing and legitimising their micro-histories, in turn disturbing the stability of the macro-history of the nation, goes right through Salústio's work and can be traced back to the novel *A Louca*. The novel is divided into twenty-three chapters and it tells us the story of Serrano, a village in a unidentified country that owes its name to a madwoman. In the introductory chapter, the narrator presents us with the setting and the historical background; allowing the reader to have a better understanding of this place, its inhabitants and their behaviours. Although no direct references are made to Cape Verde — an aspect which gives a much more universal feature to the novel as a whole — some of its cultural elements lead us to associate Serrano with this country (Gomes 2000a; Correia 2004). Through a shared *national imagination*, a parallel is created between both the fictional and the real historical worlds, suggesting the author's proposal to revisit Cape Verdean national identity from a female point of view.

The first references made to Serrano weave a portrait of an isolated, peculiar, rudimentary and forgotten village on the periphery of an unidentified capital:

> Serrano, esquecida da civilização, comprimia-se entre os caminhos remotos que levavam a uma longínqua saída para a capital e a região selvagem que se estendia até se perder as vistas, imersa num mundo povoado de seres de estranhos costumes [...]. (Salústio 1998a: 14)
>
> [A place that civilisation forgot, Serrano was squeezed between the remote roads that led to a distant exit towards the capital city and the wilderness which stretched beyond the horizon. It was immersed in a world inhabited by creatures of strange habits [...]]

If, on the one hand, this description directs us to Serrano's isolation, which might lead us to recall Cape Verde's insularity, on the other hand it exposes the gap between Serrano and the capital city, since the former appears to be an uncivilised space, as opposed to the latter's civilisation. The emphasis on Serrano's stagnant nature, from which it is only possible to escape by going to the capital city, suggests a confrontation between two distinct ways of experiencing community: one rural and one urban. Considering that the rural community appears to be depicted negatively, as obscure and obsolete, we are somehow reminded of PAIGC/PAICV's socialist discourses of modernity, as shall be observable later on. Again, this directs us to the everyday experiences of the archipelago's inhabitants.

After providing these introductory references, the narrator tells us about the legend that surrounds the creation of Serrano. This story associates the village with the destiny of an old woman, a stone giant that had been thrown into the sea. At some point in her existence, this woman threw away pieces of her own body, and these pieces became little islands that spread throughout the world. This reference clearly invokes the mythical story of the creation of the Cape Verde Islands. According to Correia (2004: 139), the legend tells us that after having created the Earth, God 'limpou as mãos uma na outra' [wiped one hands together], and the little pieces of rock that He dropped fell onto the sea, becoming the archipelago of Cape Verde. However, the fact that the author chose to recreate the myth by drawing on the indispensable contribution of an old woman's body to the foundation of Serrano reveals important features of this particular place and, simultaneously, suggests an analogical relationship between Serrano and Cape Verde. Firstly, it indicates the existence of a system of traditional authority which is based on a matriarchy, since Serrano's highest authority is a woman — the *parteira* [midwife]. Secondly, it highlights the fact that in this female-dominated context women appear as fragmented beings, since the formation of the community is only achieved through the dismembering of their bodies. Hence, a paradox is put forward: women are represented as powerful due to their reproductive ability, but their encapsulation in that representation inhibits their real access to power in society.

The narrative continues to disclose aspects of Serrano, which is described almost as a living entity: 'Serrano abraçava-se sobre si mesma, deixava-se perder no entrelaçar das árvores e das pedras e respirava tranquila, quase bela, quase mulher, quase homem' [Serrano embraced itself, letting itself get lost among the interwoven trees and rocks. And it breathed quietly, almost beautiful; almost a woman, almost a man] (Salústio 1998a: 15). It appears closed in upon itself, self-sufficient, and almost ignorant of what lies beyond its limits. As Correia (2004: 142) observes, this isolation invokes the insularity which is normally associated with the people who live on islands — and, therefore, the Cape Verdeans — who sometimes find it difficult to access other worlds. Yet, Serrano is 'um pedaço de terra forte' [a strong piece of land] (Salústio 1998a: 15), one with strong roots and a very strict cultural code, which defines traditions, behaviours, habits, and beliefs. There is a clear reference to the instinct of survival that the community of Serrano seems to have, but there is also an implication of their lack of ability to examine the village itself and its flaws:

> Era um pedaço de terra forte, sim, e não era qualquer acto de menos fôlego que a deitava abaixo, e os seus pontos fracos, tinha-os como todo o mundo, ninguém por muito prevenido que estivesse se apercebia deles, nem do que lhe ia debaixo da pele lamacenta, ou no fundo da alma rochosa. (1998a: 15)
>
> [It was, indeed, a strong piece of land, and no small effort would bring it down. It had its weaknesses, like any other, but not even the most informed of people would notice them, nor any of what was going on underneath its muddy skin, or deep inside its rocky soul.]

The Madwoman and Gremiana — a wild girl who refuses to accept living with the false image of perfection projected by the community — seem to be the only exceptions to this panorama of consensual blindness that affects the whole population, given their capacity to see beyond, and their refusal to live behind masks.

The arrival of five outsiders in quiet and peaceful Serrano completely changes the course of the story for this peculiar village. These foreigners, who do not belong to the scenario and, for that reason, look down on the villagers, interfere inopportunely in the population's way of life by imposing their different methodological approaches to the world. Regarding this specific aspect, it is relevant to observe the words the narrator uses to refer to these outsiders: 'o estrangeiro' [the foreigner] (Salústio 1998a: 17), 'os forasteiros' [the outsiders] (1998a: 17), 'funcionários públicos da cidade' [civil servants from the city] (1998a: 17), 'desconhecidos' [strangers] (1998a: 18), 'os intrusos' [the intruders] (1998a: 19). Such a selection of words emphasises the distinction between the villagers and the foreigners. Moreover, there seems to be a gradual intensification of this distinction through the words selected to refer to them in each specific moment, which themselves are progressively organised in terms of intensity. By forcing them to position themselves in an arbitrary system which is unfamiliar to them, the men from the capital entrap the villagers in a kind of *colonial* sphere that can be interpreted in different ways.

An immediate postcolonial reading of the story evokes the Cape Verdean colonial past. Salústio's depiction of the five men's behaviour could be interpreted as a reference to Portuguese colonialism, which was initially almost non-existent, and only really came into effect during the nineteenth and twentieth centuries (in the face of the possibility of losing the colonies to other nations). Initially, the 'fiéis servidores do reino' [the kingdom's faithful servers] (1998a: 20) arrive only to ensure that the territory has got a name and to observe its potential. Two hundred years later, they return with an imperialist attitude and an ideology:

> [...] quando voltou nova missão, desta vez com forte protecção militar, [os habitantes locais] ficaram a saber que aquele local tinha sido destinado a obras de importância vital para o desenvolvimento da zona e para a segurança do país. (1998a: 20–21)
>
> [[...] when the new mission returned, this time surrounded by strong military protection, they [the local inhabitants] realised that that place had been earmarked for work which would be of vital importance for the development of the area and the country's security.]

The behaviour described corresponds to the colonial policies advanced by the 1930 Colonial Act, a constitutional legislation that defined the relationship between Portugal and its overseas territories, which were thenceforth to be called colonies and form part of the Portuguese Colonial Empire (Castelo 1999: 46). It also invokes the official Lusotropicalist discourse that the *Estado Novo* presented to the world, whereby Portugal was composed of a multiracial and multi-ethnic community, distributed amongst various territories, which despite being geographically distant, shared the same culture (Castelo 1999: 97). Nevertheless, this episode in the novel demonstrates the impossibility of such a discourse, since the villagers completely fail to identify with the foreigners:

> A palavra país não lhes dizia nada e, no seu modo de pensar, os homens que os obrigaram a dar um nome à sua terra eram tão estrangeiros como as gentes que possivelmente moravam no outro lado do mundo. Não tinham nada em comum e, mesmo a língua, eles não a compreendiam muito bem e continuavam a pensar que para todos os efeitos, quanto mais afastados se mantivessem de outros povos, tanto melhor para o sossego do seu pedaço de chão. (Salústio 1998a: 21)
>
> [The word country meant nothing to them and, from their point of view, the men who had forced them to name their land were as foreign as the people who possibly lived on the other side of the world. They had nothing in common; they couldn't even understand the language that well. They persisted in thinking that, in any case, the further away they stayed from other populations, the easier it would be to keep their piece of land quiet.]

There is no cultural reciprocity. At the same time, the villagers' failure to identify with (and even to a certain extent their rejection of) the foreigners is quite revealing in itself. In this respect, Cape Verdean author Germano de Almeida claims that Cape Verde did not have the same oppressive experience of colonialism as other Portuguese colonies did 'by virtue of the fact that the Portuguese presence was more indirect and local government and bureaucracy were to a large extent in the hands of a local elite' (Medeiros 2006b: 40–41). Yet, as Medeiros points out, it is quite significant that some of the first acts of cultural resistance to colonialism emerged in Cape Verde (2006b: 41).

A second reading, however, suggests inner cultural tensions in Cape Verde. The emphasis on the return of the authoritarian colonists two hundred years later generates a parallel between the colonial and the post-colonial. Despite the importance that the post-independence one-party socialist government placed on bringing the whole nation together under a single cultural language to make it stronger, this forced unification can be interpreted as castrating in Salústio's work. Considering that the majority of leaders of PAIGC were Cape Verdean, but the imaginary of the nation had Guinea-Bissau as its reference, this episode may represent a clash between the socialist ideas defended by these elite intellectuals and the real situation of the population. Although the general belief is that there are not many cultural differences amongst the Cape Verdean people (Chabal 2002: 92) — at least not as obvious as in other former colonies such as Angola or Mozambique — each island has its own sociocultural particularities (Madeira 2015: 50–55). Furthermore, and recalling the aforementioned opening description of Serrano, these inner cultural tensions become more noticeable. As the binary opposition between urban and rural setting is emphasised, this discrepancy can be read as a reflection of the revolutionaries' alienation from civil society and its cultural references. Considering that the national space was built upon the memory of the colonial space, this postcolonial spatial reconfiguration, which clearly implies a cartographical exercise of remapping and renaming, is somehow imbued with fundamentalism and authority. The space of the city — in the novel, the capital city — which emerges as historically linked with colonial power, is recaptured as the known point of departure for the recognition and occupation of the unknown wilderness, the space occupied by *others*. Devaluing certain cultural behaviours and labelling them barbarian because they do not belong to the elite culture are still colonial acts, even if carried out in the name of a post-independence single nation ideal. The suggestion of this parallel could therefore allude to colonial continuities in the postcolonial imaginary of nationhood.

The forced positioning of the community makes it become aware of the birth of a *common* identity, which emerges from the creation of a name for the village:

> A palavra que se ouvia pela primeira vez vibrou ponderosa na cabeça dos camponeses que levaram as mãos ao peito, onde o sangue bate mais forte, e por largas horas, a montanha, as serras, o vento, a ribeira, e os animais da terra, do ar e das águas, as folhas das árvores, as flores e a fonte repetiram Serrano para que o nome da povoação ficasse gravado em tudo que tivesse vida e igualmente em tudo que não a tivesse. (Salústio 1998a: 19)
>
> [When the farmers heard the new word for the first time, it vibrated powerfully in their minds; they put their hands on their chests, where their hearts were beating harder. And for several hours, the mountain, the hills, the wind, the stream, the land, air and water animals, the leaves of the trees, the flowers and the fountain repeated Serrano, so that the settlement's name would be engraved in every living thing, and every non-living thing too.]

The *parteira* [midwife], or head of the community, is the one who has to come up with this name for the village, and in this almost exhausting task, she is assisted by the Madwoman. By giving the *louca*'s name to the village, the old woman ties up their two destinies, as will be discussed later. The most important aspect to focus on here is the (re)naming of the village. If, on the one hand, it leads to the birth of a sense of shared cultural identity, on the other hand, it reinterprets the community's history, in order to make it fit the purposes of a historicity dictated by the revolutionary discourse of nationhood. Hence, the community's *other* histories are disrupted and suspended, ultimately foretelling the end of the cultural community as it existed up to that point. Nonetheless, this sense of a newborn common identity does not generate estrangement in the population, as even the Madwoman is accepted by them, even if only for five days.

Despite accepting the Madwoman as belonging to this nation, the population confine her to the margins. Considering that, at this point, the only members of the village who are ostracised are the Madwoman and Gremiana, we can interpret this attitude as one that perpetrates sexual hostility. It suggests that despite the society being matriarchal, the elaboration of a national imagination is male-dominated.

As McClintock notes, national discourses project specific roles for both genders, and by doing so, they 'limit and legitimize people's access to the resources of the nation state' (1995: 353). Since the public sphere was continuously forbidden to women throughout history, they were imagined as the 'symbolic bearers of the nation' (1995: 354), the ones that ensure its continuity, but remain socially and politically disempowered. If, as McClintock reminds us, gender identities need to be understood within the specific project of nationhood from which they emerge, the choice of the official common cultural discourse to keep women in a stagnant conceptualisation proves to be deliberate and strategic, since a sense of cultural continuity is achieved through the maintenance of conventional gender identities (1995: 354). As such, women's uninterrupted entrapment in their colonised bodies reveals that the limits of this nation are defined in the female body. However, this projection of femininity can only be understood when confronted with the construction of masculinity. Given that they were always dominant, both in the private and the public spheres, men were responsible for the elaboration of national discourses — and they were also constructed as such. Therefore, power structures within gender can only be fully understood when placed in a particular context in which other categories interfere as well. In her analysis, McClintock (1995: 6–7) departs from the conviction that the maintenance of imperialism depended on specific constructions of gender, class and race, which emerged as interdependent categories that had to be examined relationally. In Chapter 3 of the novel, we are able to observe how class, race and gender interact in the social setting.

The chapter starts by highlighting a very important social characteristic: class differentiation. We are introduced to the San Martins, a traditional family in the capital city that has succeeded in surviving throughout difficult times of change, thanks to their ability to readjust and maintain their financial supremacy. The women from the family often promote charities along with the Church to help the poor people from the capital city. This generous act is actually a way to ensure the maintenance of the social gap between rich people and poor people. In their social acts, the rich women are supported by the Church, through the figure of the priest who struggles substantially to defend them publicly against the envious comments and acts of poor people. Having himself been an object of charity in the past, he uses the Catholic discourse to encourage poor people to accept their condition and, therefore, propagate social differentiation. Despite the emphasis on class struggle, the question of race appears to be connected to it; Joana San Martin's biggest fear is that her daughter Genoveva is in love with Roberto, a young sportsman, who, despite all his qualities, does not fit the profile that such families look for in prospective boyfriends:

> Normalmente um nome sonante e, sobretudo, um respeitável património. Encantada, a mocinha jurava que ele era o homem da sua vida e fazia contas aos anos que faltavam para o casamento, ignorando as recomendações da mãe que, inconformada, acusava o desportista de pobre, negro e ignorante. (Salústio 1998a: 46)

> [Normally a good name and, above all, a respectable patrimony. Delighted, the

> young lady swore that he was the love of her life and counted down the years to the wedding, ignoring her mother's recommendations. Refusing to accept this, the mother accused the sportsman of being poor, black and ignorant.]

Finally, gender is also contemplated, since it is through the control of the female body — a control that is asserted through the female lineage — that the class structures and the racial order are maintained.

Again, we are confronted with an analogical resemblance between the fictional social reality of the capital city — representative of the official discourse of nationhood — and the historical facts of Cape Verdean social reality. Notwithstanding the impact that Freyre's utopian Lusotropical ideals had on Cape Verde, the fact is that social stratification exists in the archipelago, and it emerges tied to people's colour and degree of miscegenation. Historically, the fact that Cape Verde has had a predominantly mixed race population has limited racial tensions in society, but, as Hamilton (1975: 236) reminds us, that does not mean that these tensions did not exist:

> [...] indeed a homogeneous, mixed-blood population in the upper stratum has helped to assuage traditional racial antipathies, although the legacy of distinctions determined by color and the presence of a black population, mostly lower class, still serve to maintain race consciousness. Cape Verde does not have the visceral racism and tensions of other multiracial societies, but traditional attitudes and socioeconomic factors do make color an important consideration throughout the archipelago.

Maria Manuela Afonso's 2002 study on education and social classes in Cape Verde also addresses this debate. Afonso (2002: 67) argues that in contemporary Cape Verdean society, racial differentiation, as well as inter-island divisions, urban and rural oppositions, or religious differentiations, although they do exist, are generally not as relevant for social differentiation as class is. Afonso concludes that since the colonial era, social classes were at the core of the structuring dynamics of Cape Verdean society. Although the class structure has changed significantly since independence, due to the widening of educational opportunities, the researcher claims that 'o acesso [à educação] não é suficientemente democratizado para disfarçar o seu papel de classe. A importância da educação como símbolo de mobilidade social é acentuada, mas também o é a realidade do seu papel como reprodutor de desigualdades' [access [to education] is not democratised enough to disguise its role in the maintenance of class structures. The relevance of education as a symbol of social mobility is highlighted, but so is the reality of its role in propagating inequalities.] (2002: 211). Hence, Afonso claims that education and the educational system privilege the social classes that belong to a 'petite bourgeoisie', which is connected with the governmental entity (2002: 207–12).

As such, because Roberto belongs to the group of black Cape Verdeans that constitute the lower class, he is not allowed to move up the class ladder, and is thus unworthy of Genoveva. It is a recurring cycle of interdependence between class and race. Therefore, all the racial prejudices that are usually attached to black people — lazy, ignorant, dumb — arise from the fact that they are poor. In addition to this, the female body is at the centre of the whole dynamic, as Genoveva is meant to marry a candidate whom her parents consider to be suited to her social status so as to maintain the social order. Once more, we observe Salústio's use of the community's self-imagination so as to spark recognition and discussion. By depicting the stagnant nature of these social dynamics, which echo colonial structures, the author promotes an intersection between fiction and historical reality, consequently questioning national identity. Simultaneously, she renegotiates these elements by building characters who neglect to identify with the established order and present subversive behaviours that demystify it.

If, as McClintock (1995: 360) reminds us, 'there is no single narrative of the nation', each specific individual and/or group that integrates into the nation experiences it in a different way. This means that nationalism is invented by a dominant group, which, at a given historical moment, *selects* symbolic and cultural elements to construct a power structure in which it has a dominant role (Yuval-Davis 1997: 4). Nevertheless, the national narrative is never closed, so it can be continuously renegotiated. Going back to the moment of awareness of community identity in Serrano, there is a clear suggestion that it is male-oriented. Not only does this imply that individuals — both women and men — imagine themselves according to predefined gender identities, but also that the female gender is sacrificed to ensure that the order remains patriarchal. Gender conceptualisation is, indeed, greatly emphasised throughout *A Louca*. From the beginning of the novel, we come to understand that despite women's dynamism in the organisation and maintenance of the social structure, every action is taken to support male social dominance. As opposed to women's dynamism, men are always portrayed as passive beings. This happens in such a way that at times it seems that the male characters are alienated, living in some kind of reality which belongs only to them and is completely out of step with what is going on around them. Despite being officially dominant in the power structure, Serranese men are disempowered by their inability to ensure the physical — and therefore social — reproduction of the community. Indeed, they are marginal to these processes, yet they must maintain the lie that enables them to remain socially dominant. Through the exposure of this reality, both women and men have the opportunity to rewrite their own identities.

Since distinct gender constructions imply different positions and expectations, in these settings — village and capital city — masculine gender is culturally constructed to project the *super-macho* ideal, an image which all men are expected to identify with. This image is primarily projected in the reproductive field — the most important one in this society. Although the men of Serrano are unaware of their infertility, they do know that something is not right regarding reproduction in Serrano. They prefer not to give much thought to the subject, which is, in fact, one of their most commonly used strategies towards the world around them. They deliberately ignore and blindly accept everything that ensures the perception of the male empowered identity as stable and continuous. Given that reproduction is their first social obligation, another strategy which men use to reject any ideas that may question their virility is to blame women:

> Sim, porque nas suas poucas falas, os homens de Serrano diziam que as mulheres é que podiam falhar na procriação, porque os machos, estes, nada tinham a ver com tal tarefa e bastava ver o mecanismo visível da sua sexualidade que, de cada vez que enchia e desenchia, um filho poderia nascer; dezenas, centenas, milhões de filhos poderiam nascer. A terra é que pode ser fértil ou não e terra eram as fêmeas e os seus úteros que às vezes não passavam de terra seca — afirmavam, frustrados, quando os descendentes demoravam a aparecer, para aceitarem com normalidade, quase com orgulho, os filhos que um dia acabavam por chegar. (Salústio 1998a: 63)
>
> [Indeed, in their few words, Serrano men said that women were the only ones who could fail to procreate, because the *machos*, they had nothing to do with such a task. It would suffice to observe the visible mechanism of their sexuality — every time that it filled up and got emptied, a child could be born; dozens, hundreds, millions of children could be born. It is the land that may or may not be fertile. The females and their uteruses were the land, which at times was nothing but dry land — affirmed the frustrated men, when procreation took longer than expected, only to normally welcome the children who were eventually born with what was almost a sense of pride.]

Hence, these men live according to a falsely projected image of themselves, neither questioning nor acknowledging the guarantees of the survival of male superiority. For this reason, the outspoken Madwoman has to be labelled as mad and kept within the margins of the community. Furthermore, Gremiana — the only woman who dares to speak openly about the fact that Serranese women are getting pregnant by men other than their Serranese husbands, in order to secure biological and cultural procreation — has to die. She is a threat to the social order and, thus, to the hegemonic national narrative of the community, which is clearly created by and for men. In the capital city the situation is the same. We become aware that husband and wife in the San Martin family are unable to have more children because the patriarch is sterile, as he caught a venereal disease from an unknown woman he slept with. Yet, the official version of this unfortunate fact is that his wife has had pregnancy complications in the past and, therefore, is unable to give birth to more children.

In *A Louca*, it is also made clear that women are required to identify with an established female conception, one that at some point will be equally deconstructed. The first image of the text is that of the *parteira* [midwife], presented as the wisest woman of the village. From a small window of her well-known house she obsessively updates her count of the number of inhabitants of Serrano, including newborn and unborn children (1998a: 67). At this moment in the text, we learn about two of the most important defining characteristics of this community. The first is that, in terms of power structures, a woman is the highest authority of Serrano and it is also she who makes the major social decisions. The second is that reproduction is very important, because this powerful woman is the midwife of the village, the one who ensures its continuity. The more we learn about the *parteira*, the more we realise how empowered she is. It is she who not only brings people into life, but also initiates boys in their sex lives, cures men's sexual dysfunctions, helps women to get pregnant, and decides on dead people's burials. Yet, this woman, who is the 'dona da única porta mágica do povoado e arredores que parecia alargar quando as dimensões do corpo que entrava ou saía o exigiam, ou quando ela assim o decidia' [owner of the only magic door in the village and its surroundings; one which seemed to widen according to the dimensions of the body that entered or left, or whenever she decided it would] (1998a: 14), is also the loneliest person in the village. Having been chosen for the position, she has to dedicate her life to serving the people, immediately annulling her individuality in order to perform the roles of *parteira* and head of the community. Hence, the survival of Serrano relies on the traditional roles of women, fully represented by this woman. However, all the *parteiras* of Serrano end up dying in bizarre circumstances that somehow recall suicides. The first one dies because she drinks too much water, although the Madwoman states that, in fact, she had been drinking *grogue*.[6] The second one is entrapped between the big door of the house and a basket that she is carrying, and ends up dying as well. And, finally, the third one disappears right before Serrano is destroyed by the waters. This may suggest the inevitability of disappearance of the female conceptualisation or, at the least, the need for it to die so that female identity can be reimagined outside the constraints of that symbolism.

This emphasis on motherhood implies that women have the responsibility of ensuring the survival of Serrano, which is an extremely stressful task in this particular setting. Therefore, they have to adopt strategies in order to adjust to the community's gender expectations. Women who cannot conceive are not considered to be complete women, as Maninha proves. Despite the authority of the *parteira*, the only power that women maintain in this society relates to reproduction. Therefore, Maninha is completely disempowered and, consequently, a subject of mockery in the community. She is despised by both men and women — the former scorn her for being unable to reinforce Jerónimo's virility; and the latter look down on her for being less of a woman:

> Maninha atravessava uma crise aguda de neurastenia depressiva e somente as famosas ervas locais conseguiam animá-la a fazer as lides da casa e a conviver com as mulheres da vizinhança que, maldosamente, conduziam as falas para gravidezes, partos e coisas estéreis. (1998a: 56)
>
> [Maninha was suffering from a severe case of neurasthenia and only the famous local herbs would encourage her to do her household chores and to socialise with the women in the neighbourhood, who would direct the conversations to pregnancies, child birth and sterile things purely out of malice.]

Although she knows that all the women in the village have given birth to children by men other than their Serranese husbands, the whole community connives in maintaining the traditions and secrets of Serrano in order to guarantee its continuity and the maintenance of the social order.

In his study of the Cape Verde islands, Basil Davidson reports on this dependence on the women:

> Hence a painful wound within this society. Its guarantee of continuity and social essence depend all the time on women. But its daily life is dominated by the wills and whims of men. [...]

> But women here become dual victims: victims of the archipelago's colonial mismanagement and ruin, and also victims of a male mastery, a rasping and most tiresome *machismo*, which even now, when things begin to be different, the visitor encounters every day. (1999: 171)

In an interview with Joana Fonseca Modesto, a local secretary for the Women's Organisation (OM) in Santo Antão island, Davidson learns that it is part of the Cape Verdean tradition that only women who have a man and children can be respected — even if that man is not their husband and does not intend to become a social father to the children. Hence, there is a kind of consensual 'sexual "liberty"' that alleviates men of any responsibilities and entraps women (1989: 172). Modesto ends by stating that regardless of the efforts made to change this situation, it has proved to be a very difficult task given the deep rooting of cultural, religious and sociological beliefs. Yet, Maria das Dores, the spokesperson of OM, told Davidson that various measures were being taken in the protective legislation for women. The great problem they were facing was, according to the spokesperson, the application of these laws among the female population, because the majority of women had to have their attitude worked on so as to accept these changes (1989: 173–74).

Salústio's emphasis on reproduction from a female-focalised perspective gives it a whole new dimension. It shows that in a patriarchal society such as this, reproduction is historically the realm of masculine realisation: male identity is defined by men's ability to procreate. At this point, it is worth mentioning a story that Davidson recalls, which confirms this statement:

> On one of my inland 'walking tours' I happened to visit an uncle of a Party leader, an emigrant living normally in Europe who comes back for holidays in the family home. [...]
>
> It transpires that our host has twenty-one living children; 'or maybe it's more', he adds with great cheerfulness, 'you can't always keep count'. His own father was thought to have had as many as sixty-three children. [...]
>
> Afterwards I ask my friend the nephew: 'But how do they support so many?'
>
> 'Oh, they don't, they support some of them. As for the rest, there's always the mother.' (1989: 171)

Regardless of the power it entitles women to in other respects, the archipelago's post-independence social and cultural existence remains patriarchal and the colonial inheritance contributes to this. In other words, women's bodies continue to sustain the community. Yet, in this Serranese setting, in which all men are sterile, women make possible the reinterpretation of reproduction, demonstrating their decisive role in the physical and social continuity of the community. They are no longer just passive wombs waiting to be fertilised: they have the power of decision over the community's faith. On the one hand, this perception demonstrates the discrepancy between the official patriarchal discourse of community and the practice of it, as women actively subvert the power structures in reproduction. On the other hand, their choice to remain silent so as not to disturb the prevailing order means that they too are contributing to the crystallisation of conventional gender identities. Although Serranese women appear to be cleverer than Serranese men, they do not attempt to surpass the boundaries of their permitted social intervention, which is limited to passive reproduction. By doing so, they end up ensuring men's social superiority. This passive behaviour of women culminates in the condemnation and death of Gremiana: 'o remorso de não terem movido uma palavra ou um gesto para a defender e salvar. Para se defenderem também' [the remorse for not having said or done anything to defend and rescue her. To defend themselves as well] (Salústio 1998a: 74).

In this context, the characters Fernanda/Genoveva, and later Filipa, behave discordantly. The former starts by failing to identify with her expected role by sleeping with Roberto and getting pregnant with his baby against her family's will. Later, because she proves that her capacity to give birth does not make her a mother, Fernanda/Genoveva shows that a committed father can also bring up a child. Furthermore, her social detachment (given her mental alienation) from Serrano opens up possibilities for her, such as, for example, her capacity to give birth without the involvement of the *parteira* or the help of any other woman. As for Filipa (Fernanda/Genoveva's daughter), she always proves that she can think for herself and make her own choices. Regardless of having had numerous families throughout the years — families who always abandoned her — she does not give up on finding her own voice and independence. The many issues that surround her birth and her upbringing — having been abandoned by her mother who she never knew; having been sent by Jerónimo to the capital city to live with her mother's family, who rejected her; having known only dysfunctional families — condition her ability to imagine herself outside this portrayal. Nevertheless, she fails to identify with any sociocultural constructions or gender predefinitions.

The author progressively deconstructs the ideal of men as *super-machos* in this context as well, by showing the falsity of this concept and the flaws that Serranese men insist on hiding. The only man who seems to be able to present an alternative in this panorama is Jerónimo. Although he attempts to conform to the ideal of masculinity projected by the community's imaginary, he finds it an extremely difficult task. After having served in the military, he dreams about a different life in the capital city. Yet, he sacrifices his dreams of liberty for the sake of the continuity of Serrano. With great effort, he gradually becomes a slave to the community's habits and avoids thinking at all, so as to minimise the suffering caused by this self-betrayal. The only thing that Jerónimo cannot accomplish is the same thing that no other Serranese man can: provide his wife Maninha with children. Naturally, the whole community and Maninha herself believe that she is to blame for the situation. The possibility is confirmed later on, when Jerónimo brings a pregnant girl into the village. The fourteen-year-old Genoveva San Martin is the amnesiac girl who Jerónimo finds wandering in the fields in the aftermath of a plane crash. Not knowing her true identity, he renames her Fernanda and takes care of her. However, the child she is carrying is not his, and his failure to reveal this fact makes him, in the eyes of the community, the first Serranese man able to reproduce. After giving birth to Filipa, Fernanda/Genoveva leaves for another city near the capital, abandoning both Jerónimo and the baby girl, who is raised by Jerónimo as his own child.

At this point, it is interesting to point out how much of a different man Jerónimo has become. Despite constantly attempting to conform to the 'laws' of survival in Serrano, he finds it extremely difficult. Moreover, he is the first Serranese man to have his *own* child and to take care of the baby, even in the absence of Fernanda/ Genoveva. Finally:

> Jerónimo era um homem respeitado na povoação, embora tivesse sido mais, se depois do trabalho ou durante a pesca, como os outros, falasse das intimidades da companheira, da Fernanda e das outras mulheres. (1998a: 101)
>
> [Jerónimo was a respected man in the village. However, he would have been even more so had he talked — after work or during fishing, like all the other men did — about the intimate matters of his partner, Fernanda, and of all the other women.]

He fails to identify with the male projection imagined by the community. Indeed, he is a 'serranês falhado' [failed Serranese] (1998a: 95). That becomes clear when Serrano is destroyed by the construction of a dam. He leaves for the capital city to become a mechanic, as he had always dreamt of doing. He also becomes the only man in the novel who is able to officially recognise and verbalise his incapacity to procreate, thus assuming his marginal place in biological reproduction. Yet, he never stops looking for Filipa, so he reaffirms his new central place in cultural reproduction. Consequently, he is able to detach himself from Serrano and its representations, and renegotiate his own identity.

In terms of male contribution to the rewriting of gender identities, it is also important to acknowledge the subversive role of the character Roberto. Although we do not know much about him, we do learn that he is considered less of a man by Genoveva's family due to his socioeconomic and, hence, racial condition. As mentioned before, he does not fulfil the ideal of masculinity that is instituted by the society of the capital city. Nevertheless, he is the only male character we know of in the novel who is fertile and Genoveva gets pregnant with his child. Thus, Roberto represents a new kind of masculinity, which emerges from the disruption of the institutionalised sociocultural orders. He emerges as the only man *worthy* of procreating and biologically contributing to the emergence of a new imagination for the nation.

Finally, it is essential to examine the Madwoman, the somewhat mythical woman who gives name to the novel:

> [A] mulher que baptizou Serrano, conhecedora de todos os segredos do vale, origem desta breve narração... uma jovem que não encontrou homem, mulher, bandido ou animal que fosse, que a tivesse chamado filha, que a tivesse feito mulher e por isso, para se vingar, amaldiçoava as criaturas do lugar que, por cumplicidade, tinham torcido o seu destino e a conheciam por Louca de Serrano. Ciclicamente, aparecia no povoado por artes desconhecidas, para desaparecer do mundo visível dos vivos quando completava os trinta e três anos e já tivesse visto tudo o que tinha para ver, e ouvido tudo o que tinha para ouvir. Depois voltava a aparecer, filha de gente nenhuma, de lugar e tempo nenhuns, criança, mulher. (1998a: 26)

> [The woman who baptised Serrano knows about all the secrets of the valley, and is at the root of this brief narration... a young woman who never found a man, a woman, a bandit or even an animal that would have called her its own, or that would have made her a woman. For that reason and to take revenge, she cursed the creatures of that place, those who conspired to change her destiny and who knew her as the Madwoman of Serrano. She always appeared in the village by unknown means, only to disappear off the face of the earth when she turned thirty-three years old — having seen everything she had to see, and heard everything she had to hear. She would then reappear, daughter of no one, of no time or place; a child, a woman.]

She represents, from the beginning, a dissonant voice that emerges from within the setting, but one which is simultaneously dissociated from it in the sense that she is not constructed by the community's hegemonic narrative. She is deviant and therefore unable to fit into a preconceived profile. For this reason, she is called Madwoman and sent to the margins of the community. The fact that she dies and is reborn every thirty-three years lends her a messianic aspect, and, as mentioned above, her destiny is linked to that of the village when the *parteira* decides to name it after her. This act can be interpreted as the condemnation of Serrano (and everything that it represents) to disappearance and subsequent rebirth with a new identity. And, indeed, when Jerónimo, Genoveva/Fernanda, and Filipa get together again as a family, the Madwoman's destiny is fulfilled. A new family arises from the margins to recreate a shared identity. It is a dysfunctional family and we do not know if it will survive in the future, but the fact that these three wanderers, who were always displaced within the community discourse, manage to succeed outside of it and finally come together shows the potential of alternative discourses. They are rewriting their identities within the community's imagination and, in doing so, they reveal a world of possibilities for society.

A Louca de Serrano: Conclusion

The work Dina Salústio develops in *A Louca de Serrano* is certainly a revisionist one. Through analogy, the author promotes the analysis of the historical, geographical, sociological and cultural aspects which intersect to originate the conceptualisation of Cape Verde as a nation. Primarily, it opens a window that looks over Cape Verde as an 'imagined community', so as to provide an understanding of how it came to be constructed, simultaneously recovering other fragments that did not make it into the national narrative. Then, through the selection and treatment of themes, in which gendered, racial and class constructions emerge entangled, Salústio invites the reader to reflect upon the colonial continuities in a post-independence setting, where socially discriminatory structures remain at the forefront of the national imaginary. Ultimately, by proposing actions and behaviours which are alien to the established national narrative, not only does she question this narrative, but she also broadens the horizons of national representation. Just like the Madwoman who gives name to it, the novel proves the potential of subversion to be a place for resistance and creativity. Salústio emphasises again the possibilities which might emerge from marginal experiences of the nation in the literary work *Mornas Eram as Noites* (1999a).

Mornas Eram as Noites

This collection of thirty-five short stories, which constitutes a kaleidoscopic representation of Cape Verdean experience, presents a wide variety of themes. The particularity of Salústio's approach to the *mornas* as an identity-reference is intimately connected with the sub-title that the author chose to add — *...De como elas se entregaram aos dias* [...Of how they succumbed to the days] — which indicates that, once again, women and the feminine perspective on Cape Verdean daily life will be at the core of the discussion. Hence, Salústio rescues these women from silence and brings alternative histories to the narrative of the nation. She guides the reader through the pages, leading her/him to assume a Cape Verdean female perspective and skin so as to analyse the different layers of which this grand narrative is composed. Fundamentally, the author's main purpose seems to be that of deconstructing female identity as it is conceived in the official national discourse of *Caboverdianidade*, in order to unveil the colonial continuities that are still visible in the post-independence setting. She does so by presenting diverse portrayals of women who come from different social backgrounds, act in different contexts and lead different lives. In her own words (Gomes 2000b):

> [...] a necessidade de publicar as inúmeras histórias de mulheres, histórias de vida que passam por mim. [...] para querer mostrar o meu reconhecimento a estas mulheres caboverdeanas que trabalham duro, que fazem o trabalho da pedra, que carregam água, que trabalham a terra, que têm a obrigação de cuidar dos filhos, de acender o lume. [...] Falo das mulheres intelectuais, daquelas que não são intelectuais, daquelas que não têm nenhum meio de vida escrito, falo da prostituta, falo de todas as mulheres que me dão alguma coisa, e que eu tenho alguma coisa delas [...] Em Cabo Verde, quando nasce uma menina, ela já é uma mulher.
>
> [[...] the need to publish the countless stories about women, life stories that pass me by. [...] I want to show my appreciation to these Cape Verdean women, who work hard, pound the food, carry the water, work the land, those who must take care of the children and light the fire. [...] I talk about intellectual women, about those who are not intellectuals, about those who are illiterate; I talk about prostitutes, and any other women who I take something from, and with whom I share something [...] in Cape Verde, when a girl is born, she is already a woman.]

These accounts will provide the reader with the necessary knowledge to understand the various places of women in postcolonial Cape Verde. At the same time, it will allow for an understanding of how these diverse feminine identities came to be formed, and how conditions such as gender, class and location interact and conflict within the national discourse so as to construct individuals' identities. At this point, we are yet again led to recall the work developed by McClintock (1995: 7–16), in which the author advocates that the reading of women's subjectivity (or its suppression) emerges from the analysis of a given national discourse — that is always gendered — and of its various relational categories at a specific moment in time. Thus, the selection of short stories explores themes that speak to the collective and they come together in a way that resembles a patchwork.

These themes will be examined against the cultural, social, historical and geographical background of the archipelagos, in order to support the argument that Salústio's *Mornas* sets out to be a work of social analysis that questions the construction of female and male subjectivities post-independence; traces women's cultural impact in the Cape Verdean nation by giving them a voice; proposes a displacement of the centrality of the official national narrative and its underlying power structures, through addressing how subjectivities are continuously renegotiated in the nation's day-to-day experiences; and demonstrates that the active engagement of these different social actors in the rewriting of the nation can produce much more challenging and democratic ways to experience the nation. As such, I will provide an analysis in the light of Bhabha's theorisation of national discourse. Bhabha (1990: 291–322) problematises the nation with a view to dismantling a historicist perception of it as a simultaneous, horizontal and homogeneous experience. In the theorist's view, this fixed conception is highly totalising, as it is incapable of representing multiple social experiences of and constant social dynamics within the nation (1990: 292). Perceiving the nation as a narrative construction, Bhabha (1990: 1–7) emphasises the temporal dimension of the discursive strategies used to legitimise a historicist conception of nation, so as to undermine it by focusing on 'a particular ambivalence that haunts the idea of the nation, the language of those who write of it and the lives of those who live it' (1990: 1). Hence, he claims that this ambivalence grows out of the gradual awareness that 'the cultural temporality of the nation inscribes a much more transitional social reality' (1990: 1).

For Bhabha, this 'discursive liminality' becomes a very privileged place for the renegotiation and rewriting of national identity, as it enables the understanding of how the ambivalent entity 'people' comes to be constructed, resulting from various discourses, in a double narrative movement (1990: 295–97). Focusing specifically on the potential of marginal discourses to contest and displace the centrality of cultural hegemonies, Bhabha emphasises the challenging nature of postcolonial and feminist temporalities (1990: 304). Thus, through a gender mapping of Bhabha's theorisation of the pedagogical and performative dimensions of national identity, this analysis will argue that the collection *Mornas* defends the non-existence of absolute and stable limits of the national narrative. By empowering those occurrences that take place outside the constraints of national discourse, the collection enables the emergence of liminality as a privileged place for the elaboration of new conceptions of the nation.

Considering the aforementioned characteristics that shape the historical evolution of *Caboverdianidade*, and focusing particularly on the post-independence setting in which *Mornas* was published (keeping in mind that the short stories were published regularly in newspapers, so they were based on contemporary occurrences in Cape Verdean society prior to their compilation and release in 1994), it is possible to state that the pedagogical discourse of the nation throughout the period represented was very much based on the assumption of masculine supremacy. Notwithstanding the socialist and post-Marxist emphasis on an equalitarian society, in which women are emancipated alongside their male peers, the imagination of a continuous and uninterrupted *Caboverdianidade* was achieved through the crystallisation of the historical power dynamics between genders, within both the private and the public spheres. As such, a supposedly stable, univocal and one-dimensional historicity of the nation emerges, imposing patriarchal constructions of femininity and masculinity as 'tradition', and ultimately shaping all social structures. Nevertheless, in *Mornas*, Cape Verdeans' daily experience of the nation continuously displaces that univocal and one-dimensional time, through the recognition of challenging social performances that attest to the fluidity of time.

Following on from these premises, it is worth starting by analysing the way in which the masculinised pedagogical conceptualisation of the nation constructs manhood, as the roles that men are expected to perform are also defined and maintained by this same pedagogical discourse of the nation. Through the analysis of various specific moments of the Cape Verdean reality portrayed, we come to realise that, in fact, the male is a shadowy presence in the short stories, rarely intervening directly or defying the sociocultural stability that legitimises his supremacy. According to the collection, there is a specific conception of manhood that all Cape Verdean men are meant to identify with: the *super-macho*. This is a man who moves across all classes and races and survives through the projection of an image of himself as centre. Honour is meant to have an important impact on the definition of manhood in the archipelagos, and this explains some of the male attitudes — such as domestic violence towards women, for example — which we will explore. According to João Lopes Filho (1996: II, 135–36), there are different sorts of honour men can relate to in this setting:

> O sentido de honra encontra-se profundamente inculcado no homem cabo-verdiano e constitui um dos valores fundamentais por que esta sociedade se rege. [...] a honorabilidade e o respeito que determinado indivíduo recebe dos seus concidadãos tem a ver, por um lado, com a conotação económica e social de honra [...] Abrange também o conceito de honra o sentido da virtude, esta especialmente associada à mulher, tendo uma conotação religiosa e sexual e portanto diferente do tipo de honra que vimos acima, intimamente associada aos valores masculinos. [...] A honra é, normalmente, uma questão masculina. [...] No entanto, a grande preocupação com o olhar dos estranhos fora do contexto familiar, recai sobre a conduta das mulheres, elementos fundamentais no que concerne à honra da família. A contribuição da mulher tem sido essencialmente de ordem passiva, para que seja positiva, diferenciando-se do papel do homem, a quem compete a acção.

> [The sense of honour is profoundly instilled in Cape Verdean men and it constitutes one of the fundamental values that guide this society. [...] on the one hand, any given individual is perceived as honourable and respectable by his fellow citizens according to a sense of both economic and social honour [...] This sense of honour also encompasses the sense of virtue, which is associated with women in particular and has religious and sexual connotations — it is, therefore, different from the kind of honour discussed above, which is closely

> associated with masculine values. [...] Normally, honour is a masculine matter. [...] Nonetheless, the great preoccupation with how things look to strangers outside the family circle lies with women's behaviour, since they are key elements when it comes to family honour. Women's contribution has been essentially passive in order to be positive, as opposed to men, who are expected to play an active role.]

Curiously, the most frequent attitude coming from men in the whole collection is absence — they remain silent and passive. Despite their social and physical dominance, men's absence from daily life — the realm where stagnant identities come to be renegotiated — demonstrates their desire to maintain their authority. As such, in these texts they are passive entities because they intend to crystallise their exercise of control over women, who appear very active in different settings of the everyday experience — so, despite their apparent stability, the power structures are being contested by women. Hence, in spite of their self-definition as the centre of the pedagogical conception of the nation — as opposed to women, who remain in the margins of the national project — they are inactive in a performative day-to-day sense, and thus marginal to the constant process of national renewal. As a result, women prove to be the real core of the nation (Filho 1996: 143).

There is one single short story in the whole collection that speaks specifically about men. It is entitled 'Campeão de Qualquer Coisa' [Champion of Everything] and it talks about an episode in which the narrator receives an outsider in a typically Cape Verdean gathering and treats him like he would treat any other man from the archipelago — so, any other man who fitted the *super-macho* profile. The guest does not associate himself with that profile and both of them end up discussing the issue, highlighting the importance of living an open life, with no disguise, and without the need to constantly prove that one is the victor. Unusually, the action takes place in a social environment which seems to correspond to the empowered Cape Verdean social class. This not only shows that the machismo we are talking about is not confined to a specific social class, but it also suggests, once again, that the alternative to this behaviour has to emerge from this empowered context as well:

> A noite ia a mais de meio. Grupos de homens e grupos de mulheres convenientemente estabelecidos. Eu fazia o protocolo e chegaste e como manda a praxe, fui-te passando um copo para as mãos e porque não te conhecia disse-te: os campeões das anedotas estão ao fundo, ao lado, os campeões da política internacional, à esquerda os do futebol, os do sexo, debaixo do abacateiro, os dos copos, junto ao bar e iniciei a retirada porque não havia mais nada que dizer [...] Foi então que me disseste que não eras campeão de coisa nenhuma e nem sequer eras bom em qualquer coisa e que eras um tipo normal. (Salústio 1999a: 11)

> [More than half the night had gone. There were groups of well-established men and women. I was following the protocol when you arrived. As is common practice, I handed you a glass, and because I didn't know you, I said to you 'the joke-telling champions are at the back; the champions of international politics are standing next to them; the football champions are to the left; the sex champions are under the avocado tree; and the booze champions are at the bar'. And I turned to walk away, because there was nothing else to say [...] It

was then that you told me you were not a champion of anything, and that you were not even good at anything, and that you were just a regular guy.]

When the narrator enumerates the groups that the guest might want to choose from, there is a suggestion of homogeneity, which is solidified through male dominance over women. Nevertheless, the outsider takes the narrator by surprise by not associating himself with that 'champion' profile, so the latter carries on insisting, almost interpellating[7] the former to fit in one of the groups predefined by the profile, telling him that all he needs to do is lie to be accepted. However, the outsider presents a whole set of alternative behaviours which are totally opposed to those underlying the conception of the *super-macho*, i.e. behaviours that expose the true face of a new man who flatters himself for being fragile and 'normal':

> Ensinaram-nos que devíamos ser heróis de qualquer coisa. Exigem que façamos permanentemente exercícios de auto afirmação [*sic*]. Não nos educaram para corajosamente debatermos os nossos medos, falhas, hesitações, infernos. Apetrecharam-nos com o mito de super-machos e esperam que sejamos sempre vencedores, fazendo-nos inimigos da própria maneira de estar, escamoteando a verdade, falseando as fronteiras. E porque somos apenas normais e temos vergonha da nossa normalidade, passamos o tempo todo a pensar numa roupagem que impressione. E vestimo-nos de atletas e mascaramo-nos de campeões, para, às escondidas, chorarmos a nossa simplicidade, a vulgaridade que enforma os nossos sentimentos íntimos. Não temos coragem para dizer não sou o melhor e não tenho que o ser, nem justificar-me da minha fragilidade. Entrar em competição com as minhas fantasias e as dos outros seria sinal de simples imaturidade e falta de respeito por mim próprio — prosseguiste descontraído, quase a rir. (1999a: 12)
>
> [They taught us that we should be some kind of hero. They demand that we constantly exercise self-affirmation. They did not teach us to talk bravely about our fears, failures, hesitations, nightmares. They equipped us with the super-macho myth in the hope that we would always be winners. By doing this, they have turned us into our own worst enemies, hiding the truth and distorting the boundaries. And because we are just normal, and we are ashamed of our normality, we spend all our time thinking of impressive clothes to wear. And we dress like athletes and disguise ourselves as champions, only to cry behind closed doors, because of our simplicity and the ordinariness of our most intimate feelings. We do not have the courage to say 'I'm not the best, I do not have to be the best, nor do I have to justify my fragility'. To compete with my fantasies and those of others would indicate sheer immaturity and a lack of self-respect — you casually continued, almost laughing.]

There is no predefined place for this outsider, no established role for him to identify with, because he realises that men's power to define gender roles according to their necessities actually works against them, as it also demands a very specific behaviour from them. Any existence outside this *super-macho* ideal is equivalent to not being a real male (as will later be discussed with reference to the episode involving the character of a sixteen-year-old boy in 'Mãe Não é Mulher' [A Mother is not a Woman]), and therefore not belonging to a particular group at the party, nor a place in that society. Nevertheless, it is also a source of empowerment: by acknowledging his social construction in the pedagogical dimension of the nation, he can build a reaction to it and disempower it, assuming the control of his destiny as an individual. Through his own renegotiated version of manhood, he himself represents an alternative behaviour: this new man emerges from the marginality of the *super-macho* and affirms himself through the friction that occurs between the pedagogical discourse and the performance of this discourse.

On the one hand, the emergence of this 'new man' in the short story is very important for presenting the male displacement of a masculinised univocal historicity, so that men's active involvement in the deconstruction of a stagnant patriarchal nation is a liberating experience for them. On the other hand, it opens up possibilities for the emergence of a 'new woman' too. 'Liberdade Adiada' [Postponed Freedom] is the first short story of the collection that introduces us to what we may call the 'typical' Cape Verdean woman, as pedagogically constructed by the nation. She is a twenty-three-year-old hardworking mother who has a moment of weakness while facing a *barranco* [ravine]. For a moment, while she contemplates it, her life flashes before her eyes and she feels that the only way to achieve her freedom is by committing suicide: 'Atirar-se-ia pelo barranco abaixo. Não perdia nada. Aliás, nunca perdeu nada. Nunca teve nada para perder' [She would throw herself down the ravine. She had nothing to lose. Actually, she had never lost anything because she had never had anything to lose] (1999a: 6). She does not do it, however. There are two major elements in her life that somehow seem to dictate her actions: her children and her *lata de água* [water can]. She is a 'symbolic bearer of the nation' (McClintock 1995: 354), although she does not have the power to make her own decisions. On the one hand, she sees motherhood as a huge burden that takes away her freedom of choice. Therefore, she hates her womb and her children, and she does not identify with either of them. Her *lata*, on the other hand, is almost an extension of herself. It is described as being her friend; they almost merge with each other:

> A lata e ela, para sempre, juntas no sorriso do barranco. Gostava da sua lata de carregar água. Tratava-a bem. Às vezes, em momentos de raiva ou simplesmente indefinidos, areava-a uma, dez, mil vezes, até que ficava a luzir e a cólera, ou a indefinição se perdiam no brilho prateado. (1999a: 6)
>
> [The can and she, together forever at the bottom of the ravine. She liked using her can to carry water. She took good care of it. Sometimes, in moments of anger or simple uncertainty, she would polish it with sand — once, ten times, a thousand times — until it was shining. And her rage or hesitation would disappear in the silver glow.]

She clearly identifies with that object, since both of them carry the faith of the land: the can carries the water, which is particularly important for Cape Verde and its people (considering the historical droughts and famine); women ensure the biological and cultural reproduction of the nation; and finally, women carry the cans of water, which demonstrates how vital they are to the physical survival of the nation.

In addition, the fact that the woman carries the can of water is presented somehow as an imposition, almost as faith, something she cannot or does not know how to escape. All she really knows is her *lata*, and that is why they are so close

— they carry each other's burdens. Simultaneously, this woman gets a kind of satisfaction from the fact that this vital aspect of the nation is controlled by her: she feels responsible for it. There is a clear interpellation being made by the conceptualisation of the nation that calls upon this woman to perform a role which corresponds to the structure that holds the nation together. Despite being physically and mentally exhausted, she cannot bring herself to give everything up because of her children, whom she loves and hates at the same time — she *must* do what she is *expected* to do. Hence, we can say that this 'Liberdade Adiada' is a contextual imposition, since she is never really given a choice. The survival of the nation as she knows it depends on her continuous acceptance of it as it is, so her freedom to choose alternative experiences of womanhood is constantly postponed. It is also important to highlight the fact that she does not have the tools to stop, through performativity, the propagation of her pedagogical construction as subaltern in this patriarchal nation, because she is poor. Due to the male economic supremacy in operation in this setting, poverty is feminised, thus causing poor women's gender freedom to be postponed on account of their class.[8] This female character is prevented from accessing the means to express herself or contest her positioning, with the alternative to her present life being suicide.

Hence, there is a clear gap between the pedagogical discourse of the nation and the performative one. The former creates an identity for this woman which is meant to be stable and to remain undisturbed, but the woman's inability to adjust to it completely (despite being forced to accept it) demonstrates that the totalising nature of the pedagogical discourse is impossible to achieve. On the one hand, she confronts the official emancipatory and equalitarian discourse of the nation with its patriarchal limitations for women, thus forcing it to acknowledge its support of a male-oriented supremacy. On the other hand, the image of her entrapment illustrates that women's complicity contributes to the preservation of their subaltern identities. This woman's postponed freedom disrupts the fixed temporality of the pedagogical discourse by demonstrating that cultural identities are always open to being renegotiated and can be altered through the empowerment of social change. Something emerges from the friction between these two interacting moments: a new way of looking at what is taken for granted — this is a constant theme throughout the short stories. As Bhabha (1990: 306) observes,

> Insinuating itself into the terms of reference of the dominant discourse, the supplementary antagonizes the implicit power to generalize, to produce the sociological solidity. [...] The power of supplementarity is not the negation of the preconstituted social contradictions of the past or present; its force lies [...] in the renegotiation of those times, terms and traditions through which we turn our uncertain, passing contemporaneity into the signs of history.

This renegotiation occurs throughout *Mornas*. As Gomes (2003: 280) notes, Salústio brings a new outlook to Cape Verdean social reality so as to debate situations that have remained the same for so long that they have become generally accepted as part of *Caboverdianidade* — which does not necessarily mean that they cannot be confronted, questioned, and changed.

A reaction to the postponed freedom explored previously emerges in 'A Oportunidade do Grito' [The Opportunity to Scream], the short story that immediately follows 'Liberdade Adiada'. The story starts with the conversation of a group of women. They express the need to disturb the pre-established order, and focus on the potential of dissident behaviours to fight the stagnation of traditional gender roles and power structures:

> Pedes a Deus? Idiota! Tens é que discutir com Ele. Enfrenta-O como mulher. Mostra-lhe [*sic*] as tuas razões. Grita se for preciso. Ele é que te pôs aqui, não é? Pois que assuma a sua parte da responsabilidade. Enfrenta-O. Deus gosta de mulheres fortes — gritou. (Salústio 1999a: 8)
>
> [Are you asking God? Idiot! You must argue with Him. Confront Him as a woman. Present your reasons to Him. Scream if necessary. Was He not the one who put you here? Well, He better take His share of the responsibility, then. Confront Him. God likes strong women — she yelled.]

God emerges as representative of a pedagogical discourse that constructs women according to the doctrines of Catholicism. From a context in which ninety per cent of the population consider themselves to be Catholic, this comes as no surprise and it makes it even harder for women to escape from their subaltern sociocultural positioning. With this in mind, it is worth mentioning Foy's (1988: 97–98) recollection of a situation in 1987, in which OMCV faced great criticism from the Catholic Church and PAICV for supporting and approving a new law on abortion. The text therefore suggests a sense of unity among women, so that together, through sharing, they can overcome the difficulties they face — that is where the strength to create an opportunity to protest comes from. Only by focusing on themselves and actively engaging in the rewriting of their own identities, can they refute the hegemony of the identities which are imposed on them by the dominant discourse. Bhabha (1990: 302) reminds us that individual initiatives are particularly confined to marginality so that they do not become dangerous. Hence, the suggestion of unity among women can be interpreted as the means to overcome this obstacle and disturb the social structure, as we shall verify further on.

It is important to point out that given their posture and concerns, these women seem to have a higher social status than the previous short story's protagonist. This suggests that women's emancipation, as well as their ability to create opportunities to rebel, depends on their social class. It is more achievable particularly for those who have greater educational and economic access to the tools that can formally dismantle the pedagogical discourse of the nation. In 'E porque havia de não gostar' [And Why Shouldn't I Like It?] there is yet another women's meeting — seven of them, who again seem to have an educated and economically empowered social background. They discuss the frustration of not being able to explore their potential as individuals and women, or to fulfil their dreams:

> Sete mulheres. Nenhuma delas notícia. Os sonhos guardados intactos, porque não vividos eram o muro onde agora se sentavam para olhar o horizonte, eternamente futuro. [...]
> — Somos o passado e por isso rejeitamos o presente.

> — Qual presente? Os outros, os outros, sempre os outros? E eu? E tu? E os sonhos? E as quedas? Os risos.... (Salústio 1999a: 29–30)
>
> [Seven women. There is nothing new about any of them. Their dreams — kept intact because they have never turned into reality — were the wall on top of which they would now sit to look at the horizon, which was forever in the future. [...]
> — We are the past and for that reason we reject the present.
> — Which present? The others, the others, always the others? What about me? What about you? What about dreams? And falls? The laughter....]

Through sharing, these women are able to state all the things they could have been, but were unable to be because even after independence they remain entrapped by a stagnant framework that the national discourse refuses to update. They are compelled to adjust to an image that refers to the past — the traditional perception of women — which clearly shows that after independence women remained virtually absent from the socialist agenda and Cape Verdean national discourse; any presence that they did have was very limited. They were prevented from living their gender in full, since they were only socially recognised when performing their roles of wives and mothers, never as women. Hence, in this scenario, when these women propose that the only sensible option is to destruct the old in order to build something new, their proposal is a performative one which disrupts the authoritarian temporality of the pedagogical order. *This* city is not enough for these women anymore: 'E se incendiassem a cidade? [...] tudo a arder e elas no bar cheio de fumo a rir e a chorar. Idiotice! Onde está a cidade? É isto uma cidade?' [What if they were to set the city on fire? [...] everything would be burning and they would be laughing and crying at a bar filled with smoke. Nonsense! Where is the city? Is this a city?] (Salústio 1999a: 92) The focus on the particular location of the city is quite revealing at this point. As an important component of both the colonial spatial occupation and the post-colonial spatial reconfiguration, the city is associated with the power of decision-making, connecting the material and the ideological dimensions. Therefore, the proposal to set fire to the city may metaphorically suggest a cartographical reconstruction that refutes any space and time essentialism in terms of the sociocultural location of women (Bhabha 1990: 306).

In order to create the conditions to reformulate their social positioning, they have to be, above all, aware of their own situation in the social sphere. This kind of awareness — that not everyone will have access to — might justify the author's insistence on the responsibility of women of a higher social status. In 'O Conhecimento em Debate' [Debating Knowledge], as the title indicates, knowledge is debated by a group of women who, once again, fit the above-mentioned social profile. Despite having access to education and being economically empowered, they are described as having their roles defined by their husbands and children. After having gone for dinner together, they all gather in private to discuss the advantages and disadvantages of knowledge. Some women find knowledge to be dangerous and somehow intimidating, given its capacity to force people to face reality as it is and subsequently to require a reaction from them. Other women, however, consider it an extremely important source of power, not only because it allows people to deal with what they really *are*, as opposed to what they *pretend to be*, but also because only real knowledge of a given issue — in this setting, of the role of Cape Verdean women and of the heterogeneous nature of this group — will allow them to dismantle the said issue and to propose alternatives. The moment they become aware of the patriarchal structure in operation is also the moment in which the existence of a power structure amongst women is exposed. This moment of knowledge is therefore also a moment of violence, in which these women strip the national narrative, expose its most disgusting aspects — its *entranhas* [entrails] — and confront it with its own monstrosity, so as to force it to rewrite itself:

> Nojo? É isso. Nojo é a palavra certa. Quando nos conhecemos uns aos outros, sentimos nojo porque o tempo todo fingimos o que não somos, o que não podemos ser, o que desejaríamos ser e o conhecimento mostra a realidade, as tripas fora, a pequenez. É por isso que querer conhecer alguém é violentá-lo, despir-lhe a armadura, exibir-lhe as cicatrizes, o intestino. (Salústio 1999a: 39)
>
> [Disgust? That's it. Disgust is the right word. When we get to know each other, we feel disgust because we pretend all the time to be something that we are not, or cannot be, or wish we could be. Knowledge shows the reality, exposes the bowels, and the pettiness. That is why wanting to get to know someone is to abuse that person, to strip them of their armour, to expose their scars, and their guts.]

Again, it is worth recalling Bhabha (1990: 299) at this point, who alerts us to the importance of knowledge for the confrontation between pedagogical and performative discourses. For Bhabha, the pedagogical gets its strength from people's traditions. Therefore, only by acknowledging that there is an ideology which interpellates them and keeps them under a unifying control are these women able to question and interrupt this tradition. Through performance they are able to build a new perspective; to provide a new time and space for the emergence of new narratives and the rewriting of their multiple identities within the nation and the national discourse; and, finally, to fight recurrent acts of ideological authoritarianism, even when they occur amongst themselves.

Concerning the second role women are expected to perform — motherhood — the collection presents descriptive examples of what it means to be a Cape Verdean mother. 'Mãe não é Mulher' [A Mother is not a Woman] brings us a dilemma in the life of a sixteen-year-old adolescent who is slapped by his mother after having misbehaved towards her. The situation gains larger proportions due to the Creole belief that 'bofetada de mulher na cara de rapaz impedia a barba de crescer' [if a boy gets slapped on the face by a woman, his beard will not grow properly] (Salústio 1999a: 33). The youngster descends into the depths of depression thinking that he will never be a *real* man again, and it is not until his mother tells him a story about Jesus and his mother Mary that he relaxes, concluding that 'se Jesus dizia que mãe podia bater na cara, mulher é que não, então não havia motivo para preocupações' [if Jesus said that women could not slap boys on their faces, but that mothers could, then there was nothing to worry about] (1999a: 34). Several indications of the conception of Cape Verdean motherhood through the pedagogical discourse of the nation are given to us in this short story. Firstly, the role of these mothers is defined to somehow mirror the image of Jesus's mother, Mary:

> Agora, pensando na minha mãe é que eu vejo como ela se identificava com Nossa Senhora e falava dela, como uma amiga. Às vezes dizia: Maria sofreu muito porque Jesus às vezes saía e nem lhe dizia para onde, mas eu não vou admitir que tu faças o mesmo.
> — Olha o que lhe aconteceu no fim! (1999a: 34)
>
> [When I think of my mother now, I realise that she identified with Our Lady and used to talk about her as if she were a friend. Sometimes she would say 'Mary suffered a lot because sometimes Jesus would go out and wouldn't even tell her where he was going. But I won't let you do the same.
> — Look what happened to him in the end!']

The construction and maintenance of women's paradoxical incorporation of Virgin Mary and Eve into their subjectivities again demonstrates the determinant influence of the Catholic tradition. Furthermore, it has influenced women's relational role within the family structure, as they are continuously defined in relation to the men in their lives — their fathers, their husbands, and their sons. Caught in this predefined complex identity, women are continuously alienated from their own selves. Secondly, mothers are presented as important cultural transmitters, not only because they have a very privileged relationship with their children (given their unique position), but also because the latter inherit their knowledge of the cultural nation from the former. As such, they have their character shaped by the pre-established roles taught to them by their mothers in the domestic sphere (Filho 1996: 129). Finally, in the archipelago setting, to be a woman implies being a mother, but the opposite is not so. Hence, motherhood emerges as a reality alienated from womanhood, demonstrating that women must live to fulfil the biological and cultural reproduction of the nation, automatically annulling any notion of them having sexual desires: 'Ao contar-vos esta história, lembro-me de uma vez em que um dos meus filhos, ainda adolescente e confuso, me perguntou: Mãe, se fosses mulher, tu gostavas de mim? [As I tell you this story, I am reminded of an episode in which one of my sons, who was still a confused adolescent, asked me 'Mother, if you were a woman, would you like me?'] (Salústio 1999a: 34).

This pedagogical effort to keep women in such a problematic position leads to performative contradictions. On the one hand, women's sexuality encapsulates them in reproduction, as cultural and biological reproducers and disseminators of the nation. On the other hand, however, they are prevented from fully experiencing their sexuality due to their above-mentioned duties towards the nation (Yuval-Davis and Anthias 1989: 7). As Filho (1996: 43–44) argues, 'Este paradoxo da condição feminina origina contradições tanto no modo como a mulher é vista pelo homem como no próprio modo como ela se vê, como tem consciência da sua individualidade e do seu papel sexual (de mulher)' [This paradox of womanhood creates contradictions, both in the way that women are perceived by men and in the way that women perceive themselves as they become aware of their own individuality and sexual role (as women)]. Hence, this episode creates tension between the pedagogical discourse of the nation and the performance of it to demonstrate that the former is impossible to achieve on a performative level, which inevitably leads to the emergence of counter-responses from Creole women.

It is also important to point out that the Creole belief that 'bofetada de mulher na cara de rapaz impedia a barba de crescer' (Salústio 1999a: 33) is clearly created to shape masculine behaviour according to a pre-conceived ideal — if a boy allows a woman to hit him, he will never become a man. Hence, the male ideal hereby explored refers to the typical *super-macho*, which is also pedagogically constructed. By utilising this comical and almost innocent episode in the lives of a young boy and his mother, the author suggests the potential for a male subversion of manhood. The mother, aware of her role within the reproduction and legitimisation of this cultural construction, is empowered to use it against patriarchy. She uses this power by teaching her son other ways to be a man outside the constraints of the traditional male identity implemented by Creole beliefs. In other words, she fights patriarchal domination from within its own limits, by getting hold of the same weapons which were given to her by the dominant discourse to reinforce it and using them to disempower it.

Accordingly, the short story 'Filho és, Pai serás' [You Are a Son, You Will Be a Father] presents a deviation from the path that is traced for women in this panorama. It describes an episode in the life of a mother who forgets about Mother's Day and is reminded of the date by her own mother's congratulatory phone call. The older woman is described in a curious manner; she is associated with 'uma série de provérbios ditos em português que, no contexto quotidiano crioulo, adquiriam um peso e um estatuto que nos amedrontavam' [a series of Portuguese proverbs which, in the everyday Creole context, acquired a weight and status that frightened us] and, thus, represented the 'sentença suprema' [supreme sentence] (1999a: 19). We see the cultural origins of the motherhood role in the archipelago invoked here, which in the text are Portuguese, and Western. As mentioned before, since the beginning of the colonisation of the islands, African women (given the absence of white women, who rarely travelled to the archipelago) were responsible for biological reproduction and this situation did not change after the abolition of slavery. They remained very much attached to the private sphere throughout the years, most of the time being fully responsible for their families. Men would often travel abroad in search of better life conditions or simply did not care about women or their children, acting according to a logic of unofficial consensual polygamy (Carvalho 2010: 66–70).

The fact that the narrator's mother ends the telephone call with one of her favourite proverbs — 'Filho és, pai serás, assim como fizeres, assim acharás' [You are a son, you will be a father, what you give today, you'll get tomorrow] — also reminds us, once again, of the importance of motherhood in cultural transmission, as well as of the strength of the pedagogical patriarchal discourse. We could read this as a means to point out that this intergenerational transfer is the perfect point of rupture with the dominant discourse, given motherhood's potential to dismantle the roles of both men and women, which are firstly defined throughout childhood, and within the domestic sphere. Hence, this indicates that the narrator, who is a mother herself, will be confronting the pedagogical and institutionalised ideal of motherhood which is represented by her own mother. As we will be able to analyse further on, through her behaviour she will displace it. Having received a congratulatory phone call from her *codê* [the youngest child], the narrator feels guilty and decides that she needs 'vingança urgente' [urgent revenge] (Salústio 1999a: 20). Therefore, she calls another one of her children and using her mother's discourse, she repeats the same Portuguese proverb she had heard from her earlier. The son starts by justifying himself, but when he hears the proverb coming from his mother, 'que lhe sabe a praga' [which sounds like a curse to him] (1999a: 20), he fails to recognise it and, thus, asks the narrator if she really means what she is saying. She immediately understands that her son is confused because she herself is different from her mother and has passed on a different cultural conception to her children. Therefore, she tells him about his grandmother's phone call and both end up laughing at the situation.

The narrator is clearly a mother who, through her behaviour, distances herself from the pedagogical conception of motherhood within the dominant patriarchal discourse, and thus from her mother, who represents it. Hence, there is a clear genealogy break in the national narrative which is achieved through the recovery of an alternative performance of motherhood. By doing this and acting through marginality, she enables the creation of an alternative universe personified by her own children — the fact that they do not recognise themselves in the dominant discourse is proof of that:

> Ao desligar, pediu-me: por favor, não voltes a dizer aquela do «Filho és, pai serás». É que me sabe a praga. A mesma sensação que eu sentia em criança, reconheci, pensando em coisas como filhos, educação, famílias. E na minha mãe. (1999a: 20)
>
> [Before hanging up, he said to me 'please don't say that proverb "You are a son, you will be a father" to me again. It sounds like a curse to me'. I recognised the exact same feeling that I used to have as a child, every time I thought about things like children, education, families. And my mother.]

We can read this as both a distancing from the traditional (colonial and post-independence) notion of cultural transference, and an embracing of cultural reinvention in the postcolonial and post-Marxist setting of Cape Verde. This focus on constantly redefining and renegotiating identity ultimately prevents the continuous recycling of essentialist and exclusivist behaviours — which are transferred from generation to generation.

Hence, childhood emerges intimately related to motherhood. In this collection, this matter is also presented to the reader in the shape of a denunciation, given that it emerges through child abandonment, abuse and prostitution. In these texts, the new post-independence generation is a lost generation — forgotten, doomed, rootless and extremely poor. There is, therefore, a reference to the situation of these children who are caught in an unescapable vicious circle due to their social and economic condition. Nevertheless, this uniformity is disrupted in 'Natal' [Christmas], a short story in which class differences are emphasised during the Christmas season. At a shop, there is a confrontation between the elite, who are making purchases, and three poor children, who enter the shop merely to look at the toys. Due to the bad atmosphere suddenly generated, the shop assistant expels the children from the shop. In general, this is a short story that demystifies Christmas as an important cultural and family celebration. It denounces it as a time to shop and to give in to capitalist values, while simultaneously unveiling the artificiality of a society which tries to maintain a European tradition that no longer has any place:

> Não estou de acordo. É bom haver Natal. É bom escrever aos amigos e dizer-lhes que estão comigo o tempo todo, apesar do meu silêncio. É bom haver Natal e poder dizer-te que tenho saudades tuas, que te amo e que te queria abraçar forte. É bom haver Natal, quando não é época de sacrifícios e angústias e dívidas, para se manter uma ridícula aparência de sucesso. (1999a: 57)
>
> [I do not agree. It is good to have Christmas. It is good to write to my friends and tell them that I think about them all the time, despite my silence. It is good to have Christmas so that I can tell you that I miss you, that I love you and would like to hold you tight. It is good to have Christmas when it's not a season of sacrifice, distress and getting into debt, all in order to maintain a ridiculous pretence of success.]

The text conveys the idea that a false image of the nation is being projected, because the real nation only exists for the elite that creates and manipulates it according to its needs. It is a nation in which only some are allowed into the imagination of a temporal simultaneity that enables everyone to have equal access to the nation's goods. Through their social position, the elite have access to all the privileges, particularly the economic ones. Therefore, the children, who are marginal due to their poverty, are excluded from the nation.

They do, however, manage to reverse the marginalising gaze of the shop customers and assistant:

> Há um sorriso nos mocinhos que eu não percebo, como se não fizessem parte de nós. Como se fôssemos uns palhaços para os divertir. Ou quem sabe, uma certa nostalgia de não serem palhaços como nós. Tranquilamente saem, em busca de outras lojas de sonhos. (1999a: 58)
>
> [The children have a smile on their faces that I cannot understand, as if they were not like us. As if we were clowns, there to entertain them. Or perhaps they just felt a certain sense of nostalgia for not being clowns like us. They leave quietly in search of other dream shops.]

Using their imaginations, they manage to escape both the margins that are built to confine them and the illusion of the centre, where the elite live, building a kind of third space for themselves. As Bhabha (1990: 307) reminds us,

> Minority discourse sets the act of emergence in the antagonistic *in-between* of image and sign, the accumulative and the adjunct, presence and proxy. It contests genealogies of 'origin' that lead to claims for cultural supremacy and historical priority. Minority discourse acknowledges the status of national culture — and the people — as a contentious, performative space of the perplexity of the living in the midst of the pedagogical representations of the fullness of life.

Their presence forces the pedagogical discourse to acknowledge its incapacity to account for the multiple experiences of the nation. In addition, their performance extrapolates the limitations of their construction as marginal, as they contribute so actively to the re-imagination of such a solid traditional holiday.

Mornas Eram as Noites: Conclusion

In sum, the short story collection *Mornas* illustrates a subtle confrontation between the colonial and the postcolonial social structures in terms of defining the identities of men, women and children in the Cape Verdean nation. Concomitantly, the short stories denounce the existence of some continuities and links between the dominant colonial discourse and the post-independence socialist discourse, in terms of the cultural identity of Cape Verde. The stories reveal the maintenance of social power structures in terms of gender and class in the postcolonial society. This means that even after independence, men continue to 'colonise', women are 'colonised', and children emerge as the result of the interaction between these identities in obsolete social structures which are ill-adjusted to the contemporary context, i.e., which are incapable of responding to social changes in the archipelago. They also reveal the maintenance of social differentiation according to class and the subsequent increasing difficulties in accessing the nation for those who are economically disempowered. Due to this identity stagnation, it becomes more difficult to keep up with the mutations that affect the nation. Hence, the author highlights the need to create new identities through the exploration of alternative and marginal behaviours, which renegotiate the traditional within the modern world, questioning the centrality of the dominant discourse and proposing new plurivocal discourses.

Conclusion to Chapter 1

Indeed, in both *A Louca* and *Mornas*, Salústio's proposal was to debate nationhood and national identity within a framework in which gender issues and perspectives were at the core. Throughout this project, her exploration of *Caboverdianidade* and how it came to be constructed exposed a set of colonial continuities which were transposed into the postcolonial conceptualisation of the nation. In doing so, they promoted the crystallisation of certain sociocultural structures and discriminatory habits which came to be perceived as Creole 'traditions'. These structures were particularly hard on women, as they fed upon a solid patriarchal culture that was constantly legitimised by women's continuous dissemination of their own subaltern subjectivities. But they also run right across womanhood, emerging in the intersection of elements such as gender, race, colour and class. Hence, Salústio's denunciation moves to expose the functioning of these social dynamics of exclusion so as to dismantle the power structures operating at their core, promote the decolonisation of the mind, and ultimately encourage the emergence of challenging behaviours that might bring about a more equalitarian and democratic society. In other words, it seems that for Salústio, national identity can only make sense as a permanently open debate.

Notes to Chapter 1

1. An earlier version of this chapter has been published in Portuguese as two separate articles (M. Tavares 2008; 2014).
2. Henceforth referred to as *Mornas*, and *A Louca*. With reference to the word *morna*, in Portuguese it can have the meaning of 'warm' or it can refer to a Cape Verdean music and dance style, which is normally considered to be the national music of the country.
3. In a study of the construction of national identity in Cape Verde through written press, Manuel Brito-Semedo (2006: 258) proposes a reflection on both Nativist and *Claridade* generations, and their respective strategies to affirm an individual cultural identity. With reference to the Nativist generation, the scholar claims that these intellectuals shared a common interest in asserting Cape Verde's autonomy through the defence of the interests of those who had been born in the islands, and in the banning of discriminatory laws that supported a power structure which privileged those who had been born in the Metropolis. Nonetheless, their love and respect towards Portugal as the Fatherland was not questioned. Regarding the group of intellectuals who gathered around the important arts and humanities review called *Claridade*, Brito-Semedo asserts that they had different, although less explicit aims. According to the scholar, their purpose was to express through literature the circumstances and specificity of Cape Verdeans, to study the particularities of their culture, as well as the socio-historical formation of the Creole islands (2006: 319). For a historical analysis of *Claridade*'s issues and how they reflected different strategies for the renegotiation of a Cape Verdean identity, see, for example, Ellen W. Sapega (2002).
4. See PAIGC (1974), in which the rhetoric of the party recovers a connection between Cape Verde, Guinea-Bissau and Africa, by focusing on: the historical trajectories of people from countries such as Mali and Ghana; European colonial systems in Africa; African liberation movements; the historical trajectories of Cape Verde and Guinea-Bissau (which always emerge interwoven); and the creation and consolidation of PAIGC.
5. It is worth highlighting the creation of the public institution ICIEG (which was initially called ICF), in 1991, and the NGO MORABI (Associação de Apoio à Auto-Promoção da Mulher no Desenvolvimento [Association in Support of Women's Self-Promotion in Development]), in 1992.
6. An alcoholic drink produced in Cape Verde, very much like rum, which is made out of sugar cane.
7. 'Interpellation' is here to be understood in accordance with Althusser's theorisation (1970). According to the philosopher, every society has a Repressive State Apparatus, which works primarily through violence, and Ideological State Apparatuses, which work primarily through ideology, in the interest of a ruling elite. Althusser defines interpellation as the process through which an individual is engaged with ideology and, thus, becomes a subject: 'ideology "acts" or "functions" in such a way that it "recruits" subjects among the individuals (it recruits them all), or "transforms" the individuals into subjects (it transforms them all) by that very precise operation which I have called *interpellation* or hailing, and which can be imagined along the lines of the most commonplace everyday police (or other) hailing: "Hey, you there!"'.
8. It is worth recalling at this point the work developed by Monteiro (2009), in which the author points out that men still emerge economically empowered in contemporary Cape Verdean society, due to their easier access to education and better jobs, and also due to the fact that they still earn more than women do.

CHAPTER 2

A State without a Nation

Reading the Utopia of the Nation in Paulina Chiziane's *Ventos do Apocalipse*, *Niketche: Uma História de Poligamia* and *O Alegre Canto da Perdiz*[1]

> The exile is a person who, having lost a loved one, keeps searching for the face he loves in every new face and, forever deceiving himself, thinks he has found it.
>
> REINALDO ARENAS

Introduction

Of the three authors under analysis in the present study, the Mozambican female writer Paulina Chiziane is the one whose work is most widely known, and also who has published the most. Given that the main emphasis will be placed on the conception of the nation during the civil war and throughout the period that followed it, this chapter will focus solely on three selected literary works, namely *Ventos do Apocalipse* [Winds of the Apocalypse] (1999), *Niketche: Uma História de Poligamia* [The First Wife: A Tale of Polygamy] (2000), and *O Alegre Canto da Perdiz* [The Partridge's Merry Singing] (2008).[2] In all of her works, Chiziane attempts to provide readings of Mozambican society, placing women and the female voice at the core of her discussions and defying the limits of their conception within the socialist nation. Through her own knowledge of the Mozambican reality and experience as a former Frelimo militant, she simultaneously challenges the limits of the socialist nation itself, revealing the cracks in the utopian ideal of a Mozambican nation and proposing a new imagination of the community project as a whole. In the author's words, 'em termos de conhecimento da realidade do meu país, eu sou especialista' [when it comes to knowledge of the reality of my country, I am a specialist] (A. M. Martins 2006a). With reference to this particularity of the author's work, Owen (2007b: 151) argues that,

> The ongoing influence of state socialist thinking, despite her critique of Frelimo, often resurfaces in her appeals for the cultural reform of community life, her endorsement of cooperative forms of social organization, and her strong

> awareness of the material realities behind the symbolic systems of exchange. It is by deconstructing the Marxist-Leninist period from within its own terms, that Chiziane points towards new, transversal directions that gender struggle might adopt within a changing national project for the post-Marxist era.

Taking the above analysis as a point of departure, this chapter will attempt to show how Chiziane updates the utopian ideal of Mozambican nation firstly by revealing its tendency to exile rather than integration, and then by proposing strategies to overcome this propensity for exile.

Using this thematic framework, I will provide a reading of all three literary works through Said's (2001a) reflections regarding exile and Guibernau's (1996) considerations of Nationalism. According to Said, exile materialises into a fracture between the human being and her/his own homeland which is beyond repair (2001a: 173). Therefore, he continues, both nationalism and exile emerge as interconnected, as two opposed realities that inevitably inform and constitute each other. Nonetheless, for Said, 'exile, unlike nationalism, is fundamentally a discontinuous state of being' (2001a: 177). The absence of a sense of belonging translates into the urgency of re-establishing uninterrupted links to the origins. At times, this act of restructuring a national identity and a nation is accomplished through the exacerbation of feelings of inclusion towards those who are the 'same' and of feelings of hostility towards the 'others' — even if they share the same condition of being exiled (2001a: 178). With Said's reflections in mind, this study will proceed first of all to the analysis of the post-independence nation as an internally exiled community. In her study on various accounts of experiences relating to the Cuban Diaspora in the USA, Andrea O'Reilly Herrera (2001: xvii–xxxiii) puts forward the term *insílio* to refer to this specific type of exile. According to the researcher, this 'inner' or 'internal' exile is a state of mind that precedes the physical parting from the homeland and translates into the refusal of or the disenchantment towards the official governmental entity and its discourse:

> In others words, they claim to have experienced a kind of exile of the inner imagination or spirit — a mental exodus, as it were — long before they left Cuba; in consequence, their initial exile experience was psychological as opposed to physical. (2001: xxii)

The specificities of Cuba, and its historical and cultural coordinates, obviously condition the experiences of *insílio* explored in the book. However, those specificities are not as relevant to this study as the concept of *insílio* itself is, since its application to the particular Mozambican context will allow us to look at the experiences of exile within the geographical limits of the nation state, as portrayed by Chiziane.

In *Ventos*, the exiled community assumes different shapes and behaviours, according to the distinct moments of the narration: firstly, the village of Mananga before being attacked; secondly, the group of survivors fighting for their lives; and thirdly, the Aldeia do Monte struggling to rebuild itself. The characters of Sianga and Emelina will also be read separately; they were exiled by the exiled and their subsequent response of disruptive behaviour produces the two great calamities that befall the communities. In *Niketche*, women, whose bodies symbolise the different parts of the state, represent the community of the exiled within the patriarchal nation due to their gender's marginality. However, because this exile is not experienced equally by all women, this study will analyse gender along with other categories such as class and race so as to explore the different exiles that coexist within the gender exile. For this reason, the construction of the polygamous husband's wives and mistresses will be observed throughout the novel with a view to understanding how each of them occupies a specific place within gender exile — a place that changes according to the economic and racial spectrum. In this context, the character of Eva will also be examined in relation to the wives as also possibly exiled by the exiled. Despite the fact that at one point this female character nearly becomes one of the polygamous husband's wives, the study explores the impossibility of redemption for Eva at the end of the novel; this could be related to both the character's race and her infertility. This reflection on the various types of exile that emerge in the intersection of gender, class and race is taken a step further in *Alegre Canto*. In this literary work, Chiziane recuperates a female genealogy by focusing specifically on the stories of three generations of Zambezian women. If on the one hand these women emerge in the novel as exiles in patriarchal and male-oriented colonial and post-colonial contexts, on the other hand their experiences of marginality differ according to the colour of their skin, demonstrating that in this novel there are new power structures in operation. Following on from the defence of memory as an act which is conditioned by social circumstances such as gender, race and class, Chiziane makes an effort to bring into dialogue complex female micro-stories of the region and a macro-history of the nation. This project not only opposes women's exclusion from the memory of continuity, but also allows for the recovery from and problematisation of the memory of miscegenation. Ultimately, by looking at the past from a postcolonial perspective, it asserts the need for the collective memory to incorporate historically marginalised memories (of the region, in general, and women, in particular) in order to 'reconstitute a diversity' (Sanches 2007: 133). Nonetheless, the absence of the character Maria Jacinta from the 'new family' that emerges at the end of the novel will be scrutinised, as this absence is justified by the character's race.

Subsequently, the analysis will focus on Chiziane's renegotiation of the nation, noting Guibernau's claims that 'the power of nationalism emanates from its ability to engender sentiments of belonging to a particular community. Symbols and rituals play a major role in the cultivation of a sense of solidarity among the members of the group' (1996: 3). In Guibernau's view, this 'national solidarity responds to a need for identity of an eminently symbolic nature, in so far as it provides roots based on culture and a common past, as well as offering a project for the future' (1996: 5). Hence, this analysis will move on to discuss the proposals advanced by Chiziane — at different moments and within various societal contexts — to recuperate a sense of community, by utilising the renegotiation of traditions, symbols and rites that speak to the population, and recovering other histories of the nation in a post-independence and modern scenario. In *Ventos*, this renegotiation occurs mostly during the journey to the village and at the 'Aldeia do Monte', because those are the moments in which the population is forced to recreate and reshape its world in order to survive. In *Niketche*, this is a transformation which develops as the characters evolve, becoming increasingly aware of themselves as individuals and of their cultural representations. Yet, it culminates in very significant moments — such as when the women get to know each other and bond in order to be able to renegotiate their social positioning; when they meet Eva; when they have to deal with Tony's fake death; and when they all dance the Niketche — which will be analysed here. Finally, in *Alegre Canto*, the recuperation of women's stories of Zambezia enables the widening of communal memory. The historical analysis of miscegenation, from a female-focalised point of view, permits the understanding of how racial representations came into being and will ultimately lead to the emergence of a new national narrative, which will also be explored.

Mozambique: A Brief Historical Retrospective

Prior to examining the realities portrayed in these literary works, it is necessary to retrospectively analyse Mozambique's history in order to understand events before and after independence, as well as to contextualise the civil war. According to Malyn Newitt (2002), there are some key factors which need to be outlined in order to achieve this understanding. The historian advances the argument that firstly it is important to go back to the pre-war period before independence and explore the colonial inheritance left by the Portuguese, who prevented the north and the south of Mozambique from ever being connected — which means that several areas of the country remained isolated — and also selected a capital city which was located in the extreme south of the country. This act led to the widening of the cultural gap between the people from the north of Mozambique, who are mostly matrilineal, and the people from the south, who are patrilineal, thus reinforcing the transformation of the ethnic, linguistic and cultural multiplicity of Mozambique into fragmentation. The amplification of this situation came in the shape of communication systems which were built to bring various regions of Mozambique closer to their neighbouring countries (Rhodesia and Nyasaland) than to other parts of Mozambique itself (2002: 186–88).

The growing dissatisfaction towards the authoritarian and centralised Portuguese colonial rule culminated with the formation of FRELIMO, in 1962, and the beginning of the war of independence, in 1964. However, the formation of the front was not peaceful, due to the difficulties in bringing together fighters from distinct ethnic backgrounds under one single line of thought and strategy against the coloniser — which leads us to the second key factor. In order to solve this problem and achieve unity and stability, FRELIMO banished some of the movement's founding members. In his study on the Mozambican socialist experience, João Mosca (2005: 155) observes that

> Muitos dos militantes expulsos na crise de 68 da Frelimo eram do centro, entre os quais Uria Simango, que pertenceu ao triunvirato da direcção do movimento de libertação após a morte de Eduardo Mondlane; posteriormente o MNR (depois Renamo), possuía uma importante base de cidadãos pertencentes às

> etnias do centro do país (sobretudo *ndaus*). Nos processos eleitorais é ainda possível identificar o 'voto étnico'. André Matsangaíssa e Afonso Dhlakama são naturais do centro de Moçambique.
>
> [Many of the militants who were banished from Frelimo during the 1968 crisis were from the centre of the country. Among them was Uria Simango, who was part of the trio that managed the liberation movement after Eduardo Mondlane's death. Subsequently, the MNR (later to become RENAMO) had an important base of citizens from the ethnic groups that inhabit central Mozambique (especially the *Ndau*). During the elections, it is still possible to identify the 'ethnic vote'. André Matsangaíssa [the first leader of the MNR] and Afonso Dhlakama [the leader of RENAMO 1979–2018] are originally from the centre of Mozambique.]

Hence, after 1969 the majority of effective FRELIMO members and leaders came from the south of the country, which not only increased hostility between southern and northern groups, but also laid the foundations for RENAMO's vehement support in the centre of the country (Newitt 2002: 190). Notwithstanding the impact that this reality came to have in the post-independence panorama, it is imperative to highlight the fact that the so-called civil war that erupted in the newly born nation state was not an ethnic war, since it was largely externally funded by both Rhodesian and South African regimes — I shall go back to this matter later.

The third factor that contributed to the post-independence scene is related to the strategies implemented by the colonial entity in order to combat FRELIMO's impact. According to Newitt (2002: 190), the Portuguese started by concentrating the population into *aldeamentos* [villages] to assure their continuous access to education and health services; to defend them; and, most importantly, to prevent them from having any kind of contact with FRELIMO, thus guaranteeing their political support. Then, they looked for the specific support of traditional chiefs, religious organisations, and Special Forces (groups of soldiers who were recruited from the African population). This structure proved to be much more rooted and difficult to dismantle than Frelimo could ever have expected it to be. After the military coup in Lisbon on 25 April 1974, independence came for Mozambique on 25 June of the following year. That would not represent the end of the problems for the new-born nation state, however, both internally and externally. Aware of its frailty as a movement that was supposed to represent the entire nation's interests and wary also of the opposition that might emerge in the immediate post-independence period, Frelimo sought to consolidate its position rapidly by becoming a party and having power transferred to it directly. This would come about through the signing of the Lusaka Agreement in September 1974, which established a transitional government that strengthened Frelimo's positioning. Once in power, Frelimo began to put into practice its programme for the restructuring of Mozambican society. Due to its openly socialist affiliation, this programme consisted of the immediate nationalisation of all social areas and the development of a central economic plan — measures both aimed to forge a centralised government that would be less vulnerable to enemy assaults from inside and outside the country (2002: 194–95).

The construction of a new Mozambique implied sacrifices in the name of a cohesive nation. This leads us to another important measure of Frelimo that would leave a permanent mark on the trajectory of the country: the non-recognition of ethnic and racial difference with the purpose of conveying a consistent image of national unity and simultaneously fighting regionalism and tribalism — which were associated with colonial structures. Notwithstanding this effort, Mosca (2005: 153) reminds us that an examination of the party's representatives shows that, indeed, Frelimo had very specific social alliances with certain ethnic and minority groups that worked together to secure and maintain its exclusive control of power. In Mosca's perception,

> A questão étnica foi sempre um tabu dentro da Frelimo. A preocupação da unidade nacional aparecia no discurso político para consumo das massas. [...] parecem existir evidências que a Frelimo, pelo sistema de alianças e também como resultado das lutas intestinas, pela decisão de constituição num partido marxista-leninista e pelas opções económicas, não contribuiu para uma efectiva unidade, sobretudo ao nível das elites. [...] Alguns observadores conhecedores de Samora acreditam que o presidente era um convicto anti-racista e antitribalista, mas também um defensor intransigente do poder; outros não duvidam de o considerar um ditador e tribalista em defesa do poder. (2005: 154–56)
>
> [The ethnic question has always been taboo within Frelimo. The concern over national unity emerged in the political discourse for mass consumption. [...] there seems to be evidence that Frelimo did not foment an effective unity, particularly among the elite, due to its alliance system and as a result of internal fighting; due to its decision to become a Marxist-Leninist party; and its economic options. [...] Some observers who knew Samora [the first president of Mozambique] believe that the president was a firm believer in anti-racism and anti-tribalism, but also uncompromising in his defence of power. Others do not hesitate to regard him as a dictator and a tribalist in defence of power.]

Consequently, Frelimo took various economic and social steps with the purpose of imposing a unique programme to be followed by the entire nation state. According to Newitt (2002: 196), Frelimo's incitement to the suppression of the 'tribe' with a view to enabling the rise of the 'nation' consisted of the exclusion of 'traditional chiefs (*régulos*) and heads of families, and religious organisations as well as plantation companies and industrial complexes controlled by Portuguese or multinational companies', and of any entities assumed to have been actively connected to colonialism (regardless of whether this connection was real or not). In order to guarantee the successful implementation of this programme and also to facilitate people's access to services such as education and health, Frelimo decided to adapt one of the most polemical measures that the Portuguese had employed during the war of independence: the *aldeamentos*. In these villages, the people were to follow a very rigorous political and social programme and, thus, to identify with a specific ideal of *Moçambicanidade* [*Mozambicanness*; Mozambican cultural identity] which did not recognise ethnicities, races or sex differences as political (Mosca 2005: 149).

In reality, this imposed standardisation meant two very important things. Firstly, it meant that the image of Mozambican citizenship that people should embrace was markedly influenced by southern culture, which dominated Frelimo's composition. As such, all other cultures should 'dissipate' and people were to assimilate to the habits which were considered to be characteristic of a 'modern' nation. Secondly, it meant that women's liberation was always regarded as primarily economic, that is, alongside men's. Despite the emphasis that both the revolutionary movement and the political party put on women's independence, on the elimination of practices that were considered to be oppressive to women (such as polygamy, arranged marriages, *lobolo*[3] and initiation rites), and on the creation of legislation for women's rights, their liberation was always perceived as something that all citizens are entitled to, and not gender-specific. As Owen (2007b: 33) advocates, women were conceptualised by Frelimo within a classic Marxist-Leninist framework, which was largely gender blind:

> Frelimo endeavoured to put into practice the classic Marxist-Leninist conceptualization of women's emancipation in economic terms, emphasizing women's historical and sociocultural oppression by colonial capitalism. This often-cited 'productivist bias' advocated the economic liberation of women through their integration into the forces of production, particularly in non-traditional areas of waged labor. What the Marxist-Leninist project ignored, however, was the significance for women of the conditions of sexual reproduction since it notoriously lacked a theory of gender struggle, equivalent to the discourse of class struggle, with which to critique the patriarchal practices of men within the liberation movement itself.

Although women were being called upon to participate as fully recognised citizens in the construction of the nation, their role and place were highly contradictory within Frelimo's discourse. As Stephanie Urdang (1989: 160–61) points out in her study on the place of Mozambican women in both the war for independence and in post-independence contexts, the party refused to update this debate by discouraging its discussion, thus devaluing its importance, and asking women to carry on patiently performing their lifelong duties within the household while happily embracing their new roles outside the household. They were not to confront their husbands, expect them to share the household tasks or to demand equality in the domestic sphere — they should always 'speak with kind words' (1989: 161).

Following the same line of thought, the social researchers Isabel Casimiro (2005) and Kathleen Sheldon (2002) assert that the agency of OMM (Organização da Mulher Moçambicana [Mozambican Women's Organisation]) itself might have been very significant for the consolidation of these measures amongst society. Formed in 1973, the organisation opened up a space for the debate on women's place within Mozambican society. Nonetheless, OMM was a Frelimo structure, so it followed the party's political, economic and social policies. As Frelimo's spokespeople, the members of this organisation regarded the emancipation of women and their integration in all levels of Mozambican life within a framework which was defined by the male-dominated socialist party. As a result, OMM was a channel that linked the party and the people, ensuring the application of Frelimo's directives and never specifically discussing gender-related issues outside the constraints of the party's Marxist-Leninist stance (Casimiro 2005: 73–74). Inevitably, OMM's agency reflected the party's contradictions in the representation of women within society, which, on occasion, translated into the reproduction of a more traditional social depiction of womanhood. In this respect, Sheldon (2002: 142) observes that

> OMM projects included classes in crocheting, teaching newly urban how to care for their apartments, and sewing infant clothes for sale. One of OMM's priorities in preparation for Frelimo's Fourth Congress in 1983 was to clean the city. [...] These activities involved women in the endeavour of developing a socialist Mozambique without raising more disturbing questions about gender inequality and power relations.

OMM's agency in the villages was no less contradictory and faced several difficulties, as did Frelimo's establishment of a socialist society in general.

Throughout this early socialist reform period Frelimo was very successful in terms of the results achieved. Nevertheless, these efforts to consolidate the party's concept of a modern nation led to the alienation of various social groups that became increasingly numerous and began to form a loud opposition that Frelimo continuously struggled to silence. Due to the characteristics of the party's agency, this antagonism rapidly assumed an ethnic and regional dimension. Although the organised resistance to Frelimo was not formed inside Mozambique, the fact is that many of its members had been exiled by Frelimo. Plus, once it got inside the country it found a lot of support amongst those who were unhappy with Frelimo's actions (Meneses 2012: 315–16), and/or who had been pushed away from power and excluded from the modern nation (Urdang 1989: 199–200). In this regard, Mosca (2005: 144) reminds us that André Matsangaíssa and Afonso Dhlakama escaped from Frelimo's highly controversial re-education centres.[4] The MNR (later RENAMO) was founded in 1975, in Rhodesia, although its most effective supporter would be South Africa. Having had strong Western and anti-communist influences, it was supported by white minority governments from the surrounding areas of Mozambique to whom Frelimo's agency — within the country and towards other African guerrilla movements outside this area — was regarded as highly threatening (Nordstrom 1997: 36–73). In a study on the twentieth century in Mozambique, Allen and Barbara Isaacman (1983: 176–77) highlight the fact that the coalition formed by Rhodesians and South Africans proceeded by recruiting people who might somehow be interested in preventing Frelimo from being successful in its intentions. As a result, it looked for the support of individuals who had been connected to the colonial regime in Mozambique (Portuguese settlers and former members of the Portuguese *Estado Novo*'s PIDE (Polícia Internacional e de Defesa do Estado [International and State Defence Police]) and colonial army, among others) and, as mentioned before, it also targeted alienated ex-Frelimo members. Its anti-Frelimo strategy was based on the infiltration of the country, the progressive destruction of the socialist government's project and structures, and ultimately the annihilation of the sense of collective identity and of the population itself. Hence, given that it set out to question, subvert and destroy Frelimo's authority, RENAMO's practical point of departure on the ground was the retrieval of those who had somehow been marginalised by the former, in order to create a network of loyalty and troops. Traditional chiefs were among those used by the guerrilla movement to achieve its goals.

In a study on the Mozambican war and its impact on people and society, Nordstrom (1997: 101–10) references one of the first field analyses, which was conducted by the social scientist Christian Geffray in the 1980s, in two villages in Nampula province, affiliated to Frelimo and RENAMO respectively, with a view to gaining an understanding of the conditions that facilitated the consolidation of RENAMO's ideals amongst the population in the countryside (Geffray and Pederson 1986; Geffray 1990). Nordstrom states that

> Geffray attributes much of village Mozambican's disenchantment with Frelimo, and the early successes of Renamo, to Frelimo's practice of implementing socialist policies in the countryside. Problems revolved around two central tenets of Frelimo strategy: the production of communal villages and the proscription of traditional power structures and culture. (1997: 101–02)

With respect to communal villages, Geffray concluded that regardless of the emphasis placed by Frelimo on the advantages arising from the construction of co-operative villages in the countryside, the real intention behind their creation was to maintain ideological control over those areas. Yet, not only were they incapable of meeting the population's needs, but they were also highly disruptive of people's lifestyles in the majority of cases observed (Nordstrom 1997: 102). As for Frelimo's exclusion of traditional power structures and condemnation of traditional culture as obscurantist, such policies provoked what Geffray views as 'a battle between the old power and the new' (1997: 102). Frelimo banned traditional chiefs from positions of power within the villages, but RENAMO promised to reinstate their power, if these chiefs would commit to their cause. Hence, RENAMO — which, according to Geffray, presented few characteristics that would allow for its classification as a political group — started to exert its authority over the villagers it controlled through these traditional chiefs, who were responsible for their local areas and had to assure RENAMO'S needs were met and its directives were followed (1997: 102–03).

Later, some of the traditional chiefs came to realise that RENAMO'S aim was not to propose an alternative governmental agenda, but to undermine Frelimo's; this became particularly clear when they were confronted with the violent nature of the group. RENAMO carried out a horrendous war against the civilian population and the infrastructures that guaranteed communications, education, farming, and economy within the country, forcefully fragmenting it, isolating communities and causing thousands of people to become refugees. These destructive attacks that contributed to the progressive downfall of Frelimo's Marxist programme coincided with floods and famine throughout the country, specifically in the 1980s, worsening the already critical situation for communities in the affected regions. Regardless of their awareness of RENAMO'S terrorist nature, traditional chiefs could neither demonstrate their dissatisfaction towards its agency nor go back to the areas which were occupied by Frelimo, as they feared retaliation from both sides (1997: 103). Therefore, as Nordstrom highlights in her interpretation of Geffray's findings, it is important to understand the traditional chiefs' positioning in the midst of this confrontation, which was a 'war of power and politics':

> Geffray stresses that the chiefs did not rebel against the state because it was a state per se, but because they had been marginalized from power and dignity. They thought Renamo offered them a means toward an independent existence where they could maintain a valued lifestyle. But chiefs, too, became pawns in a larger military contest, and people, freed from the communal villages, found they were yet again displaced to Renamo control areas for security reasons. Little if any improvement was gained under Renamo, and the enthusiasm for Renamo promises waned. (1997: 104)

Hence, as proven by Geffray's study, regardless of whether they were under Frelimo's or RENAMO'S control, the villagers were always victimised and from their point of view this minimised the apparently major differences between both entities. As Nordstrom brilliantly points out, the villagers were caught in a crossfire that unravelled into 'a continuing cycle of violence' (1997: 104).

Notwithstanding the fact that Frelimo did not initially regard RENAMO'S opposition as a threat, the party soon realised that it could not ignore it any more. By the late 1980s, Frelimo's inability to respond and simultaneously deal with all the internal issues that were affecting Mozambique forced it to look for external help from Western countries and, subsequently, detach itself from the Eastern Bloc. Obviously, this help came at a cost: Mozambique had to act according to a Western agenda (Urdang 1989: 213). From the mid-1980s on, the conflict between Frelimo and RENAMO assumed different forms, given that both initiated diplomatic offensives with international projection and sought to consolidate these offensives internally, by finding firm supporters. In 1992 the signing by both parties of the General Peace Agreement (which was prepared and mediated by the UN) would put an end to this internal conflict, so that within two years the country would have its first multiparty elections. It would lead to the recognition of Frelimo as the legitimate government, given that the party won the elections, and of Renamo as a legitimate political party (Urdang 1989: 214–22). Although the 1994 elections passed off peacefully and reaffirmed the legitimacy of Frelimo's government, the task of bringing together such a fragmented society was not a simple one. In Newitt's (2002: 218) words:

> What, however, emerged most clearly after peace was eventually established was that Mozambique was divided very much along regional lines, with Frelimo commanding overwhelming support in the south and Renamo receiving strong backing in the central provinces north and south of the Zambesi.

Hence, one of the biggest challenges of the post-civil war period is precisely that of redefining the concept of *Moçambicanidade* — debating it and allowing it to be flexible, pluralist and adjustable to a democratic setting. The present analysis will, thus, attempt to show how the work developed by Chiziane in *Ventos*, *Niketche* and *Alegre Canto* portrays this framework in the sense that it reflects on the post-independence, modern condition of *Moçambicanidade* by exposing and renegotiating the different forms of exile co-existing within the Mozambican society, with a particular emphasis on exile connected to gender, ethnicity and race.

Ventos do Apocalipse: An Introduction

In *Ventos* the main emphasis is placed on exile as 'a contemporary political punishment' (Said 2001a: 175), although not in the exact sense that Said describes it. As mentioned before, Said's theorisation associates this punishment with the forced abandonment of the homeland, as a geographical space to which it is impossible to return, and, consequently, with a deprivation of the history, roots and identity that are attached to it (2001a: 175–77). The literary work, however, focuses on this same deprivation within the limits of the state. This *insílio* (Herrera 2011: xvii–xxxiii) is a point of departure for the disruptiveness which will spread into a variety of exiles within that exile. Taking these nuances into consideration, Said's theorisation will be read alongside Nordstrom's anthropological research, which was carried out in Mozambique throughout the post-independence war. As mentioned before, in her work Nordstrom (1997) analyses the creative strategies employed by the civilian population to dismantle the structures of violence that surrounded them; these structures were put in place as much to strangle their culture and identity as to annihilate the people. Analysing the literary work through the filters of Said's theorisation and Nordstrom's social findings will, for that reason, allow us to observe the limitations of the application of Said's reflections on exile to the specific context of the Mozambican nation state throughout this particular period.

The novel is divided into three sections: the prologue (*Vinde todos e ouvi / Vinde todos com as vossas mulheres / e ouvi a chamada. / Não quereis a nova música de timbila*[5] */ que me vem do coração?*) [All of you, come and hear / All of you, come with your wives / and listen to the calling. / Do you not want the new *timbila* music / that comes from my heart?]; the first part (*Maxwela ku hanya! U ta sala u psi vona* — Nasceste tarde! Verás o que eu não vi.) [You were born late! You will see what I have not seen.]; and the second part (*A siku ni siko li psa lona* — Cada dia tem a sua história) [Each day has its story]. In the first section, the readers are called to listen to the stories which are about to be told. This is a clear reference to the tradition of storytelling around the fire, which brings together the eldest and the youngest to share knowledge and ensure its propagation from one generation to the other:

> Quero contar-vos histórias antigas, do presente e do futuro porque tenho todas as idades e ainda sou mais novo que todos os filhos e netos que hão-de nascer. Eu sou o destino. [...] é época de vindima [...] Chegam todos ao mesmo tempo. Preparam a fogueira e quando tudo está a postos dizem em uníssono: aqui estamos, avô. Conte-nos bonitas histórias. (Chiziane 1999: 15–16)
>
> [I want to tell you old stories, from the present and from the future because I am all ages, and I'm still younger than all the unborn children and grandchildren. I am the destiny. [...] it is harvesting season [...] Everybody arrives at the same time. They prepare the fire and when everything is ready, they say in unison, 'Here we are, grandfather. Tell us beautiful stories'.]

These references direct the reader to a common and shared knowledge that bestows verisimilitude on the short stories, approximating them to a recognisable reality. There are three stories in this prologue and they are entitled 'O marido cruel' [The cruel husband], 'Mata, que amanhã faremos outro' [Kill it, we'll make another one tomorrow], and 'A ambição da Massupai' [Massupai's ambition]. Each story is retrieved and incorporated into the main narrative — each of them appearing at one of the three distinct moments in which the narrative is subdivided. The second section explores the first moment of the narrative by telling us the story of the community of Mananga up until the point when it is attacked. Finally, the second and third moments of the narrative — that refer respectively to the journey of the group of refugees and to their arrival, adaptation and reintegration into the Aldeia do Monte — are explored in the closing section of the book. Hence, the choice of structure for this book, which is unique among Chiziane's works, also seems to be quite revealing as it discloses a latent discontinuity that surfaces intimately related to the theme explored, as the main narrative unravels. I will come back to this later, when analysing the latent disruptions that emerge throughout the book.

First Moment of the Narrative or '*O Marido Cruel*' [The Cruel Husband]

As mentioned above, the first moment of the text introduces us to the village of Mananga in a particularly difficult scenario. We acknowledge that this population is in great distress due to drought and consequent famine, and also to the rumours of an approaching war. These factors lead to many younger people departing in order to survive, leaving elders, women and children behind. A sense of isolation, abandonment and ultimately of annihilation surrounds the village, not only suggesting that the people are left to deal with their issues on their own, without any kind of governmental support, but also that they might not succeed in surviving what lies ahead, which will forcefully bring about the reformulation of their world. Minosse, one of the main characters, describes this environment as follows:

> Chegou a perdição de Mananga. Já não há remédio que sirva; nem Deus, nem espíritos, nem defuntos. A terra abre violentas fendas ávidas de água. Será necessário desabar o céu inteiro para dar de beber à terra e aos homens com ela. Se isto continua assim morrerá o último homem e a última mulher, predigo eu — pensa Minosse — , aí Deus vai aprender a lição. Terá a grande maçada de recriar de novo o Licalaumba e a sua companheira Nsilamboa mas, antes disso, será necessário reinventar a paisagem original, trabalho que ele pode evitar enviando alguns grãozinhos de chuva. (1999: 31–32)
>
> [Mananga's ruin is upon it. There is no longer any remedy; not God, nor the spirits, nor the deceased. Massive fissures eager for water split open the earth. The whole sky would have to collapse for there to be enough rain to water the earth and give the people a drink. Minosse thought to herself, 'If things go on like this, I foresee the last man and the last woman dying. Only then will God learn His lesson. He will have to go to the great trouble of creating the Licalaumba and his partner Nsilamboa again. But, before that, the original landscape will need to be reinvented, which is work that He could have avoided by just sending a few little drops of water.]

As we are progressively introduced to the main individual characters we realise that each of them represents a specific type of exile that is closely related to the exile of

Mananga as a community and that each form of exile develops in different ways.

The first characters we encounter are the couple Sianga and Minosse. Sianga is the former *régulo* [traditional chief] of the village who has been doubly disempowered — as a man and as a leader, that is in both the private and the public spheres — after independence. This happens due to the revolutionary state's determination to dismantle the former structures of power and eradicate traditional cultural practices associated with them in favour of a centralised and modern government — and of modern collective villages as well. He, therefore, represents the present's alienation from the past, as he now spends his days meditating on his bitterness and hostility towards the modern nation that, in his view, ostracised him:

> Vê o trono a ser arrastado pelos ventos da revolução e independência. São as oito esposas que abalam, ficando apenas a mais nova e a mais desprezada. [...] A minha boca transpira agruras, frustrações. Sabes bem que não consigo conciliar o passado e o presente. Fui árvore, fui flor e régulo desta terra. Agora não sou mais do que um ramo seco ou fruta podre. Já não sou nada nem ninguém, minha querida esposa. Comprei-te com dinheiro vermelho a ti e às outras oito. Veio o vendaval e carregou as que partiram pelo mundo levando cada uma todos os filhos que geraram. (1999: 30–31)
>
> [He sees his throne being swept away by the winds of revolution and independence. And then the eight wives who rush away, leaving only the youngest and most despised one behind. [...] The bitter taste of grief and frustration is puckering my lips. You know well enough that I cannot reconcile the past and the present. I was tree, flower, and traditional chief in this land. Now I'm no better than a dry branch or rotten fruit. Now I'm nothing, I'm nobody, my dear wife. I bought you and the other eight women by sweating blood. A violent storm came and carried off around the world the wives who left, each one taking all of their offspring with them.]

Sianga has been excluded from the new conception of the nation, thus becoming an exile within it; ultimately, it is his strong awareness of this fact that prompts the disclosure of the Mananga community's exile.

Minosse is Sianga's ninth wife and the only one who does not abandon him after independence. She is a 'esposa dos velhos tempos' [wife of the old days] (1999: 27) who still maintains and propagates the traditions of a patrilineal culture that have been inculcated into her. Stripped of any sense of individuality in order to perform the role that is expected from her, she is a devoted wife and mother who maintains the household at any cost. When the land refuses to provide food for her family, she assumes this task by selling sex for some food in return: 'Ai, Deus, homem que se preza, morre de fome preservando a honra, mas o meu vende-me para encher a pança' [Oh Lord, a real man would rather die of hunger and preserve his honour, whereas my husband sells me to fill his belly] (1999: 29). This is the only reality Minosse knows, and the only one that she can make available to Wusheni, her rebellious daughter. Regardless of her silent thoughts of protest against patriarchy and old patriarchal practices, Minosse remains entrapped in a profile that is still to be renegotiated. As the sexual power structures unfold, she appears before us as an exile within the nation on account of her gender. Minosse materialises a specific type of exile that travels through time, bridging both past and present, and also future, as we will discuss later.

Her space for self-reinvention is opened up by Wusheni's strong reaction against her own entrapment. Notwithstanding her vehement refusal of a traditional arranged marriage, it is only when she is made pregnant by her beloved Dambuza — a man other than the one her father had chosen for her — that she is finally able to open a breach in the chain of patriarchy. Motherhood, which usually works as a device that traps women in patriarchy, is hereby presented as a weapon that backfires:

> Minosse fica radiante. A existência de uma vida no ventre da única filha coloca de lado todos os preconceitos que tem sobre a origem do homem que a engravidou. Todas as possibilidades estavam vedadas ao Muianga, esse cretino. A tia Rosi cai fulminada. O jogo está perdido. (1999: 84)
>
> [Minosse is thrilled with the news. The existence of a life in the womb of her only daughter makes her set aside all her prejudices against the origins of the man who impregnated her. All possibilities were now non-existent to Muianga, that idiot. Aunt Rosi is struck down by the news. The game is lost.]

At this point, the shield provided by motherhood allows both mother and daughter to make use of the specificity of gender to present an active opposition to the economic dynamics of the patriarchal lineage. This opens up possibilities for a new reality in which women regain power over their bodies and rewrite the feminine identity outside the constraints of a wholly male-oriented conception. Although Wusheni's act does not disrupt women's dependency on men, as she remains a possession that is transferred from her father's to her husband's household, the expression and imposition of her choice successfully disturbs this process. Such a gesture evidences women's awareness of their own condition and, simultaneously, their engagement in actively subverting it within the limits of the imposed patriarchal frame. We shall come back to this very specific type of exile later.

We learn about another important characteristic of Mananga's community through the description of the character Dambuza, namely its isolation. Despite being the nephew of someone who belonged to the community, he was regarded as a foreigner, and therefore unworthy of equal treatment: 'É da nossa tribo mas não é do nosso clã. [...] Para quê tratá-lo bem se ele não é do nosso clã? É um estrangeiro, e se se sente mal que regresse à sua origem' [He is part of our tribe, but not of our clan. [...] Why treat him well if he doesn't belong to our clan? He's a foreigner, and if he feels uncomfortable, he should go back to where he came from.] (1999: 38). This attitude on the part of the villagers reveals the consequences of the modern nation's discourse for the creation of national unity so as to consolidate the nation state. Mozambique's civil post-independence discourse refuses to recognise cultural difference, promotes ethnic assimilation, and repudiates multiplicity in favour of a univocality that emerges from a specific ideal of community to which everyone is expected to adjust. In its urgency to create a united nation 'Do Rovuma ao Maputo' [From Rovuma to Maputo],[6] it deliberately refuses to acknowledge the existence of cultural realities that precede the formation of the nation state and, consequently, ends up being unsuccessful in its project. At the same time, this proves the untranslatability of Anderson's 'imagined community' in the particular context of independent Mozambique. In Meneses's words (2012: 312),

> A aplicação da proposta teórica de 'nação imaginada' (ANDERSON) ao Moçambique independente revela-se problemática. Com efeito, o sistema de produção de uma identidade nacional estava pouco estabelecido, tendo sido alvo, ao longo do último século, de permanente contestação, face à diversidade cultural do país.
>
> [The application of the proposed theory of 'imagined community' (ANDERSON) to independent Mozambique proves to be problematic. In effect, the scheme to produce a new national identity was not very well established, having been subject to constant contention throughout the past century, due to the country's cultural diversity.]

In this sense, like the character Sianga, Dambuza embodies the present's exile of the past.

Again, it is worth stressing that despite the fact that, in the particular case of Mozambique, political power was almost entirely in the hands of southern ethnic groups, it would be wrong to say that the post-independence war was an ethnic war, especially if we take into consideration Renamo's open self-characterisation as anti-Frelimo (Isaacman and Isaacman 1983: 171–88). However, in *Ventos* there is a suggestion of fraternal annihilation through the deaths of Wusheni and Manuna, who are brother and sister and end up killing each other during the attack on the village (Chiziane 1999: 117–18). This disruption coming from inside the family structure points towards an exile that might emerge from the treatment afforded to the issue of gender in this setting. Manuna, one of the sons of the village (and the *régulo*'s son) is manipulated by the RENAMO terrorist cell to become one of the soldiers who is responsible for the destruction of Mananga. So, in *Ventos* he can be read as the outcome of the exploitation and manipulation of all the nation state's frailties, in a very vulnerable context (famine and drought), by a group whose only intentions were to discredit the Frelimo government and, subsequently, to destroy the nation from within. By resorting to the forced recruitment of young males to eradicate every structure that supports their own community and the prospective collective entity that the modern nation seeks to create, the RENAMO group succeeds in exposing and capitalising on the specific weaknesses that characterise this conceptualised nation, namely its internal fragmentations and its patriarchal family structure.

In Mananga we can observe these internal fragmentations through people's behaviour, as those whom the community consider to be outsiders are immediately marginalised. Regardless of being part of the community, someone that no one would have denied some food to in the good days, Dambuza is openly discriminated against. His is an empowering exile, nonetheless. His continuous struggle for survival makes him physically stronger and more independent than all the other young men of the village. In addition, the fact that he lives on the margins of the community makes him develop a critical perspective of the community values, as well as a strong individual identity detached from its flaws (1999: 42–43). So, in the eyes of the population, he is repulsive for his difference and for being able to successfully survive outside the community's rules, but his independence and ability to readjust are simultaneously very attractive and an object of envy. Dambuza emerges as the representative of a disruptive male identity. He does not fit the social profile that would make him eligible to belong to the traditional patriarchal lineage, because he is a poor foreigner and, so, unable to pay for Wusheni's *lobolo.* Yet, he is portrayed as a 'real' man, much cleverer, more capable and generous than all his male counterparts. He is shown to be worthy of Wusheni and together they try to impose a new order that disempowers all the other discourses imposed — traditional and modern — by moving beyond class and gender constraints in the reinvention of their identities. These two potential agents of change for the future (given that Wusheni is pregnant with Dambuza's child) have, however, a tragic end. Wusheni and the baby die at her brother's hands and Dambuza commits suicide when confronted with this reality. They represent a project that was brutally interrupted just when it was being set in motion. On the one hand, this reveals the population's powerlessness before the incomprehensibility of a war that overtakes them very suddenly. On the other hand, it demonstrates the overwhelming need to suspend the various struggles (such as gender and class struggles) that were taking place, because survival had to be prioritised (Casimiro 2005: 74–75). Nevertheless, Chiziane seems to indicate how gender and class equality would help survival too, if only they were prioritised as well.

Indeed, the study of the above-mentioned characters allows us to have a better understanding of the elements that compose the particular setting of exile in which Mananga is embedded. As famine, drought and rumours of the proximity of war become the villagers' daily reality, a sense of abandonment increasingly grows for each of them. In this vulnerable condition, an emerging oppositional discourse infiltrates the village through a group of soldiers seeking the support of those who had not been protagonists of the Frelimo state's national discourse, supposedly to fight the modern nation which was, according to their understanding, highly dissatisfying and elitist. Not surprisingly, Sianga is the first person to be contacted by members of this group of opponents who promise to restore his power and the traditional structures, revealing a persuasive and markedly traditionalist speech. Although Sianga and his *compinchas* [buddies] understand that both these discourses are in opposition, they perceive them to be unexpectedly similar at this specific moment in the text due to the discourses' emphasis on the same issues — oppressiveness, obscurantism, liberty, fraternity, unity — from distinct angles (Chiziane 1999: 50–51). This brings the confrontation between discourses down to a question of power seizure, a struggle between traditional and modern: 'A linguagem dos homens é curta, imperfeita. O secretário da aldeia e o comandante das armas dizem a mesma coisa com sentido diferente. Só o cérebro mais do que inteligente pode entender tamanha bagunça' [The men's language is short and imperfect. The Village Secretary and the Commanding Officer say the same thing in a different way. Only the brain of a genius could understand such a mess] (1999: 51). Again, we are driven to consider the conclusions of Geffray's study, which showed that these traditional chiefs' quest for cultural dignity and social empowerment led them to become entrapped between two opposing discourses that alienated them (1986). This explains Sianga and his friends' perception of the discourses of both the *secretário da aldeia* (Frelimo) and the *comandante das armas* (Renamo) as similar (Nordstrom 1997: 104). In other words, it is possible to say that Sianga and his friends were also victims.

In an interview given to the present author and Ana Martins (M. Tavares & Martins 2008), when asked about the process of construction of her characters, Chiziane made a very precise and interesting remark about the construction of Sianga:

> Então, às vezes, construo personagens que dão trabalho. Quando fiz o *Ventos do Apocalipse*, o Sianga. Comecei a descrevê-lo de uma forma tão feia. Comecei a descrevê-lo de uma forma muito feia e eu dormi a pensar 'Será que fiz bem? Como é que vai ser? Que final é que vou dar?' Quando dormi, sonhei que o Sr. Sianga, que a pessoa que eu criei levantou-se e começámos a dialogar. Pronto, e ele me pergunta... eu ainda me lembro tão bem! 'É o Sr. Sianga?' 'Sim, sou eu. Gostaria de saber porque é que a senhora me tratou tão mal, se já lhe fiz mal algum dia'. Olha, acordei e disse 'Meu Deus, dormi a pensar nisto e o sonho se tornou real'. Então, no dia seguinte acordei e voltei a arrumar um bocadinho melhor. Melhorou um bocado a história, para aquilo que era a minha previsão. De vez em quando me acontece isto. [...] Sim, imagina, eu estou a trabalhar num texto durante uma semana, a escrever a mesma coisa, o mesmo nome, a dialogar com isto. É lógico que quando vou dormir as pessoas aparecem. Perfeitamente. Mas, nunca mais me vou esquecer do Sianga. O Sianga perguntou-me mesmo 'Mas, minha senhora eu nunca lhe fiz mal nenhum. Porque é que me trata assim?'

> [So, sometimes I create characters that are hard work. For example, Sianga from *Ventos do Apocalipse*. I began by describing him in such an ugly way. I described him in a really ugly way at first, and then I went to bed thinking 'Did I do the right thing? How is it going to develop? What will the ending be like?' When I fell asleep, I dreamt that Mr. Sianga, the person who I created, got up and we started talking. OK, and then he asked me... I still remember it so well! 'Are you Mr. Sianga?' 'Yes, I am. I would like to know the reason why you've treated me so badly. Have I ever done you any wrong?' Well, I woke up and said to myself 'My God, I went to bed thinking about this and the dream became real'. So, the following morning, I got up and tidied it up a little bit. It improved the story a bit, in relation to what I had in mind before. Sometimes this happens to me. [...] Yes, imagine that I've been working on a text for a week; writing the same thing, the same name, entering into dialogue with it. It's perfectly logical that when I go to sleep the characters are going to appear to me. Of course. But, I'll never forget Sianga. Sianga really asked me 'But, lady, I've never done you any wrong. Why are you treating me like this?']

Sianga's demand for some more dignity in his construction and treatment as a character was viewed as legitimate by the author. On revising the character, Chiziane clearly points to the need to look more closely at the duality of Sianga's positioning. Interestingly, Chiziane's first impulse was to create Sianga as a very 'ugly' character, which, taking her own personal formation and active involvement in Frelimo's socialist activities as a youngster into consideration, can be read as an unconscious bias against the action of traditional chiefs. Nevertheless, her increasing reflection on the subject led her to view Sianga's exile and perhaps his actions as a reaction to his being deprived of an identity and his subsequent need to feel reintegrated and re-empowered.

In this respect, it is relevant to point out that the eloquent spokesperson who meets Sianga and his most loyal former subjects in secrecy is a very young man disguised as an elder. He persuades them to betray their community in order to recuperate their positions, in what is a clear suggestion of an alluring use of a traditionalist discourse in a particularly fragile setting to achieve ends other than those revealed, i.e., to subvert the modern programme in practice:

> O homem desfeito do disfarce era mais jovem que o milho tenro. [...] Disse que os régulos são os verdadeiros representantes, medianeiros entre os desejos do povo e os poderes dos espíritos. [...] Sianga, [...] Todo o mundo se ajoelhará aos seus pés, e quanto às mulheres, nem há necessidade de falar'. (Chiziane 1999: 50–51)
>
> [Without his disguise, the man was as young as the morning. [...] He said that the traditional chiefs were the real representatives, since they mediate between the people's wishes and the spiritual powers. [...] Sianga, [...] The whole world will kneel before you, not to mention the women.]

The promise of empowerment leads the former *régulo* and his associates to progressively convince the population that the present drought situation is a result of their detachment from ancient traditions and it can only be solved through a reaffirmation of their belief. As Said reminds us, the awareness of their own exile, as opposed to what they perceive to be the population's non-exile, generates feelings of resentment in the *régulo* and his associates. Those feelings compel them to somehow reverse this situation so as to be able to imagine themselves as 'part of a triumphant ideology or a restored people' (Said 2001a: 177–81). Inevitably, they end up exiling the already exiled population of Mananga.

In a context of despair, the population are led to believe that the gods are their only hope, so they agree to empower the *régulo* once again in order to persuade him to perform the *mbelele*. In this important rain-making ceremony women have a primordial role, given that they must run naked through the village. This illusory return to the origins confirms the entrapment of the community in between two worlds without any kind of balance or negotiation: 'O grosso da população, livre de compromissos ideológicos, rogava livremente a qualquer deus [...] Os deveres que não cumpriram durante mais de um século, procuram realizá-los em apenas poucas luas' [The bulk of the population, free of any ideological commitments, prayed freely to any god [...] They tried to accomplish in only a few moons the duties that they had not fulfilled for over a century] (Chiziane 1999: 60–61). In order to survive, they are pushed to change their beliefs according to the situation they are facing. As the Mozambican critic and thinker Lourenço do Rosário (2007: 200–21) argues in his essay on the construction and consolidation of democracy in Mozambique, before hunger, the famished are deprived of their agency. As they are forced to depend on charity, they also succumb to it — regardless of its form or source — in order to survive (2007: 210). However, in the text, both discourses that allegedly exist to ensure the endurance of the community seem to be working against the population itself. This happens due to the fact that the groups that make up what Said (2001a: 176) calls the 'rhetoric of belonging' — which guarantees the binding of the collective — are fighting each other in the seizure of power. This assumption becomes clear later on, when the *mbelele* produces no results whatsoever and the desolate situation escalates.

Indeed, the population of Mananga is shown to be ideologically exiled in the 'perilous territory of not-belonging' (2001a: 177). The villagers are incapable of building a stable community identity because their 'collective ethos' (2001a: 176–77) is shifting: it changes according to distinct political stances. Frelimo's modern ideal of the nation imposed the detachment from, and in some cases the denial of, historical, cultural and traditional coordinates. At the same time, it enforced the incorporation of new practices, behaviours, values and beliefs, which constitute what Pierre Bourdieu calls '*habitus*, the coherent amalgam of practices linking habit with inhabitance' (Said 2001a: 176).[7] While they were still struggling to conform to their modern imagining as a community, the population are induced by RENAMO to believe that they should invert their identity trajectory and retrieve their traditional self-images — although, in reality, RENAMO never engaged in the advancement of an alternative communal identity strategy (Nordstrom 1997: 103). In other words, the population continuously oscillate between opposing modern and traditionalist discourses, having no *apparent* possibility of negotiation, since both discourses force the choice of a positioning upon people. As a result, the instability of their 'collective ethos' and subsequent incoherence of their habits prevent them from achieving the *habitus* which would enable their self-imagination as part of a triumphant nationalism. They are, therefore, trapped in an identity exile which is placed beyond the binomial 'us' and 'others' — a discontinuous state of being that, in such a context, leaves the people to suffer in the most complete solitude, as they realise in the aftermath of the false *mbelele*:

> Esse mbelele foi uma farsa vergonhosa e nojenta. Mungoni, o célebre adivinho, disse a verdade desde a primeira hora e não o quisemos escutar. Estamos a definhar, estamos a morrer, fomos aldrabados pelos capangas do Sianga, minha gente, ah, cegueira humana! Por que cerramos sempre os olhos a quem nos mostra o caminho da razão? Fomos bem enganados. Sianga é um rato, engorda à custa do nosso sangue enquanto nós lambemos as crostas da nossa sarna, minha gente! (Chiziane 1999: 108–09)

> [That mbelele was a shameful and disgusting farce. The famous diviner, Mungoni, had told the truth right from the beginning, and we didn't want to listen to him. We are starving, and we are dying. We were deceived by Sianga's henchmen, my people! Oh, human blindness! Why do we always close our eyes to those who show us the path of reason? We were well fooled. Sianga is a rat. He gets fatter at the expense of our blood, while we lick our wounds, my people!]

When the population of Mananga become aware of their exile, the arrival of refugees from the village of Macuácua with news of the proximity and inevitability of war accentuates their alienation and, simultaneously, gives rise to a new attitude towards exile within the community. Due to the current panorama, the influx of refugees is generally regarded as a great burden that is imposed on the Mananga people. They are now forced to share the already sparse food with them, to take care of *their* wounded and to deal with *their* reality of war:

> Estão aglomerados como porcos no canto norte da aldeia. Bem-vindos a Mananga, diríamos nós, se boas novas nos trouxessem. [...] A recepção é hostil e as atitudes fratricidas. O nosso povo sente o desejo louco de defender o território à força de ferro mas as autoridades impõem-se, malditas autoridades. [...] Vieram apenas para roubar-nos os alimentos, a paz e o sossego com os seus problemas. (1999: 109)

> [They are clustered like pigs in the northern corner of the village. We would say 'Welcome to Mananga', if they were bringing good news. [...] The reception is hostile and the attitudes fratricidal. Our people desperately want to defend the territory with an iron hand, but the authorities impose themselves, the damn authorities. [...] They came with their problems just to rob us of food, peace and quiet.]

From this behavioural frame, it is possible to infer that Mananga does not possess a sense of extended community, i.e., an attachment with a national entity (Meneses 2012: 312). The refugees with whom they share the same nation state are considered to be 'foreigners' not only because they do not belong to the village, but also due to their differences. In addition to this, the community's understanding of its own condition of exile leads it to become closed in on itself by drawing a very precise, inclusive line around the Mananga villagers, that inevitably separates them from the 'foreigners'. In an act which reproduces the same attitude that Sianga and his followers previously had towards them, the population exiles another community in an attempt to change its own self-perception. In this regard, Said (2001a: 178) remarks that since exile is 'a jealous state', it will eventually end up producing 'an exaggerated sense of group solidarity, and a passionate hostility to outsiders, even those who may in fact be in the same predicament as you'. Soon the people from Mananga come to understand that, in reality, they share the same exile with the refugees. This happens when the population acknowledges that Sianga has recruited young people from within the community (including his own son, Manuna) to be trained and to attack the village — something which had already happened previously in Macuácua. Through the destruction of the village, the line of division is blurred, revealing the equality of exiling circumstances that surround both communities. In addition, the death of Wusheni and Manuna is particularly revealing as it materialises the exile of blood, the ultimate form of exile that the whole population faces, by being destroyed from within. Suddenly, the fratricidal nature of the war — and, consequently, of all the behavioural patterns that preceded it — becomes a physical reality.

In the aftermath of the attack, the absent Frelimo head of the village finally arrives, only to reaffirm the isolation and abandonment left to Mananga by the governmental entity. Not only was he away at the time of the attack, but he had also heard rumours of a conspiracy prior to the attack — rumours that he chose to ignore along with the village itself:

> O sangue sobe-lhe aos olhos, não consegue acreditar na destruição do seu império. Nunca antes avaliara a importância que tinha na sua vida aquela aldeola pobre e pacífica. Pensa em si. Nunca fizera nada por aquela aldeia e sempre negligenciara todos os problemas a ela referentes. Ouvira falar de uma infiltração inimiga e não ligara a devida importância. Esperam-no agora dificuldades e talvez desemprego. (Chiziane 1999: 120–21)
>
> [He feels a rush of blood to his head: he cannot believe the destruction of his empire. Never before had he valued the importance that that poor and peaceful village had in his life. He thinks of himself. He had never done anything for that village, and he always neglected any problem concerning it. He had heard talk of an enemy infiltration, but he did not give it the attention it deserved. He would now face difficulties and perhaps even unemployment.]

He reduces the destruction of the village and the killing of the population to his own disempowerment as a representative of political power. In the end, the people appear as mere casualties in a war for power which is alien to the vast majority. His detachment is made even more evident through his inability to take action. All he can do besides crying is smoke weed — which is lit by the fire still consuming the huts — in a desperate attempt to escape reality. However, he manages to be empowered once again in the eyes of the survivors of the attack and bond with them for the first time by resorting to revenge. By finding scapegoats on whom the population could focus its anger — thus, forgetting his negligence — and letting them decide the traitors' fates, he allows the people the temporary illusion of power. Consequently, Sianga and his followers are sacrificed twice: for the sake of the credit of the regime in power, represented by the head of the village, and also for the sake of preserving what is left of a sense of community within the group of survivors.

As mentioned above, the character Sianga emerges as connected with a traditional structure that was wholly ridiculed and catalogued as outdated by the post-independence state. As such, when the younger generations of the village make fun of him, they are also mocking their ancestors, their roots and their culture. Hence, Sianga is also an exile and, because of this exile, he becomes an instrument of the struggle for power. After the attack on the village, the population acknowledge their own exile and feel the urge to sacrifice Sianga and his accomplices in order to diminish it, regardless of their awareness of their own responsibility and of the cruelty of this act:

> O ódio do povo acende-se como uma fogueira de sândalo. [...] Ontem este povo proclamou e coroou Sianga. Depois crucificou-o. Voltou a realizar uma coroação clandestina e agora o crucifica de novo. As ocasiões alteram o comportamento dos homens. Como as estações do ano. Como o camaleão. (1999: 124–25)
>
> [The hatred of the people lights up like a sandalwood fire. [...] Yesterday this group of people proclaimed Sianga king and crowned him. Then, they crucified him. Later, they carried out a clandestine coronation, and now they crucify him again. Men's behaviour changes according to the situations. Like the four seasons. Like the chameleon.]

Although they know that Sianga himself is an exile, they feel the need to exile him further in a frantic effort to fight the discontinuity that inevitably characterises their existence. Hence, their awareness of their broken 'selves' and the urgency of gluing them back together leads them to 'otherise' Sianga (Said 2001a: 177). They feel entitled to take justice into their own hands so as to try to re-establish some of the connections with their roots that have been damaged and might never be recovered again. These are the connections that will ensure that the imagined community does not cease to exist: 'É preciso preservar a continuidade da tribo' [It is necessary to preserve the continuity of the tribe] (Chiziane 1999: 131). This continuity is negotiated, only for the people to conclude that the solution for the physical and cultural preservation of the community entails travelling to a village they have heard of, a peaceful territory where they hope to be able to reconstruct their *habitus*.

Although at this point they are still not fully aware of it, the structural existence that they knew and had somewhat taken for granted had already been destroyed. It is true that the community, as it was conceived by Frelimo's modern discourse and consequently the whole ideal of the Frelimo nation, proved to be unstable and was easily deconstructed from within. This emphasises the danger in attempting to delete an entire community's sense of historical continuity. One particular passage underlines both Frelimo's detachment from the population's reality of war and its inability to react to this reality. When a truck is sent to Mananga to collect the wounded and incapacitated villagers and take them to a city-based area controlled by the governmental forces, the population is completely *otherised* by the truck driver's gaze (1999: 150–54). The spectacle makes him feel nausea. Not for a single moment does he identify or sympathise with them — in fact, he acts in completely the opposite way. Objectifying the population, he remains detached from them, only addressing them to give orders:

> Metam os tipos dentro, que já é demasiado tarde. Tenho que atingir a vila antes de anoitecer, rápido, lesmas. [...] Esboça um sorriso nervoso, satisfeito, as suas ordens são cumpridas a contento. [...] Tapa os ouvidos. Não quer ser incomodado pelos ais dos moribundos. (1999: 150)
>
> [Put the guys in, it's getting late now. I have to reach the village before nightfall. Faster, you slugs. [...] A hint of a nervous smile crosses his face, and he is satisfied. His orders are happily followed. [...] He covers his ears, as he doesn't want to be bothered by the cries of pain coming from the dying villagers.]

In a clear allusion to the material dimension of the official discourse that he represents, the driver makes sure that all the wounded persons are piled up like dead bodies so as to economise on space, because 'não há tempo nem combustível para fazer uma segunda viagem' [there is not enough time or fuel for a second trip] (1999: 151).

In this setting, the image of this old truck emerges as a metaphor for the socialist government in Mozambique. Notwithstanding the fact that it is a piece of advanced machinery, the truck is so old that it will not move unless it is pushed by men. It bounces like a boat down a road full of holes, and all the noise and smoke that it produces illustrate its imminent collapse. Hence, we can read it as representative of the unfeasibility of mechanical and technical revolution in the countryside — which is to be the basis of the socialist administration — and, thus, of the economic vulnerability of Mozambique (Isaacman and Isaacman 1983: 145–70). In addition, this truck carries dying people who are described as a huge mass of bodies. What binds this collective entity, in which it becomes impossible to distinguish individualities, is the experience of violence — death; loss of material and cultural dignity; loss of a sense of belonging; interruption of a sense of continuity; and constant fear of what lies ahead. Their situation is presented as a hopeless one. Those who might survive will get separated from their families, and those who might die will end up in a mass grave, their families never being able to find out if there they are still alive due to the lack of records (Chiziane 1999: 151–52). This description exposes the disintegration of these people's identity and their consequent exile. On the one hand, they are the object of RENAMO's violence which, as Nordstrom (1997: 122) reminds us, is something that unfolds into a variety of ramifications which affect all areas of the individual's human and social reality:

> It is a violence, Mozambicans tell me, that goes far beyond the physical bloodshed to injure family stability, community sustainability, and cultural viability. The continuity of the historical present is obliterated, respected traditions are dismantled, values rendered moot. Psychological peace and emotional security are bygone memories. Tomorrow, once taken for granted, now becomes a tenuous proposition.

On the other hand, they are also *otherised* by Frelimo, an entity whose conceptualisation of the nation they fail to recognise and which, therefore, is unable actually to help them. There is an immense gap between the governmental entity and these villagers for whom they are supposedly building a nation. In the text, this becomes evident through the relationship between the wounded villagers, who represent the majority of the population living in the countryside, and the truck driver, who represents the city-based leaders who rule over the nation state from a distance. There is no relationship between them — the driver merely instructs and conducts them, without any intention of listening to them or even looking at them. Even their views on what lies ahead (i.e., the road that will take them all to the city) are completely opposed. Although both look for familiar elements that give them a sense of continuity, the villagers desperately look for a house, a person or a friendly animal, whereas the driver is reminded of war concerns, such as bullet wounds and hiding places.

Second Moment of the Narrative or '*Mata, Que Amanhã Faremos Outro*' [Kill It, We'll Make Another One Tomorrow]

Indeed, Frelimo's ideal of the nation is described as not having reached all people. Nevertheless, RENAMO's effort to create what Mozambican Frelimo leader Sérgio Vieira described to Nordstrom as a *nonsociety* (Nordstrom 1997: 130) was equally unsuccessful, regardless of its efforts to have a war that was meant to institute a culture of violence and ensure the impossibility of imagining any feasible future.

The population in the novel respond to the violence being imposed on them by engaging in practices of survival, which inevitably lead them to rethink and rebuild their individual and collective identities. Throughout the villagers' twenty-two-day journey, renegotiation and readjustment are forced upon them, prompting the rise of a new order from chaos — which takes us to the second section of the text. Although the community is now detached from any geographical space where it can settle, the possible re-establishment at the Aldeia do Monte opens up possibilities for the active reconception of their habits and subsequent restructuring of their *habitus*. As the sixty survivors carefully plan their journey, they feel it is necessary to recreate some kind of behavioural structure which would be familiar to the collective. They do so by selecting a 'leader', a person who is meant to guide them, and also set up some norms to be followed. At this stage, the choice of Sixpence for the leadership is quite revealing, on account of his individual characteristics, his strong awareness of the community and his propensity for change. Firstly, as opposed to the young Commanding Officer (RENAMO) disguised as an elder who convinced Sianga to sacrifice the village of Mananga, Sixpence is a 'homem jovem a quem as turbulências da vida envelheceram' [a young man turned old by the adversities of life] (Chiziane 1999: 154). Various events on his personal journey are described in the text along with references to important historical events, which evoke the experience of the nation. Through the creation of this parallel, this character appears to incorporate the past, the present and the future of the nation, which suggests that he is the perfect leader:

> Conhece a aldeia do Monte e já lá viveu. Já esteve na guerra dos portugueses e está familiarizado com as longas marchas e os mistérios dos caminhos. Como homem que se preza, trabalhou nas minas do Rand, condição exigida para realizar o matrimónio com a mulher ideal. Antes desta maldita guerra exercia as funções de caçador e domina os segredos das matas. Sixpence ficou surpreendido com a eleição. Teve vontade de dizer que não, mas não teve coragem. [...] Embora a situação lhe desagradasse, acabou dizendo o sim para cumprir um dever moral e social. (1999: 154)
>
> [He knows the Aldeia do Monte and has lived there before. He fought in the war against the Portuguese and is familiar with long marches and the mysteries encountered along the way. Like any man worth his salt, he worked in the Rand mines, a necessary requirement for marrying the ideal woman. Before this cursed war he was a hunter and mastered the secrets of the woods. Sixpence was surprised by the election. He wanted to say no, but he did not have the courage. [...] Although the situation displeased him, he ended up saying yes to fulfil a moral and social duty.]

His experience of working in the South African gold mines — a typically but not exclusively southern experience — suggests that Sixpence belongs to a southern ethnic group. However, the fact that he fought for the independence of his country in the armed struggle and emerged victorious not only endows him with national dimension, but also demonstrates triumphant nationalism. In addition, the fact that he knows the country very well, is used to long marches from a soldier's perspective, and is very familiar with life in the bush brings him closer to the experience of the majority of the population who live in the countryside, and makes him the ideal candidate to guide them to survival. Finally, he is the only person in the group who knows the Aldeia do Monte; he has already been there and is therefore more capable of ensuring the success of their venture. In other words, Sixpence incorporates a sense of continuity which is highly attractive for those who are struggling to restructure their shattered identity. His past experience makes him the person most capable of leading others in the present situation and of guiding the population to the possible future that awaits them at the Aldeia. Secondly, although he dislikes the idea of having to assume leadership in the journey, Sixpence silences his individual interests in favour of the collective's needs. By regarding his position of power as one that carries with it responsibility towards the people, he acts in an entirely different way from the preceding leaders, Sianga and Mananga's Frelimo head of the village. Finally, it is important to highlight that Sixpence is considered to be a foreigner, as he is a native of Macuácua. Interestingly, we only access this information after the group's successful arrival at the Aldeia do Monte. This suggests that the emphasis is now being placed not on what separates the survivors, but on what brings them together, i.e. the experience of violence under RENAMO and survival. As a result, in the new conceptualisation of the nation, whose renegotiation begins during the journey, this differentiation is not relevant anymore, because Sixpence effectively subverts it. For all of the reasons mentioned above, the new leader emerges as a unifying element, the community of survivors' point of departure for rebuilding their collective ethos and, subsequently, their successful community in exile. He somehow becomes the image of a triumphant ideology which, according to Said (2001a: 177), is vital for the reconstruction of a community in exile.

In her reflections on nationalism, Guibernau (1996: 80–84) asserts that community conscience implies the use of certain symbols and rites which individuals can identify and relate to and that simultaneously represent their unity, leading them to focus on the collective over the individual. When the author mentions 'symbols' she is actually referring to objects, signs or words. However, I believe that in this context the character of Sixpence can himself be read as a symbol, given that he invokes the history of the extended community, with episodes of his personal life intersecting with some of the nation's historical moments that the population can relate to individually. By doing so, he is able to lead the people to bond through the sharing of a common experience and to consequently feel a sense of community. In Guibernau's words (1996: 82),

> I shall argue that the nation, by using a particular set of symbols, masks the differentiation within itself, transforming the reality of difference into the appearance of similarity, thus allowing people to invest the 'community' with ideological integrity. This, in my point of view, explains the ability of nationalism to bind together people from different cultural levels and social backgrounds. Symbols mask the difference and highlight commonality, creating a sense of group. People construct the community in a symbolic way and transform it as a referent of their identity.

This successful intersection between the individual and collective levels achieved by Sixpence not only allows the dissipation of difference in equality within the community, but also inspires the population to strive for the community's continuity — a community they intend to actively rebuild in a particular context and beyond the surveillance of any specific ideological discourses.

Accordingly, the leader is determined to bring about change as he mediates the community's assimilation to new behavioural norms, in order to adjust to the new circumstances. Throughout the journey, the survivors face various trials that put their renegotiation skills to the test. When Doane realises that his pregnant wife is going into labour during an air raid he panics, because he understands that in that setting, the birth of one child can lead to the community's annihilation. Doane's positioning suggests that there is no space for renewal in this community — the only way to ensure its survival is by preventing it from expanding. It is overpowered by the demands of the here and now, because only the present can guarantee the survival of both past and future. At this point, the exile of the community is reaffirmed as the people suddenly realise that the war has spread, which necessarily implies that the reasons for the emergence of that war go beyond the specific circumstances that brought about the destruction of Mananga. As they hear the approaching sounds of gunfire, they wonder 'Se a terra é verde e fresca e de certeza chove, por que é que os homens se batem? A complicação da guerra é muito maior do que o entendimento do aldeão comum' [If the earth is green and fresh and rain is a certainty, why do men fight each other? The complexity of war is far greater than the understanding of the common villager] (Chiziane 1999: 161). This exile is accentuated by a growing sense of isolation amongst enemies. Nonetheless, the whole group survives the bombing and Doane's wife gives birth. As for Doane, he cannot bear the sight of such destruction; he loses his mind, and ends up being eaten by a boa constrictor. It is therefore possible to read Doane's fate in the text as a punishment for his behaviour towards the collective project. The community should be able to expand, regardless of its contextual restraints. On the one hand, the hostility that surrounds the population in the jungle *animalises* some of them — it challenges their ability to be flexible, to adjust and to develop survival techniques. On this subject, in her presentation of the multifaceted reality of violence, Nordstrom (1997) provides several accounts in which victims described the worst act of violence that was enacted towards them. One of these accounts states the following:

> But you want to know what I think is the worst thing about this war, the worst violence I suffer? It is sleeping in the bush at night. [...] Forcing us to sleep out with the animals makes us no better than them — these Bandidos, they take away our humanity, our dignity, they make us like animals. My marriage bed is the centre of my family, my home, my link with the ancestors and the future. This war, these soldiers, have broken my marriage bed, and with that they try to break my spirit, break what makes me who I am. This is the worst violence you can subject someone to. (1997: 125)

On the other hand, the hostility progressively reinstates the need for the villagers to invest in the cohesion of the group to maintain an identity. Ultimately, it takes their capacity to resist all the violence that they are suffering to the limits, forcing them to develop resistance strategies.

In order to strengthen the people's self-confidence in this complex and discouraging situation, Sixpence teaches them self-defence techniques in a move that proves to be double-edged. It is productive in the sense that it gets the villagers involved in the improvement of the group dynamic, but at the same time it is dangerous as it generates a defensive attitude of self-assertion in them. As Said (2001a: 184) points out, the exiles' agency tends to reflect a defensive nationalism precisely because they feel the need to reassure themselves as a community. Accordingly, in their urge to ensure the community's stability, the population react immediately by once again drawing an inclusive line around the members — 'us' — thus excluding those who might somehow threaten their survival — 'the others'. When they are confronted with a group of unknown wounded people they express the desire to just ignore them, but are given a lesson of solidarity by their leader. Not only does Sixpence remind them of the whole population's condition of exile in this war's setting, but he also alerts them to the counter-productive nature of such attitudes in the process of collective identity reconstruction: 'Sixpence defende-os. Ele diz que já que a vida tudo lhes negou, que tenham ao menos a felicidade de morrer rodeados pelos seus semelhantes' [Sixpence defends them. He says that since life has denied them all, they should at least be granted the happiness of dying surrounded by their peers] (Chiziane 1999: 169). The children found are subsequently taken along, as well as the wounded, who get treated by the villagers. The continuous trials that beset the consolidation of the community do not stop here. For instance, after having successfully ambushed a group of enemies, the survivors realise that one of them is the son of Mani Mossi, one of the members of the group of survivors. And, once again, the population are confronted by their own condition of exile, this time by reverting towards themselves the othering gaze that they had previously directed towards the people who did not belong to the group. In doing so, they reaffirm their entrapment within the 'territory of not-belonging', the impossibility of going back home by restoring unbroken links to their cultural identity, and the reality of their interrupted existences: 'A arma do mal ergue-se e divide a família. Mas para onde foi o amor e a liberdade que nos ensinaram os nossos antepassados? Onde ficou enterrada a moral e a vergonha deste povo?' [The weapon of evil rises and divides the family. But where was the love and freedom that our ancestors taught us? Where was the morale and shame of these people buried?] (1999: 174). The villagers gradually become able to adjust to their new circumstances through Sixpence's constantly vigilant attitude. Patiently, he leads them to continuously reflect on these issues as part of a structured survival project. Hence, they are able to carry on fighting for their survival, for the renegotiation of a set of habits which could be somewhat coherent in this setting (thus allowing them to maintain a sense of community), and for the non-reproduction of the violence that is being imposed on them.

At this point it is worth going back to Nordstrom's (1997: 4–31) investigation, which ultimately shows us that despite all the contradictions and repressive acts that the Mozambican population had to deal with, the majority were actively engaged in rebuilding their world by strengthening the bonds of humanity amongst them:

> [...] violence is about the destruction of culture and identity in a bid to control

> (or crush) political will. People at the epicentres of violence demonstrated to me that resistance emerges at the first sign of oppression, and is most powerfully coded in re-creating culture and identity against the vicissitudes of violence and oppression. It is in creativity, in the fashioning of self and world, that people find their most potent weapon against war. [...] Far from finding a dog-eat-dog survival mentality in the absence of all institutional and governing supports, I found most people operating according to a strong code of humane ethics. (1997: 4; 13)

In the text, the villagers still lack some of the means and tools to wholly reshape their worlds due to their condition as refugees; however, their awareness of their exile allows them to engage in the process. The consciousness and internalisation of their alienation allows the villagers to move to the next step, which is to turn the space of exile into a space of renegotiation and reconstruction. Therefore, on the twenty-first day of the journey, the group that has been reduced to less than forty members by this point finally reaches the Aldeia do Monte. At that moment, Sixpence collapses, as he realises that not only has he been successful in leading the survivors there, but also that the villagers have actually internalised his teachings of resistance against the oppressive violence that had set out to crush their cultural identity:

> Os companheiros transportam-no aos ombros, comandados dirigindo o seu comandante num gesto de máxima gratidão. [...] São todos iguais. Não há velhos nem novos, a turbulência da vida nivelou-lhes as idades. Não se distingue o homem da mulher pelos contornos do corpo. [...] A fidelidade aos defuntos, as leis da tribo, o orgulho do homem, as normas mais elementares da vida humana, tudo quebraram. (Chiziane 1999: 183–84)
>
> [The fellow travellers carry him on their shoulders — those who were led before are now leading their leader in a gesture of utmost gratitude. [...] They are all the same. There are neither elders nor youngsters, for life's turbulence has levelled their ages. Men and women can no longer be distinguished by the contours of their bodies. [...] Loyalty to the dead, the laws of the tribe, the pride of man — they have broken all of the most elementary rules of human life.]

Indeed, the success of this venture provides the population with the necessary strength to begin a reconstruction project that will allow them to imagine themselves as a 'restored people' (Said 2001a: 177), which takes us to the third and final section of the text.

Third Moment of the Narrative or '*A Ambição Da Massupai*' [Massupai's Ambition]

Having rethought and renegotiated a new set of habits throughout the journey, which can now be territorialised, the community feels sufficiently stable and willing to actively re-establish its *habitus*. Upon their arrival at the Aldeia, they are warmly welcomed by its community, who receive them as equals. They then feel prepared to start rethinking a new world and refashioning new identities with a view to compensating for the loss they had experienced (Said 2001a: 181). Yet, the awareness of this loss makes them eager to build a new world which is somehow similar to the one they knew before — and that can never be retrieved again. Although hope seems to lead the population to engage in a collective effort to move beyond the conditions of extreme poverty, expand, and rebuild a sense of community that is managed mainly by solidarity, the people also somehow feel that they can recreate the world they knew before in this new territory. As a result, at this point in the narrative, the community is confronted with situations which test its ability to be flexible and incorporate new practices. The first occurrence involves Sixpence and Mara, who get together to form a subversive couple in the most unlikely context. She is a young girl from the Aldeia who is determined to take care of a moribund Sixpence and bring him back to life. Despite being engaged and *lobolada*, she ends up falling in love with him, which leads her to reject her predefined identity as a woman and to impose her will and choice. It is impossible not to create a parallel here between the agency of the couples formed by Mara and Sixpence and Wusheni and Dambuza, given that both of them defy the establishment to affirm their own will. Hence, this reunion not only accentuates the potential of a balance between past, present and future — a future marked by solidarity, tolerance and acceptance — but it also reopens the debate about the place of women within the new emerging community. It is worth pointing out that nobody in the community opposes the formation of this new couple, apart from Mara's fiancé, for obvious reasons. In the first instance, this episode could suggest women's prominence in this society. Nonetheless, it might also be related to Sixpence's status of 'hero' within the community, which would exempt him from any sanctions.

The second occurrence takes place when a new natural catastrophe comes to disturb the fragile structures of this newly constructed society. This time, ironically, rain and floods destroy the majority of shelters which had been so carefully built, thus forcing the population into a new process of reconstruction. Once again, the community's cohesion and solidarity are trialled in adversity. When José Nuvunga dies during the storm while sleeping in his hut, his death discloses certain aspects which demonstrate a relapse into some of the behaviours which jeopardised the community in the past. His description suggests that he lived on the margins of this society and somehow chose to give up fighting for survival (Chiziane 1999: 214–15). For this reason, the whole population is disgusted with the sight of his dead body and they feel eager to bury it. They prepare everything to do it as quickly as possible, but when the head of the village arrives he decides that the deceased should not be buried in his clothes, given that they were good clothes which could still be worn by others. Again, we are confronted with a disjuncture between the population's and the government's ideal of the community's identity. Although the people want to give Nuvunga a traditional burial in which the deceased is respectfully treated and mourned, the head of the village ignores their perspective and dictates an order that depicts him as a mere casualty. He completely dehumanises Nuvunga, depriving him of his identity even in death. On the one hand, Nuvunga becomes a disposable object because he cannot contribute to the collectivity anymore: 'José Nuvunga desce à terra mais nu do que no momento em que viu a primeira luz no mundo dos tormentos' [José Nuvunga descends to the earth even more naked than when he saw light for the first time in this world of torment] (1999: 216). On the other hand, he becomes useful *because* he dies, since his clothes can be worn by someone else. Furthermore, the head of the village selects and keeps the best pieces of the deceased's clothing for himself, ignoring Nuvunga's nephew's claims of an entitlement to the 'inheritance'. His behaviour clearly highlights the gap between the governmental entity and the population it claims to represent, simultaneously emphasising the materialistic nature of the modern nation's discourse — particularly of some of its representatives to whom, in the end, it was all a matter of having the power to control everything. It is important to point out that although the population are shocked at the head of the village's demands and disapproves of them, they accept them, so they contribute to their own entrapment in exile: 'A ordem é uma selvajaria, vandalismo puro. O chefe da aldeia faz ouvidos de mercador e ordena. E o povo cumpre, palavra de rei não volta atrás' [The order is an act of savagery, of pure vandalism. The head of the village turns a deaf ear to their comments and proceeds with the orders. And the people comply, for a king's word is supreme] (1999: 216).

This episode is of particular relevance as it reveals two very significant aspects that facilitate a better understanding of the Aldeia's dynamics up to this point and its subsequent annihilation. The first is connected with the gap between a stationary conceptualisation of community, as imposed by an elitist governmental entity, and the day-to-day experience and renegotiation of this conceptualisation, which is performed by the population. Through her observation of people on the front lines of war and violence in Mozambique, Nordstrom (1997: 13) concluded that many of the most creative solutions proposed to readjust to these complex and permanently shifting settings were actually advanced by average citizens, meaning that 'Society and culture were sculpted from the ground up'. Up to this point of the narrative it is clear that the population is, indeed, actively engaged in reshaping a sense of community which is not necessarily synchronised with the government's ideals. The second aspect refers to how this process of what Nordstrom calls 'worldbuilding' is conducted (1997: 13). The researcher claims that this is a central issue to focus on, given that

> [...] if people rebuild their lives and worlds as they are, they will simply be open to re-attack. Survival, then, involves crafting a new universe of meaning and action. [...] Truly to create is to bring in a wholly new world — to add something that has not been before. (1997: 13; 15)

Although they do intend to reconstruct a sense of community and adjust it to their present reality, which is in permanent mutation, it is impossible to say that the population of the Aldeia reaches this state of identity development. Their eagerness to rebuild their *habitus* leads them to recuperate some of the habits they used to have before in a move that inevitably causes the reiteration of certain counterproductive behaviours. These acts lead us once again towards Said's (2001a: 181) claim that exiles need to rebuild, as soon as possible, a new world which is somehow similar to the old one that is lost forever, in an attempt to compensate themselves for their loss. Caught in this negotiation, the population neglect to update some of the structures that will later come to expose their frailties, and ultimately bring about the Aldeia's destruction. Far from being an innocent coincidence, the Aldeia's being destroyed because of a woman's betrayal is a particularly revealing aspect of the story. It prompts a new reading of the events from a different perspective, forcing further analysis of the discussion of gender issues throughout the diverse stories that intersect. From early on in the text we understand that gender is hardly ever an openly discussed issue, and when it is (in social environments such as the one that preceded the Mbelele ceremony) the potentially questionable established structures remain undisturbed. Despite the well-aimed and successful attacks that are performed by individual characters such as Wusheni and Mara, their positions are isolated and they demonstrate that the role of women inside the community is still to be debated and renegotiated. It is worth pointing out that, eventually, both of them end up being filled with the same silence that keeps Minosse and Emelina alienated, and leads the latter to inform the enemy of the Aldeia's exact location. Hence, gender emerges in the text as a very precise type of exile, different from those that have been explored so far.

In his theorisation on exile, Said omits to focus on gender. By defining exile as 'a discontinuous state of being' and intersecting it with nationalism, the theorist assumes that exile is a disruptive state that follows a continuous one, i.e. the condition of belonging precedes that of being in the 'perilous territory of not-belonging' (2001a: 177). Hence, despite recognising that exile is not experienced in the same way by all the refugees and dislocated people, when he argues that 'nationalism is an assertion of belonging in and to a place, a people, a heritage', Said somehow assumes that nationalism is generally experienced in the same way, regardless of factors such as gender (2001a: 176). However, where to place those who did not feel the sense of belonging in the first place within the national conceptualisation which was supposed to be continuous and stable to them? Such displacement will forcefully change their experience of exile in a community rebuilt later — one that sets out to erect a new world based on the one they knew before. It is a trajectory of uninterrupted exiles that overlap and emerge condensed in *Ventos* in a space of silence, absence and alienation. This space, which is sporadically disrupted by individual voices that speak up, is occupied by all the women throughout the various stories, as the characters Minosse and Emelina demonstrate. As we have already acknowledged, Minosse is a 'traditional' wife, according to patrilineal culture. After the death of all her family members, she ceases to exist as a woman, as she is unable to fit the only female definition she knows. Sianga's death liberates her from his tyranny, but at the same time she feels that there is no place for her in the world anymore, since she can no longer be any of the things she used to be — a wife, a mother and a grandmother. Consequently, throughout the journey to the Aldeia do Monte, Minosse appears to be completely absent from the survival project, not only because she feels self-alienated, but also because there is no room for difference or individuality in this project. The urge to stay alive and rebuild a community identity that keeps it cohesively together prevails over all other needs, including that of considering gender difference (Casimiro 2005: 75). Throughout this period in the narrative, various episodes occur which precisely highlight this need to address gender difference in its specificity. Good examples include: the episode in which Doane feels like killing his wife because she is in labour (Chiziane 1999: 157–60); the one in which a *capulana*[8] is removed from the dead body of a woman, exposing the deceased's genitals, because it was in perfect conditions to be reused (1999: 169–70); or the one in which children who are found wandering in the forest are handed to women in the group who had lost their own children (1999: 169). As mentioned before, by the time the population reaches the Aldeia they were 'todos iguais' [all equals]: a huge mass of bodies which were impossible to distinguish between in any way (1999: 184). Therefore, despite surviving the journey, Minosse remains completely detached from her own body and alienated from the community — she does not eat, does not sleep, nor does she talk to anyone. She spends her days staring at birds flying through the sky, remembering Sianga and daydreaming of all the things that Wusheni was unable to experience (1999: 207–11). Her total displacement in the new setting is reflected in this constant reminiscing movement that keeps her trapped in the past, which is the only reality she knows.

Just when she is sure of the insurmountable nature of this incompatibility, she comes across a little boy who has been ostracised by the entire community. Minosse understands that he is openly neglected because no one wants to be responsible for an extra mouth to feed in times of scarcity. Like a cycle that repeats itself endlessly, the population replicates the same violence which is performed against them (1999: 219–21). On recognising her mirrored image in this child, both as a woman and as an elder, she decides to subvert the cycle of violence by taking him into her care. This humanitarian gesture enables her to rebuild a sense of community in which she has an active voice: 'A velha não está disposta a perder a batalha. Esgota a língua, esgota as carícias que não são correspondidas' [The old woman is not willing to lose the battle. She uses up all her words, and all her tenderness, even though these gestures are not reciprocated] (1999: 221). This is a turning point in the evolution of this character, as she is able to step up and act in accordance with her own independent beliefs for the first time. The awareness of her exile as a woman enables her to engage in the reformulation of her identity by taking on the roles of mother and grandmother to children that are somehow exiled by the exile community itself — which is also the case of Sara and her brothers, who had been enslaved by a female villager (1999: 229–31). By doing this, Minosse is simultaneously proceeding to the reconstruction of the family concept, which is built upon solidarity, love and bonding between older and younger generations in the modern world:

> Nunca antes imaginara encontrar no desterro a família sepultada nas areias de Mananga. [...] Os meninos órfãos confiam nela. Vivem sob a sua protecção. Semeiam os campos orientados por ela. Ensina-lhes as manhas da terra, os segredos da semente, as voltas da água e os movimentos do vento. (1999: 231–32)

> [Never before had she imagined finding in exile the family that had been

> buried in the sands of Mananga. [...] The orphan children trust her. They live under her protection. They sow the fields under her guidance. She teaches them the tricks for cultivating the land and passes on her knowledge of the secrets of the seed, and the movement of water and wind.]

Notwithstanding the fact that her agency builds an alternative sense of community within her new family, Minosse is quite aware of the fact that hers is no more than an isolated act — like Wusheni's and Mara's. In itself, that act will not affect the conceptualisation of the extended community, as long as it refuses to debate gender difference and continues to allow bridging between past and present so as to provide itself with a sense of continuity — as can be observed later on. As she reflects on life as she knows it, she fears for her children's faith — Sara's in particular — because she realises that the one thing that remains immutable, regardless of all the other contextual changes that occur, is the fixed roles assigned to Mozambican men and women within society.

While looking back on her own life, she is now able to understand that men always emerge as active, the ones who lead, decide and experience pleasure, whereas women are never allowed to intervene beyond passively observing those same decisions and pleasures, constantly being alienated from their bodies and themselves. Hence, women's continuous gender exile within the exiled community itself will inevitably keep them in positions of vulnerability and dependency, in a repetitive chain that appears to be unbreakable, in Minosse's point of view. It is worth mentioning at this point that this idea of repetitiveness is reinforced by the description of the harvest season at the Aldeia. When it starts, women are called upon to cook for and serve men, who are sitting under a tree, chatting: 'Todas as mulheres casadas vão em procissão e levam comida e mais comida para os seus senhores e estes não cabem em si de contentamento porque as suas esposas são as melhores cozinheiras do mundo' [All of the married women move in procession and bring more and more food to their masters. And they couldn't be happier, because their wives are the best cooks in the world] (1999: 263). The use of the expression 'os seus senhores' [their masters] is also quite revealing, as it creates an immediate association between men and colonisers — in this case, men are depicted as colonisers of women's bodies. This image also evokes the ceremony of Mbelele that took place at Mananga, because while the selected women were performing the ritual, those remaining were serving men, who, for their part, were playing 'ntchuva', while eating and drinking under the trees (1999: 100–01). So, in both situations, each of them evocative of a modern and traditional scenario respectively, the elements that refer to the definition of gender roles remain invariable — men are associated with the public, progressive and active space, whereas women emerge related to the private, stagnant and somewhat retrograde sphere.

In her reading of Stuart Hall's definition of cultural identity, Herrera (2001: xxvi–xxviii) underlines the need to articulate both the collective cultural identity and the various identities that emerge within it according to gender, class, sex and age factors in order to truly account for the multiple experiences of exile. Despite agreeing with Hall that cultural identity is influenced by history, culture and power, and acknowledging its fluidity and dynamism throughout history, Herrera makes a very interesting point in adding that 'one cannot ignore the role that desire plays in the conscious construction or acquisition of cultural identity' (2001: xxvii). In other words, Herrera is hereby emphasising the active role of individuals, who are not passive in the entire process, and also their responsibility. Following this line of thought, it is possible to argue that in the text the community *chooses* not to renegotiate gender roles in the Aldeia, because the reproduction of their past existence gives them the illusion of a safe continuity. Furthermore, the maintenance of a patriarchal society would be much more convenient for a male-dominated community such as the one in question here. According to Casimiro (2005), despite the emphasis put on women's emancipation and gender equality, theorisation of this subject was non-existent within the modern conceptualisation of the nation, which led to the re-enactment of old stereotypes. In addition, by immediately reading the private sphere as retrograde, marginalising it, and focusing solely on the male-dominated public one, the modern conceptualisation of the nation neglected to debate the sexual division of labour within the household, and at the same time forced women to accumulate contradictory roles. They were to be actively engaged in the public sphere like their male peers, but should simultaneously be silent and obedient housewives, mothers and wives within the private sphere (2005: 67–68). Hence, these women were never really given the opportunity to decide on their destinies. As Casimiro (2005: 69–70) reminds us, women's citizenship was still designed as a constrained one within the 1975 Constitution, which leads the scholar to affirm that theirs was a 'cidadania restrita, como se elas continuassem seres inferiores e incapazes de decidir sobre as suas vidas' [restricted citizenship, as if they were still inferior and incapable of making decisions about their own lives]. On the one hand, the Constitution gave women the right to vote, the right to two months of maternity leave, and equality with men in terms of employment, salary, education and justice. Yet, on the other hand, it forced women to relinquish their Mozambican citizenship if they married a foreign citizen — a measure that only applied to women (2005: 69–70).

Nevertheless, Emelina's agency brings this structure into the open, exposing it as one which will ultimately provoke the annihilation of the Aldeia community. Taking into consideration the trajectory of all the characters in *Ventos*, it is possible to say that Emelina is the most exiled character, as she embodies the three types of exile that we have explored so far: she is exiled for her gender, for being a refugee, and for being rejected within the Aldeia's community. Emelina lives on the margins of the community with her baby girl, from whom she is never parted. Due to her silence, isolation and detachment from inclusive social habits (such as bathing, for example), she is regarded as crazy and is completely ostracised by the community (Chiziane 1999: 228; 244). Yet, when the nurse Danila comes to the village and invites her into a conversation, Emelina immediately accepts and is eager to tell all of her story, demonstrating that the only reason that she does not talk is because no one is interested in listening to her, nor are they willing to comfort her (1999: 246–47). We learn that in the past, Emelina killed her three children in order to make herself available to the powerful man she was in love with. However, when she asked him to return this demonstration of love by killing his other two wives, he abandoned her while pregnant. After that, she was captured by the RENAMO enemies and lived with them for over a year, subsequently returning to the community which did not forgive her for what she had done in the past. Clearly, Emelina is far from fitting the traditional female profile that was expected of her, which prompts the whole community — other women in particular — to marginalise her. Nevertheless, the community ends up acting in a contradictory way towards her. Despite recognising that she symbolises a disruption in the traditional construction of women, they are unable to imagine her outside that frame, i.e. they cannot see her as active and even able to reproduce violence, because she is a woman. Hence, the fact that her open bitterness towards those who refuse to forgive her and reintegrate her into society is never regarded as threatening, becomes an advantage for Emelina in her pursuit of revenge:

> Os poetas cantam a mulher como símbolo de paz e pureza. Os povos veneram a mulher como símbolo do amor universal. Porque ela é uma flor que dá prazer e dá calor. [...] O que os poetas esqueceram é que, para além do símbolo do amor, a mulher é também parceira da serpente. (1999: 249)
>
> [Poets sing about the woman as a symbol of peace and purity. People regard the woman as a symbol of universal love. Because she is a flower that emanates pleasure and warmth. [...] What the poets have forgotten is that, in addition to being the symbol of love, the woman is also the serpent's partner.]

Refusing to remain trapped in an outmoded passive identity, Emelina shows the villagers that as a woman she is able to *give* and also to *take*, i.e. to be both passive and active. We observe, in addition, that her need to reproduce violence is a direct consequence of the community's marginalisation of people who had been kept under the enemy's influence for long periods of time. According to Nordstrom (1997: 51), this was a strategy very frequently used by RENAMO: sending women and even children to villages in order to get information for later attacks, which brings us back to the researcher's claim that 'if they [Mozambicans] refashion their lives as they knew them, they create conditions as vulnerable to attack as existed previously' (1997: 190). RENAMO's knowledge of the stagnant conceptualisation of women within Mozambican national discourse allowed them to use it against Mozambicans themselves. This does not mean that RENAMO itself viewed women in a different way, as we are aware that not only was the group's view of women highly traditionalist, but also that RENAMO did not have an alternative sociocultural programme. RENAMO was, however, able to understand that Mozambican society's patriarchal nature could be a weak spot to be used in the group's favour. In addition to this, the community's inability to deal with the violence that surrounds Emelina dehumanises her. Throughout her analysis of the creative worldbuilding techniques applied by Mozambicans to build cultures of resistance, Nordstrom (1997: 209–11) points out, precisely, that the processes of unmaking violence were one of its main underpinnings. Given that Mozambicans were aware that violence can only generate violence, they paid particular attention to the healing of all victims of violence, as a community effort, especially those who had been kidnapped by RENAMO. In the end, it is paradoxically Emelina, in a gesture of profound individuality and deeply internalised violence, who forces the community to face its own flaws, bringing about its destruction. These flaws are, of course, connected with the ideal of community identity that emerges in the Aldeia in this context of war. As already mentioned, the population were trapped between two opposing discourses that prevented them from attaining a stable identity. Yet, through its efforts to imagine itself as a restored community, it did come to understand the need to rethink itself and look for a balance between tradition and modernity — to bridge past and present in order to build the future — because acting otherwise would deprive it of a sense of continuity and make it vulnerable to manipulation, by both internal and external forces.

Focusing primarily on the external forces, these emerge in the aftermath of the heavy rain and floods that devastate the Aldeia. Due to the government's inability to respond to the desperate situation that several areas of the country are going through, international help is called upon. Despite the youngsters' enthusiasm towards this 'mão desinteressada' [unselfish hand] (Chiziane 1999: 238), the elders regard it as suspicious and similar to a colonial gesture, since they understand that this act inevitably places them once again in a position of dependency towards other nations. International help comes from all over the world in the shape of all sorts of items, but it ends up by othering the population and providing conditions for the rise of structures that profited from the war. With reference to these structures, Nordstrom (1997: 5) points out that

> Everything from development dollars to human rights organizations, from covert operations specialists to illegal industries that gain from conflict, builds on the linkages of these networks that shape war and peace as we know it today. And in all this a powerful set of cultural prescriptions develops around the concept and conduct of war. It is at once international and localized [...] This global flux of information, tactics, weapons, money, and personnel brokers tremendous power throughout the warzones of the world.

The underlying criticism at this point of the text seems to suggest that the over-reliance on these structures places the country in a vulnerable position within the networks of power that operate on a worldwide scale. At the same time, the instability of the community's identity is exposed when the population recognise themselves in this othering gaze that is launched upon them. The villagers dismiss their traditional behavioural habits and also their history of colonisation from their minds, as if they did not have a past:

> Todos comem até saciar e esquecem o trabalho da machamba, para quê trabalhar se os homens bons nos dão tudo? [...] O povo não exerce os seus deveres, as suas tradições, e espera pela esmola, nova forma de colonização mental. [...] Alguns indivíduos neste grupo de boa gente com o pretexto de ajudar, ajudam-se. [...] Os desonestos enriquecem. Os pobres depauperam. (Chiziane 1999: 238)

> [They all eat until they are full and forget about working the land. Why work if the good men give us everything? [...] The people do not perform their

> duties, their traditions, and they wait for a hand-out, a new form of mental colonisation. [...] Some individuals in this group of good people help themselves under the pretext of helping others. [...] The corrupt ones get richer. The poor ones get poorer.]

Hence, following these events, the population is once again led to reflect upon its own group identity as a way to guarantee its survival.

It is important to highlight the fact that this debate is proposed primarily by Minosse and Mungoni. These two characters are present in the three distinct sections of the narrative, so they accompany the evolution of the community in its various stages. Both of these elder characters who are somewhat connected to a traditional conception of the community (Minosse as the *régulo*'s last wife and Mungoni as soothsayer who predicts Mananga's destruction) are transposed into a modern context, having survived all the challenges that the population is continuously confronted with. For this reason, they represent not only the impossibility of erasing the past, but also the need to respect and integrate it into the reconceptualisation of identity that occurs in the present, so as to open the possibilities for its stabilisation in the future. They are, for that reason, cultural mediators in the renegotiation of the community's identity. As mentioned above, Minosse is one of the characters who acknowledges the need to renegotiate the community's identity in a much more active and independent way. While pondering her children's future, she realises that the population's general passivity regarding its own conception as a community will generate a much more disturbing exile for the generations to come. This is due to the fact that the rupture between past and present will imprison them in an identity limbo that deprives them of a sense of continuity and belonging, subsequently making them socioculturally vulnerable (1999: 258–59). Notwithstanding her hope for a more dynamic governmental agency towards youngsters, she envisages her own children as part of a 'lost generation' (Nordstrom 1997: 40) who will inevitably remain prisoners of this vicious circle.[9]

Following the same line of thought, Mungoni defends the view that the only way to offer resistance is for the population to take their identity renegotiation into their own hands and to attempt to find a balance between past and present — traditional and modern — in order to make possible their projection into the future: 'Deve-se procurar melhorar a vida tendo como base o que há de bom na nossa cultura. A mudança rápida de hábitos provoca decadência e a instabilidade será o preço. [...] Que saibam harmonizar o velho e o novo' [We must look for a better life based on the good aspects of our culture. Suddenly changing our habits causes decline and instability will be the price to pay. [...] May they know how to balance the old and the new] (Chiziane 1999: 265–68). By challenging the community to develop its own strategies of cultural survival, Mungoni seeks to detach it from any constitutive political discourses and, thus, stop the dehumanising violence that exiles it and prevents it from expressing its own will. According to Nordstrom (1997: 143), it was this same creativity that ultimately enabled Mozambicans to deconstruct the signifying systems that instituted violence as a 'fixed entity'. Their redefinition of violence is representative of their own future political will. In the researcher's words, 'in de-legitimizing violence, people reconstruct a new political culture, one that delegitimizes the politics of force. Such political reconstructions are a serious threat, for they simultaneously delegitimize the political systems that rely on force to maintain power' (1997: 143–44).

Despite their efforts to imagine themselves as a restored community, the population fail to redefine themselves culturally outside the socio-political positions that ultimately reduce this war to a struggle for power. In the final episode, a priest goes to the Aldeia to celebrate mass and the population are attacked during the ceremony. Inevitably, we are led to draw a parallel between this mass and the Mbelele ceremony, which was performed at Mananga and ultimately brought about the destruction of the village. Again, the community is shown to be trapped between two discourses. If in Mananga the ceremony was sponsored by the enemy forces so as to discredit the government, in the Aldeia the mass was supported by the government so as to reaffirm its ideal of the nation and its dominance over the rural areas. In both situations, the community was incapable of rethinking itself outside the constraints of the prevailing discourses, which not only reaffirms its exile, but also its incapacity to turn this exile into a privileged place of worldbuilding. The community's identity emerges irremediably fragmented. A clear reflection of this fragmentation and discontinuity can be found in the peculiar structure of the literary work. Firstly, with regard to the narrative's formal structure, it is important to highlight the presence of elements that refer to the oral tradition. As a result, the novel form is destabilised, as the self-legitimation of the oral element undermines, disrupts and inevitably enhances the novel's closed format from the Western literary tradition's point of view. Sílvio Renato Jorge (2008: 177–86; p. 182) describes this movement as follows: 'somos convocados a vislumbrar traços de formas tradicionais do narrar que se inserem na matéria romanesca para desestabilizar as condições de isolamento próprias da produção textual como a compreendemos hoje, reagenciando sentidos e perspectivas' [we are invited to glimpse into traces of the traditional narrative forms embedded in romanesque texts, to destabilise the isolation which is characteristic of textual production as we understand it today, renegotiating meanings and perspectives]. In addition, orality, as an element which emerges immediately related to tradition, disturbs, intersects and ultimately fuses with writing, an element which is immediately related to modernity. In this sense, we can read this interaction as a confirmation not only of the impossibility of deleting history, but also, as Jorge (2008: 177) states, of humankind's need to recognise history in order to evolve as human beings. It is therefore possible to affirm that in its structure, on the one hand, the narrative advances the proposal of a balanced articulation of both elements, which are imbued with cultural connotations. In other words, the narrative suggests that cultural *métissage* should be the basis of *Moçambicanidade*. On the other hand, if we take into account the fact that Owen (2008a: 164) reads Chiziane's appropriation of oral and traditional forms to voice women's experience as a gesture that 'contranarra o exotismo antropológico' [counter-narrates anthropological exoticism], we could interpret the narrative's structure as a call to dismantle women's representation in both the traditional and modern discourses — and the binary itself. We can also read it as suggestive of the urge to legitimise a new representation for women, one that emerges from the intersection in which gender roles are articulated and equality rewritten.

Ventos do Apocalipse: Conclusion

Hence, a new format is presented to reflect the Mozambican identity experience in a much wider sense. In this sense, the disruptions in the narrative's structure can be understood as part of a meditation on the discontinuities of *Moçambicanidade*, its renegotiations, and its changing nature. *Ventos*'s three-part configuration suggests that each section of the book refers to the community's renegotiation of a discontinuous identity in specific moments in time, i.e. past, present and future. Section one of the prologue immediately conveys an introduction to the story, but it simultaneously focuses on a state that historically precedes the developments which will follow. In other words, by invoking a particular *habitus* that refers to the Mozambican identity and to the community that materialises it, Chiziane emphasises the need to focus on what precedes Frelimo's imposition of an ideal of modernisation — hence the reference made to storytelling around the fire and intergenerational knowledge transference. History and the stories which make it up emerge as the main cultural components of a community. They are the unifying elements within a community because they provide it with a sense of continuity. That continuity is reinforced by intergenerational sharing. Section two, however, reveals a rupture with the preceding section, thus suggesting the present's alienation from the past. The repetition of the stories of self-destruction, which were previously presented, puts forward the population's general detachment from a historical past. Furthermore, the community is shown to be trapped between the two discourses which are imposed on it. This identity exile reveals the population's incapacity to build a stable and continuous identity in their present setting. Finally, section three explores the community's attempt to attain balance between past and present in order to build the future in a scenario of physical and identity survival. In their attempt to recapture a sense of continuity to ensure the survival of the community's identity, the population are tested several times with regard to their beliefs and their ability to adjust to a new context. They are also confronted with the need to be more active in the recreation of their identity. Eventually, they succeed in maintaining a sense of community, and they do so by attempting to rebuild a world which is similar to the one they had before. Yet, this is a world which is lost forever and the attempt to recapture it in its essence leads the population to relapse into the same mistakes that contributed to their collapse in the past. By failing to recognise the relevance of the struggle for gender equality, the community brings about its own destruction.

Hence, the repetition of the stories portrayed in section one, in both segments that follow it, discloses that forgetting one's historical past leads to the repetition of this same history, which becomes particularly dangerous when this history is abundant in stories of exile. The fact that all three stories are about women (each of them referring to a specific role traditionally performed by women, as wives, mothers and lovers) uncovers the uninterrupted exile that they have lived in throughout history. Gender exile exists in the past, in the present and, consequently, in the future. Therefore, it transverses and conditions all other exiles, and in the text, it ultimately proves its insurmountable influence by exposing the fact that a patriarchal community is a fragile one as well. Indeed, in *Ventos*, Chiziane accentuates the importance of renegotiating gender exile. The reading of the novel through the lens of Said's reflections on exile allows for the exposure of Said's omission of gender as an element that not only refutes the homogeneity of the experience of exile, but also unfolds into myriad exiles when analysed alongside other factors, such as race and class.

Introduction to *Niketche: Uma História de Poligamia*

Following on from the premise that women do not experience gender exile equally, in her novel *Niketche* Chiziane proceeds to the deconstruction of gender exiles in their specificity, especially regarding ethnicity, race and colour. In other words, the author explores the extent to which these categories influence and condition the experiences of womanhood, simultaneously examining how they interact in a problematic coexistence that produces various forms of exile. The emphasis is placed, therefore, as much on women's exile within a patriarchal framework as on women's exile by other women within a female power structure which, in itself, is informed by social constructions such as race, colour, class and ethnicity. The story, which is set in the post-independence and post-internal conflict democratic era, introduces us to Rami, a woman who at the end of twenty years of marriage finds out that her husband Tony has got four other unofficial families. From this point, the character engages in a journey of self-discovery and exposition of the four wives' marginality that reveals the politics of gender differentiation at work in the national discourse, simultaneously discussing gender's different cultural conceptions within the nation state and proposing new identities for both women and men in the intersection of tradition and modernity.

At this point it is important to refer back to the work by Owen (2007b) on the debate over gender difference which is put forward throughout *Niketche*. Focusing on the role played by gender in the management of regional and ethnic differences within the official unity discourse of the Mozambican nation, Owen demonstrates that the process of 'southernisation' and subsequent masculinisation of Mozambique was achieved through the female body (2007b: 186–99). On reading Chiziane's depiction and subversion of Frelimo's discourse of national unity, Owen highlights a characteristic of this discourse which will be very relevant for the present analysis: its reproduction of the Lusotropical ideology of harmonious racial *mestiçagem* and cultural reciprocity among the different black ethnic groups of wives in *Niketche*. Following on from the premise that '*Niketche* reveals how a Lusotropical legacy of sexualized racial fusion lived on in Frelimo's attempts to unify a state of many "nations" from the Rovuma to the Maputo' (2007b: 187), Owen dismantles the disempowered role of women in this process of unification and, simultaneously, the active strategies advanced by Chiziane so as to propose a 'third space' (2007b: 194) where women's empowerment enables them to recreate cultural and ethnic exchange as a space of difference. Considering Owen's discussion of ethnicity in terms of a very specific gender exile, the present study will focus on race as a social construct that also represents a particular type of gender exile. Hence, this analysis will attempt to prove that, in *Niketche*, Chiziane initiates a debate on the specific intersectionality between race and gender — given that in the novel the main emphasis is placed on the dynamics between ethnicity and gender — which will be further analysed in *Alegre Canto*. Through the analysis of the female characters and their relationships with the polygamous husband that bonds them, the study intends to provide a multidimensional perspective in which race emerges at the core of the intersection of social categories such as class, ethnicity and colour, that co-exist within gender exile.

Race, Racial Representations and 'Situated Feminism' in Mozambique

According to the Mozambican sociologist Carlos Serra (1997: 110–11), the modern conception of race has less to do with the individual's particular biological characteristics than with her/his social status and the nature of her/his social relationships. As such, race emerges inextricably linked to power and elitist social relations, meaning that in a competitive environment, racial connotations will differ according to the level of access to resources. Serra states that 'a raça torna-se fenómeno sociológico quando, em situações de confrontação e de tensão social e de luta por recursos, componentes fenotípicas são rapidamente, "instintivamente" e estrategicamente invocados, manipulados e sujeitos a um tratamento estigmatório' [race becomes a sociological phenomenon when, in situations of confrontation, social tension and struggle for resources, phenotypic components are rapidly, 'instinctively' and strategically invoked, manipulated, and subjected to stigmatisation] (1997: 111). Therefore, as Michel Wieviorka (2000) reminds us, racial constructions are dangerously disruptive in the sense that they imply social practices of inclusion towards those who fit the profile of acceptance and also of exclusion towards those whose inadequacy might be interpreted as threatening.

As a young nation state with a solid pre-colonial tradition, a long colonial past and a post-independence socialist history, Mozambique's society is highly complex in many respects, particularly as concerns racial matters. According to Anna Maria Gentili (1999: 285–93), the consolidation of the colonial state (which only occurred at the end of the first quarter of the twentieth century) was achieved through reshaping political and social structures so as to centralise power, keeping it in the hands of Portugal and its internal and external allies. In this context of domination, this centralising move obviously implied that power was a privilege for a minority, who maintained its power and differentiation through the creation of racist ideologies and practices, and a strict legislation that supported them. Nevertheless, this colonial discourse suffered many adjustments throughout history due to different contextual circumstances, as Cláudia Castelo (1999) points out. In her study, Castelo provides an excellent analysis of the political stances and imperial discourses created and adopted by Portugal — the Lusotropical in particular — so as to justify its maintenance of the African colonies both internally and externally, especially in the second half of the twentieth century, when the majority of African countries were already engaged in decolonisation processes. Salazar's rise to power from 1926 onwards and the subsequent creation of the *Estado Novo* in 1933 through the approval of the new Constitution was, indeed, a very significant turning point in terms of colonial policy. Castelo moves on to identify three specific historical moments in the evolution of this colonial policy, which emerge related to distinct social practices (1998: 45–67). During the 'anos da *mística imperial*' [years of imperial mystique], the Portuguese colonial administration was highly centralising, unitarian and imperial. The Colonial Act, a political project that reaffirmed Portugal's vocation for colonisation, was implemented in 1930 to concentrate all the Portuguese domains under the aegis of the *Império Colonial Português* [Portuguese Colonial Empire] and to assert the general belief in the inferiority of the indigenous populations, according to Darwinist social theories. Although they were considered to be Portuguese subjects, they were not part of the nation. In his work entitled *The Struggle for Mozambique*, the father of the Mozambican revolution, Eduardo Mondlane (1983: 40–41), explains that from 1930 onwards, the colonial state instituted the *regime do indigenato* [indigenate regime], which basically divided the population into two distinct groups: the *indígenas* [natives], Africans who had no citizenship, for whom it was mandatory to carry an identity card (*caderneta do indígena*) at all times, and who were subject to very strict labour obligations and social rules; and the *não-indígenas* [non-natives], who had full Portuguese citizenship and were entitled to all the privileges attached to it.

However, by the end of World War II the experience of German Nazism and the Holocaust had changed world politics, and the creation of the UN reflected that in practical terms (Castelo 1998: 48). Due to the application of measures that reinstated the right to autonomy to everyone in the world, a very strong anti-colonialist movement emerged and all colonial powers were compelled to engage in the processes of recognising the colonies' autonomy. Faced with the prospect of losing its colonies, the Portuguese government initiated the second historical moment in the evolution of its colonial policy by effectively carrying out a revision of the Colonial Act in 1951. This revision proposed the replacement of imperial terminology and the implementation of assimilationist practices so as to generate an image of 'unity' that would satisfy international opinion. In addition, the colonial regime mounted a very efficient campaign which argued that there was a unique relationship between Portugal and the African territories attached to it, through the 'adaptation' of the Brazilian sociologist Gilberto Freyre's Lusotropical theory (1998: 48–61). As mentioned in the previous chapter, Freyre (1986; 1961) argues for the specificity of the Portuguese social relations with the peoples that they have encountered in the tropics, which ultimately led to the emergence of a Lusotropical civilisation. This civilisation is characterised by the harmonious symbioses of cultures, ethnicities and races in a perfect *mestiça* unity. So, the *mestiço* emerges as the symbol of perfection (Castelo 1998: 35–43). For obvious reasons, this theory was highly attractive and useful for Portugal in terms of its foreign policy — at least the part of it that did not jeopardise the sovereignty of the Portuguese nation (Klobucka 2011). Hence, in order to reinforce this assimilationist tendency and demonstrate the non-racist nature of the Portuguese people, the *Estatuto do Indigenato* was abolished in 1961. In legislative terms, this measure was the most important one taken in the third moment of the colonial policy's evolution, as identified by Castelo, and it coincided with the period of decolonisation and independence for the majority of British, French and Belgian former colonies. It meant that the individuals who had the conditions to do so could stop being *indígenas*, acquire Portuguese citizenship, and assimilate to Portuguese culture. According to Castelo (1998: 60), the conditions to become an *assimilado(a)* [assimilated person] were the following:

> [...] ter mais de 18 anos; falar correctamente a língua portuguesa, exercer profissão, arte ou ofício de que aufira rendimento necessário para o sustento próprio e das pessoas de família a seu cargo, ou possuir bens suficientes para o mesmo fim; ter bom comportamento e ter adquirido a ilustração e os hábitos pressupostos para a integral aplicação do direito público e privado dos cidadãos portugueses; não ter sido notado como refractário ao serviço militar nem dado como desertor.
>
> [to be over 18 years old; to speak the Portuguese language correctly; to have a job, trade or profession which provides the necessary income to sustain herself/himself and any dependants, or possess sufficient assets for the same purpose; to behave well and to have acquired the education and the customs expected for the full application of the public and private rights of Portuguese citizens; to not have evaded conscription or been considered a deserter.]

As Gentili (1999: 275) points out, these privileges were aimed at a bourgeoisie minority from the colonies who would ensure Portugal's maintenance of power. Nevertheless, the application of these laws based on Lusotropicalism, which was intended to attenuate racial tensions, actually worked in the opposite way, as it revalidated the immediate association between access to power and colour of skin. In other words, these were official juridical mechanisms that transformed the category of race into class. Based on official data from the *Junta de Investigação do Ultramar* [Overseas Research Board] published in 1964, Mondlane (1983: 38–39) shows that the composition of Mozambican society had three layers. The highest layer was occupied by a minority which represented approximately 2.5% of the total population and was composed of 'European whites, Asians, Mulattos and a few Africans concentrated in the urban areas and in the agricultural and mineral developments' (1983: 38). This was a Westernised and urbanised elite connected to the society's modern sector. The second social layer comprised a numerical minority of approximately 3.5% of the total population and it was 'composed of elements of various races but above all of Africans' (1983: 38). According to Mondlane, they represented the proletariat, given that they had rural origins, they were concentrated in the peripheral areas of the most expanded population agglomerates and they generally turned into wage labourers. Finally, the last and widest social layer, representing about 94% of the total population, was composed of what Mondlane calls Africans and we assume this to be black Africans, the majority of them peasants and/or migrant workers living 'under a regimen of subsistence economy' in tribal areas (1983: 38–39). Although it is important to bear in mind that ultimately Mondlane's analysis is more concerned with the category of class and with economics than with race and colour related-issues (which is visible through his lack of precision in the definition of the various racial groups involved in the social hierarchisation), this data enables us to view the new legislation as a simple means of camouflaging the real discriminatory nature of the social dynamics in these African territories.

Mondlane moves on to analyse how this discrimination is visible in economic terms, i.e. how the socioeconomic scenario is prepared with a view to ensuring the crystallisation of social positions and circumstances. Indeed, the unassimilated African is highly regulated so as to be unable to escape her/his economic inferiority, so that she/he reproduces the social stratification. According to Mondlane (1983: 43), not only are commercial activities barred to them, but they are also unable to have a profession due to their limited or non-existent education. Furthermore, the author presents data which shows that wages were paid according to a racial spectrum, so that the white population earned the best wages and the African population the worst; this reinforces the idea that race goes hand in hand with access to resources — simultaneously exposing the mythical and utopian nature of Lusotropicalism.[10] Taking into consideration the fact that Mondlane's analysis places an emphasis on social occurrences in the public sphere, it is important to point out that the absence of the gender and sex categories in his data examination suggests the crystallisation of the place of women within the private sphere. This reading is reinforced by the fact that Mondlane only seems to acknowledge the central role of women as regards miscegenation.

Indeed, Mondlane's demystification of Lusotropicalism is also achieved through his problematisation of social phenomena such as assimilation and miscegenation in the particular context of Mozambique. Regarding assimilation, he emphasises the fact that an *assimilado(a)* is completely stripped of her/his previous African identity in order to embrace Portuguese citizenship: 'according to the law, he must live in an entirely European style; he must never use his own language, and he must not visit unassimilated relatives in their own homes' (1983: 50). However, this citizenship was a limited one, as the *assimilado(a)* was meant to identify with the white Portuguese, but was never treated as one. With respect to miscegenation, Mondlane highlights the colonial discourse's exaggerated depiction of it as representative of Freyre's Lusotropical community, given that this mulatto minority, which was much more representative in qualitative terms, rather than in quantitative terms, represented only 0.5% of the Mozambican population.[11] He adds that notwithstanding the fact that miscegenation was a constant practice since the first contact between the Portuguese and Mozambicans, the mulatto community and the white community were not considered to be equals (1983: 50–54). A few mulattos did possess Portuguese citizenship, access Portuguese education, and achieve better work positions than the *assimilados*, but they were kept under close surveillance by colonial social mechanisms and by the colonial community itself — being protective of its own power — to make sure that they did not achieve what was meant for the white Portuguese only.[12] Furthermore, Mondlane (1983: 51) continues, they were still representative of a transgression, given that 'it is miscegenation not intermarriage which is accepted'. Considering also that relationships between Portuguese women and African men were unacceptable — which underlines the patriarchal nature of the colonial policy — this highly celebrated miscegenation was achieved through the unofficial possession of the African women's bodies. Although she was central to the process, she was confined to a marginal role — always a mistress and/or a servant — as the opposite would represent a subversion of the established social structure. In addition, the fact that the African mother was associated with an inferior class meant that she was forbidden from having access to her mulatto child. The mulatto was therefore trapped in an identity gap, given that she/he was never fully accepted by either the white or the black African communities (1983: 52).

In 1974, after a liberation struggle that would last for a decade, Portugal finally recognised Mozambique's sovereignty and independence through the signing of the Lusaka Agreement, which established the beginning of the transfer of power that culminated in the country's independence on the 25 June 1975. The Frelimo government was finally able to implement its programme in the new nation state, using strategies and structures which had already been put in motion in liberated zones during the armed conflict. This new political programme set out to achieve a radical break with the colonial machine at all levels, but that proved to be more difficult to achieve than Frelimo had expected, as the new government inherited an extremely complex structure to manage. As Gentili (1999: 314) points out, not only did they inherit a centralised, hierarchical and selective political structure, but they also acquired all the regional, territorial and racial asymmetries of colonialism. Most importantly, they inherited the colonial conceptualisation of political management and the social representations that ensured the maintenance of the colonial power structures. Finally, as mentioned before, its official adherence to socialism and centralism led the independent state to deny all forms of intracultural differences — based on racial, ethnical, sexual and class differences — in favour of a national stance of unity. This policy *dehistoricised* the society, thus in this sense reproducing the same ideology that had characterised the colonial stance throughout history. At this point, it is worth mentioning Boaventura de Sousa Santos and Teresa Cruz e Silva's view on the matter (2004). In their reading of the Mozambican state, they qualify it as a heterogeneous state at many levels. Referring specifically to the political and juridical culture, they state that:

> A cultura político-jurídica colonial, apesar de rejeitada da maneira mais incondicional — como demonstram paradigmaticamente as ideias do 'escangalhamento do Estado' durante o período revolucionário — acabou por prevalecer até hoje, não só sob as formas mais óbvias da legislação colonial que continuou em vigor, ou da organização administrativa, mas sobretudo em hábitos e mentalidades, estilos de actuação, representações do outro, etc. (2004: 34)

> [Although the colonial political-juridical culture was rejected wholeheartedly — as paradigmatically demonstrated by the ideas of 'breaking up of the colonial state' during the revolutionary period — it has ended up prevailing up to now, not only in the most obvious forms of colonial legislation (still in force), or administrative organisation, but above all in habits and mentalities, ways of acting, representations of the other, etc.]

In other words, the independent state builds its new representations largely upon the colonial state's representations. As such, some of these representations, which survive through culture, will also outlive both the colonial state and the socialist period, making their way through to contemporary society.

Hence, considering the above-mentioned historic framework, it is important to analyse how racial representations are conceptualised within the Mozambican setting in the democratic era. In 2000, a team of social researchers led by the Mozambican sociologist Carlos Serra published the results of a study made in five Mozambican cities in order to analyse the people's perceptions of racism and ethnicity, and to verify tendencies in opinions and behaviours towards these two phenomena in urban settings. This was the first ever study of this subject to be carried out in Mozambique. According to Serra (2000: 20–21), it is the combination of three specific phenomena — social interaction, dispute for power resources and education — that produces racism and ethnicism. It is at that intersection that people make sense of social elements, thus creating their social references, structuring their social categorisation and naturalising what, in reality, is socially constructed. Both racism and ethnicism advocate the belief in the natural superiority of given groups whose characteristics make them the most eligible to access specific power resources or tools. Hence, in Serra's words,

> É racista quem defende a superioridade genética de um grupo; é étnico quem defende a superioridade da sua comunidade imaginada de origem. Em ambos os casos se monopoliza os recursos de poder em função de marcadores, pigmentação num caso, comunidade imaginada de origem no outro. Racismo e etnicidade são exercícios sociais de inclusão/exclusão sociais que, interiorizados e assumidos, funcionam como os semáforos (o verde para os *nossos*, o vermelho para os *outros*). (2000: 21–22)

> [Racists are those who defend the genetic superiority of a group. Ethnicists are those who uphold the superiority of their imagined community of origin. In both cases the power resources are monopolised according to markers — pigmentation in one case, imagined community of origin in the other. Racism and ethnicity are social exercises of inclusion/exclusion that, once internalised and assumed, function like traffic lights (green for *ours*, red for *others*).]

Because the distribution of power is asymmetrical, processes of *othering* take place and stereotypes are created to support them. In this sense, the relationship between those who maintain power — the *estabelecidos* [established ones], to use Serra's denomination — and those who are peripheral to it — the *intrusos* [intruders] — is always very tense (2000: 23–24). The former will always struggle to preserve their positions and, consequently, envision the latter as threatening, whereas the latter will regard the former resentfully and will always attempt to question their status.

It is, therefore, possible to affirm that both phenomena are strategically constructed in relation to access to power (2000: 26).

Considering the main hypothesis that Serra's social study puts forward, Serra and the other researchers give it the following three-level structure:

> 1. Racismo e etnicidade são duas variações identitárias (com o seu corpo de reacções de inclusão e de exclusão) de um mesmo fenómeno: desigual distribuição de recursos de poder;
> 2. Os seus potenciais estão em relação directa com o apego à tradição;
> 3. Percepções sobre racismo são urbanas, percepções sobre etnicidade são rurais. (2000: 27)
>
> [1. Racism and ethnicity are two identitarian variants (with their reactive framework of inclusion and exclusion) of the same phenomenon: the unequal distribution of power resources;
> 2. Their potential is directly related to their attachment to tradition;
> 3. Feelings of racism are urban, whereas feelings of ethnicity are rural.]

The study was conducted across the whole country, in Lichinga (north), Beira (centre), Tete (centre), Inhambane (south) and Maputo (south), and the methodologies applied were direct observation, questionnaires and archive research. The analysis of this study's results led the researchers to believe that, in general terms, there is a debate amongst Mozambicans over the distribution of and access to power, in which perceptions of racism and perceptions of that distribution emerge as interconnected (2000: 79–83). In other words, for the majority of those who participated in the study, the question of racism is defined much less by colour than it is by education, social class and wealth. As for the specific levels defined within the main hypothesis previously advanced, only the first level was proven by the results. In the end, regardless of the study's limitations (for example, the chosen methods for data collection or the fact that the study only refers to five Mozambican cities), it successfully showed the '"pensamento médio" das cidades moçambicanas' ['average thinking' in Mozambican cities] regarding racism and ethnicism (2000: 100).

It is, therefore, very important to rely on this study as our main reference point as it reflects the specific, situated reality of the Mozambican experience. At the same time, reading this information through the lens of gender, which is largely absent from Serra's view, will allow us to access another very particular set of social relations that unfolds into a variety of gendered experiences of the nation that change according to variants, such as race, class and ethnicity (I. M. Casimiro and X. Andrade 2005; Owen 2007b: 169–213). Hence, through the analysis of Said's (2001a: 177) theorisation of exile as a 'discontinuous state of being', as well as the theorist's failure to focus on gender, the present study aims to articulate both Said's considerations on exile and Serra's perspective on racism and ethnicism — which also lacks a view on gender. The aim of this is to reveal how in both *Niketche* and *Alegre Canto*, the confluence of the above-mentioned variants — gender, class, colour, race, ethnicity — which inevitably influence and change each other, permits the emergence of the various forms of what I will call gender exile, that are represented by the different female characters. In these literary works, all the female characters share a similar place of exile in relation to the patriarchal institution represented by the male characters. Nevertheless, this unique place unfolds into a variety of experiences when, for example, the race, colour, class or ethnic grouping of the different women is taken into consideration. Acknowledging this permits the exposure of the internal forms of exile that might arise from the friction between these distinct situational contexts. In other words, because women do not experience gender exile uniformly, they might be led to exile other exiled women, like themselves, in order to protect the imagination of their own identity stability. Hence, the analysis of these dynamics in the light of Said's and Serra's works proves to be extremely productive, thus highlighting the advantages of a multidimensional approach to the subject of gender.

According to Sonia Nhantumbo and Maria Paula Meneses (2005), this intersectional approach is fairly recent in Mozambique. Having analysed a range of activities related to the research on women and gender which was carried out at Universidade Eduardo Mondlane between 1975 and 2000, the researchers were able to distribute the activities into three main periods, according to the theoretical frameworks used and the methodologies applied. These three periods were the following: 1975 to 1982, the post-independence period that corresponds to the socialist experience; 1982 to 1990/92, which refers to the introduction of neo-liberal policies and the PRE (Programa de Reajustamento Estrutural [Structural Adjustment Program]); and, finally, 1993/94 to 2000, corresponding to the post-war period, in which the national reconstruction was in motion (2005: 106–07). The analysis of the works developed in each period shows that it was not until the second period identified by Nhantumbo and Meneses — that is, from 1982 to 1990/92 — that they began to present multidisciplinary approaches to the themes of women and gender. Not only did the approaches developed throughout this second period enable the deconstruction of the standardised representation of the socialist New Woman — that was so strongly advertised during the first period identified — but they also prompted the exploration of what Casimiro and Andrade (2005: 20) define as 'Feminismo Situado' [Situated Feminism]. This positioning has been shown to enhance the quality of the works developed in the last and most recent period, as these works reveal in-depth theorisation and reflection.

Taking into consideration the state of research conducted in Mozambique on the subject, it is possible to state that Chiziane's work affords a literary reflection on it, due to her snapshots of women's multiple lived experiences of gender through the intersection of various social categories. Indeed, as this study will attempt to demonstrate later on, in *Alegre Canto*, Chiziane constructs a genealogy for Mozambican women by advocating the genderisation of memory, simultaneously problematising the impact of the race variable on women's experience, a discussion that can be traced back to *Niketche*.

Niketche: Uma História de Poligamia — Of *Estabelecidos* and *Intrusos* [Established And Intruders]

As mentioned before, in *Niketche*, Chiziane initiates a debate on gender and race which is conducted by the five wives and two mistresses of Tony, who eventually becomes the polygamous husband of the novel. The first character to be introduced to us in this literary work is Rami, and it is from her perspective that we initially access the facts of the story. Through her initial self-portrayal, we learn that she is a southern Shangaan woman living in Maputo, a traditional wife who is married to a police commander named Tony (António Tomás) and the mother of his children. These introductory revelations show that she has been most unhappy since her husband was promoted to that position due to his various affairs with other women, which have kept him away from home for long periods of time. Having presented her predicament, Rami decides to engage in a search for identity that will take her on a journey, in the course of which she will face her fears, get to know herself and acknowledge as well as mock her husband's multiple lives. This is how she ends up learning about the existence of his four unofficial wives and families and is forced to deal with all the tensions that emerge from this revelation. The analysis of Tony's five wives — official and unofficial — the social dynamics amongst them and their evolution as characters facilitates the identification of two distinct moments in the narrative in which the experience of womanhood is shown to be heterogeneous, varying according to the impact of other elements in its intersection with gender, namely ethnicism and race. Taking into consideration Serra's (2000: 23–25) conceptualisation of the phenomena of racism and ethnicism as being informed by the struggle for access to power resources, we can affirm that in each of the two distinct moments identified, there is a relationship between the *established* and the *intruders*, as the characters that occupy these positions change according to the logics of inclusion and exclusion at work.

Hence, early in the text Rami appears as the 'established' wife, at the centre of the power relations, as opposed to the 'marginal intruding' wives whose apparent intention was to disrupt her establishment and, thus, her entitlement to power. Although they have no means of legally disrupting the power which Rami has as the official wife, they subvert it in a parallel unofficial level of everyday existence (by resorting to witchcraft, for example, in their attempt to keep Tony away from Rami), which escapes the scope of the official legal monogamous marriage. At this point, and as Owen (2007b: 192–99) proves, the conflict is ethnically informed, since the tension between ethnic groups appears at the core of the problematisation of the multiple feminine experiences in Mozambique, along with the struggle for resources within the feminine gender. Following this line of thought, several cultural elements that derive from the specific context of the city of Maputo emerge as markedly influenced by southern patterns, to confirm Rami's position. Leading a life embedded in it — with all its patrilineal and patriarchal tradition, its Christian tradition and its Marxist influence — she is an official black African wife in a Christian monogamous marriage. The fact that she is black becomes very relevant when we acknowledge that the other four unofficial wives are also black. That generates a horizontality amongst them, mediated by Rami, which will ultimately allow them to imagine themselves as equals. This imagination of levelled equality is only possible because they are all black, as the introduction of the *mulata* character Eva will subsequently prove.

Considering herself to be a perfect wife, Rami is an obedient housewife who depends emotionally and economically on her husband, and she has a privileged life due to her husband's social position. She does belong to an elitist bourgeoisie, having easy access to the world through her husband. Therefore, her power cannot be quantified against or in comparison to his, because it only exists through him, which demonstrates her subalternity in relation to Tony. Aware of this reality and also of her inability to reverse this situation, Rami is left with only one way to preserve her power: to affirm it before the 'intruders'. First and foremost, Rami decides to look for the unofficial wives and get to know them in order to assert her own entitlement to Tony by establishing their position as the intruders, as opposed to her own position as the legitimate wife. Hence, she acknowledges that Julieta, *a enganada* [the woman deceived], is a southerner, just like herself, whereas Luísa, *a desejada* [the woman desired], Saly, *a apetecida* [the woman fancied] and Mauá Sualé, *a amada* [the woman loved], are northerners (Chiziane 2016: 83–84). Having been deceived by Tony in the past, Julieta, from Inhambane, is the mother of six of his children. This housewife, who depends on him economically and emotionally, still believes all of his promises and waits for the day when he will divorce Rami to marry her. Interestingly, Rami finds her very familiar, which suggests a link that might potentially emerge from a shared cultural background: 'Sofro com ela. Coitada, ela é mais uma vítima do que uma rival. Foi caçada e traída como eu' (Chiziane 2002: 26) ['I suffer with her. Poor thing, she is more of a victim than a rival. She was pursued and betrayed like me' (Chiziane 2016: 30)]. Both Rami and Ju are presented as being originally from Maputo and Inhambane respectively, provinces in which the lineage groups are markedly patrilineal. The three unofficial wives from the north, however, are different women with a very distinct position which complies with the matrilineal tradition in which they were educated.[13] Coming from a place where men are shared because they are so few, the Zambezian and Makua Lu is totally aware of her gender disempowerment in that setting and, thus, openly shows that she looked for a man who could maintain her. She is the mother of two of Tony's children and depends on him economically, but not emotionally. Indeed, when he does not tend to her, she goes in pursuit of her own sexual fulfilment and even has a lover. When she first meets Lu, Rami feels immediately attracted to her, as Lu reminds her of something that she was, but is not anymore: 'Ela tem todos os encantos que eu perdi' (2002: 60) ['She had all the charm I had lost' (2016: 82)]. The Makonde Saly, from Cabo Delgado, mother to two of Tony's children, openly states 'eu sou pobre. Sem pai, nem emprego, nem dinheiro, nem marido. Se não tivesse roubado o teu marido, não teria nem filhos, nem existência' (2002: 68) ['I'm poor. No father, no job, no money, no husband. If I hadn't stolen your husband, I'd have neither children nor any life whatsoever' (2016: 95)]. In doing so, she implies that her choice was solely made according to what Tony could offer to her, i.e. a way into society through maternity. Finally, the Makua Mauá Sualé, from Nampula, was the most recently acquired wife and the youngest in the group, being only nineteen years old.

The differences in the representation of each woman are significant, and become particularly relevant when read against the specific cultural backgrounds from which they emerge. In an important study on sexuality and gender politics in Mozambique, Signe Arnfred (2011) argues that the distinct kinship systems — matrilineal and patrilineal — reacted differently to the influences of external processes of modernisation (economic, religious, ideological) introduced since the nineteenth century. Basing her argumentation on substantial data collected in the country from 1975 to 2005, Arnfred contends that this modernisation was largely detrimental for women, particularly central and southern women, as it facilitated an increasingly larger space for the emergence and affirmation of male dominance, very much attached to the patriliny promoted (even if inexplicitly) by Frelimo (2011: 24–61). According to Arnfred,

> The women living under terms of patriliny tend to be much worse off in many respects, compared to their sisters of the north. First and foremost, marriage is much more binding and divorce is much more difficult, seen from women's points of view. This is linked to lobolo. [...] In the south of Mozambique it is the woman who leaves her family in order to settle with the husband's kin in the first years of marriage. [...] For a woman to divorce, she must persuade her own family, receivers of the lobolo, to return it to her husband. As very often the lobolo has already gone, this is no easy task. Consequently there will be pressure on the woman to stay and endure even a bad marriage. For the man divorce is easy. He just sends the wife away, back to her own parents; he stays in the house, with the kids (excepting the very young ones, who follow the mother) and with the couple's belongings. (2011: 46–47)

Traditionally, under matriliny, the female lines inherit the land and marriage is matrilocal, which means that the husband is the one who moves into the lands of the wife's family. Divorce is easy for both parties, since there is no *lobolo* involved, but it is the woman who stays in the house and with the couple's children (2011: 46–47). Even though this kinship system is not matriarchal (the paternal authority is the uncle, that is, the woman's brother, rather than the father), it does allow women more access to social authority (2011: 30). All aspects considered, Arnfred continues, it becomes easier to understand why the principles of matriliny would clash with Frelimo's promotion of the nuclear family at the basis of a modernising society, which was much more in line with the principles of patriliny.

As such, in Rami's point of view, Tony's unofficial wives emerge as 'intruders', as marginal to the institution represented by the official and monogamous Christian marriage. Due to their deliberate denial of this institution, and consequently of the cultural structure that supports it, they fail to recognise her power as legitimate wife, thus questioning her rights. Furthermore, since Tony mediates their economic access to the world, they are able to aspire to Rami's positioning, even if not consistently: 'A minha casa é dos lugares mais agradáveis deste mundo. [...] Mas esta casa é melhor ainda. Foi construída com o dinheiro do meu marido, por isso é minha. Esta mulher imita-me e tenta ser mais perfeita do que eu' (2002: 21) ['My house is one of the nicest places in the world. [...] But this house is even better. It was built with my husband's money, which is why it's mine. This woman is imitating me and trying to be better than me' (2016: 23)]. Finally, Rami understands that none of the unofficial wives have a job — their income source is their relationship with Tony. That is the moment in which Rami realises that what brings her close to these women is much more than what separates her from them, as they all share the same condition of exile in relation to their promiscuous husband. Despite coming from distinct cultural backgrounds, the women are united by their experience of womanhood in relation to Tony and the patriarchal society that he represents, an experience that is marked by alienation and silence. Hence, once again recuperating Said's (2001a: 177) definition of exile as 'the perilous territory of not-belonging', the unofficial wives appear as exiles in the sense that they are prevented from entering the community due to their status of unofficial. Furthermore, Rami, just like the unofficial wives, is unable to access the material world without Tony's mediation. They all appear to be entrapped between an official, openly masculinised cultural discourse and some very specific practices that materialise Tony's manipulation of the cultural systems, which serve him in the propagation of his wives' subalternity (Owen 2007b: 189).

On the one hand, as southern Shangaan women, both Rami and Ju are immersed in this *habitus* that keeps them in a highly controlled position of inferiority to the patriarch. Rami problematises this position when she reflects on women's total incapacity to access ownership of both their names and their own bodies, as those are relationships that are always mediated by men:

> Na terra do meu marido sou estrangeira. Na terra dos meus pais sou passageira. Não sou de lugar nenhum. Não tenho registo, no mapa da vida não tenho nome. Uso este nome de casada que me pode ser retirado a qualquer momento. Por empréstimo. Usei o nome paterno, que me foi retirado. Era empréstimo. A minha alma é a minha morada. Mas onde vive a minha alma? (2002: 92)
>
> [In my husband's land, I'm a foreigner. In my parent's land, I'm merely passing through. I'm from nowhere at all. I'm registered nowhere on the map of life, and I have no name. I use this name given to me at my marriage, and that can be taken away from me at any moment. I've borrowed it. I used my father's name, but this was taken away. I had borrowed it. My soul is my dwelling. But where does my soul live? (2016: 129)].

On the other hand, the three unofficial wives from the north (Lu, Saly and Mauá) are forced to leave their customs behind, eliding their identity difference so as to conform to the local *habitus*, which does not recognise it. This non-recognition translates into the incorporation of these women into the southern social, sexual and economic dynamics. The scenario described corresponds to the form that polygamy acquires in contemporary Mozambican cities, identified by Arnfred as *amantismo* [having mistresses] (2011: 89–90). The scholar claims that in pre- and early colonial Mozambique, polygamy was a system of production and reproduction in a country whose economy was strongly based on farming (2011: 76). These practices remain very much the same in the countryside, even after modernisation. In the cities, however, the economy is much more based on wage labour, which means that men do not need to get more wives to increase production. What tends to happen is *amantismo*, meaning that married men have mistresses and other families, for whom they have no responsibilities — a situation that clearly favours men:

> It is he who profits from the setup and from the competition between the wives. He can play one woman off against the other, and he does so. In the 'polygamy of the city' there is no shared daily life and no work relation between the wives. They do not live together; they do not help each other. They may know (of) each other, but only indirectly, through the husband. They are not related as closely and importantly as are co-wives in the countryside, and thus the main advantage of polygamy seen from the women's point of view, has gone. 'In the countryside women are united', the factory women said. This is not the case in towns. It seems to me that, much more than in traditional rural polygamy, the 'city polygamy'-women are exploited by men. (2011: 89)

As Rami learns about gender and sexuality in matrilineal tradition, a new world opens up to her, with multiple possibilities that surpass the construction of women in the south. Through this newly acquired knowledge, Chiziane proposes the creation of a space where women's empowerment enables them to recreate cultural and ethnic exchange as a space of difference (Owen 2007b: 187). Therefore, in choosing to recuperate patrilineal polygyny and extending the benefits that she was entitled to as official wife to the unofficial ones and respective families, Rami prompts a process of social levelling between the wives, whose consequences will be verifiable in terms of their access to power as opposed to Tony's. Upon being officially recognised as members of a polygamous family, the wives proceed to the recovery of polygamy as a very specific structure of traditional power, which will ultimately allow them to restrain the fast spreading hegemonic masculinised forces of modernity in this urban setting, and claim back some of the space that they lost throughout the processes of modernisation (Arnfred 2011: 47).

Sousa Santos and Cruz e Silva (2004) shed light on this tendency of recovering tradition as a way of proposing an alternative modernity, which is revealed as a strategy to resist the forces of globalisation in African societies. According to these two social scientists, this feature puts forward a rewriting of tradition in modernity with a view to presenting an alternative paradigm in the democratic era:

> Uma das áreas onde esta reapropriação e resignificação tem vindo precisamente a ocorrer é na área do poder tradicional. Nesta medida, o tradicional é recuperado como uma estratégia moderna de resistência contra uma modernidade global excludente. Recuperação do tradicional hoje em dia em África é, em geral, um exercício bem moderno. Longe de ser uma alternativa à modernidade, é expressão da reivindicação de uma modernidade alternativa. É uma forma de globalização que se apresenta como resistência à globalização. (2004: 29)

> [One of the areas where this re-appropriation and resignification has clearly been taking place in is the area of traditional power. In this respect, the traditional is reclaimed as a modern strategy of resistance against an excluding global modernity. In contemporary Africa, the recovery of the traditional is, in

> general, a very modern practice. Far from being an alternative to modernity, it expresses the demand for an alternative modernity. It is a form of globalisation that presents itself as resistance to globalisation.]

As such, the women take three very important steps that lead to the legitimisation of their power as 'established' and, ultimately, to the collapse of the polygamous family, which becomes obsolete in that context. This proves the point that, in terms of production, polygamy is not necessary in the urban setting. Firstly, they force the officialisation of the polygamous marriage; then, they successfully achieve economic independence through inter-loan and *xitique*; finally, they manage to get their *lobolos* paid for.[14] Considering that the wives use their differences to become stronger as a group, it is possible to state that they successfully manage to compensate for their previous losses by creating a new space for themselves (Said 2001a: 181), in the intersection of both matrilineal and patrilineal cultures. This joint action allows them to ascend as a group to the position of 'established', as opposed to the patriarch, Tony, who becomes the 'intruder' who constantly tries to disrupt their empowerment. When Tony realises that, as representatives of polygyny as an institution, his increasingly established wives have disempowered him, he attempts to reverse this tendency.

Eva and the Problematic Representations of Miscegenation

The subsequent introduction of the female character Eva into the plot comes to destabilise and put into question the wives' recently consolidated establishment due to two important features: she is infertile and a *mulata*. In the aftermath of the polygamous family's officialisation, Tony is forced to adjust to the new rules that impose a strict schedule and ritualistic share between the wives: 'Poligamia é isto mesmo. [...] Passar o homem de umas mãos para outras mãos com a delicadeza de quem segura um ovo' (2002: 128) ['Polygamy is precisely this. [...] Passing the man from one set of hands to the next with the care of people carrying an egg' (2016: 187)]. However, when he starts failing to accomplish his sexual obligations, the wives soon come to realise that he has found a new way to escape the monitoring control exerted by the new family structure, by getting himself another woman. Due to the recently acquired status of the wives, this new woman appears as a lover, an intruder who comes to question the authority of the official wives and to disrupt their power, given that she allows Tony to escape from the constraints of the polygamous marriage. For this reason, the wives' primary focus is the husband's attempt to re-appropriate and shift the power structures. Nonetheless, they react in a completely different way when they learn that Eva is a *mulata*. The introduction of this character is a turning point in the narrative, since from then onwards the debate on gender is informed racially — as opposed to culturally and ethnically, as it had been previously. It simultaneously confirms the existence of a racial hierarchy within the category of gender, which in turn is informed by and informs economic status: 'O entusiasmo desaparece. Uma mulata é uma rival a sério. Os homens negros são obcecados pelas peles claras, como os brancos são obcecados pelas cabeças loiras' (2002: 133) ['Our enthusiasm vanishes. A *mulata* is a serious rival. Black men are obsessed with lighter skin, just as White men are obsessed with blondes' (2016: 194)].

As they try to make sense of this woman, they gather some information about her that will enable them to present her as an 'intruder' in these power relations. As Said (2001a: 178) reminds us, exile is a jealous condition in the sense that

> What you achieve is precisely what you have no wish to share, and it is in the drawing of lines around you and your compatriots that the least attractive aspects of being in exile emerge: an exaggerated sense of group solidarity, and a passionate hostility to outsiders, even those who may in fact be in the same predicament as you.

In other words, it is the wives' eagerness to affirm the stability of their identity that leads them to exile Eva, without even realising that she too might be an exile before the patriarch. As they attempt to find out more about her, they learn that she is a wealthy divorced woman who has her own car and was rejected in the past by her husband for being sterile. Due to her ability to access the material world directly, without the mediation of a man, Eva's position as a woman is associated in the wives' imagination with race and colour. Firstly, she emerges as an oversexualised and deterritorialised woman. As the embodiment of hybridity, the *mulata*'s body acquires many connotations that change through time, inevitably going back to Portuguese colonial policies. As the anthropologist Miguel Vale de Almeida (2004: 65–82) points out in a study on hybridity and miscegenation in colonial and postcolonial Portugal, *mestiçagem* was always connoted negatively in the sense that it materialised the excessive sexual extrapolation of the established hierarchical racial order, regardless of its ideological uses by the various imperial discourses. Furthermore, the *mulato* is conceptualised as being able to navigate between and thus extract the best from two distinct worlds, which is not necessarily true if we consider the unequal power relations that feed the idea of *mestiçagem*, and consequently the 'hierarchical discourse on whitening' that the Lusotropicalist discourse is based on (Almeida 2004: 71). In spite of these facts, the mulattos are regarded as socially privileged, given that they can access certain power resources which are denied to or are at least less easily accessible to other 'races'.

With this in mind, the economic distinction between Eva and the polygamous wives becomes even clearer, as we learn that not only was she educated and married to a politician in the past, but she also has a very high position at work: 'Tem dinheiro, essa mulher, manda chuva. Tem estatuto. No emprego dela, é chefe. Manda nos homens. Conduz um carro que é um paraíso' (Chiziane 2002: 137) ['The woman's got money and power. She's got status. She's a boss in her job. She tells men what to do. And she drives a flashy car' (2016: 200)]. Hence, since she represents the best of both worlds, she emerges as the vehicle for the polygamous husband to engage in a socioeconomic whitening process and, subsequently achieve a status that will enable him to extrapolate the ethnic and ultimately the geographical and cultural limits of the nation. When the five wives confront Tony asking him to justify his relationship with Eva, on which they had the right to be consulted according to the laws on polygamy, he uses a highly racist and colonial expression to simply state that he felt 'vontade de variar, meninas. Desejo de tocar numa pele mais clara. Vocês são todas uma cambada de pretas' (2002: 140) ['A desire for variety, girls. A wish to touch some lighter skin. You're all dark, a bunch of black women' (2016: 206)]. Regardless of his attempt to turn the issue into a simple matter of pigmentation, it is not so much the colour of the women that is at stake here, as the power that emerges attached to it. Although his wives and children ironically allow him to perceive himself as the perfect patriarch who 'embraces' the entire country, thus turning into the national husband who makes perfect use of his own body as an instrument of power, his relationship with Eva lends him a different but related form of power, resting on his class ascendency. By possessing Eva, Tony goes through a whitening process which will ultimately allow the patriarch's internationalisation, as he is able to go to Paris with another woman — Gaby — for some short holidays due to Eva's help. Thus, he becomes the ultimate Lusotropical male.

Eva's origins in the intersection of two different cultural worlds also reinforce her appearance as an 'intruder' in the eyes of the official wives because they associate her with deterritorialisation. From their point of view, Eva is incapable of respecting their status as official wives because she does not recognise the cultural rules that apply to that context — they are foreign to her. In addition, as a person who is able to extract the positive aspects of two realities according to her needs, she might jeopardise the wives' positioning. In this representation, her space of enunciation appears to be acultural and deterritorialised; for that reason, she is interpreted as dangerous and threatening to a pre-established order. In this respect, Serra (2000) points out that the results of the study on racism, ethnicity and power in Mozambique confirmed that the mulattos were a social group whose stigmatised conceptualisation dissociated them from a homeland, a *pátria*. In the words of one of the interviewees from Tete, 'eu sou mulato, nós somos uma mistura e apanhamos dos dois lados, não temos inserção nos dois lados, os próprios chefes desprezam-nos porque o mulato não tem bandeira, não tem pátria' [I am a mulatto; we are a mixture and we are beaten by both sides, as opposed to being integrated into both sides. The Chiefs themselves despise us because the mulatto has no flag, no homeland] (2000: 52). Therefore, in the wives' eyes, Eva appears as someone who is not to be trusted due to her mixed-race origin. Her skin colour leads her to be immediately associated with race and class betrayal, as she threatens the national borders of the national husband.

Nevertheless, Eva's position comes to be levelled with that of the polygamous wives in the second instance of their analysis of the potential threat that she might constitute. On learning that she was abandoned by her husband due to her infertility, the wives sympathise with Eva: 'Assolou-nos um momento de piedade. Mulher estéril é um ser condenado à solidão, à amargura. Qual a vida da mulher estéril? Marginalidade, ausência' (Chiziane 2002: 136) ['We were swept by a momentary feeling of pity. A sterile woman is condemned to solitude and bitterness. What life does a sterile woman have? Being marginalized and forgotten'] (2016: 199). Indeed, as the Mozambican anthropologist Ana Maria Loforte (1998) points out, since the female body is associated with reproduction in this particular setting, it acquires a special connotation that gives women a certain status — so, women are only considered to be women if they can give birth. As an infertile woman, Eva is therefore disempowered, both in the extended male-dominated social arena and within the private circle composed of the official wives; this reveals not only the dynamics of gender domination, but also the important role that women play in the propagation of their own subalternity. Conceição Osório (2007d) claims that in Mozambique, sexuality and power are interconnected, as the correspondence between sexuality and reproduction presupposes the total control over women's bodies, thus highlighting their importance as places of domination, but also of counter-domination. In the Mozambican anthropologist's view,

> No caso de Moçambique, a fertilidade/infertilidade são critérios que classificam uma situação não apenas de ordem biológica mas constituem um elemento fundamental do modo como o poder se exerce. Em torno deste binómio (fertilidade/infertilidade) produz-se um discurso de sanções e de permissões [...] reveladores de uma representação em que se nega às mulheres, fora do contexto permitido pelo modelo cultural, o exercício da sexualidade. (2007d: 327–28)
>
> [In the case of Mozambique, fertility/infertility are criteria that not only classify a biological situation, but that also play a fundamental role in how power is put to use. Around this binomial (fertility/infertility), a discourse of sanctions and permissions is produced [...] revealing a representation in which women are denied the right to exercise their sexuality outside the context allowed by the cultural model.]

Hence, the fact that Eva is marginalised by the whole of society for being incapable of performing one of the major roles that defines Mozambican womanhood diminishes the sexual excess that is associated with her as a *mulata*, thus emptying her representation and bringing her down to a level at which it is possible for her to be absorbed by the polygamous family. In other words, her racial demystification allows for an alteration of the rules of exclusion and she is allowed into the national family — at least to a certain extent, as will soon be discussed.

When Tony fakes his own death, Eva appears for the first time, telling her side of the story and bringing proof that Tony is still alive. We learn that she is a Makonde from Palma, in the far north of the country, who was tricked by Tony on two occasions. The first time was when he told her that the only wife he had was Mauá; and the second was when she made all the arrangements for them to travel to Paris together, and he ended up travelling with another woman named Gaby instead. The empathy between Rami and Eva is clear right from the beginning of their conversation. Despite not being an official member of the polygamous family, Eva is forced by the other wives to participate in the mourning procedures, which she does by offering to pay for the coffin and the funeral reception. She is, therefore, offered a temporary position inside the polygamous family, which is much more than we can say about Gaby. The plot reveals very little about this female character. However, her name suggests that she might be a foreign woman. In addition, considering Tony's escalating trajectory into the racial spectrum, which runs parallel to economic power, we may speculate that Gaby is a white woman who ends up serving Tony in his intentions to become what Owen calls a 'multi-national husband' (2007b: 195). I would add that he also intended to become the ultimate multi-racial husband, in a movement that clearly replicates the Lusotropicalist ideology of a pluriracial and multicultural society, and a pluricontinental nation — in this specific case, husband — built on unequal power relations. Indeed, he accumulates women of different ethnic groups, races and colours (the five black wives, the *mulata* and possibly the white woman), bringing them all together under the big patriarchal umbrella, which elides the specificities of their various feminine experiences and consequently reproduces the politics of southern gender domination.

Although the patriarch is unsuccessful in creating his own Lusotropical family, due to the wives' active engagement in their own empowerment and increasing direct access to the economic world without his mediation, it is impossible not to focus on the specific case of Eva in relation to them. As mentioned before, she is offered a partial position in the polygamous family, but is never formally incorporated into it, thus retaining connotations of exclusion. After Tony's fake death and burial, he returns to the city only to find out that he now has to deal with the repercussions of his acts. Having shown his wives that he is willing to do everything to make it up to them for the chaos he created, he is confronted with Rami's suggestion of incorporating both Eva and Gaby into the family. Although he refuses to accept this change, the wives insist on Eva's integration, given that they are now able to view her as an equal. Yet, he shows that he believes that Eva would never accept joining this family, suggesting that she would not do it precisely because of a racial tension:

> — Ela te usou. Era justo que ele assumisse a perda. Por isso achamos que ela tem que ser a tua nova mulher.
> — Nunca. Mesmo que eu tente, ela nem iria aceitar.
> — Já lhe fizeste a proposta?
> — Não.
> — Porquê?
> — Não tenho coragem. (Chiziane 2002: 244–45)
>
> ['She used you. It's only fair that she should share in the losses. That's why we are of the opinion that she should be your new wife.'
> 'Never. Even if I asked, she'd never accept.'
> 'Have you ever proposed to her?'
> 'No.'
> 'Why?'
> 'I haven't got the courage.' (2016: 361–62)]

It is important to note that despite the wives' visible inflexibility towards the resolution of incorporating Eva into the family in this context, we never find out what happens, because the story is dropped. We continue to accompany the development of the five wives' stories, but we do not have any kind of access to Eva any more.

At this point, there are two very important aspects that must be highlighted. Firstly, the polygamous husband is intimidated by Eva's power. He is fully aware that, due to her economic condition, she does not need him as a mediator to access the world; this might suggest that he only existed in her life because she had been rejected by other men for being infertile. Hence, because she successfully dissociates women's sexuality from reproduction, Eva's potential as a disruptive female character is revealed. In this line of thought, she represents a threat to the stability of the patriarch inside the polygamous family, because she contributes to neither his empowerment nor his progeny — on the contrary. Tony's acceptance into the family of a woman who is unable to ensure the continuity of the group would represent his self-annihilation as a patriarch. Secondly, the *mulata* is once again described as someone who is external to that and any other world described in the novel. The fact that both Tony and his wives did not believe that Eva would agree to join the polygamous family suggests that they are reading her in terms of both her race and colour. As Osório (1998) reminds us, the social relations built inside the family are relations of power. This means that if she were to accept becoming the polygamous husband's most recent wife, she would have to respond to a very specific hierarchical order in which her racial superiority as a *mulata* would be elided. Furthermore, it suggests that although Eva alters the wives' self-perceptions as women as they realise that her inferiority for being infertile is a social construction, they never actually dismantle it. This leads us to wonder if, indeed, there is any kind of redemption in the novel for this character.

Niketche: Uma História de Poligamia: Conclusion

As the story unravels, we realise that the world changes for every character. Interestingly, as time passes, the women gradually lose interest in the polygamous family. As each wife affirms her individuality, the polygamous family starts to collapse progressively, starting with Lu's decision to abandon the family in order to build her own monogamous one with Victor, her lover. At their wedding celebration, there is a symbolic occurrence which conveys the idea that the women have successfully built a 'third space' for themselves, where they renegotiate their sexual and cultural identities as women, and consequently their condition as 'gender' exiles. While dancing the *niketche* — a dance which is characteristic of northern culture and marks sexual initiation for women — and singing to liberate Vuyazi — the protagonist of a southern tale who was punished for her insurrection against women's traditional role — they celebrate the construction of a modern conceptualisation of traditional culture that emerges from the intersection of north and south. Simultaneously, they celebrate the construction of a new postcolonial space, one that rewrites the unity of post-independence by proposing a cartographic reconfiguration which decentralises the south as the unique representative of the national space and includes the peripheral areas of the geopolitical space in the national map, through the recuperation of the women's alternative cultural backgrounds. As a consequence, the process of national decentralisation coincides with the disavowal of the Lusotropical patriarchal nation. However, Eva is excluded from this manifestation, and therefore also from the new national cultural mapping. As all the wives progressively abandon Tony to engage in relationships with other men whom they have chosen, their liberation does not extend to Eva, who remains trapped in her representations as hyperfeminised and deterritorialised. Although she is no longer seen as an 'intruder', she remains a stranger in this setting, a fact that echoes the *mulata*'s problematic sociocultural positioning. On the one hand, one could argue that Eva's positioning is reversed, as she successfully brings about Tony's disempowerment by acting as a barrier to his attempt to become a Lusotropical national husband, and also as she changes the wives' self-perceptions as sexual beings. On the other hand, one could argue that her positioning remains undisturbed, given that her exclusion from the new cartography of the nation, a space which is mediated, reconfigured and brought into modernity by black women, raises the question of the racial mapping which is being proposed by this literary work. Hence, the *mulata*'s absence from the new racial mapping represents the rejection of a colonial, Lusotropical and miscegenated nation, unified by sex. Nonetheless, not only does it bring about her deterritorialisation, but it also suggests that the cartographic reconfiguration of the nation should be exclusively black. In other words, there is an underlying attitude that invokes an ideology of Negritude, in which the exultation of the black women's values leaves no room for any non-black women, thus reproducing the same essentialism that found it hard to represent *mestiços* as anything other than threatening. Therefore, a problematic and non-conciliatory reading of the novel arises, as in an effort to escape the essentialist representation of women in the gendered power structure, a new essentialism is created when the five black wives' attitude towards the mulata Eva, in turn, reproduces an essentialist racial and colour ideology. Again, the 'third space' created by the wives emerges as a highly problematic one in the sense that the reversal of their exile is built upon the exile of Eva.

The novel's inability to provide redemption for the *mulata* Eva, along with the remaining black wives, sheds light on the complex power structures that operate in the intersection of gender and race. This indicates the need to further explore the dynamics which support the miscegenation that characterised the composition of what has now been the Mozambican social fabric for centuries, before the institution of the colonial state. These issues find a special space for reflection in Chiziane's 2008 novel entitled *O Alegre Canto da Perdiz*; it puts forward a reflection on the cultural nation which emphasises the dialogic relationship between Mozambique and Portugal (that is, the colonial and not the pre-colonial contact), to the detriment of other relationships (such as the relationships developed by Mozambique within the Indic course, for example; see Meneses 2012: 316).

Introduction to *O Alegre Canto da Perdiz* — Women and/in Memory

Placed in the setting of the northern province of Zambézia, in the cities of Gurué and Quelimane, the story unravels 'exiles' throughout time, across three distinct historical moments, focusing particularly on the intersection of questions of race, colour, ethnicity and gender, and their relevance in the constitution of both men's and women's identities. In a clear allusion to matriliny as the sociocultural system which is normally attributed to the societies of the north of the country (Arnfred 2011), the main plot emerges from the stories of three generations of Zambezian women — Serafina; Delfina; Maria das Dores and Maria Jacinta. These stories inevitably transverse, interact with, and reflect on the official history of the province and the country, in a gesture that not only discloses the potential for marginal and counter-narrations of the nation, but that also accentuates the need to regard the act of remembering as a mental act which is markedly gendered. According to John Neubauer and Helga Geyer-Ryan (2000),

> [...] even if we agree that remembering is not biologically determined, we can assume that memory is influenced by the particular social, cultural, and historical conditions in which individuals find themselves. And since men and women generally assume different social and cultural roles, their ways of remembering should also differ (2000: 6).

Indeed, taking into consideration that the official history of what is now the Mozambican nation state was always written and maintained by intellectual and political elites — both colonial and post-colonial — which were primarily made up of men, it is possible to affirm that *Alegre Canto* is a novel that demonstrates how the experience of gender determines practices of memory. It simultaneously recaptures hidden or forgotten memories which, although repressed in certain male-dominated contexts in the past, are still a relevant part of the collective memory and, therefore, need to be recognised (Sanches 2007: 131–33). In other words, the novel proceeds to reposition an unbalanced cultural system by recovering what was marginalised for a long period of time: the female experience of the nation.

Anne Pitcher and Scott Kloeck-Jenson (2001) corroborate and demonstrate the applicability of Neubauer and Geyer-Ryan's hypothesis in the specific Zambezian context in a text entitled 'Homens, Mulheres, Memória e Direitos aos Recursos Naturais na Província da Zambézia' [Men, Women, Memory and Rights to Natural Resources in the Province of Zambezia]. By interviewing twenty-two people, eleven women and eleven men, the researchers came to realise that the interviewees' memory was gendered. When confronted with the need to evoke images of a specific moment in the past, such as the internal conflict between Frelimo and RENAMO forces, both women and men would remember different aspects of it. Men tended to express their grief towards the loss of certain objects and/or belongings, as well as how that loss led to their present condition; whereas women tended to regret the loss of knowledge and information, the intergenerational transfer of which was brutally interrupted throughout the conflict, inevitably conditioning the maintenance of their identity (2001: 163). The researchers' conclusions highlight the need to recognise the memories of both men and women so as to bring back a more inclusive and reliable portrayal of the past and the present (2001: 175), which again takes us back to the aim of *Alegre Canto* and to Chiziane's attempt to bring back *other* memories. Nevertheless, as Neubauer and Geyer-Ryan point out, the act of remembering is not solely conditioned by the gender factor, since circumstances such as class and race influence it as well (2000: 6). Given that they alter each other when they come into contact, as they shape people's identities, these are important features to take into account when analysing those identities. Again, we are led to make use of a multidisciplinary framework — by recuperating Said's theorisation of exile and Serra's work on racism and ethnicism in Mozambique — which considerably opens up the possibilities for analysis of the novel. The deployment of this multidisciplinary approach reveals the complexity of the act of remembering, a process which, in itself, echoes the construction of the distinct female characters in *Alegre Canto*.

In the literary work's Postcript, Nataniel Ngomane (2008) identifies two highly complex female 'characters' in the novel — 'a mulher zambeziana' and 'a Zambézia' [the Zambezian woman and Zambézia] — highlighting the fact that the former character is formed by multiple experiences of womanhood in the *mestiça* province of Zambézia:

> Tendo-nos habituado a personagens femininas como a Sarnau da *Balada de Amor ao Vento* (1990), Minosse e Wusheni do *Ventos do Apocalipse* (1995), Vera de *O Sétimo Juramento* (2000) e Rami do *Niketche* (2002), apresenta-nos agora — em simultâneo com a construção de Maria das Dores, Maria Jacinta, Delfina e Serafina — duas novas personagens femininas, mais complexas na sua concepção e, talvez por isso, desempenhando papéis igualmente complexos e cruciais para a compreensão da trama narrativa: de um lado, a mulher zambeziana, resultante da projecção metonímica e metafórica em que se vão desdobrando Maria das Dores, Jacinta, Delfina e Serafina, cada uma com as suas ambições e conflitos e, de outro, a Zambézia, província moçambicana do centro-norte, onde a autora viveu durante anos e que, por sinal, se configura agora como uma das personagens principais deste livro. (2008: 340–41)
>
> [Having acquainted us with female characters such as Sarnau, from *Balada de Amor ao Vento* (1990), Minosse and Wusheni, from *Ventos do Apocalipse* (1995), Vera from *O Sétimo Juramento* (2000), and Rami from *Niketche* (2002), [the author] now introduces us to two new female characters — simultaneously with the construction of Maria das Dores, Maria Jacinta, Delfina and Serafina — who are more complex in their conception and, perhaps because of that, play equally complex and crucial roles in the understanding of the narrative's plot. On the one hand, we have the Zambezian woman, derived from the unfolding metonymic and metaphoric projections of Maria das Dores, Jacinta, Delfina and Serafina, each one of them with their own ambitions and conflicts. On the other hand, we have Zambézia, a north-central Mozambican province where the author lived for years and, incidentally, is now one of the main characters of this book.]

At this point, it is imperative to focus on three very important and interrelated aspects which are revealed by the close proximity and overlap between these two characters. The first aspect concerns the relevance of women in the history of Zambézia; the second aspect refers to the impact of that same history in the construction of feminine identity; and, finally, the third aspect alludes to the reality of *mestiçagem* in Zambézia, or in Ngomane's words, to the fact that 'a província da Zambézia é apelidada de Brasil de Moçambique' [the province of Zambézia is nicknamed Brazil of Mozambique] (2008: 342). Therefore, in this sense, it becomes possible to affirm that these two 'characters' — Zambezian women and Zambézia

— relate to each other reflexively, given that the colonial formation of the province had traditionally been achieved through the control and usage of women's bodies for different ends, according to the demands of particular historical moments.[15] Both characters highlight how the economic development and the sociocultural *mestiçagem* in Zambézia could only be achieved through women; how women can appear disempowered even in a matrilineal kinship system, i.e. in a context in which 'matriliny and matrilocality is a source of social authority to women' (Arnfred 2011: 30); and how despite the recognition of women's vital role in Zambezian society, these various experiences of womanhood have been absent from the official history of the province. This open effort to disclose the feminine face of Zambézia might, in addition, suggest a parallel between the marginality of women's genealogy in Mozambique and the marginality of the history of Zambézia (or, perhaps other northern/central provinces, as opposed to the southern ones, which are generally more well-known due to their historical association with political power since the nineteenth century) in the delineation of official contemporary historiographic discourses of the nation.

Nevertheless, it is important to underline that the immediate association of the Zambezian women with the Zambezian land is highly problematic, as it reproduces the same essentialist feminisation of the land that characterised the imperial discourses of the nation, as McClintock reminds us (1995: 21–74). Simultaneously, the fact that the Zambezian province is compared to Brazil links the experience of racial *mestiçagem* in both contexts. As mentioned before, the Brazilian anthropologist Gilberto Freyre was the main theorist to be associated with the spread of both the conception of Brazil as a 'racial democracy' and the representation of Portugal's former colonies as examples of 'mixed' and therefore positive racial experiences (1986; 1961). Nevertheless, the real situation was much more complex than that, as proved by the Brazilian social scientist Marcos Chor Maio in a text about the role of UNESCO's 1950s project on the process of institutionalisation of social sciences and race studies in Brazil (2001). Basing his work on numerous studies carried out since the 1950s, the researcher shows that those studies produced by sociologists who were engaged in the project proved that racial prejudice did indeed exist — it just had 'more subtle manners of manifesting itself' (2001: 58). This realisation required the development of research strategies to understand the nature of this prejudice and, ultimately, to combat it. Hence, the comparability of Zambézia and Brazil might also suggest that the debate over the composition of Mozambican social and racial fabric needs to take place in an appropriate setting, at an official level. Only this discussion will allow for the understanding and ultimately the resolution of some of the social problems identified by the previously mentioned study on racism, ethnicism and power which was coordinated by Carlos Serra in 2000. In accordance with the above, the present study sets out to analyse *Alegre Canto*'s deployment of racial exile in Zambézia across time — in the colonial and post-colonial eras — within a matrilineal tradition and through the recuperation of a female genealogy, which is achieved by way of gendering the communal memory. Hence, in this process the remapping of the nation will be achieved in the intersection of the black women's experiences, the *mulata*'s territorialisation, and the cartographic reconfiguration of feminine memory, given that the recuperation of Zambezian history through the recovery of a female genealogy is also the retrieval of the memory of miscegenation, which is hereby territorialised and problematised.

O Alegre Canto da Perdiz

As is typical in Chiziane's works, the first chapter of the novel reveals the thematic framework to be approached, and sets the tone of the narrative. Hence, the first character we encounter is Maria das Dores in the form of a naked woman bathing on the banks of the Licungo river, a spot which is reserved exclusively for men. This behaviour obviously provokes a reaction from the local female population, whose feeling of threat leads them to attempt to somehow make sense of the situation and try to reason with her. But Maria das Dores is portrayed as different from all the other women and external to their rules, a fact which immediately directs us both to her transgressive nature as a character and to the multiplicity of exiles within gender. Maria das Dores experiences a form of exile in relation to the women — she is not considered to be one of them because she does not conform to the same social rules. This means that she needs to be *otherised* and made aware of that marginalisation so as to internalise it and, ultimately, conform to the collective social rules:

> Mulher, não tens vergonha na cara? Onde vendeste a tua vergonha? Não tens pena das nossas crianças que vão cegar com a tua nudez? Não tens medo dos homens? Não sabes que te podem usar e abusar? Oh, mulher, veste lá a tua roupa que a tua nudez mata e cega! (Chiziane 2008: 14)
>
> [Woman, have you no shame? Where did you sell your shame? Do you not feel sorry for our children, who will be blinded by your nudity? Are you not afraid of men? Do you not know that they can use and abuse you? Oh, woman, put on your clothes now, for your nudity kills and blinds!]

The women's urgent need to identify Maria das Dores and exile her is intrinsically linked with their need to feel secure within the limits of their imagination as women. As a woman, Maria das Dores is defying their cultural representation as women, which is a profoundly threatening gesture in the sense that, as Said reminds us, exiles feel the urge to imagine themselves as part of a triumphant ideology (2001a: 177). Hence, they can only be comfortable with their womanhood if they exile Maria das Dores for having gone beyond the limits of female representation.

Indeed, when we learn about her name (which translates as Mary of Sorrows), some further directions of the novel are revealed:

> Maria das Dores é o seu nome. Deve ser o nome de uma santa ou uma branca porque as pretas gostam de nomes simples. Joana. Lucrécia. Carlota. Maria das Dores é um nome belíssimo, mas triste. Reflecte o quotidiano das mulheres e dos negros. (Chiziane 2008: 16)
>
> [Maria das Dores is her name. It must be the name of a saint or a white woman because black women like simple names. Joana. Lucrécia. Carlota. Maria das

> Dores is a beautiful but sad name. It reflects the daily lives of women and black people.]

In fact, her name points towards two distinct realities that are carefully positioned in opposition on the racial spectrum. Although she bears a name that refers directly to the reality of the privileged white Portuguese population, its meaning alludes to the lived experience of the underprivileged population, namely women and black people. There is a clear suggestion that she is somehow caught between these two worlds. In addition, the association between women and black people constitutes a reference to the intersection of two exiles, which is to be explored throughout the novel. Gender and race emerge at this point in the novel as factors of social discrimination, suggesting that women and black people occupy the lowest positions within the power hierarchy, and implying that Maria das Dores brings together both forms of exile. This produces a very specific type of exile, which surfaces at the intersection of the two variants that inevitably shape and alter each other. If as a woman Maria das Dores lives in gender exile in a male dominated context, as a black woman she will also occupy a less privileged place within the racial spectrum (that is, compared to women of different colours), which will predictably have an impact in terms of her social positioning in the class hierarchy.

Interestingly, all of this takes place in a matrilineal context, and involves a woman of the third generation of females whose stories form the novel's plot. This might suggest that, as Arnfred defends, matriliny is changing, under the pressures of modern society, and that 'this development means an erosion of female power' (2011: 249). This idea is further reinforced when the women of the village look for the support of the *régulo*'s wife so as to convince Maria das Dores to abide by their sociocultural rules and not to defy society. Yet, the elder alerts the women to the fact that they are exiling the foreign woman, and proposes a new perspective on her. In order to support her argument, the elder tells all the other women one of the many myths that transverse the novel. All of these invoke the historical matrilineal tradition and maintain that at the beginning of everything, the world was ruled by visionary and forward-thinking women who, at some point, ended up having their power stolen by men:

> Os homens invadiram o nosso mundo — dizia ela — , roubaram-nos o fogo e o milho, e colocaram-nos num lugar de submissão. [...] Ó gente, ela veio de um reino antigo para resgatar o nosso poder usurpado. Trazia de novo o sonho da liberdade. (Chiziane 2008: 22)
>
> [Men have invaded our world — she said — stolen our fire and corn and put us in a place of submission. [...] Oh people, she came from an ancient kingdom to recover the power that was taken from us. She brought the dream of freedom back again.]

The recuperation and rediscovery of these myths forces the women to confront their own gender exile, their discontinuous female identity and the need to engage in the rewriting of their own *habitus*. Furthermore, it overlaps with both a retrieval of Zambezian history and its simultaneous revision. According to Newitt (1995: 217–42), the historical interweaving of different peoples in Zambézia led to the installation of a patriarchal tradition there, which in turn caused the corruption of the matrilineal ties that had always been a local institution. Hence, the novel proposes a retrospective look at the history of Zambézia as a cultural community so as to prove that it was built through the bodies of women:

> As mulheres violadas choravam as dores do infortúnio com sementes no ventre, e deram à luz uma nova nação. Os invasores destruíram os nossos templos, nossos deuses, nossa língua. Mas com eles construímos uma nova língua, uma nova raça. Essa raça somos nós. [...] Lembrem-se de que somos todos filhos do longe, como essa Maria que viram nas margens do rio. Lembrem-se sempre de que a nudez é expressão de pureza, imagem da antiga aurora. Fomos todos esculpidos com o barro do Namuli. Barro negro com sangue vermelho. (Chiziane 2008: 23–25)
>
> [The raped women wept over the pain of their misfortune with seeds in their wombs, and gave birth to a new nation. The invaders destroyed our temples, our gods, our language. But with them we built a new language, a new race. This race is us. [...] Remember that we are all children from afar, like that woman, Maria, that you saw on the riverbanks. Always remember that nudity is an expression of purity, the image of the ancient dawn. We were all carved out of the mud of the Namuli mountains. Black clay with red blood.]

It simultaneously advances the analysis of women's role in the mediation of race relations, and in the maintenance of the institutionalised racial spectrum throughout different historical and cultural moments in time, an investigation that needs to take the black woman as its point of departure. The examination of these important mechanisms will permit an untangling of what lies beneath racism and the techniques it uses to reproduce itself, ultimately leading to the disclosure of the conditions that ensure the crystallisation of certain social contexts and prevent social change from taking place.

Taking the aforementioned points into consideration, it is important not to forget the role of literature in the portrayal of this situation. The literary critic Pires Laranjeira (2008) asserts, with reference to the novel *Alegre Canto*, that the author has moved on from writing a novel to creating something that he calls *ficção ensaística* [fictional essay]:

> Vendo esse livro, atrevo-me a dizer que a autora, de facto, deixou de escrever um 'romance' e passou àquilo a que chamarei *ficção ensaística*. Não que ela queira demonstrar, em ficção, uma tese, que entre pela demonstração, como na velha narrativa naturalista, mas porque se trata de uma pungente expedição aos recessos da memória das mulheres do povo moçambicano, em forma de grande alegoria imaginativa sobre a mestiçagem, a hierarquia das raças, a vileza humana, o colonialismo, a manipulação de adultos e crianças, a mentira, o assassínio institucional sem culpa individual, a traição política e conjugal. Uma tragédia em força de exorcismo veemente. Nua e crua, sem romantismos ou ademanes cultistas, tão próprios de alguma literatura bem-comportada. (2008: 25)
>
> [Regarding this book, I would go as far as to say that the author didn't, in fact, write a 'novel' but instead produced what I shall call a *fictional essay*. This is not because she wants to demonstrate, through fiction, a thesis, that starts

> through demonstration, as in the old naturalist narrative. It is because the book engages in a harrowing delivery of the depths of the memory of Mozambican women, in the shape of a great imaginative allegory about miscegenation, racial hierarchy, human vileness, colonialism, the manipulation of adults and children, lies, institutional assassination without individual blame, political and marital betrayal. A tragedy by virtue of a vehement exorcism; naked and raw, without the romanticism and cultist affectations which are so typical of some well-behaved literature.]

Indeed, Laranjeira's assertion is partly correct, as the novel does have a very clear and straightforward ambition. Nevertheless, it is inaccurate to affirm that Chiziane does not produce a literary work in her decision to focus completely on a very specific sociocultural problematisation. This assertion deliberately ignores other parallel occurrences that take place in Chiziane's literary production, given that the literary dimension of any literary work emerges from the junction of various components, such as the linguistic and the ideological. For instance, it is important to highlight the author's writing of orality as a literary proposal, in the sense that it recuperates peripheral paradigms (of Bantu origin) and integrates them into the Western symbolic representation codes of the novel. Furthermore, the transnational thematic framework chosen and its approach are also relevant, because, as Leite reminds us, 'a grandeza de uma obra literária está na sua capacidade de ser simultaneamente local e global' [the greatness of a literary work lies in its ability to be both local and global].[16] Hence, Laranjeira's reduction of the novel's reading to its historical and social dimensions reproduces the legitimisation of a stereotypical approach to Chiziane's work, given that the author's work has proven to question, as well as represent, reality, simultaneously. As the author herself put it, 'contar uma história significa levar as mentes no voo da imaginação e trazê-las de volta ao mundo da reflexão' [telling a story means taking minds on a flight of imagination and bringing them back into the world of reflection] (Chiziane 2008: 21–22). Similarly, in the words that Neubauer and Geyer-Ryan (2000: 6–7) chose to define the contributions to the *Gendered Memories* volume, 'remembering via literature becomes [...] a quasi-Freudian archaeology, a reworking of the past that aims at reshaping identity in the present'. It is, therefore, important to focus on the way in which the act of remembering is conducted throughout the novel. As mentioned above, given that each of the four main female characters in the novel is immediately related to a specific historical moment and, thus, the evolution of their development can be read diachronically, the present study will analyse each of them as representative of an exile placed in the intersection between the exiles of gender and race throughout time.

Serafina

Although Maria das Dores is the first female character that we access, Serafina, her grandmother, is the first character that we need to look at within the genealogy. Serafina emerges as a female character who is representative of a very long period of time in which Zambézia was violently disturbed by the experience of slavery.

This experience took all the native black men away, leaving women with the responsibility of producing this work force, and providing all the conditions for foreigners to come and engage in all sorts of business in the region (the main ones being the trade of slaves, ivory and gold). In this particular context, the racial question emerges inevitably connected with class and gender issues for several reasons. Firstly, as Newitt (1995: 298–316) clearly points out, for many centuries Zambézia was controlled by the Afro-Portuguese and wealthy families of Indian origin who would also seek intermarriage with the local African wives. This meant that only a very specific part of the population would be enslaved, first, and contracted for labour later (either inside or outside the geographical limits of Mozambique). This was the indigenous black population, which was the poorest as well. In the words used in an 1898 report regarding labour legislation, 'the black and only the black can fertilize Africa' (1995: 384). Furthermore, women were considered to play a vital role in all contexts of expansion, as they were the main providers of the labour force, initially ensuring the maintenance of the slave trade, and later the labour recruitment for both the South African mines and the Rhodesian farms. Therefore, they were historically seen as very valuable, even becoming slaves and objects of trade between the traders (1995: 285). In spite of their relevance, black women were still poor and had to struggle for their survival. This means that the idea of 'improving their race' would be a very appealing one in the setting of the years of imperial mystique in which the 'empire-nation' divided the population into two different racial groups: the indigenous and the non-indigenous. For women — particularly after the Portuguese imperialist state took full charge of Mozambican affairs under *Estado Novo* — improving their race meant accessing better economic and life conditions, given that the lighter one became in the racial spectrum, the higher one could climb up the social ladder (Matos 2006: 148–59).

Regarding the character Serafina, she is markedly representative of this belief in racial improvement through a whitening process. It is important to begin by saying that her representation is not a constant one, as she evolves, thus changing her way of thinking according to the shifting perceptions of her own exile. As a black woman who knows little beyond this particular condition and all of its implications (belonging to the lowest social layer, due to both her underprivileged race and her disadvantaged gender), she is completely involved in the colonial economy — which, again, is the only one she knows. In order to survive and conform to the demands of colonial practices, she is forced to give up her three sons for slavery and her only daughter for prostitution. As a mother who saw her children being kidnapped and taken to other countries without any hope of ever returning home, the living experience of slavery made Serafina fully aware of her condition's limitations. In her perspective, these could only be surpassed temporarily through the rental of her daughter's body to white men. Although this gesture revealed her scorn for her own race, it also shows that she does not accept her condition silently, as she struggles to access the white people's world, even if temporarily, in order to achieve some kind of illusion of freedom which would enable her to bypass the unilateral nature of the colonial economy's laws. It is this urge to escape the inevitability of race that makes Serafina refuse to consent to Delfina and the black man José do Monte's wedding, in favour of miscegenation. In this highly stratified society, both the *mulato* and the white people have predefined places within the core of the imagined community, whereas the black population is immediately sent to the margins: 'ser negra é doloroso. Negro não tem deus nem pátria' [being a black woman is painful. Black people have no god or homeland.] (Chiziane 2008: 82). As such, they can only renegotiate that position through processes of physical, cultural and social whitening, such as miscegenation or assimilation. Having a child by a white man would, therefore, simultaneously represent an escape from the destiny of black people and access to the white world in the long run:

> Vamos, arranja um branco e faz filhos mestiços. Eles nunca são presos nem maltratados, são livres, andam à solta. Um dia também serão patrões e irão ocupar o lugar dos pais e a tua vida será salva, Delfina. Felizes as mulheres que geram filhos de peles claras porque jamais serão deportados. (2008: 97)
>
> [Come on, find yourself a white man and have mestizo children. They are never arrested or mistreated; they are free, they go unhindered. One day they will also be bosses and they will take their fathers' places, and your life will be saved, Delfina. Blessed are the women who bear fair skinned children, because they will never be deported.]

This strategy, exclusive to women, provided the guarantee of a more dignified life — even if that implied the child's rejection of the black mother in the future — and it simultaneously demonstrates the social relevance of the *mestiços* in this setting, at least compared to the black community. Hence, as an 'exile' who is jealous of the white and *mulato* stable social situation, Serafina feels the need to exile the black community in order to be able to imagine herself as socially ascendant and, thus, somehow established.

It is not until she becomes aware of the conditions under which the engagement between Delfina and José do Monte is going to take place that she has a change of heart. Her acceptance of the wedding arises, on the one hand, from the fact that the ceremony is to be carried out according to Portuguese religious tradition, which would enable a display of status before the black community. This mimicry would allow an approximation to the white people's world through an assimilative gesture that would immediately be recognised and interpreted by the black community as distinctive. On the other hand, marriage as an official institution, particularly with a black man, would erase the stigma of the black woman as the white man's sexual slave that hung over Delfina's body. As she starts reflecting on Delfina's choice, Serafina recognises her own lack of knowledge of the white community, as well as her fear of them. All that she knows about them concerns the material factors that emerge interconnected with their race, i.e. what they own and what they allow the black population to access, according to the networks of interests created. For that reason, there is a turning point in her behaviour at this stage, as she acknowledges the gap that exists between her own reality as a black woman, the white population's reality and even the dilemmas that the *mulatos* face in their everyday lives. The fact that the white population emerges as established and empowered makes them threatening in the eyes of Serafina, leading her to distrust other realities and value her own:

> Genro negro, netos negros, harmonia da família. Do futuro, só Deus sabe. Será que esses netos mulatos que tanto sonho, será que me iriam amar? Não me iriam desprezar? Talvez me ignorem por representar as raízes que se pretendem eliminadas. Foi melhor assim. (2008: 106)
>
> [A black son-in-law and black grandchildren mean harmony within the family. Only God knows what the future holds. Would these mulatto grandsons, who I dream of having, love me? Would they not despise me? Perhaps they would ignore me because I represent the roots that ought to be eliminated. It was better this way.]

This protectionist attitude towards her own race becomes Serafina's first step towards her imagination at the centre of the community as a black woman, through her descent and as opposed to the white population, which is something that she had never had the opportunity or the means to do before.

She finally learns not to hate her own race, and that becomes even clearer for this character in the aftermath of Delfina and José do Monte's official assimilation to Portuguese cultural identity. Through this process, the latter are forced to let go of their former identities as members of the black population and, thus, to break the link with their past, their ancestors and their lived and cultural experiences as black people. Serafina's awareness of the new situation's implications leads her to start dreaming of racial purity as the only means of achieving freedom from colonial power. In other words, the Portuguese dream of racial purity, which never gets to be fulfilled, ends up generating the black dream of racial purity, which would be at the origins of the liberation movement (2008: 145–48). Yet, this moment of revelation coincides with Delfina's disruption of the intergenerational transmission, which means that she is unable to absorb Serafina's new teachings, and by doing so, she inevitably prevents both Maria das Dores and Maria Jacinta, her daughters, from accessing them in the future.

Delfina

The complexity of this character, Delfina, arises from the fact that she provides the debate over the intersection of the categories of race, gender and class with a whole new dimension. She provides the *leitmotiv* for the greatest developments in the plot and in the lives of the other main characters. Having learnt from a very early age about the impact of racial distinction and the construction of social roles according to race in everyday life, Delfina inherits from Serafina a fascination with the lives of the white population. Being born into a family whose patriarch refuses to become assimilated, which would facilitate her integration into the whitening process, she dreams about becoming white herself, through marriage and miscegenation:

> No seu sonho é senhora e habita uma cidade de pedra. Com vestidos de renda. Criados tão pretos como ela que tratará como escravos. Um marido branco e filhas mulatas a quem irá pentear os cabelos lisos e amarrar com fitinhas de

> seda. Terá a grandeza das sinhás e das donas, apesar de ser negra, ela sente. Receberá favores do regime. As mulheres negras que casam com brancos sobem na vida. Comem bacalhau e azeitonas, tomam chá com açúcar, comem pão com manteiga e marmelada. (2008: 77–78)
>
> [In her dreams she is a lady and lives in a city of stone. She has lace dresses. And servants as black as she is, who she will treat as slaves. She has a white husband and mulatto daughters whose straight hair she will comb and tie with little silk ribbons. She feels that she will be as great as the *sinhás* and *donas*, despite being black. She will receive favours from the regime. Black women who marry white men get on in life. They eat cod and olives, drink tea with sugar, and eat bread with butter and marmalade.]

Delfina's dreams about becoming white are closely related with her need to access the material goods and privileges that are denied to the black population. Hence, she begins an escalating trajectory, with the help of three men, which in her imagination will ultimately allow her to achieve her total racial redemption. Having had her virginity sold to an old white man in exchange for a glass of wine, Delfina becomes a prostitute, thus accepting the condition of sexual object in order to escape the irredeemable poverty of black women. At this point in the text, the description of her body is imbued with motifs that clearly refer to the Zambezian land, which, once again, redirects us to the proximity and fusion between both histories, as they overlap and mutually constitute each other:

> Numa luta desigual, vale mais a pena a rendição que a resistência. [...] Prefiro oferecer as doçuras do meu corpo aos marinheiros e ganhar moedas para alimentar a ilusão de cada dia. A natureza deu-me um celeiro no fundo do meu corpo. Uma mina de ouro. Para explorá-la com trabalho duro, pensam que não trabalho? (2008: 81)
>
> [In an unequal struggle, surrendering is worth more than resisting. [...] I prefer to offer the sweetness of my body to sailors and earn coins to feed the illusion of each day. Nature gave me a barn deep in my body, a gold mine to exploit with hard work — do you think that I don't work?]

It is under these conditions that she meets and falls in love with José do Monte, a poor black man who works at a palm tree plantation and apparently has nothing to offer her. As mentioned before, given that their wedding is a Westernised celebration, their marriage appears in the eyes of the black population as the primary marker of Delfina and José do Monte's social detachment from the black margins. However, in the eyes of the local white female population it re-establishes both the power hierarchy amongst women and the racial equilibrium that had been disturbed and jeopardised before, when Delfina was a prostitute who could freely have relations with their white husbands (Castelo 2007: 283–330).

As for the character Soares, who represents the white male population in this particular setting, we learn that he has had a relationship with Delfina in the past and is the one who, along with his wife, organises and pays for the whole wedding celebration. This is quite a telling aspect if we take into consideration the fact that Soares will be the father of two of Delfina's children in the future. If, on the one hand, it suggests that Soares never intended to really give up seeing Delfina, on the other hand, it reveals an action, premeditated and calculated by Delfina, regarding the management of racial relations. Despite being in love with José, she confesses that she wants to get married in order to organise her own life, a process that involves different stages (Chiziane 2008: 110). Hence, José becomes the first stage of the process, as he turns out to be Delfina's ticket out of marginal blackness when he agrees to become assimilated — the only means available to him to engage in a whitening process. At this particular moment, only assimilation would enable them to acquire a higher social status. Therefore, José is compelled by Delfina to reject all his previous lived experiences as a black African so as to embrace Portuguese culture and identity, and to become a *sipaio* [sepoy; an indigenous soldier serving under Portuguese orders] and earn much more money than he would as a hired employee. Naturally, Delfina was not worried about José's moral issues regarding turning his back on others like himself: all she cares about are the goods that she will be able to access as she ascends socially. Although he finds it difficult to adjust to his new condition at the beginning, José ends up realising that that is the only way to ensure their survival and the maintenance of his wife, who completely embraces their new identity. He, thus, ends up following her example and goes through a process of transformation:

> Dos olhos do casal escorre o despertar dos assimilados. Caminhar de cabeça erguida e olhar o mundo do alto, mergulhando no prelúdio da História e tentando abortar o amanhã de liberdade. E José descobre que as folhas das palmeiras têm um verde-vivo e o voo das andorinhas é de plena liberdade. Delfina experimentou a sua saia longa, de seda, com entretela e forro. Gosta da sua nova imagem. Da imagem do seu José. (2008: 120)
>
> [The assimilated awakening flows before the couple's eyes. To walk with one's head held high and to look at the world from above, plunging into the prelude of history and trying to abort tomorrow's freedom. And José discovers that the palm tree leaves are a lush green and the flight of the swallows is completely free. Delfina tried on her long silk skirt with lining and buckram. She likes her new image. And her José's image as well.]

Although José faces a constant inner struggle throughout the adjustment to their new social reality (one that emerges from the fact that he must prey on his own race, to conform to the demands of the colonial enterprise), the same does not happen to Delfina. Completely detached from José's reality as a *sipaio*, she keeps on demanding more and more from him, always asking him for valuable goods, even when he leaves to go to war. When Maria das Dores is born to Delfina and José, an official intergenerational rupture occurs between Delfina and Serafina, as the former refuses to take part in any manifestation of a non-Portuguese culture demanded by the latter. Assimilation emerges, therefore, as the most disruptive form of identity subversion and alienation, even able to break the matrilineal lineage, which evidences Delfina's, and consequently her children's exile from their roots: 'A vida entre as gerações transformou-se nisto. Sempre discutindo ideias, vivências. Sem consenso. Pisando areia movediça na viagem ao desconhecido' [Life between generations has turned into this. Always discussing ideas, experiences, without any common ground. Stepping into quicksand on the journey into the unknown] (2008: 151). It also confirms their entrapment in an in-between place that prevents them from ever having a stable identity, as they are constantly faced with the limitations imposed by the colonial entity.

As they both evolve, the characters of José and Delfina engage in escalating searches for white power. He destroys everything and everyone who stands in his way to become the ultimate black whitened hero, whereas she does the same in order to overcome all racial and colour barriers. Hence, as he kills Moyo, his spiritual guide, she engages in a relationship with the white man Soares and gives birth to Maria Jacinta. Both seem to completely destroy the deepest marks of their black identification as they engage in social experiences that take them further and further away from their black origins. Delfina's calculated choice of acquiring a white lover and having his *mulato* child is actually a very interesting act in the novel, because at some point we realise that the encounter has been fed by different motivations. We know that she aimed to use miscegenation as a means to overcome socio-racial boundaries and escape the colonial control instituted to ensure the white supremacy of the metropolis. As Castelo (2007: 289–90) reminds us, *mestiçagem* was only common in Mozambique until the 1920s/1930s, because from that period on white women were sent to the colony as a strategy to ensure colonial control and continuity. As a result,

> A presença das mulheres brancas justificava que a comunidade dos colonos cerrasse ainda mais as suas fileiras, não tanto para precavê-las dos indígenas, mas para impedir que os homens brancos pusessem em causa a sua supremacia sexual e doméstica (vd, Stoler, 1989, p. 138 e 148), isto é, de reprodução biológica e social. (2007: 290)
>
> [The presence of white women justified the colonist community's decision to further close their ranks, not so much to take precautions against the indigenous, but to prevent white men from calling their sexual and domestic supremacy into question (see Stoler, 1989, pp. 138 and 148), that is, in terms of biological and social reproduction.]

Nevertheless, the colonial state was unsuccessful in its attempt to end mixed race relationships and, thus, ensure the eradication of *mestiçagem* as a threat to the stability of colonial power. It is, therefore, in the battle against Soares's white Portuguese wife that Delfina is able to affirm the supremacy of the subversive bio-social reproduction that she represents — thus anticipating the impossibility of the colonial regime's perpetuation through racial segregation — subsequently attaining a new identity through her *mulata* daughter. This new identity allows her to imagine herself and her family at the centre of the community, as in practice, the birth of the *mulata* would also rescue her black children from the *indigenato*: 'Por isso a mulher negra buscará um filho mulato. Para aliviar o negro da sua pele como quem alivia as roupas de luto' [That is why the black woman will seek a mulatto child. To ease the black from her skin, like someone easing their mourning clothes] (Chiziane 2008: 184).

If on the one hand we recognise that Delfina successfully subverts colonial power, on the other hand we learn that the encounter between Delfina and Soares is provoked by José's superiors in the army. We come to understand that José becomes so good at performing his tasks as a *sipaio* that he actually becomes a threat to the social hierarchy. That is the reason why his sergeant decides that the only means to restrain his rising trajectory is to remind him of his inferiority, something which can only be achieved through the domestication of his ego. Indeed, Delfina proves to be the easiest and most efficient way to attack José. When he sees the *mulata* baby child, José is confronted with the reality of his wife's betrayal with his white boss. He is thus doubly attacked, in both his gender and race, and after considering suicide, he vanishes only to reappear at the end of the novel as the mute cook who rescues Delfina from her solitude. In this setting, the subversive power of mixed-race relations and, of course, the reproduction of the uneven racial powers at work within them are being used by the official colonial entity in order to ensure the maintenance of colonial domination. In the eyes of the black man, miscegenation appears as the most irrefutable proof of his disempowerment before the white man, whose power is reassured; the black wife, who herself goes through a whitening process that revokes his reproductive power; and the *mulata* child, to whom he will never be more than a subordinate, according to the racial spectrum. Nevertheless, it is important to add that regardless of being a solution which served the purposes of the regime in the short term, miscegenation was precisely what would help to bring an end to it, as the impossibility of its eradication in the long term represented the unfeasibility of the colonial dream of uniformisation (Castelo 2007: 290). Due to their positioning in the socio-racial hierarchy, which entailed both privileges and limitations, the *mestiço* middle classes ended up becoming some of the earliest anti-colonialist and nationalist thinkers, who formed an active opposition to the colonial regime (Gentili 1999: 276).

With the help of Simba, who was a sorcerer and her former pimp, Delfina is able to scare Soares's white wife away back to Portugal and occupies her place in the household, the ultimate step to climb on the whitening ladder. In Delfina's imagination, she and her own family are now at the core of what she believes to be the imagined community. This movement, which implies access to the world where the white population lives and to the kind of lifestyle it has, leads her to perceive herself as being white, regardless of her true colour:

> Minha preta, negrinha. Uma expressão ofensiva, humilhante, redutora. Porque já tinha ultrapassado as fronteiras de uma negra. Ela já tinha um homem branco e filhos mulatos. Ela já falava bom português e tinha a pele clareada pelos cremes e cabeleira postiça. Sou preta, sim, mas só na pele. Já sou mais do que uma preta, casei com um branco! (Chiziane 2008: 225)
>
> [My negro, little black woman. An offensive, humiliating, reductionist expression. Because she had already crossed the boundaries of what it means to be a black woman. She already had a white man and mulatto children. She already spoke good Portuguese; her skin had been made fairer by creams and she had fake hair. Yes, I'm a negro, but only through my skin. I'm already more than just a negro woman, I married a white man!]

It is the access to the material aspect of whiteness that leads her to affirm herself to be white, regardless of Soares's constant reminders of her racial origins, which I shall return to later. As such, entering the white world causes the reproduction of the white world's principles, which means that from that moment on, the racial structure imposed by the white colonial regime is reproduced within the domestic sphere of Delfina's household — the public racial conflict then becomes private and familial as well. Having had two black children (Maria das Dores and Zezinho) with José and another two mulatto children with Soares (Maria Jacinta and Luisinho), Delfina proceeds to the reorganisation of the domestic space by diminishing the importance of the former and praising the latter. Hence, due to her lower racial status, Maria das Dores, the eldest daughter, becomes the housekeeper:

> — Maria das Dores, esfrega-me os calcanhares e corta-me as unhas dos pés.
> — Sim, mãe.
> — Agora traz os meu chinelos, a minha toalha, a vaselina, traz o pente, traz o creme.
> — Estão aqui, mãe.
> — Vê se a mesa está posta, vê se a Jacinta comeu, se o Luisinho dormiu.
> — Sim, mãe. (2008: 228)
>
> ['Maria das Dores, rub my heels and cut my toenails.'
> 'Yes, mother.'
> 'Now bring me my slippers, my towel, the Vaseline; bring the comb, and bring the cream.'
> 'Here they are, mother'.
> 'Check if the table is set; check if Jacinta has eaten, and if Luisinho is asleep.'
> 'Yes, mother.']

Her life begins to mirror her mother's, as she is a constant reminder to Delfina that she cannot escape her race, which might also explain her mother's urge to sacrifice Maria das Dores whenever it is necessary.

It is at this point that Delfina's life as an imagined white woman reaches its peak, subsequently starting to collapse. This collapse begins when Soares decides to abandon her and return to his former white family, in Portugal. We understand that since he assumed a relationship with Delfina, Soares has had to deal with all sorts of charges from a regime that regarded miscegenation and 'cafrealisation' (the acculturation of the Portuguese in the African context) as highly disruptive and worthy of condemnation. He proves himself able to face all of these difficulties, but fails to deal with his own image mirrored in Delfina. His need to constantly reaffirm Delfina's blackness rises out of the need to crystallise an image that is reassuring to him as a white colonial subject. However, the confrontation with everything that he represented within his own household and with Delfina's mimicry of his whiteness causes an insurmountable estrangement in Soares. As Delfina's mental state of detachment towards her predefined identity — or, in other words, her 'insílio' — deepens, Soares's exile widens (Herrera 2001: xxii). Suddenly, he is fully aware of himself as a foreigner and starts feeling nostalgic about his white ex-wife: 'Somos ambos emigrantes, Delfina. Eu, da Europa para esta Zambézia. E tu saindo de ti para parte nenhuma. Nenhum de nós tem poiso seguro' [We are both immigrants, Delfina. I, going from Europe to this Zambézia. And you, coming out of yourself and going nowhere. Neither of us have a safe haven] (Chiziane 2008: 228). He therefore decides to go back to Portugal, leaving his mixed-race family behind, in a gesture that predicts the inevitable disintegration of the colonial structure. Soares's choice has major consequences for Delfina, because in the absence of the white husband, the black whitened woman becomes disempowered, left alone within her blackness once again. This means that she is once again unable to attain all the commodities of the white world, given that she has no job, and no husband to provide for her. Nor does she have any inheritance, as Soares has left it only for the four children to access on their emancipation. Delfina, thus, becomes one of the assets that the white population leaves behind on their departure, which is to be fought for and redistributed amongst those who remain in the land. For this reason, in the aftermath of Soares's departure, a *sipaio* who has been paid to avenge Delfina and Soares's defiance of the colonial society's rules invades Delfina's household and reclaims it as his own: 'Já não tens dono, Delfina, o teu branco foi-se embora, não volta mais. O teu dono sou eu a partir de hoje. Temos que dividir o dinheiro do branco. Queres segurança? Protejo-te. Queres briga? Esmurro-te. Queres um confronto? Mato-te' [You no longer have a master, Delfina. Your white man has gone, and will not return. From today onwards, I am your owner. We have to split the money from the white man. Do you want safety? I will protect you. Do you want a fight? I will punch you. Do you want a showdown? I will kill you] (2008: 237).

As the representative of a very successful whitening process (that involved the rejection of black marginality and the reclaiming of commodities that should only be available to white people), Delfina had to be sacrificed for the sake of the continuity of the colonial society's dream. Nevertheless, she ends up poisoning this *sipaio* and turning to her friend Simba for assistance once again, in order to attempt to bring Soares back from Portugal. Delfina's *insílio* prevents her from being able to have a stable identity, as she is trapped between two worlds which she does not want or cannot belong to anymore. As a result, she struggles to keep hold of what is left of the white world so that she is not forced to go back to the black margins. Indeed, it is the fear of recognising herself in Maria das Dores that leads her to sell her daughter's virginity to Simba in exchange for a spell that can bring Soares back — or in other words, in exchange for a temporary illusion of power. Delfina ends up reproducing the same colonial economy through which her mother had sold her virginity in the past, in a final attempt to maintain her social status, which did not correspond to her race:

> Na sua terra a mulher é peça que se compra e se vende. Selo de contrato. Moeda de troca. Hipoteca. Multa. Sobrevivência. Ela também foi usada pela própria mãe, na infância distante. Entregue aos brancos das lojas a troco de comida. (2008: 243)
>
> [In her homeland, women are items that can be bought and sold. They are the seals affixed to contracts. Exchange currencies. Mortgages. Fines. Means of survival. She too was used by her own mother throughout her distant childhood. Handed to the white shop owners in exchange for food.]

With his mind set on Maria das Dores's inheritance, Simba tricks Delfina and kidnaps her daughter after deflowering her. Delfina's loss of Maria das Dores is also the loss of herself, all of her other children, her servant and the access to Maria das Dores's inheritance: it is the dismembering of the family as well of Delfina's dream of achieving the ultimate whiteness. Simultaneously, it represents another intergenerational disruption in the matrilineal lineage, as the bond between the mother and the eldest daughter is destroyed, only to be mended twenty-five years later. From this moment on, Delfina engages in the mediation between the black and the white worlds by exploiting the gender economy. To do this, she builds a brothel where she sells the virginity of young black girls to white men, under the aegis of the myth of racial improvement. In other words, Delfina proceeds to the creation of her own 'miscegenation machine'. Oddly enough, her open investment in miscegenation backfires when Maria Jacinta turns her back on her, rejecting her for what she has done to Maria das Dores (her much beloved sister), for everything that she represents, and for all the lessons on racial hierarchy that she forced upon her children. The *mulata* child's rejection of the black mother is another intergenerational disruption, one that in the novel is not revoked.

Maria das Dores

Indeed, the analysis of this third generation of women reveals new dynamics in the intersection of gender and race. Looking at the interesting trajectory of the character Maria das Dores, we have access to the metaphorisation of a very specific black female experience in Zambézia. As mentioned above, when we first meet Maria das Dores she is naked, bathing on the edge of the Licungo River, ignorant of the social rules that prevent women from doing this in a space which is reserved for men only. This ignorance of behavioural norms and of her own body as a cultural subject arises from her loss of memory, or incapacity to remember events diachronically. Although she can remember certain aspects of her own life, they appear discontinuously, as if fragmented in her head. They are reminiscences of what her identity might be, according to the social roles she used to perform as a daughter, as a mother, as a sister and as a wife — but never as a whole woman. It is possible to affirm, indeed, that she is ignorant of what any notion of feminine identity might be. Appearing, at this point, in the eyes of the community as a mentally ill woman due to her transgressive behaviour, Maria das Dores's freedom exposes the other women's confinement within a predefined gender identity. This is why they want her to masquerade as a woman in order to eliminate her difference:

> — Maria, tens que te vestir.
> — Para quê?
> — Para te protegeres e seres igual às outras mulheres.
>
> A nudez de Maria era o regresso ao estado de pureza. Da transparência. As mulheres ficam escandalizadas porque o nu de uma se reflecte no corpo da outra. (2008: 33)

['Maria, you must get dressed.'
'What for?'
'To protect yourself and to be like other women.'
Maria's nudity was the return to the state of purity, of transparency. The women are shocked because the nakedness of one woman is reflected in the body of another.]

Hence, when she engages in this journey in which she attempts to return to her mother's womb, she is, by analogy, attempting to recover a gender identity that is strange for her in the beginning, due to her amnesia. Simultaneously, she is proceeding to the cartography of female memory through the recuperation of a female genealogy within the matrilineal Zambezian context, with all the racial inheritance that this move will necessarily reveal.

The first accounts of Maria das Dores's life come to us in the form of fragments that she remembers, but we only learn about the most significant parts of her past through her family history, that is through the voices of the narrator and remaining characters. She, therefore, rarely intervenes in the telling of her own history, one that reaches us through a collective memory in this first instance. It is also important to point out that the marks on her body — which are equivalent to the slaves' tattoos — also speak for her: 'No corpo desenhando-se o mapa da terra. Da aldeia. Da linhagem. Em cada traço uma mensagem. Árvore genealógica' [The map of the land is drawn on her body. Of the village. Of the lineage. There is a message on each line. The whole family tree] (2008: 31). The reading of these tattoos not only unveils the identities of a female genealogy, but it also reveals the geographic, political, and identity map of the community as it appears printed on women's bodies. Born in 1953 to an assimilated family, Maria das Dores is Delfina and José's firstborn child. Raised by both of them in the reality of assimilation, she has access to all of the commodities that were made available to this social group by the colonial state (the fact that she was born at a hospital for white people, for example, is indicative of that) and is unaware of any social hierarchies. It is not until José abandons the family, to be replaced by Soares, the white father who raises her, that Maria das Dores becomes aware of the reality of racial demarcation. Actually, when she describes her memories of both houses — the black father's and the white father's — the former appears surrounded by fantasy and pleasure, in an environment of unfinished projects, whereas the latter is imbued with feelings of sadness and solitude that suggest a harsh reality, despite it being a more expensive and more beautiful house:

> Recorda a casa do pai preto. De forma cónica, como um cogumelo dos contos da Alice no País das Maravilhas. Árvores frondosas e um verde muito verde. Mosquitos. Comida com fartura. Risos e sonhos. Felicidade pura. A casa do pai branco, muito bela. No bairro dos brancos. Com janelas largas e vidro fosco. E jardim com muitas flores. Electricidade. Mobílias mais altas que as pessoas, que à noite se confundiam com os fantasmas. Comida boa, e muita tristeza. (2008: 49)
>
> [She remembers the house of the black father. Conical, like a mushroom from the tales of Alice in Wonderland. Leafy trees and a very lush green. Mosquitoes.

> Plenty of food. Laughter and dreams. Pure happiness. The house of the white father was very beautiful. Located in the white neighbourhood. With wide windows and frosted glass. And a garden with lots of flowers. Electricity. Furniture taller than people, which at night could be mistaken for ghosts. Good food and a lot of sadness.]

The description of the house of the black father is rendered in a somehow essentialist fashion, associating it with a state of purity that precedes the arrival of the white father and, thus, of the conflict. His arrival is described in materialistic terms, as the emphasis is put on all of the goods that the family could suddenly access. Furthermore, it has negative connotations, from Maria das Dores's point of view, because from that moment on, her mother institutes a hierarchy according to race within the household, which was something that Maria had never experienced before. In the urge to delete her own blackness and difference through an economic and social makeover, Delfina sets out to act as the white population would. In order to do this, she transposes the public racial conflict into the household, where the black father's children must be sacrificed. Indeed, Maria das Dores is exiled between two worlds: one that she knew before and will never be able to return to, where she was central; and a second one, that is highly exclusive, to which she is marginal. In this world where she is raised, Maria is the reflection of everything that Delfina wishes to eliminate in herself and, therefore, she becomes her mother's main target. She becomes threatening to Delfina because she does not allow her to imagine herself as being fully successful in her whitening process. Hence, Delfina does not bring her daughter with her in this social ascension. Rather she prefers to exile Maria because to do so will reinforce her own identity. Maria thus acquires both forms of exile, given that it is due to both her race and her gender that she occupies the lowest position in the hierarchy. In addition, since labour tasks are defined in the public sphere according to race, as well as studying, she must take on the role of servant within the household, taking care of everything and everyone as a true housekeeper.

The black mother's selection of the mulatto children to the detriment of the black ones is merely a strategic choice, as in her imagination the former will mediate her entrance and guarantee her permanency in the white population's world. In order to reach this goal, Delfina will sacrifice Maria das Dores; she will end up reproducing the action of Serafina (who had previously sold Delfina's virginity in exchange for a temporary illusion of empowerment). Interestingly, the business is conducted with a black man this time around, the sorcerer Simba, who, despite his cruel behaviour towards Maria, earns a place in the dysfunctional family that emerges at the end of the novel, as will be discussed later on. Pretending to be willing to help Delfina in her quest, he steals one of the most obvious means to access the economic privileges of the white world from her, given that he is the one who will now manage Maria's inheritance. Delfina is, thus, progressively buried in the inevitability of her blackness, from which she cannot escape anymore. Using Maria to get his revenge on Delfina, Simba kidnaps her at the age of thirteen and forces her to become his wife. Hence, Maria is forced to move from her mother's house to that of Simba, in a trajectory that annuls the premises of matrilocality and reinstitutes the economy of gender that places women in a fragile place of inferiority. Furthermore, she is forced to deal with a tyrannical husband and his two wives in a polygamous marriage framework, in which, again, she is in a subjected position as the youngest and most recent wife. After years of torture, Maria is able to finally escape Simba's household, bringing along her three children: Benedito, Fernando and Rosinha. Although they all survive the difficult journey, they are taken to a hospital for treatment and, in a moment of mental alienation, Maria das Dores ends up losing her children. Due to this loss, she spends years trying to find them. The more we learn about Maria das Dores, the stronger and more individualised her voice becomes, and the less fragmented and more consistent her story becomes. Finally, as the narrative evolves, she starts verbalising her own story, proposing an individualised stance, as opposed to the collective one that was more frequent before, in a gesture which is characteristic of Chiziane's work. Interestingly, Maria's memory returns with the mediation of her children Benedito and Fernando. They assume responsibility for recuperating a memory which is also a genealogy. This retrieval of the past by the last generation of the family is very significant if we take into account the message of the novel, which clearly emphasises the need for the younger generations to question, scrutinise and acknowledge a past that inevitably conditions the place that they occupy in the present; in Sanches's words, 'the contemporary reworking of a common past, as history, or memory, in order to make sense of the postcolonial condition' (2007: 131). Hence, when the dysfunctional family reunites at the end of the novel — Delfina, José do Monte, Simba, Maria das Dores, Benedito, and Fernando — there are two important aspects to highlight. The first aspect concerns a genealogical recovery and re-establishment of the matrilineal lineage. The intergenerational connection that was interrupted when Delfina exiled Maria das Dores is once again restored when the former reattributes her inheritance to the latter, one which proceeds from the money that Delfina gathered herself, from the day that Maria left her mother's house, and not from the white father's assets. There is, therefore, not only a return to an essentialist state of purity in the sense that the white man does not interfere in the patrimonial transference, but also the recovery of the matrilineal lineage, through a power transference from mother to eldest daughter.

At this point it is worth mentioning as well that it is not until Delfina and Maria das Dores come to terms with each other that the latter is called solely *Maria* for the first time in the novel, thus assuming a new identity which excludes *das Dores* [of Sorrows]. By doing so, she is embracing her black womanhood and detaching herself from the condition of entrapment between two realities. Simultaneously, the fact that Maria's two sons, and not her daughter, are the ones who mediate their mother's process of memory recovery indicates, in parallel, the establishment of a lineage which despite invoking a disrupted patrilineal tradition, combines harmoniously with the matrilineal lineage, which, in turn, calls upon a Zambezian tradition of cultural miscegenation. The second aspect to highlight regarding the dysfunctional family that emerges at the end of the novel, with prospects of continuity, refers to the absence of the *mulata*. Indeed, this absence, although it is justified in the novel, provides the constitution of the new family emerging in 'the post period' (postcolonial, post-independence and post-civil war) with a certain essentialism: 'Queremos agora celebrar a reunificação da família. [...] Esqueçam as lutas antigas e enfrentem as novas. Selemos agora o pacto de coabitação. Construímos o novo mundo, vamos fortificá-lo' [We want to celebrate the reunification of the family now. [...] Forget about the old struggles and face the new ones. Let us seal the cohabitation pact now. We have built the new world, let us fortify it] (2008: 330). Hence, there is, again, the suggestion that in spite of accepting and making peace with its history of miscegenation, harmonising coexistence within the new family cannot be inclusive of it. In other words, harmonisation is only possible at an intergenerational level, but not at an interracial one, which leads us to the analysis of Maria Jacinta, the *mulata* daughter.

Maria Jacinta

Ever since the day she was born — or we could even say ever since the day she was projected to be born — Maria Jacinta was defined solely by her race: 'Do interior da casa de José, o choro de uma recém-nascida rasga espaços como salvas de canhão. Os soluços dela têm a sonoridade de comando, característica das crianças que nascem para governar o mundo' [From inside José's house, the cry of a newborn fills the air like cannon salutes. Her sobs sound like commands, a defining characteristic of children who are born to rule the world] (2008: 181). As a *mulata*, she has a consistent (albeit often limited) connection with both the white and the black worlds. Those connections allow her to have direct access to a lifestyle that escapes the constraints of both the white and the black worlds, due to its location in a grey zone of power. It is precisely due to her positioning on this intermediary platform that the *mulata* becomes the materialisation of the conflict between two opposed worlds — what is praise-worthy miscegenation (or racial improvement) for the black population becomes contemptible 'cafrealisation' (or racial disfigurement) for the white population. She is permanently exiled in between two worlds, and condemned to be perceived according to the amount of power that she has in each one of them. She, thus, exists on a platform which is neither margin nor centre, and therefore, cannot be territorialised:

> Diante dos pretos chamavam-lhe branca. E não queriam brincar com ela. Afastavam-na, falavam mal da mãe e diziam nomes feios. Diante dos brancos chamavam-lhe preta. Também corriam com ela, falavam mal da mãe e chamavam-lhe nomes feios. Um dilema que crescia na sua cabecinha: afinal de contas, qual é o meu lugar? Porque é que eu tenho de me ficar entre as duas raças? Será que tenho que criar um mundo meu, diferente, marginal, só com indivíduos da minha raça? (2008: 247)
>
> [The black kids called her white. And they did not want to play with her. They would exclude her, speak ill of her mother, and call her names. The white kids called her black. They would also push her away, speak ill of her mother, and call her names. A dilemma was growing in her mind: in the end, what is my place? Why do I have to be stuck between the two races? I wonder if I will

> have to create a world of my own, different, marginal, where only individuals of my own race exist?]

Due to this experience, Maria Jacinta learns from an early age that the concept of race corresponds to demarcation and hierarchy, and she suffers because that conceptualisation entraps her in a racial limbo. She, therefore, hates both her white father and her black mother for having transgressed the instituted behavioural norms and created a human being who, apparently, cannot be culturally defined.

In the aftermath of the departure of the white father and Maria das Dores, Maria Jacinta rebels against the black mother. As the materialisation of Delfina's successful engagement in the process of whitening, Jacinta comes back to haunt her for all the things that she did in order to achieve this status of temporary whiteness. Interestingly, when Maria Jacinta affirms that she suffers due to Maria das Dores's absence, in her head the latter is not just the beloved sister who used to take care of her. She is also the openly needed and much missed servant, who ensures the maintenance of the household. Therefore, in the eyes of Jacinta, Maria das Dores is always a black woman, who performs certain service tasks due to her race. The way she looks at the members of her family is inevitably conditioned by the way she is taught to envision the world. Thus, when she abandons Delfina's household, taking her two brothers Luisinho and Zezinho with her, she leaves the black margins decisively behind in order to integrate into the white world as deeply as possible. This suggests that although she was trapped between two worlds, she could, to a certain extent, choose which world she wanted to live in. In this context, her choice might be read as strategic. When, at the age of nineteen, Jacinta gets married to a white man, she completely fulfils her mother's dream of whitening through her daughter. Yet, at the moment of its accomplishment, the dream loses its utopian aspect and backfires to attack Delfina. At the altar, Jacinta repeats all the discourses of demarcation that Delfina had taught her in the past, leading the latter to confront her own blackness, which returns to haunt her in the shape of Jacinta's whitened reflection.

O Alegre Canto da Perdiz: Conclusion

Alegre Canto is, indeed, a novel that aims at gendering the communal memory of the nation by recovering marginalised female experiences from within the province of Zambézia. It recuperates a female genealogy through the construction of four complex female characters — Serafina, Delfina, Maria das Dores and Maria Jacinta — as representative of four distinct exiles which develop in the intersection between the exiles of gender and race and are attached to different moments in time. In the novel, the recuperation of Zambezian history is a process which entails not only the recovery of black women's experiences in specific historical moments, but also the retrieval and problematisation of the memory of miscegenation.

It is important to observe that ultimately the novel successfully portrays the territorialisation of miscegenation, thus recuperating Maria Jacinta and, by extension, Eva in *Niketche* as well from both the racial and cultural limbo in which they were trapped as *mulatas*:

> Sou de todos e de ninguém. Sou diferente e igual. Amai-me e odiai-me, à altura da vossa paixão e da vossa raiva, mas atenção: sou vossa, eu vos pertenço! Esta é a minha terra. Aqui é o meu céu e este o chão dos meus antepassados. (2008: 323)
>
> [I belong to everyone and to no one. I am different and the same. Love me and hate me, with all your passion and all your anger, but know this: I am yours, I belong to you! This is my land. This is my sky and this is the ground of my ancestors.]

Nonetheless, the notion of community that emerges by the end of both novels (in the shape of the new monogamous families in *Niketche* and the dysfunctional family in *Alegre Canto*) does not incorporate the *mulata*. As such, in *Alegre Canto* there is, therefore, a repetition of the essentialist ending that characterises *Niketche*, suggesting that despite being part of the nation and having an irrefutable place in it, the *mulato* is yet to be incorporated into the ideal post-independence, post-internal conflict and post-Marxist community, which is black.

Conclusion to Chapter 2

The analysis of Chiziane's literary works *Ventos do Apocalipse*, *Niketche: Uma História de Poligamia* and *O Alegre Canto da Perdiz* demonstrates that the author proposes portrayals of the post-independence ideal of Mozambican national narrative, from a female point of view, in order to deconstruct it and expose its limitations, therefore reopening the debate on *Moçambicanidade* in the post-Marxist era. In the novels, discourses of community appear as utopian, as the author demonstrates their propensity for exile through the recuperation of voices and experiences that have no place in them. In other words, Chiziane focuses on their utopian nature by revealing and analysing the dystopias they generate throughout their processes of legitimisation and survival. The study of these literary works through the lens of Said's theorisation on exile, as well as Herrera's proposal of internal exile has enabled us to expose myriad experiences of exile within the geographical limits of the Mozambican nation, according to Chiziane's perception. Furthermore, the application of these theories to the specific Mozambican context and to Chiziane's particular project allows us to identify the limitations presented by those theories, as their problematisation opened up various possibilities.

In *Ventos*, the emphasis is placed on exile as an internal condition, a mental state of detachment towards an imposed communal imaginary that occurs within the geographical limits of the nation, as Chiziane portrays the precarious living conditions of the rural population throughout the internal conflict in the country. If on the one hand this portrayal demonstrates that exile can be a potential place for the renegotiation of identity, on the other hand it reveals that exile, like nationhood, is not uniformly experienced by all members of the imagined community. This perception reveals one of the limitations of Said's theorisation as regards its application to the particular contexts under analysis — that is, its failure to focus on gender as a form of exile. Hence, Chiziane's reflection not only sheds light on women's continuous exile within both patriarchal experiences of nationalism and exile, but also illuminates the fact that gender as a form of exile is experienced differently, according to variants such as race, colour, class and ethnicity. The complexity of these layers within gender exile exposes other power structures in operation within it, which ultimately come to impose hierarchies and define identity representations amongst women.

In both *Niketche* and *Alegre Canto*, the focus on women's marginality in male-oriented conceptualisations of the nation runs parallel to the observation of the power dynamics occurring within the experience of gender exile, in a continuous effort to dismantle these structures and propose new conceptions of identity in/and collectivity. In *Niketche*, notwithstanding the differences in terms of ethnicity, culture, origin and even age between the official wife and the unofficial ones, they manage to find a balance amongst themselves, which emerges from their common race, as well as their common experience and subsequent condition of exile in relation to the patriarchal polygamous husband. Nonetheless, the insertion of the *mulata* character Eva in this context comes to disrupt that fragile equilibrium, thus demonstrating the existence of a racial power structure (which corresponds to a class structure as well) within gender and, simultaneously, allowing miscegenation to arise as problematic in the negotiation of the cultural imagination of the nation. Eva's exclusion from the polygamous family, the women's escape from the polygamous patriarchal surveillance and their subsequent celebration of their successful redefinition of the national map (through the affirmation of their cultural differences) demonstrates that the *mulata*'s representation is not updated. Her female peers' celebration of womanhood in its difference is exclusively black, therefore not allowing the *mulata* to be rescued from exile.

The complexities of miscegenation, as well as racial divides within gender, are analysed in depth by Chiziane in *Alegre Canto*. Through the recovery of a generational lineage of Zambezian women, the author not only reintegrates women's memories into the macro-history of the nation, but also forces that macro-history to reconfigure itself by incorporating other experiences of the nation that go beyond the limits of the politically dominant southern history. Considering the historical and cultural specificities of the Zambezian context, miscegenation emerges in Chiziane's perception as a story that is inscribed in women's bodies — therefore, it is told through the recovery of diachronically organised female memories. On the one hand, as women's continuous exile in relation to men (in colonial and postcolonial contexts) unravels, the voicing of these silenced memories gradually leads to the redemption of the female characters. On the other hand, as the intricacies of the dynamics between gender and race (and, of course, class) are untangled in their specific historical context, we come to realise that this redemption only extends to black women (and black men as well), as again the *mulata* character, Maria Jacinta, is excluded from the new national family which is proposed by Chiziane at the end of the novel. Again, we are led to believe that although Chiziane's portrayal suggests the need for the macro-history of the nation to come to terms with its history of miscegenation, ultimately the 'national family' which emerges from the identity negotiations is black. Hence, gender exile, and women's refusal of it, are not, indeed, consistently experienced in Chiziane's perception, as the *mulata* is still to be rescued from the margins.

Notes to Chapter 2

1. The first part of the title is borrowed from the title of Chapter 6 of the work by Guibernau (1996).
2. Henceforth referred to as *Ventos*, *Niketche* and *Alegre Canto*. All translations from the Portuguese of Chiziane's *Niketche* (2002) from this point are by David Brookshaw (Chiziane 2016), who has recently translated this work under the title *The First Wife: A Tale of Polygamy*.
3. Arnfred (2011: xvi) defines *lobolo* as follows: 'usually translated as "bride price", but better translated as "traditional marriage" in the patrilineal south of Mozambique. Without *lobolo* the ancestral spirits are not informed about the marriage, and the children do not properly belong'.
4. In the process of bringing about a socialist revolution and a New Society, Frelimo created the re-education centres. These were centres in which 'dissidents' could learn to adjust to the paradigms of New Men and New Women. Very little is known or has been published to date about these centres, or the duration of the project. Having traced the theme in the local and foreign press at the time, historian Colin Darch (2010) notes that the announcement of the project took place in November 1974, and its suspension in late 1981. President Samora Machel was a firm believer in the value of the re-education centres, but he suspended the project after a tour of the Cabo Delgado province, in which he observed various problems with the way the centres were functioning.
5. The *timbila* is a xylophone traditionally associated with the Chopi communities from the south of the Inhambane province, in southern Mozambique. In 2008, the Chopi *timbila* was inscribed on the Representative List of the Intangible Cultural Heritage of Humanity (UNESCO 2008).
6. 'Do Rovuma ao Maputo' was a slogan created by Frelimo with reference to their intention of freeing the entire country, given that the Rovuma river is at the extreme north of the country and the Maputo river is at the extreme south, thus conveying the idea of the geographical territory of Mozambique as a whole. It also appears in both of the National Anthems that Mozambique has had to date: 'Viva, Viva a Frelimo' [Long Live Frelimo], from 1975 to 2002, and 'Pátria Amada' [Beloved Homeland], adopted in 2002 to reflect the multiparty era.
7. Bourdieu (2010: 166) defines habitus as follows: 'the habitus is necessity internalized and converted into a disposition that generates meaningful practices and meaning-giving perceptions; it is a general, transposable disposition, which carries out a systematic, universal application — beyond the limits of what has been directly learnt — of the necessity inherent in the learning conditions... Because different conditions of existence produce different habitus — systems of generative schemes applicable, by simple transfer, to the most varied areas of practice — the practices engendered by the different habitus appear as systematic configurations of properties expressing the differences objectively inscribed in conditions of existence in the form of systems of differential deviations which, when perceived by agents endowed with the schemes of perception and appreciation necessary in order to identify, interpret and evaluate their pertinent features, function as life-styles.'
8. A *capulana* is a piece of cloth made of cotton, which is used by women all over Mozambique and wrapped around their bodies as a skirt. According to Arnfred (2011: xv), 'in the coastal culture of northern Mozambique *capulanas* are sold in pairs, one to be used as a skirt and (part of) the other as a scarf'.
9. According to Nordstrom (1997: 40), 'the physical harm, plus the severe psychological, socio-cultural, and interpersonal traumas provoked by the war, have prompted many Mozambicans to refer to the children born during the post-independence war years as the "lost-generation"'.
10. Mondlane (1983: 43–44) states that agricultural annual wages were the following (in *escudos*): white people — 47,723.00; coloured [i.e. mixed race] — 23, 269.10; assimilated Africans — 5,478.00; unassimilated Africans — 1,404.00. In terms of industrial daily wages, they were as

follows: white (unqualified) — 100.00 minimum; coloured (unqualified) — 70.00 maximum; Africans (semi-skilled) — 30.00 maximum; Africans (unskilled) — 5.00 maximum.

11. When mentioning these numbers, the author does not specify the year in which the data was collected. Hence, we assume that the percentage refers to the year in which the book was first written, i.e. 1969.
12. It is important to highlight that despite not being institutionalised, the social mechanisms of racial distinction which run parallel to the institutionalised ones, such as assimilation, were equally effective. Community surveillance, for example, which was carried out by the colonists regarding the colonised, is a move that replicates an intragroup exile, in the sense that it requires the members of the same group — the colonists — to keep an eye on each other so as to prevent infractions that will result in social exclusion.
13. According to Arnfred (2011: 40–47) kinship relations follow matrilineal lines in the provinces of Niassa, Cabo Delgado, Nampula, Zambézia and the north of Tete. The central provinces of Manica, Sofala and the south of Tete follow patrilineal lines, as do the southern provinces of Gaza, Inhambane and Maputo.
14. On *xitique* and the re-inscription of this traditional savings scheme in modern economy by women, see Owen (2007b: 190–91).
15. A good example of this would be, for instance, the construction of the great Afro-Portuguese households through reproduction, from the sixteenth to the twentieth centuries, which would ensure the survival of the community (Newitt 1995: 127–385).
16. Oral communication given at the VIVA of Elena Brugioni at Universidade do Minho, on 4 June 2009.

CHAPTER 3

Women in the Contact Zone in Rosária da Silva's *Totonya*

> Coitados dos cordeiros,
> quando os lobos querem ter razão
>
> [Poor lambs,
> when the wolves want to be right]
>
> Cabinda Proverb[1]

Introduction

The Angolan writer Rosária da Silva is the third and final author whose work is under analysis in the present study. Of the three authors, she is the one who has published the smallest amount of literary works, as the novel *Totonya* (2005) is the only one that Da Silva has made available to the public to date. Having completed a degree in Educational Sciences with a focus on Linguistics, Da Silva has dedicated herself to teaching Portuguese Language and writing in various genres (essays, short stories, poetry and plays), in different publications. The literary work *Totonya* was first published in 1998 and republished in 2005, 2014 and 2017. This novel not only marked Da Silva's debut as the first female novelist of independent Angola, but also won her a *menção honrosa* [honourable mention] in the 1996 literary competition named after the Angolan poet António Jacinto, which was promoted by the INALD (Instituto Nacional do Livro e do Disco [National Book and Disc Institute]). Having been released in a decade in which the most horrific civil wars were taking place in Angola (the first from 1992 to 1994 and the second one from 1998 to 2002), the novel was published by the Brigada Jovem da Literatura de Angola [Angolan Literary Youth Brigade]. This was a literary movement created in 1981, of which Da Silva was a founding member. Its main aim was to give visibility to a new generation of writers who, in turn, were aiming to create a new voice in the immediate post-independence Angolan literary arena. As a consequence, at this stage the literary production of the writers who were engaged in the movement was markedly ideological and it openly acknowledged their political affiliation to the MPLA (Movimento Popular de Libertação de Angola [People's Movement for the Liberation of Angola]), the overtly Marxist-Leninist ruling party at the time. It this therefore not surprising that, for instance, the printing and publishing of *Totonya*'s first edition was sponsored by the National Bank of Angola, the Eduardo dos Santos Foundation, the Port of Luanda and the Ministry of Fishing — all of them entities which, as will be discussed later on, are connected to the MPLA government (Hamilton 2000).

Although at first glance *Totonya* seems to suggest an affiliation to the dominant ideology, the present analysis will argue that the use of this Marxist-Leninist ideological discourse undermines itself, exposing its limitations, internal paradoxes and inconsistencies. By revealing the strategies of exclusion in this discourse, which are set in motion in order to consolidate its position of power and, thus, perpetuate it in time, the novel focuses specifically on cultural, ethnic and gender marginalisation. Cultural and ethnic marginalisation, emerge in the delimitation of two Angolas that are in direct confrontation, in the twin cities of Luanda and Benguela. Taking into consideration Angolan history and the specificities of the formation of Angolan society, this confrontation becomes an ethnic one in the novel. As for gender marginalisation, this arises from the representations of femininity and masculinity in both of the Angolan contexts being explored, revealing a structure of power in operation that clearly positions women in a subordinate place, as opposed to men's dominance. Hence, this reading of Da Silva's novel will be informed by an intellectual framework composed of two main theoretical concerns that will allow a better understanding of the process through which *Totonya* analyses, appropriates, subverts and recreates the post-independence discourses of the nation. Firstly, and expanding on the research developed by Phyllis Peres (1997) on the works of contemporary Angolan fiction writers, it will be informed by Mary Louise Pratt's theorisation of contact zones, autoethnography and transculturation (1991). In *Transculturation and Resistance in Lusophone African Narrative*, Peres focuses specifically on the narrative works of Luandino Vieira, Pepetela, Uanhenga Xitu and Manuel Rui as narratives of resistance that textualise and problematise Angolan national identities and communities. According to Peres, the analysis of these narratives through the lens of Pratt's understanding of transculturation enables a thorough appreciation of the work developed by these authors, with a view to analysing in more detail the acculturation imposed by the Portuguese dominant culture. They do so through the appropriation and adaptation of this discourse to specific Angolan realities, simultaneously problematising the complex construction of an Angolan national identity — one that emerges from the continuous negotiation of sociocultural elements such as race, gender, class, generation, ethnicity, region and tribe (Peres 1997: 10–15). Taking the work developed by Peres as a point of departure, this analysis sets out to take the exploration of sex and gender issues much further. Hence, considering *Totonya*'s focus of interest, perspective and intellectual proposal, Pratt's theorisation becomes extremely useful in the present reading as well, as will soon be confirmed.

In 'Arts of the Contact Zone', Pratt uses the term 'contact zone'

> [...] to refer to social spaces where cultures meet, clash, and grapple with each other, often in contexts of highly asymmetrical relations of power, such as colonialism, slavery, or their aftermaths as they are lived out in many parts of the world today. (1991: 1)

She moves on to analyse positive examples of contact zone — such as a classroom of students from different backgrounds in which their cultures are juxtaposed and a space of interaction, dialogue and knowledge exchange can be created — and negative examples as well — such as colonialism, in which a power structure operates, clearly imposing a dominant culture upon a subordinate *other.* Hence, according to Pratt, through the occurrence of specific phenomena, these contact zones enable the questioning of instituted models of community. In the specific case of negative contact zones (for instance, in colonial environments), the scholar notes that autoethnographic texts have an important role in the deconstruction of predefined representations, as they 'are representations that the so-defined others construct *in response to* or in dialogue with those texts [ethnographic texts]' (1991: 2). This dialogue takes place through transculturation, another phenomenon that occurs in the contact zone. Pratt reminds us that this term, created by the Cuban sociologist Fernando Ortiz, refers to the active role of marginal groups in selecting and appropriating certain features of the dominant culture (1991: 2). This gesture will forcefully refute the homogenisation of Anderson's 'imagined community' (1991) in its application to the Angolan context, and, thus, prompt the imagination of new representations within the changing community — in Sanches's words, 'substituting *an* imagined community (Anderson 1991) by diverse fragments of the nation (Chatterjee 1993), restoring a multiplicity of histories that postcolonial studies and subaltern studies have been demanding' (2007: 133).

In this sense, *Totonya* will be read as a novel that deconstructs representations of culture and gender in the discourse of the dominant ideology, ultimately exposing, through autoethnography, the limitations of postcolonial assimilation. Considering that the novel can be read as a strategic autoethnography of the female experience in postcolonial Angola, it becomes relevant to simultaneously focus on Graham Huggan's study of the Post-Colonial Exotic (2001: 34–57). When exploring the reception of African literature among Western audiences and its treatment by the publishers, Huggan observes the occurrence of a phenomenon that he describes as 'the anthropological exotic' (2001: 37), which implies the representation and advertising of Africa as a more familiar and homogeneous context for the consumption of Western readers:

> Thus, the perceptual framework of the anthropological exotic allows for a reading of African literature as the more or less transparent window onto a richly detailed and culturally specific, but still somehow homogenous — and of course readily marketable — African world. Anthropology is the watchword here, not for empirical documentation, but for the elaboration of a world of difference that conforms to often crudely stereotypical Western exoticist paradigms and myths ('primitive culture', 'unbounded nature', 'magical practices', 'noble savagery', and so on).

Huggan then moves on to analyse three examples of what he calls 'ethnographic counter-discourse' in contemporary African literary production (2001: 40). The first example, which arises from the literary work *Things Fall Apart*, by the Nigerian author Chinua Achebe, proposes the strategies of 'ethnographic parody' and 'celebratory autoethnography'. The second example, focusing on the *Le Devoir de*

Violence, by the Malian author Yambo Ouologuem, presents 'ethnographic satire'. Finally, his third example is based on the South African writer Bessie Head's work, which attempts to generate a dialogue between anthropology and oral literature. It is, therefore, made clear that in Huggan's perception both the anthropological exotic and the ethnographic counter-discourse are strategies that emerge as representative of the opposition between the colonised and the coloniser, within colonial versus anti-colonial or postcolonial contexts. Despite the emphasis on cultural perceptions and representations, the focus on the aforementioned binary opposition implies the centralisation of one single power structure, to the detriment of all others in operation within both strategies under discussion. Considering the scope of the present reading, I intend to take Huggan's theorisation a step further by focusing on the emergence of ethnographic counter-discourses within a post-independence and postcolonial scenario, with sex and gender power structures at the core of the analysis.[2] In other words, the emphasis is not so much on having the colonised African writing back to the Western coloniser, as it is on Angolan women writing back to Angolan men within a postcolonial Angola that is itself negotiating the construction of its national identity (Mama 2001).

Taking into consideration the particularities of *Totonya*, the present study will focus specifically on the strategy of 'celebratory autoethnography', which, according to Huggan (2001: 43),

> [...] turning the language of Western evolutionist anthropology against itself, enables an allegedly 'subordinate' culture to regain its dignity; and to reclaim its place, not within the imagined hierarchy of civilization, but as one civilization among others — and a sophisticated one at that.

Hence, this study will argue that by directing the anthropological gaze back towards the identity construction of the nation imposed by the male-oriented dominant ideology, the novel not only critiques but also resists the cultural and gender representations created by that imposed imagination of the nation. Considering its emphasis on the construction of what Peres (1997: 12) calls 'Angolanness', with all of its complexity and in a very particular moment of the Angolan history, *Totonya* is a novel that needs to be understood in a historical and contextual framework, as a brief analysis of its graphic design makes clear.

Totonya: Some Brief Considerations

As mentioned above, *Totonya* was first published in 1998 by the Brigada Jovem da Literatura de Angola and it was sponsored by governmental entities and a private foundation which belongs to the Chairman of the MPLA and former President of Angola, José Eduardo dos Santos. According to Hamilton (2000) the cover of the book's first edition features a *Chokwe* mask and a *Chokwe* wooden sculpture, consisting of a set of three statues, against a red background in which there is a picture of part of a female face. This illustration, which was created by José Mendes Fernandes, is interpreted by Hamilton as being suggestive of a discussion of the Angolan indigenous societies through the eyes of the female character who gives her name to the literary work, Totonya (2000: 64). I would add that the juxtaposition of the red background, the *Chokwe* cultural items and the female face is highly suggestive in the sense that it might indicate a confrontation between two distinct conceptions of the nation — a modern and markedly socialist one against a traditional and pre-colonial one — in which women and female representations appear in the intersection of both worlds.

In addition, and focusing specifically on the presence of the *Chokwe* mask, its reading can point us in two directions. On the one hand, and on a more general level, the mask can be taken to indicate precisely the need to analyse the hidden layers of the new official nationalist discourse. In the words used by Leite (1996) to refer to some of the literature produced in post-independence Angola,

> This was the moment when authors started to take a step back and gain perspective on their country, casting a critical look at some of the new national myths. A new phase in Angolan literature began in which the tautologies of an invented unity were replaced by the masks and mirrors of diversity. The mask denounces duplicity, ambiguity and contradiction. It does so by means of deconstructive irony. (1996: 123–24)

On the other hand, and on a more specific level, this *Chokwe* mask may invoke the *Mwana Pwo*. According to Manuel Jordán's account on *Chokwe* masquerades and ceremonial celebrations, this is one of the most important *makishi* (spiritual guides) masks, given that it symbolises feminine identity as culturally conceived by the ethnic group (1998). *Mwana Pwo* is a masquerade character who emerges in the specific context of the *Mukanda* boys' initiation rites and whose performance is devoted to the entertainment of women and the homage to motherhood. What is interesting to note about this character is that, despite representing an ideal of femininity, it is created by men. Hence, notwithstanding the fact that, as Jordán points out, they may reject this male conceptualisation of the feminine identity if they feel somehow dishonoured by it, women are only allowed to intervene directly in the ceremony through *Mwana Pwo*, who 'speaks on behalf of all women in the community' (1998: 68–69). Considering that '*Makishi* often serve to sanction and validate social and political institutions, which are generally perceived as the domain of men', women's ability to renegotiate their identity appears constrained by a masculine imagery represented by this gender-ambiguous character (1998: 67). Hence, the combination of the *Chokwe* mask and the female figure on the novel's cover may suggest an incitement to women's empowerment through the performance of their own initiation. It seems to propose that they should impose themselves as agents, as their own spiritual guides — subjects and objects of their own representation in the ongoing renegotiation of the nation.[3] This gesture reinforces the importance of the female autoethnographic journey as the means to analyse the dynamics of gender relations in everyday life; to expose women's self-conceptualisations within historically male-oriented discourses of community; and, simultaneously, to resist and overcome them, through women's active involvement in the transculturation process.

It is interesting to note the changes that were made in the second edition of the novel, namely the illustration on the cover and the sponsorship. In the 2005 edition, which emerged in a completely different historical context, the front cover illustration, for which José Mendes Fernandes is once again responsible, presents only the drawing of a female face. The references to *Chokwe* culture disappear, as well as the red background, thus highlighting the question of female representations over the others previously identified. Furthermore, although the publisher remains the same, the sponsorship changes, as the second edition is not supported by a governmental entity. This time it is Gemac Lda, a private national enterprise with investments in tourism and entertainment, which sponsors the 2005 edition. It is made clear that different moments in history dictate distinct priorities in the agenda of the dominant ideology. If in the 1990s the MPLA government's fragile condition led it to give in under international and internal pressure and make political concessions, its comfortable position in the world economy in 2005 might explain its lack of interest in supporting the work of the first female novelist of independent Angola.[4] On the subject of the expectations of the parties that opposed MPLA in the multiparty, democratic and post-civil war era, Vidal (2007a: 154) states that

> A particular disappointment for the parliamentary opposition was directed at the international community, in particular the World Bank and the IMF, for reducing the pressure that was being exerted on the government in terms of accountability and transparency in the management of public funds and respect for human rights. This was likely due to the increased demand for oil that came from the new Asian partners of the Angolan government — China, India and possibly South Korea — oil that the West also desired.

Therefore, the emergence of the first edition in the particular context of the year 1998 needs to be understood in its specificity. To this end, some historical considerations will be examined for a better comprehension of the literary work, its emergence, and its deconstruction of cultural identity and representations — all of this taking place at a time in which the conceptualisation of the nation and an imposed imagination of the community as horizontal were at the core of contemporary debates.

Totonya: Notes on History and Society

The examination of such issues implies a review of key moments in the history of Angola. One of the biggest and wealthiest of Portugal's former colonies, the young nation state of Angola achieved its independence in 1975. Angola has many particularities that make it unique within the universe of Portugal's former African colonies, not only in terms of a common Portuguese colonial experience, but also through the perspective of a postcolonial idealisation of the nation. Chabal states that three sets of factors are usually highlighted in the attempt to understand the complexity of the Angola's present-day reality (2007). The first set of factors concerns the pre-colonial and colonial structures of social and political power, in which it is necessary to underline the very important and influential role of the Luanda Creole community. Angola (just like Mozambique) was a settlement colony with a very important and influential Creole community. Despite having lost most of their privileges during the period of white settlement (mostly from the 1930s to the 1970s; see Castelo 2007), this community had a determining role in the formation of the MPLA, a pro-liberation front that would eventually come to constitute the post-independence government of the newly born nation. According to Newitt (2007), this community dates back to the end of the fifteenth century. The history of these Afro-Portuguese people, who established themselves as a separate and economically powerful ethnic group, is strongly connected with the slave trade. Hence, they were responsible for the creation of the two important Angolan Atlantic cities of Luanda and Benguela. Due to their origins, their development and their location, these cities acquired what Newitt calls

> A distinct identity, which was deeply rooted in the history of the people of the coast and at the same time shared in the creole cultures of the Atlantic world. The late nineteenth century was to see the attempt by the peoples of the coast to conquer and colonise the interior. The civil wars, which occurred after the withdrawal of the Portuguese in 1975, also assumed the character of a conflict between the old Afro-Portuguese coastal states and the inland people. (2007: 36)

Although it would be incorrect to affirm that the neo-patrimonial governance which the MPLA instated in post-independence Angola is Creole-dominated, Chabal argues that, this Portuguese-speaking elite does, indeed, enjoy a privileged position within the spheres of power, as it is best positioned to access power in the network created by the political party and its former President, José Eduardo dos Santos.

The second set of factors regards the specific type of colonial rule developed by the Portuguese in the territory that would later become the Angolan nation state, which would decisively influence the postcolonial conceptualisation of the nation. At this point, Chabal starts by emphasising the racial, ethnic and regional tensions fomented by the colonial entity through the nature of its economy. These tensions would ultimately be incorporated into nationalist competition between the pro-liberation fronts, not only in the context of the anti-colonial conflict, but also in the post-independence setting, in the form of a civil war that would last for twenty-seven years. As Newitt demonstrates, in the aftermath of the Berlin Conference, Portugal began to make serious attempts to demonstrate effective control over its colonies through strategies such as the pacification wars (which implied the use of traditional ethnical rivalries to strengthen the colonial government), the revitalisation of the Catholic missions, and the incorporation of a settlement policy (2007: 42–50). Hence, this change in colonial positioning, based on the strengthening of racial boundaries, led to a gradual decrease of influence for the Afro-Portuguese community. The *Estado Novo*'s reinforcement of these boundaries was effected through the introduction of the assimilation policy in 1954. Additionally, the subsequent stipulation of the social statuses of *indígena* [native] and *não indígena* [non-native] led to the development of social distinctions that would outlive the colonial government and, thus, have a major ongoing impact on the postcolonial ideal of the nation (Newitt 2007: 52–53).[5]

Consequently, there were tensions generated not only between the white and the black populations, but also amongst different ethnic groups. The most visible example of this tension would be the dichotomy between the Portuguese-speaking, Catholic, urban-based and socially privileged Creole elite, and the mission-influenced (Protestant or Catholic) and socially marginalised Africans from the interior. These tensions would be echoed in the formation of the distinct nationalist movements — on the basis of different colonial experiences — that would engage in the post-independence civil war (Newitt 2007: 64). Chabal points out that if the struggle for Angola's autonomy ended in 1976, from that moment on the conflict assumed the characteristics of a 'struggle for power', which had distinct phases and was less of an ideological confrontation than a struggle for the domination of the nation state and its resources (2007: 6). Chabal also underlines the bureaucratic nature of the colonial administration, which the postcolonial socialist government created by the MPLA would inherit. In addition, as Newitt highlights,

> [...] the government of independent Angola inherited an economy in which the state had a very large stake. The temptation to use the state-owned enterprises as sources of revenue and patronage was not resisted, with the result that a once strong and diverse economy was reduced to ruin in only two or three years. (2007: 63)

Finally, Chabal turns his attention to the violent and repressive nature of the Portuguese regime, which would leave a deep mark on post-independence and postcolonial forms of political expression. Suffice it to say that the MPLA, which had 'always been construed, and used, as the crucible for a national, supra-ethnic, political "machine"', became profoundly authoritarian and intolerant after the 1977 attempted coup led by Nito Alves (Chabal 2007: 5). As for the political organisation UNITA (União Nacional para a Independência Total de Angola [National Union for the Total Independence of Angola]), which was designed and created by Jonas Savimbi, it rapidly developed into a 'war machine' (Chabal 2007: 7).

The third set of factors is related to the uniqueness of Angola as a former colony. Although the country is very often regarded as having been more Portuguese than other Portuguese former colonies (mostly due to the existence and historical development of the Luanda Creole community), Chabal continues, it is important to contextualise Angola locally, i.e. within the African continent. Similarly to other African oil-producing countries, Angola is conditioned by the fact that it is rich in mineral resources. However, as Chabal highlights, three main factors make up the specificity of Angolan economic power: the fact that the oil is offshore and, therefore, can be protected; the fact that the oil revenues are entirely controlled by *Sonangol*, which is dominated by the President (who uses these revenues outside the constraints of the governmental structure); and finally, the fact that the government has maintained financial deals outside the supervision of the state, i.e. which depend on the regime rather than the state (2007: 8). Chabal (2007: 4) adds that a particularly relevant issue to be taken into consideration for the understanding of the contemporary Angolan situation is what he calls the 'foreign actor involvement', notably visible throughout the Cold War period and responsible for the intensification of social symptoms, such as internal rivalries and intolerance that would ensure the perpetuation of the civil war.

Bearing all of the above-mentioned factors in mind, it is important to explore further the nature of the post-independence government of Angola, as well as its different configurations across diverse moments of history. One of the main distinctions between the trajectories of the nationalist movements that emerged in Angola and in the two other countries under analysis in the present study — i.e., Cape Verde and Mozambique — is precisely that the three movements that were created (MPLA, FNLA and UNITA) were never able to reach any understanding and, therefore, form a single movement or united front. The same did not happen in relation to both PAIGC (Partido Africano da Independência da Guiné e Cabo Verde [African Party for the Independence of Guinea and Cape Verde]) and FRELIMO, which successfully managed to generate united fronts in their respective areas of action, at least in the context of the anti-colonial struggle. As mentioned before, one of the first nationalist movements to come to life amongst Angolans was generated by members of the educated and urbanised *não-indígena* elite. The MPLA was created in 1958 by Angolans who were studying in Lisbon and Paris. According to Newitt, their proximity to the Portuguese Communist Party, and the fact that they did not have a political base inside what was to become the Angolan territory, led them to look for the international support of Marxist states — a choice that would inevitably have major social and political repercussions in the post-independence period:

> Most of them were Marxist inclined — and it has been pointed out that the mestizos, whites and *assimilados* who formed the MPLA needed a class-based ideology to deflect the accusations that they were not really African at all. The lack of any organization or even any firm constituency of support within Angola was to force the MPLA to rely on its international friends, initially among the members of the non-aligned bloc, but later the Soviets and Cubans. This was to be a major factor dictating the patterns of the civil wars that followed independence. (2007: 73–74)

Much closer to Angola, in the Belgian Congo, another nationalist movement was born in 1956: the FNLA. This front was firstly called UPNA (União das Populações do Norte de Angola [Union of the Populations of North Angola]) and later UPA (União dos Povos de Angola [Union of the Peoples of Angola]), before finally becoming the FNLA. The movement defended an openly Africanist nationalism and it was responsible for the first armed attacks on the Portuguese colonial government, in 1961. Finally, UNITA, the third Angolan nationalist movement, was formed in 1966 by a group of FNLA dissidents. Regarding the impossibility of these movements creating a united front (in the image of PAIGC and FRELIMO), Newitt argues that there were two main reasons. The first is that the three movements were being supported by distinct newly independent African states, which had no interest in prompting the creation of a united movement (2007: 75). The second reason, as defended by Newitt, refers to the three movements' different positionings regarding the major powers involved in the Cold War, the USSR and the USA:

> The MPLA was fairly consistently supported by the USSR after 1964 while the US lent support to UPA and intermittently to UNITA. Yet, it is fairly clear that the ideological positions of UPA and UNITA were as much the result of the split with the MPLA as the cause of it. (2007: 76)

Hence, Newitt continues, although the ethnic and racial rivalries were to play a very important role in the long run in the definition of the basis for the three-way opposition between the three movements, this was not something cultivated from the beginning, whilst their authoritarian and totalitarian nature was (2007: 76–77).

The liberation war that lasted from 1961 to 1975 placed the Portuguese government and the nationalist movements in opposition within the international political arena. On the one hand, the former struggled to convince international opinion of its entitlement to the colonies, simultaneously taking action to undermine any possible unification between the three nationalist movements. On the other hand, these three nationalist movements pursued their strategies in direct opposition to each other, as they struggled to strengthen their international credibility and their military forces, and to create links with the major world powers involved in the Cold War. It is, therefore, not surprising that in the immediate aftermath of the collapse of the *Estado Novo* regime in Portugal, on the 25 April 1974, a civil war erupted in Angola. This was the real struggle that all three movements had been preparing for. As Newitt argues, it was not until 1963 that the MPLA, under the leadership of Agostinho Neto, became an openly Marxist movement, creating a corresponding political programme and aligning itself with both PAIGC and FRELIMO, and projecting a convincing image of a modernising party:

> It presented itself as a modernising party, opposed to tribalism and racism, which planned to create a new socialist society based on scientific principles, where there would be equality between men and women and in which traditional authorities, traditional religion and practices like polygamy would have no place. In contrast, it branded the FNLA as a tribal party, identified with outdated and backward-looking Africanist values. Like Frelimo and the PAIGC, the MPLA claimed to have begun to create the new society in the areas it controlled by setting up modern health and educational services and a newly structured peasant economy. (2007: 83)

The reality, however, was completely different, as it would impose its ideology on the population by force in the areas it controlled, through an effective 'policy of terror' characterised by executions of those who might somehow oppose the MPLA's ideology (Newitt 2007: 84). Growing dissatisfaction towards the MPLA's stance amongst some of the movement's supporters was one of the reasons for the creation of UNITA. Jonas Savimbi, its leader, had formerly been connected with Holden Roberto's FNLA, the growing weakness of which might also have been behind Savimbi's decision to create his own movement. According to Newitt (2007: 84), Savimbi's ideological discourse was largely built on racial and ethnic factors, as he attacked MPLA's mestizo leadership and both MPLA and FNLA's ethnic exclusivity and military incapacity. Yet, UNITA's discourse shifted according to the movement's solidarities. Furthermore, although it projected an image of a modernising anti-socialist movement, it looked to the support of the traditional authorities and, like the MPLA, UNITA persecuted those who did not align themselves with its ideals.

Hence, after the fall of the *Estado Novo* in Portugal and the signing of the Alvor Agreement in January 1975, the Civil War erupted in Angola. Although the Civil War would last for twenty-seven years, the MPLA was able to impose itself as the dominant party in the Angolan post-independence setting. This was due to the foreign intervention of its Cuban and Soviet allies, to its influence amongst the Luanda population, and to its advantageous connections with Portugal, in the form of Admiral Rosa Coutinho, its governor up until the signing of the Alvor Agreement (Newitt 2007: 86–87). Once it reached this position of power, the party set a programme in motion to consolidate a socialist political system, which Chabal (2002) describes as follows:

> [...] the regime rapidly put in place a singularly 'Stalinist' or 'orthodox' one-party state. The main features of such a system were: the concentration of power in the hands of a very small group at the apex (the party's central committee and political bureau run with an iron hand by the president); the absolute dominance of the party over the organs of the government (including the prime minister and his ministerial colleagues); the supremacy of the party within all essential state, administrative, military and economic institutions; the reliance on ideology as a weapon of political control; the re-shaping of the economy according to the rigid principles of nationalisation and 'primitive socialist accumulation'; and, finally, the attempt to exert total (party) political control over the principal (religious, social, academic and cultural) institutions of civil society. (2002: 66)

This system opened space for corruption and major socioeconomic disparities. Nevertheless, Chabal continues, the MPLA was confronted with many difficulties in the consolidation and legitimisation of such an ambitious socio-political programme. Firstly, its alignment with the Soviets prevented its recognition by the Western bloc. Secondly, UNITA's armed opposition prevented the consolidation of MPLA's power across the country. Finally, the party faced opposition from among its own supporters. As a consequence, the party's administration was very much city-based, proving ineffective outside the main urban areas (2002: 101).

Christine Messiant (2007) argues that the distinctiveness of Angola's socialism rests on its oil wealth and on the internationalised character of the civil war which was taking place. In her view, only these two factors could explain, on the one hand, the fact that the MPLA was supported by a substantial part of the population (who would not dare to oppose the regime); and, on the other hand, the regime's policy of repression and exclusion to maintain its power and ensure that the economic and political gains would rest in the hands of a few (2007: 96). This means that, although the regime's policies proved to be ineffectual for the majority of the population, the single party structure only grew stronger and became more powerful. Messiant moves on to identify a change in the political system from 1985, as follows:

> From that period onwards, a transition occurred to what I would call 'savage socialism', combining the dictatorship of the single party, the 'dollarisation'

> of the economy — in effect, the sanctioning of illegal practices — and the transition to a political economy of clientelism. (2007: 97)

Yet, the changes that were occurring inside and outside the country (such as the end of the Cold War; the end of the Apartheid; the increasing international pressure for a peaceful resolution to the internal conflict; and UNITA's military victories) dictated the regime's change of strategy. Not only did it go on to generate policies protective of the single party, but it also attempted to reach an understanding with UNITA with regards to democratisation. As Messiant put it, 'this entailed negotiation without recognition but with co-optation, the best way of incorporating individuals from the other side without jeopardising single-party rule' (2007: 98).

In 1991 the two opposing parties signed the Bicesse Peace Agreement, which would pave the way for the first elections to take place, the following year. Following MPLA's victory and the subsequent legitimisation of the single-party regime, both internally and externally, Savimbi's refusal to accept the results led to the reactivation of the armed struggle. Yet, on this occasion the MPLA had the support of the international community, as Savimbi had refused to demilitarise UNITA, on the grounds of the Lusaka Agreement.[6] It is in this context that José Eduardo dos Santos (who replaced Agostinho Neto after his death in 1979 and held the presidency until 2017) started to take measures with a view to ensuring the protection of his own positioning, as well as to eliminating any form of defiance towards the regime. He, therefore, kept civil society organisations under tight control and even moved to build his own civil society, materialised in the José Eduardo dos Santos Foundation:

> He sought to neutralise Angola's autonomous civil society — the activities of which by implication have exposed government failures — with an ambitious scheme to create his own 'civil society'. To that end, he set up the José Eduardo dos Santos Foundation, whose main aim was to ensure that support for social, health and educational activities would be credited to him, not to the extensive independent NGO sector, which was financed by donors. (Messiant 2007: 104)

Having reaffirmed the legitimacy of its power before the international community and ensured its maintenance internally through ideological surveillance and social control, the MPLA was perfectly positioned to seek UNITA's destruction — not only as a military opponent, but also as a political threat. In order to do this, it intensified the military campaigns against UNITA and, simultaneously, it proceeded to the recognition of the UNITA-Renovada, a new party which the elected representatives of UNITA were forced to form. This recognition not only allowed the government to bring UNITA's political arm under surveillance, but, as Messiant reminds us, it also enabled the MPLA to reinforce the illusory image of their dedication to the construction of a democratic society (2007: 105). Messiant (2007: 107) moves on to explain how the defeat of UNITA by the MPLA in 2002 did not mean that any changes would actually occur in terms of the economic and political democratisation process, as the transition to post-war politics was entirely fashioned by the regime, according to its own interests. Although, generally speaking, the life conditions of the population improved with the end of the civil conflict, social inequalities remain and are still being fomented by the regime. These facts show that, as Vidal asserts, the existence of a multiparty structure in Angola's politics does not necessarily translate into a democracy (2007b).

In this sense, it is important to focus on the emphasis placed by the MPLA regime on the construction of a civil society since independence. According to Vidal (2007b), despite the emphasis placed in the first years following independence (that is, during the socialist period) on the design and development of specific programmes that would ultimately lead to the enhancement of the social sector (education, housing, health, community services and social security), these had a very short existence. Hence, social services within a government-devised plan of actions were practically non-existent in Angola, particularly throughout the years of the civil war. This meant that the great majority of the population became increasingly marginalised. In other words, throughout both the socialist period and the Dos Santos administration, the governmental entity felt comfortable enough to neglect its responsibilities towards the population — urban and rural — as it was feeling increasingly secure, both in economic and political terms. The transition to the multiparty system, Vidal continues, enabled the emergence of internationally funded Civil Society Organisations which came to perform the tasks and assume the roles normally attributed to the state (2007a: 204–18). The regime's inability to assert effective control over all of these organisations and their demands led it to develop another strategy: the creation of 'government-friendly CSOs', such as the already mentioned José Eduardo dos Santos Foundation (1996) and the Lwini Social Solidarity Fund (which was set up by Dos Santos's wife, Ana Paula dos Santos), which are organisations created entirely as vehicles for presidential propaganda. Through them, the President not only emerged separate from the state, but also appeared to work to provide services for which the state should be responsible (Vidal 2007b: 225).[7] According to Vidal, despite the decrease in international funding for humanitarian aid, the Angolan regime continues to neglect the social sector and refuses to invest in social infrastructures.

The social structure imposed by the MPLA government since independence is, therefore, one that is based on a hierarchical network which places a select elite at the centre of access to the nation and to determining the concept of nationhood. This leaves the great majority of the population in the peripheral and passive areas of the performance of the community, as dictated from above. Vidal (2007b: 203) states that 'this inhibited the appearance of an alternative social logic based upon notions of citizenship or class (where people place themselves horizontally in relation to the state) and therefore hampered the emergence of civil society as understood in the West'. Hence, this neo-patrimonial logic is sustained by a general refusal of equity, which becomes visible at all of the levels that compose the social arena: political, cultural, racial, ethnical, economic and gender.

The 'Woman Question' in Angola

As mentioned before, the MPLA's alignment with Marxism from an early stage led it to develop gender-oriented policies that would ensure the construction of a society based on ostensible gender equality. Indeed, ever since the first programmes of the pro-liberation movements, they have incorporated the struggle for equality between genders — focusing specifically on the emancipation of women — in their causes through the creation of particular women's organisations which, in the logic of modernisation, were to play a very important role in the struggle for liberation. According to Henda Ducados (2004), the OMA (Organização da Mulher Angolana [Angolan Women's Organisation]) was born in 1962 as an extension of the MPLA that was meant to work towards the incorporation of women into the liberation war. Although the leadership of OMA was composed of educated women who were somehow connected with the leadership of the MPLA, the truth is that the organisation was very successful in reaching all types of women, from different sociocultural and ethnic backgrounds, and actively incorporating them into the struggle. As Ducados points out, their role was decisive mainly in the support of the guerrilla movement (in terms of education, health, nourishment and arms transportation), but even so many women actually fought on the battle fronts. Running parallel to OMA, within the UNITA movement there was another women's organisation, which was created in 1973 — the LIMA (Liga Independente de Mulheres Angolanas [Independent League of Angolan Women]). Contrary to OMA, LIMA's leadership had no familial connections to the UNITA's leadership, which, according to Ducados (2004), was 'due to fear of repercussions against men if women failed in their endeavours'. Having an agenda similar to OMA's, LIMA's members were also very active in the political engagement of the population, a characteristic that the organisation maintained even throughout the post-independence conflict.

The MPLA's rise to power provided OMA with the opportunity to actively propose measures towards the construction of a more gender-equal civil society. Indeed, Ducados argues that in the 1980s the organisation successfully achieved many victories, such as the introduction of the Family Code, the provision of free family planning to women, and the creation of a space for debate over issues which were normally considered to be part of the private sphere — and, therefore, taboo (2004; OAW 1984).[8] Nevertheless, as David Birmingham (2002: 161) points out, these achievements did not produce real gender equity, as the governmental structure itself and society in general remained very much male-oriented:

> Women sympathetic to the MPLA were able to hold such relatively prestigious posts as that of university rector or national librarian. Even UNITA had a woman as one of its economic advisers. In the government, tokenism led to the appointment of some women as junior ministers though none played a role in the running of the oil sector or the management of the army. The party's organisation for women appeared to put women on a pedestal while effectively removing them from any real access to power. High-profile women were more likely to play a role in the dynastic politics of the Luanda families than in any

> real power struggles, and women with authority were commonly deemed to be an offence to African male pride [...].

Furthermore, in the civil war context the government proved itself to be ineffectual both in the protection of the population (within which women, children and the elderly were the most affected) and in the formulation of policies that were socially and economically protective of women. Indeed, Birmingham continues, women were specifically victimised by the civil war in many senses (2002: 158–62). Many died during the conflict; others were raped and kidnapped; some others were injured by landmines; others lost their children and/or husbands to the war, taking on the sole responsibility for their households. Hence, as Ducados highlights, their workload increased, as they had to combine their husbands' tasks with their own and ensure the survival of their families (2004). In addition, the war had a major impact on gender power structures within the family, as the shortage of men led to polygamy becoming a socially acceptable practice — one that left women and children in vulnerable positions.

Another major consequence of the war was migration. Instability and the urge to survive forced many women to move to the cities on the coast (particularly Luanda), in search of protection and employment. Given that the great majority were illiterate, they ended up being absorbed by the informal market, which, as Aline Pereira notes, offered no economic protections or guarantees to these women (2005). Focusing specifically on the question of literacy, it is important to point out that regardless of the valid efforts of the post-independence government to develop educational policies and actions, the fact that there was a civil war in progress (as well as all of the socio-political instability that it caused) heavily conditioned the execution of those plans. According to Pereira, women were particularly affected in this conjuncture, as in the context of deprivation they were never prioritised. Hence, boys were sent to study and girls were kept in the domestic sphere, reproducing the same gender stereotypes which were meant to be resisted (2005: 11–12). After the transition to multipartidarism, OMA stopped being connected with the government to become a mere branch of the MPLA, which inevitably led to a decrease in its influence and the decline of its credibility. The governmental institution that came to replace OMA in 1991 was the SEPMD (Secretaria de Estado para a Promoção e Desenvolvimento da Mulher [State Secretariat for the Promotion and Development of Women]), which was turned into the MINFAMU (Ministério da Família e Promoção da Mulher [Ministry of Family and the Promotion of Women]) in 1997. As Pereira argues, the existence of this ministry does not translate into the government having a greater concern for gender equality issues or women's rights, rather to the contrary. The MINFAMU is one of the least-funded governmental ministries and its actions are limited, not having any real impact on the lives of Angolan women. Hence, Pereira continues, the Angolan government does not regard women's participation in society at all levels as a priority — despite having signed the agreement by CEDAW (Convenção sobre a Eliminação de Todas as Formas de Discriminação Contra as Mulheres [Convention on the Elimination of All Forms of Discrimination against Women]) and the Declaration on Gender and Development of SADC (Southern African Development Community) (2005: 9–10). In a discussion on Postconflict Gender Policy Reform in Angola, Aili Mari Tripp (2015: 140) supports this view, adding that the lack of channels for political expression in the country led to the emergence of a 'cultural renaissance' through which male and female artists address 'some of the deepest sorrows, silences, and divisions within society'.

Totonya: A Reading

The contextual characteristics of the Angolan historical process pre- and post-independence, which I have taken the time to describe above at some length, will shed an important light on the reading of *Totonya*, the main story of which develops throughout the first half of the 1980s. The initial lines of the literary work direct us to a precise date and location — October 1981, at Benguela's airport. At this point, we are immediately led to recall some of the determining facts of Angolan history throughout this period. Following what was to be called 'The Second Liberation War', the 1977 attempted coup d'état led by Nito Alves and the death of Agostinho Neto in 1979, this was a time in which the Angolan MPLA government adopted an openly Marxist-Leninist centralising and dictatorial stance in ideological, political and economic terms, under the guidance of its president, José Eduardo dos Santos (Wheeler and Pélissier 2009: 362–63). This was also a time during which the civil war was ongoing, now polarised between the MPLA and the UNITA forces, which, in turn, reflected the opposition of the political and ideological powers involved in the Cold War. The former were being supported by the Soviet Union and Cuba, whereas the latter had the USA and South Africa as their main sponsors. Hence, given the Dos Santos administration's inability to respond to the population's social and economic requirements, while having to deal simultaneously with the destabilising actions of the UNITA front, dissatisfaction towards the government grew intensely. This was visible not only in the urban areas, amongst those who were external to the Luanda elite, but also, indeed, mostly in the countryside, which was seriously neglected. As Birmingham (2002: 171) reminds us, the strong efforts made by the MPLA to guarantee the maintenance of Luanda, and the consequent centralisation in the capital city, generated the widening of the gap between the rural and the urban worlds:

> The antagonism between the town and the countryside had paved the way for the war of the 1980s to spread like bush fire from neglected province to neglected province. Regional distrust remained a dreadful burden as the nation sought a sustainable peace for the 1990s.

These are very important facts to consider when we go back to *Totonya* and acknowledge that in October 1981, Maria Antónia Paixão Jerónimo — an educated woman from Luanda who was also known as Totonya (her nickname) — was travelling with her three children from the capital city to Benguela, to meet her husband. At this point, there are two main aspects to focus on regarding this trip. The first refers to the decentralising movement itself. At a time when Luanda was increasingly consolidating itself as the centre of Angola in political, economic, social and cultural terms, this flight to Benguela suggests a decentralisation movement not only in the sense of acknowledging the existence of the peripheral ethnic areas of Angola, but also in terms of testing the limits of the MPLA nation outside the confines of the capital city. In addition, the flight itself recalls the ethnographic journeys, so frequent during the colonial times, in which the narratives built by Portuguese explorers created representations of the Angolan *others* under analysis (Wheeler and Pélissier (2009: 99–101). Hence, there is a clear allusion to the occurrence of an autoethnographic journey, as the imposed community, as imagined by the governmental entity for the whole Angolan territory, is about to be analysed and deconstructed by one of its members. The second aspect refers to the fact that it is a woman who is undertaking this autoethnographic journey, which obviously means that women's day-to-day life will be at the core of this experience. The fact that she is travelling by plane highlights her socially privileged position. Furthermore, she travels without her husband's knowledge (as she wishes to surprise him), which in itself is an indicator of the modernity that the new nation state wishes to stand for, as she is able to determine her own choice and mobility. Nevertheless, as we will acknowledge later, this apparent liberation is only achieved through her husband, a fact which will ultimately determine the occurrences in Totonya's life.

As mentioned before, the story begins at Benguela's airport, when Totonya arrives with her children to join her husband, Joaquim Mendes, also known as Quim, who is a veterinary technician. Having been transferred from Luanda (his hometown) to Lobito-Benguela, Quim had lived there for four years before the couple decided that they should not be apart anymore. Because Totonya was then a student, she would request her transfer to the Instituto de Mecânica de Benguela [Benguela Institute of Mechanics] and move to the city with the couple's children. The family reunion was a happy and reassuring moment, and the family was about to expand shortly, as Totonya was pregnant. Nevertheless, after only seven months of pregnancy, she gave birth to a child, who died a few days later; this event would mark the turning point of Quim's behaviour, and subsequently the disintegration of the family. As Quim progressively detaches himself from his family in an attempt to embark on an unofficial polygamous relationship with both Totonya and Joana, he alienates and disempowers Totonya and their three children, focusing solely on his new family. Furthermore, he starts beating Totonya up frequently in order to persuade her to accept his polygamous behaviour. Throughout this process, a whole new world is revealed to Totonya, who thought that Benguela would be an extension of Luanda in all aspects of her existence. Hence, she is forced to struggle in it in several ways in order to survive. Not only does she become fully responsible for the survival of her family, but she also attempts to fight for her husband by consulting sorcerers. Although at times she is able to persuade Quim to come back home and leave Joana, his decision never lasts for more than a few days, after which he returns to his previous behaviour. Not even when Totonya decides to inform her own family and that of Quim back in Luanda of the occurrences in order to seek their intervention is she able to find help. She then discovers that other men from Quim's family display the same behaviour, but that the women cover for them. Finally, not even the OMA, the party representatives and the judicial system's agents are able to help Totonya. Ultimately, Quim expels her from their previous home, hands their children to her and abandons the family. Left with no other option, Totonya decides to move away from both Benguela and Luanda to restart her life with her children.

From the beginning of the story, we understand that the narrative sets out to deconstruct hierarchies of cultural power and power relations within gender. Therefore, although the factual ongoing civil war is never named, it comes into being through the delimitation of two Angolas — Luanda and Benguela — which confront each other, as well as through the analysis of both the female and male representations within the two scenarios. Hence, as Totonya's autoethnographic journey unravels, we can identify three distinct perceptions of the relationship between the two communities involved, which, in turn, imply different insights into gender relations. When Totonya begins her journey from Luanda to Benguela, she perceives both communities to be equal, so that the latter would be an extension of the former. At this point, the sense of continuity is emphasised by the indication of familiarity, as the similarities between the two contexts are denoted. An example would be the first person who Totonya comes into contact with on her arrival at Benguela: a nameless *mestiço* gentleman who kindly helps her and her children to sort themselves out at the airport and to get in touch with Quim. Indeed, Totonya notes the uniqueness of his surprising behaviour as a man, although she does not do so in opposition to Quim's. Yet, the fact that he is a *mestiço* who remains anonymous directs us to the historical perception of Luanda and Benguela as the twin cities, both of which were constituted by the Afro-Portuguese community and should therefore share the same Creole culture. Another example would be the privileged house that Quim set up for his family: 'A casa era realmente linda. Uma espécie de mansão de dois pisos à beira mar, rodeada de cedros e girassóis fora do vulgar' [The house was truly beautiful. It was a kind of two-storey mansion by the sea, surrounded by unusual cedars and sunflowers] (Da Silva 2005: 22). Quim is entitled to this house through his professional connections with the party (he had been transferred from the Ministry of Agriculture in Luanda), which obviously shows this to be an elite family in both cities. In theory, Totonya would be able to maintain her lifestyle and social status in the new setting. A final example would be the maintenance of their gender representations, as well as the expectations attached to them. Quim, the male provider for the family, has his gender identity reassured in the eyes of the community through the arrival of his family from Luanda:

> — Vizinha... olha, a minha esposa e os meus filhos vieram...
>
> Pouco depois, a vizinha, o marido, os filhos todos vinham e eram apresentados aos recém-chegados. Um sorriso de escárnio e triunfo desenhou-se no rosto de Quim. Totonya estudou o perfil másculo, enquanto ele continuava entusiasmado a fazer as apresentações. (2005: 22)
>
> ['Neighbour... look, my wife and my kids have come...'
>
> Shortly afterwards, the neighbour, her husband, and their children all came

> and were introduced to the newcomers. A smile of contempt and triumph marked Quim's face. Totonya observed the masculine profile, while he enthusiastically carried on with the introductions.]

As for Totonya, she is also meeting the expectations of her gender identity through her performance of the correct roles as a soon-to-be highly qualified woman (a student), and as a devoted wife — 'O marido era tudo p'ra ela e os filhos' [The husband meant everything to her and their kids] — and mother, who enabled the expansion of the family with a new pregnancy (2005: 23). From her point of view, up to the point at which Quim's behaviour towards her and the children changed, there were no differences between Luanda and Benguela, as her expectations as a member of the dominant culture and ideology were being met. In other words, she assumed everything to be the same, as the cultural community was supposedly one and the same for everyone — at least in the areas that the MPLA controlled, as was the case for both cities — according to the government's ideological impositions. However, she would soon be confronted with the limitations of this univocal modern conception of community, as the government had formulated it without any regard for the contextual specificities of each geocultural area and for gender equality.

Interestingly, it is the death of the premature child that triggers the changes which occur both within this family and in Totonya's perceptions of the surrounding cultural space. As such, a disturbance in the private sphere shows the public sphere in a whole new light. The death of the child seems to represent a strong blow to Quim's conception of manhood, as it disrupts his perception of himself as national reproducer. When he gets himself a lover, Joana, thus embracing unofficial polygamy, everything changes in Totonya's life. She is confronted with a set of behaviours and habits which are unfamiliar to her and which imply a deviation in her autoethnographic journey, as she suddenly encounters a reality that is marginal to that advocated by the discourse of the dominant ideology, that both she and her husband are meant to represent. Hence, at this point both communities begin to diverge, as the emphasis is put on what distinguishes them, setting them against each other in a hierarchy of power which is obviously conditioned by Totonya's own perceptions and cultural background. Although Quim has the same cultural background and is directly connected with the party and, thus, should be following its guidelines, he is aware of the fact that his gender allows him to circulate freely between the two communities without ever risking his social position of power. He does so for as long as he is able to ensure the maintenance of his private life in the private sphere — to prevent it from having an impact on the public one: 'Sabias que se isso fôr ao conhecimento do partido ainda posso cair?' [Did you know that if the party found out about this, I could fall?] (2005: 33). Therefore, in order to force Totonya to assimilate to a different set of behaviours within the new cultural setting, which will ultimately allow him to maintain his own mobility, he engages in the progressive emptying out of her gender identity as she knew it before. In order to do this, he eliminates the things that make her a woman, so as to leave her with no option but to accept his distinction between private and public life and, thus, embrace unofficial polygamy on his terms. Firstly, he prevents her from having a sex life (at least inside the marriage), which not only elides Totonya's female desire, but also suspends her ability to reproduce again. Secondly, he disempowers her as the official wife. When he is sent to work at Dombe for a year, he leaves his family behind and takes Joana along. Thirdly, through continuous violence, he exerts control over Totonya's body, simultaneously asserting the structure of gender power before Totonya and the community — and this is a situation that repeats itself for three years. Finally, he completely abandons the entire family, forcing Totonya to become fully responsible for the whole household. During this process, she gives up her studies to become the breadwinner.

Indeed, Totonya's 'expedition' to Benguela leads her to understand that despite the centralising governmental entity's efforts to promote an image of national unity and continuity, there is no single community model or cultural discourse of the nation. Again, we are confronted with the limitations of Anderson's 'imagined community' in the context of Angola. Totonya starts conceptualising Benguela neither as an extension of modern Luanda nor as representative of a traditional 'backward' countryside: Benguela emerges as a contact zone, and a very negative one at that. As such, this community offers a social arena in which two different cultures interact within a power structure that defines the dominant, official and imposed order, as opposed to the dominated, unofficial and subjected order. The same binary opposition of the pre-independence Angolan contact zone, which placed the coloniser and the colonised in direct confrontation, is reproduced in Benguela, this time setting the dominant culture against all of the other cultures, which are considered to be comparatively marginal. The intransigent nature of the dominant ideology manifests itself through the attempt to carry out post-colonial cultural assimilation, which is unsuccessful due to its inability to completely erase and substitute dominated cultures. Hence, the awareness of the occurrence of the contact zone as a cultural phenomenon exposes the limitations of the unifying imagination of the nation. At the same time, it underlines the significance of Totonya's autoethnographic trajectory as the means to demystify gender constructions. By focusing on the materialisation of the dialogue between the dominant and dominated cultures, the autoethnographic journey emphasises the active role of marginal groups in the performance of transculturation, a process that, ultimately, translates into a cultural negotiation in which the dominated culture selects and incorporates specific features of the dominant culture.

As we learn more about the Benguela community, we come to realise that it puts forward a cultural paradigm that enables the population to access a sense of belonging to the national community, without sacrificing the cultural model that preceded it. However, the balance of this negotiation depends on the maintenance of the opposition between the private and public spheres, given that in the former the community is able to maintain cultural behaviours considered obsolete by the dominant discourse, whereas the performance of this dominant ideology takes place in the latter. As Catherine Scott (1995: 105–19) reminds us in her important study on gender and development theories, the revolutionary discourse of the MPLA (in accordance with its Marxist-Leninist influences) envisioned modernity and women's liberation within it as a revolutionary process that could occur only within the public space. This implied the immediate association of the private sphere with obsolete and oppressive traditional structures and practices, and, therefore, the deliberate disregard of the household as representative of that same marginal space. The preservation of this opposition is particularly oppressive to women, given that the household — the place with which they have been historically associated — is clearly sacrificed for the sake of the survival, consolidation and assimilation of the official male-oriented public discourse of the nation:

> OMA, presumably as a result of the pressures from the male-dominated MPLA, has avoided open opposition to bride-price because it would evoke hostility from 'traditionalists' (Wolfers and Bergerol 1983: 126). In addition, bride-price and other practices such as polygamy are characterized as 'feudal practices' by both parties [MPLA and Frelimo], which has the effect of equating such practices with dehistoricized 'tradition' rather than inextricably bound up with social organization and the relations of production. (1995: 113)

Hence, in *Totonya* this immediately implies the continuity of gendered power structures. In the public sphere women emerge as emancipated (having mobility and jobs; being able to study and to make their own choices), but in the private sphere they are subjugated (adding domestic tasks to their professional ones; being completely responsible for their offspring; being forced to accept unofficial polygamy; and not having the means to make themselves heard in a male-oriented society). They appear to have no place in the contact zone, which makes the autoethnographic journey twice as relevant: on the one hand, it dignifies an 'allegedly "subordinate" culture' (Huggan 2001: 43), thus demonstrating the potential of a positive contact zone; and on the other hand, it claims a place for women within the nation, by denouncing the male-oriented character of the hegemonic national narratives created.

Predictably, Totonya's first reaction when she becomes aware of the contact zone and, subsequently, of the non-hegemonic position of the dominant discourse, is to assimilate the cultural paradigm postulated in Benguela. When she realises that her Luanda Catholic God is powerless in Benguela, she does not abandon Him, but she does 'conceal' both Him and her religious practices in the private sphere. Indeed, it is particularly interesting to observe here that as a representative of the official socialist discourse of the nation, she is so obviously connected with the hidden practice of Catholicism, a fact that immediately suggests two different lines of reading. The first refers to the limitations in applying an orthodox Marxist-Leninist ideology to the specific context of Angola, in which religion, and particularly the Catholic Church, had such a major cultural impact historically. According to Birmingham, many members of Luanda's political elite maintained their religious connections and practices throughout this socialist period, albeit at a private and secret level (2002: 174–75). The detection of such behavioural characteristics in Totonya reveals a certain duplicity in the performance of the official discourse of the nation which exposes its instability, as shall be discussed later on. The second line of reading directs us to the importance of Totonya's open affiliation with Catholicism (regardless of the contradiction it entailed in ideological terms) in the eyes of a reader in 1997. By the end of the Cold War period and after the signing of the Bicesse Peace Agreement in 1991, the government changed its attitude towards religion and officially reactivated its connections with the Catholic Church. Birmingham (2002: 175) points out that the Luanda elite had a central role in the making of this decision, as it was eager to 're-build the country's traditions of power and subordination' through the reactivation of 'the Catholic church's authoritarian hierarchy'. In other words, the stronger the association with the Catholic Church, the greater the access to power. Given that the government aimed to use the Catholic Church's support while simultaneously restraining its power, particularly in the period that followed the signing of the Lusaka Accord in 1994, this reference to Totonya's religious faith is, by no means, innocent. Reading this faith, as it is presented by Da Silva at the end of the 1990s, does suggest a primary illusion of uninterrupted continuity, as if, in essence, the MPLA government — and, by extension, the Luanda elite and the whole of Angola — had always been religion-friendly. Yet, by portraying religion in a very specific historical moment to an audience which is sixteen years away from that moment, and living under a supposedly distinct ideological regime, the novel simultaneously incites the reader to create a parallel and, thus, question the role of religion as one of the ideological instruments of the governmental entity. As Messiant (2007: 103) reminds us,

> During this post-Lusaka period, the regime consolidated the domination gained by military means. It ensured that UNITA failed to get a toehold, either in politics or within society, which might have been threatening to the MPLA. It also made sure that no political opposition was allowed to surface and that civil society remained unable to challenge the prevailing predation, destitution, injustice and impunity.

Although she feels torn and disempowered as a cultural agent, the struggle for survival in the new cultural setting compels Totonya to publicly embrace the new power structure by agreeing to look for help from sorcerers (Da Silva 2005: 45). Notwithstanding her reluctance, Totonya ends up visiting various sorcerers over the years, and spending all of her money on them, although they continuously prove ineffectual. All of the sorcerers tell her the exact same thing: that Quim is not to be blamed at all for the situation, given that Joana has bewitched him. Hence, Quim emerges completely discharged of any responsibility for his actions, as if although he does not *want* to be a polygamous husband, he is *obliged* to be one by forces that command him, which are ultimately controlled by Joana. The public tension between both genders arises disguised as a private domestic strife between women, a portrayal in which the position of men clearly remains unquestioned. At this point, and given the emphasis that is put on the discourse's very specific use of witchcraft, it is impossible not to see a parallel with the historic witch-hunt that the MPLA — as well as the UNITA — carried out against those who positioned themselves against the party's stance at various times (Newitt 2007: 82–85; Birmingham 2002: 183; Messiant 2007: 103–06). In order to consolidate its power as incontestable, the party persecuted and killed many of its opponents under accusations of witchcraft and sorcery, practices which, allegedly, were contrary to the regime's ideology and conceptualisation of the modern nation. The discourse on witchcraft was then used to create scapegoats, who in turn, would be sacrificed to ensure the MPLA's hold on power. In this context, the reasons for the support given by FESA (Fundação Eduardo dos Santos [Eduardo dos Santos Foundation]) to the publication of the novel *Totonya* become even clearer, especially if we take into account the specific context of 1996. This was a time in which the MPLA government was facing vast popular discontent and, thus, conducted a clever racial/ethnic campaign that would enable the people to release some of their frustration, without losing their support to UNITA (which, at the time, was also preparing for war). Messiant (2001: 307–08) states that

> The President himself, through police and legal measures and aided by the media, directs the process of suggesting certain recognisable groups as targets or scapegoats, on which popular anger may be vented. This serves the common interests of the regime and the nomenklatura and can also be used to manipulate internal divisions and contradictions. Designated scapegoats are as far as possible external to the regime but may even, when necessary, include internal segments of the power elite as well. Examples of designated scapegoats include so-called 'foreign speculators', Ovimbundus, mulattoes and whites.

Furthermore, it is important not to forget the fact that, as an 'obscure' and 'backward' practice, witchcraft is represented in revolutionary discourse as being part of the traditional world, the realm inhabited by women. In the words of Samora Machel, with reference to the liberation of Mozambican women, 'all superstitions and religions find their most fertile soil among women, because they are immersed in the greatest ignorance and obscurantism' (1981: 24; quoted in Scott 1995: 111). In *Totonya*, specifically in the Benguela context under analysis, men's conduct towards those who are peripheral and therefore threatening to power — namely women — is analogous to that of the Marxist regime as a whole. They also make use of the discourse on witchcraft to exempt themselves from any behavioural responsibility, thus keeping the gender power structures intact. For years, Totonya is persuaded to believe that the person who is responsible for her own and her family's situation is not Quim, but Joana, in a clear recollection of the ancient colonial rule of 'Divide et Impera' [Divide and Rule] (Gentili 1999: 7–36). Again, women are shown not to have a voice within the contact zone, as here too the process of transculturation is being manoeuvred by men. As such, all of Totonya's energy is spent on trying to win Quim back. Compelled to live in unofficial polygamy, she becomes a constant victim of Quim's rage attacks and she accepts them without question, as she believes that he is not responsible for them:

> A surra passou a ser o pão de cada dia. Surrar Totonya, para Quim deixa de ser um hábito para se tornar um vício. Assim era a vida de Totonya, vida essa que aguenta cerca de três anos. Não podia sair. Ainda tinha esperanças que Quim voltaria p'ra ela. Porque as pessoas que conheciam o tradicionalismo assim o diziam. Diziam que a amante lhe dera drogas, que fazem os imbanda e que adormecem totalmente o passado, para dedicar-se sòmente à quem lhe deu a droga. Mas diziam também que esta droga, mas diziam que mais tarde

> ou mais cedo acabaria e ele voltaria para casa. Por isso Totonya se encontrava ali. Para receber o marido de braços abertos, quando ele voltasse, para que os filhos desamparados e tristes como estavam, voltassem a ser felizes. (Da Silva 2005: 39–40)
>
> [The beatings became her everyday reality. For Quim, beating Totonya up ceases to be a habit and becomes an addiction. Such was Totonya's life, a life that she endured for about three years. She could not leave. She still hoped that Quim would come back to her. Because the people who knew about traditionalism said so. They said that his lover had given him drugs that produce a spell which makes people completely forget about their pasts — so that they dedicate themselves solely to the one who gave them the drug. But they also said that the effect of this drug would wear off sooner or later, and he would then return home. This is why Totonya stayed there: to welcome her husband with open arms on his return, so that the children, forsaken and sad as they were, could be happy again.]

She completely neglects herself so as to adjust to the new order in the contact zone. Due to Quim's total alienation from the family, she is forced to assume all manner of responsibilities within the household. In addition, the fact that she is constantly injured due to the beatings prevents her from attending her classes and, thus, carrying on with her studies. Yet, she continues to consult different sorcerers, who are recommended to her by other women, as they provide her with the temporary illusion of having the power to change Quim. It is, thus, made clear that in this setting women can only exert any sort of action through the intervention of men, but these sorcerers manipulate the small fragments of illusory power given to women, in order to consolidate the male network. As individuals who are perceived to have the power to change people's destinies, the sorcerers are portrayed in the novel as having a major influence on the way people conduct their lives. By leading women to believe that other women and not men are responsible for polygamy, not only do they divert women away from the reality of the gender power structures in operation, but they also manipulate them to reinforce this reality and ensure its propagation. Although Quim's behaviour keeps Totonya imprisoned in the passive private sphere, the whole of society expects her to contribute to the maintenance of the modern community in the public arena.

Another very important aspect to focus on is the evolution and subsequent elimination of Totonya's desire. This begins when Quim decides to get himself another wife in the aftermath of the newborn child's death, and it is never fully revoked in the entire novel. Interestingly, when Totonya first arrives at Benguela and meets the *mestiço* man who helps her, she expresses desire for him, which demonstrates her awareness of her own body and pleasures:

> Totonya achou-o interessante.
> — Que bacana! — pensou — como é que eu não o tinha reparado antes? Ai se eu fosse solteira... juro que esse tipo não me escapava... — e sorriu por dentro ao imaginar o que diria Quim, se lhe dissesse o que estava acontecendo com ela naquele momento. (Da Silva 2005: 20)
>
> [Totonya found him interesting.

> 'Cool!', she thought, 'How have I not noticed him before? Oh, if only I were single... I swear that this guy would not escape me...' And she smiled to herself, imagining what Quim would say, if she told him what was happening to her at that moment.]

Nevertheless, she only does this in her mind, and always in a very self-censored manner, thus adopting a behaviour that is indicative of both a conservative Catholic and a classic Marxist stance. From the moment in which Quim prevents her from having a sex life, Totonya gradually loses control over her body and it becomes exclusively the passive receptacle of Quim's violence. And she never claims her desire back. Given that the markedly masculine process of modernising the new nation state depends on women's cultural sacrifices to succeed, female desire is elided for the sake of maintaining male hegemonic authority within the household — and, consequently, in the outside world as well. It is, therefore, not surprising that the sorcerers use their status to reinstate the colonisation of the female body. As soon as they become aware of the fact that Totonya has not had any sexual activity since Quim found himself a new lover, most of the sorcerers that she meets offer to replace him as sexual partners. Hence, despite acknowledging the total elision of female desire and sexuality, they do so with a view to replacing the hegemonic male with another hegemonic male, thus allowing the sexual economy to remain undisturbed. Nonetheless, Totonya's refusal to have sex with the sorcerers either to voice her sexual desire or to guarantee Quim's return to the household can, thus, be read as a move towards taking back the female body in the sense that it represents her choice of actively disrupting the propagation of the sexual economy. As a consequence, the autoethnographic journey becomes celebratory, as it exposes women's sexual representation as passive and exchangeable items in a male-dominated sexual circuit, simultaneously subverting this same representation through Totonya's choice to place herself in a position of decision making as regards her own sexuality and desire.

Quim's constant violence towards Totonya also represents a strategy to confine her sexuality and ensure that she remains within the limits of the household, the official non-existence of which, within the official discourse of the nation, guarantees men's mobility and uncontested power. In the aftermath of another beating, Totonya ends up being taken to hospital by some female neighbours, who do not mention the truth about her injuries to the doctors for fear of retaliation. When questioned by the doctors and nurses, Totonya lies. Despite knowing that she could put an end to her misery by making public a private matter, she chooses not to do so because she still believes in the excuses for Quim's behaviour (Da Silva 2005: 60–62). Throughout this process of assimilation to the new cultural setting, Totonya loses her *self*, and her female cultural identity: she does not know who she is anymore, nor does she know how she is meant to behave. Her self-alienation reaches a point at which she harms herself, while praying to her Luanda God (Da Silva 2005: 84). In fact, in moments of despair, Luanda is immediately called upon as the place of salvation, in clear opposition to Benguela. Apart from Totonya's obvious connection with Luanda, the city is the place where her family (who can supposedly do something to help her) lives; the place where her children want to escape to; the place that connotes modernity. Luanda is portrayed as her safety net, the place where there is a positive and stable order, as opposed to the complex and obscure reality of Benguela. This takes us to the third moment in Totonya's autoethnographic journey, in which the perceptions of the relationship between Luanda and Benguela change once again. Tired of waiting for change, she decides to travel to Luanda in order to inform both her own and Quim's family of the couple's situation and request their assistance. Totonya's return to Luanda implies a deviation in the autoethnographic journey which, in turn, materialises her response to her own identity construction within the Benguela contact zone. In an effort to confront and ultimately deconstruct her *other* gender identity in the *other* community, she attempts to recuperate her former *self* identity, as she knew it before entering the contact zone. Given that, in Totonya's perception, the Luanda-instituted model of community has always seemed horizontal, the reaffirmation of its universal validity appears to be the only way to claim a space for women in the contact zone and, thus, oppose the male-dominated transculturation process that takes place in Benguela.

In Luanda, once Totonya's family learns of her situation, they decide to call Quim's family so that both families can think of a solution together. Despite demonstrating that they are shocked at and ashamed of the state of affairs, Quim's family direct their frustration at the women, condemning their behaviour. Firstly, they direct it at Quim's mother, given that she had previous knowledge of the situation, but had asked Totonya not to tell anyone about it, as she would bring shame on the family. Subsequently, they direct it at southern women, disapproving of their behaviour and generally associating them with witchcraft. In the end, both families decide that one member of each family should be sent to Benguela, along with Totonya, to force Joana to undo the spell and to make sure that Quim gets treatment, and that normality, according to their terms, is restored. However, when Quim's uncle, Francisco Alfredo Dudas, fails to join the other members of the party on the scheduled date, the multiple hidden layers of Luanda men's behaviour begin to be unveiled before Totonya's eyes. Soon she finds out that Dudas also practises unofficial polygamy, having four wives. By hiding in a different house every day, he escapes Totonya's family, thus refusing to make his contribution to the dismantlement of a structure that he also benefits from. Eventually, Totonya's family gets tired of the wait and decides that the best thing to do is not to send anyone at all — Totonya would have to be patient and accept her situation:

> A Totonya vai ter paciência. Desta vez vai ainda sòzinha. Depois, nós aqui vamos ver se conseguimos mais convocar a família do tale marido. Depois agente telefona pra Totonya pra dizer como é que foi. Ouviu mana? Deve ser tua karma já, vamos fazé mais como? Não fica zangada, nós vamo resolver. (Da Silva 2005: 147)

> [Totonya, you will have to be patient. This time you will have to go back alone. Then we'll see if we can get your husband's family together again. We will call you afterwards, to let you know how it went. Did you hear me, sister?

> This must be your karma, anyway, so what else can we do? Do not be angry, we will sort this out.]

This episode in Luanda represents a very important stage in the autoethnographic journey. At this point the proximity between Luanda and Benguela is portrayed, once again, as irrefutable; this time the continuity between the two distinct communities is achieved through the efforts made to ensure the maintenance of the gender power structures. The separation between the private and the public spheres is preserved by the connivance of Totonya and Quim's families, which demonstrates the limitations of the nation's official revolutionary discourse of nationhood for women's emancipation. It reveals, in addition, an awareness of the need to sacrifice women to ensure the success of the transculturation process. They are meant to silently accept their contradictory positioning within the negotiated identity of the community as 'karma', as a destiny which is not open to renegotiation. Hence, Luanda, just like Benguela, emerges as a negative contact zone, in which the postcolonial conceptualisation of the nation responds to the colonial one, by attempting to overcome it — despite being aware of the impossibility of (completely) erasing the previously instituted models of community. As Scott points out, the political elite responsible for the revolutionary discourse was aware that maintaining their hold on power would entail negotiation with other social elites. The discourse of unity would, thus, be achieved through the sacrifice of women, as the class and economic liberation of women so emphasised during the pro-liberation war would have to be deprioritised in the post-independence setting. As Scott puts it, 'in this sense, both governments [the MPLA and Frelimo] have attempted to maintain political support by conceding the terrain of the household to male authority' (1995: 110). It is therefore made clear for Totonya that in the Luanda contact zone the prevalence of the dominant ideology also depends on the preservation of a patriarchal hierarchy within the family structure. Once more, her autoethnographic journey allows her to comprehend that, indeed, there is no place for women in this contact zone either, as the transculturation process is, again, produced by and for men.

Powerless, Totonya returns to Benguela only to find a very well-behaved Quim expecting her at their place. Eventually, she realises that he does so in anticipation of the consequences of Totonya's trip to Luanda — he is scared that his freedom might be jeopardised if the private becomes public. Obviously, a month later, when he is sure that none of his family members will reprimand him, he feels comfortable enough to go back to his old ways. At the same time, he starts devising a plan to completely disempower Totonya in the public sphere, so as to prevent her from ever becoming a threat to him, in his position of an official representative of socialist ideology, who is openly subverting it. It becomes clear at this point that Quim is working consciously and opportunistically towards the preservation of a gender power structure which cuts across all community discourses. Nevertheless, Totonya is incapable of any reaction. She seeks the advice of OMA, but when its secretaries suggest calling in Quim for a conversation, she refuses to allow them to interfere. She knows that Quim's public image, as the prototype of the socialist, revolutionary and modern New Man, depends on his control of the private sphere. Therefore, she sacrifices herself to keep his projected masculinity intact, and, following the advice of a friend (who, curiously enough works at the Municipal Committee of the MPLA), she carries on consulting *kimbandas* in an attempt to undo Joana's bewitchment. Having been completely deprived of any identity in both the Luanda and the Benguela settings, Totonya is willing to fully assimilate to the new cultural setting to safeguard some sense of continuity, as she is still unable to recreate her identity outside any imagination that defines her *self* in relation to her husband. In her perception, Quim leaving their household represents her complete loss of identity:

> Não sei porquê a Joana fez isso comigo. Não devia fazer essa partida pra... pra mim. Devia vir só e ficávamos as duas. Não é... não é proibido um homem ter duas mulheres. Ago... agora por cima do que é meu, va... vai ficar com ele as... assim. Vai enfei... feitiçar o meu marido pra ficar só... só dela, de cor... de corpo e alma? Oh! Não. Não Lúcia, é muito pra mim. Que mal é que fiz nesse mundo, pra merecer tanto castigo? (Da Silva 2005: 156)
>
> [I do not know why Joana did this to me. She should not play such tricks on... on me. She should just come over and the two of us would be here together. It's not ... it's not forbidden for a man to have two women. Now... now she takes over what's mine, and she's going to keep... keep him just like... like that. She puts a spell... a spell on my husband to keep him just... just for her, body... body and soul? Oh! No. No, Lúcia, this is too much for me to handle. What harm have I done in this world, to deserve such a punishment?]

Aware that Totonya still has the power to destroy his public image by exposing his treatment of her in the private sphere, Quim seeks to disempower her. He does so by reversing the situation. Taking advantage of the fact that Totonya travelled to Luanda without his knowledge, he proceeds to destroy her public image by questioning her behaviour in the private sphere. He, thus, spreads the rumour that Totonya was unfaithful to him in order to discredit her publicly, subsequently creating a reason to expel her from the household, or even to kill her if she refuses to leave (Da Silva 2005: 171–73). Totonya's refusal to disempower Quim ends up providing him with the tools he needs to disempower her. Left with no other option, she ends up escaping the household and even considering suicide, but the image of her abandoned children prevents her from doing so. Dona Andresa, Totonya's devoted friend, provides shelter for both her and her children. It is in this new household that Totonya makes contact with different conceptions of femininity for the first time, as she learns more about D. Andresa's six daughters. D. Andresa, who became a widow at the age of twenty-seven, has struggled all her life in order to provide her daughters with the best education they could get. Hence, her first daughter, Carla, who is twenty-seven years old, is studying Economics in London and is single. Dora, the second daughter, twenty-six years old and a final-year medical student in Uambo, is also single. The third daughter, Lala, is a divorcee who had been sent to study in Switzerland straight after her divorce, and is now working in Luanda, at the Ministry of Foreign Affairs. She has one daughter, who is living with D. Andresa. Mima, the fourth daughter, is twenty-one years old and has two children. She studied in Cuba, but was unable to complete her course due to her pregnancy. She is now living in Benguela with her soon-to-be husband Walter, with whom she is very happy, and both of them have resumed their studies. Isa, the fifth daughter, is a twenty-year-old dance student in Portugal. And, finally, Maria José is eighteen years old and studies in Luanda. Of all six daughters, D. Andresa is only concerned about the older ones (who refuse to get married, and consequently, do not achieve the social status that marriage provides to women), and Mima (who, in her mother's view, did not take full advantage of her opportunity to study abroad and, because of that, now has to share a home with her mother-in-law and sisters-in-law).

In the novel, these women incorporate experiences of femininity which are very distinct from all of the others that Totonya comes into contact with throughout her autoethnographic journey. All of D. Andresa's daughters seem to be very aware of the limitations of revolutionary ideology for women. Therefore, from within their (class and economic) public liberation, they subvert the patriarchal imagination of the nation through their refusal to reproduce the male sexual economy of women's exchange. The absence of the patriarchal male in this female-dominated household can be read as a prediction of the disturbance of the male sexual economy. Decisions are made by women who, once in that position, are able to bring forward challenging female identities which are highly disruptive to convention. Hence, there are, at this point, three important aspects that the novel focuses on regarding the female identity. Firstly, there is a clear reference being made to education as the means to allow women to rewrite their identities, which echoes the socialist ideals of women's emancipation in the public sphere for their engagement in the revolution. Secondly, education also emerges as the means for women to attain freedom — not only in terms of physical and sociocultural mobility, but also in terms of personal choice. Finally, the majority of female subjectivities proposed here emerge as detached from men, as if to suggest that women's rewriting of their own identities is something that they have to undertake on their own. Although women are analysed here within a markedly masculine context, feminine identities never really get to be renegotiated alongside masculine identities. Hence, the description of the six daughters' diverging paths adds to Totonya's autoethnographic journey in the sense that it reveals alternative female subjectivities. These subjectivities respond to and are in dialogue with predefined representations, thus actively engaging in the renegotiation of the ongoing transculturation process in the national narrative.

Once Totonya starts feeling part of this family, some changes begin to emerge in her behaviour. She starts by getting the courage to file a formal police complaint. Nevertheless, the police prove to be completely useless, as they lose the official documents of Totonya's denunciation five days later. And even when Totonya looks for the party's help, she is confronted with the same inefficiency:

> — Não sei quais foram os problemas que fizeram com que ele te pusesse na rua — disse — de qualquer forma, acho que, pra um homem agir assim tem que ter motivos fortes. Vou ver o que ele vai dizer. Vou tentar ajudar. Mas fica já a saber, que não posso obrigar um homem a viver com uma mulher que não quer. (Da Silva 2005: 183)

> ['I do not know what problems prompted him to throw you out on the street,' he said. 'Anyway, I think that for a man to act like this he must have strong motives. I'll hear what he's got to say. I'll try to help. But let me tell you, I cannot force a man to live with a woman he does not want.]

Again, the household is portrayed as a blind spot that is beyond the limits of influence of official discourse, where male hegemony is not to be contested. Furthermore, the fact that both the police officer and the party assistant are men suggests that they work together to maintain this order. In the aftermath of these frustrating meetings with the representatives of the official nation state, Totonya visits a *kimbanda* for the last time. After begging the old sorcerer to help her, he tries to rape her, but she manages to escape. Although at this point she can only envisage her sexuality within her marriage, which is over, by resisting the *kimbanda* she also rejects the circuit of the male sexual economy. When Quim looks her up to tell her that she is not a threat to him anymore because the party would not force him to take her back, Totonya finally gives up on him and starts focusing solely on her own survival and that of her children. Totonya's disconnection from Quim materialises in the restoration of her desire, when for the first time she feels attracted to another man, Lino, D. Andresa's eldest nephew. Finally, when she discovers that Quim has ruined her reputation across the entire town, she decides to place a request for a work transfer and moves away with her children. We do not know whereabouts in Angola she moves to, but the text does mention that she chooses neither Luanda, nor Benguela, but herself and her children. The last few lines of the novel suggest that Totonya rebuilds her identity, but never again is she able to fall in love, for fear that another man may steal her identity from her — again reinforcing the idea of the emergence of an alternative female identity being conditioned by women's disconnection from men.

Conclusion to Chapter 3

Scott (1995: 9) claims that, 'class relations and subordinate relations between centre and periphery in the world capitalist economy thus take precedence in dependence theory; other locations of struggle, contradiction, and conflict are given less attention'. In a move that seems to reinforce Scott's view, the novel *Totonya* proposes the household as an*other* location of gender struggle, in a very specific historic moment in which the renegotiation of communal identity was occurring. In this continuous renegotiation, balance depends on the stabilisation of the male identity as somehow continuous (in a permanently and rapidly changing world) in the private sphere. This means that the stabilisation of the male identity is achieved through the sacrifice of the female identity, which becomes contradictory. On the one hand, women become representatives of the modern world in that they leave the 'backward' traditional world behind to occupy a space in and validate the male designed/oriented revolutionary public space. On the other hand, women become representatives of the traditional world in that it is the maintenance of their identity in the private sphere that provides the male identity with a sense of continuity.

Hence, it is women that bear all the responsibility for maintaining a continuous and stable communal identity, which is meant to be simultaneously adaptable and modern. This perception gives a whole new dimension to the revisiting of this particular socialist and revolutionary context in 1998, especially if we take into consideration the fact that in this period the Angolan government was attempting to respond to the international directives of the World Bank and the IMF. As Scott (1995: 18) reminds us, although the World Bank targeted women specifically in their development policies from 1989 onwards, their directives came to put more pressure on women, given that 'women continue to be defined in terms of procreative, childrearing, and "household economy" functions, but they are also made the new "targets" of government policies and the recipients of greater bureaucratic discipline and control'.[9]

The novel, thus, seems to ask, 'when will Angolan women have a place in the ethnography of the nation?' Totonya's autoethnographic journey sets out to make this blind spot visible in the continuous imagination of *Angolanidade* [Angolanness]. The clear deconstructive gesture of 'celebratory autoethnography' (Huggan 2001: 43) claims a place for women in the narrative of the Angolan nation through the historicisation of the female experience. Furthermore, it exposes the limits of the dominant national discourse, simultaneously exposing the Luanda and Benguela communities as negative contact zones which are maintained through the male dominance of the household. It also reveals how the transculturation processes which occur in both settings are recreations of a masculine modernity that limits women's options within cultural identity. And, finally, it attempts to resist preconceived female representations by proposing new forms of female subjectivity which are able to engage in the active renegotiation of the nation. Although Da Silva is less optimistic than Chiziane, for example, in the proposal of new female representations, the novel does open the way for some alternatives (D. Andresa's daughters and even Totonya, by the end of the story), which might suggest a process of transculturation which is inclusive of women who, alongside men, should proceed to the definition of 'Angolanness'.

Notes to Chapter 3

1. Portuguese translation of a Cabinda Proverb, quoted in A. P. Tavares (2004: 49).
2. On the strategic use of gender and sexual difference to deconstruct structures of exoticism, see A. M. Martins (2012).
3. See Ganho (2004). Ganho provides a discussion of gender, sexuality and ethnicity within the rewriting of Angolan nation and imagery, as depicted in the works of the Angolan poets Lopito Feijoó and Ana Paula Tavares.
4. For a discussion of the role of the World Bank in the (counterproductive) definition of 'the woman question' as one of the priorities of the 1990s development plan for African countries that underwent structural adjustment (so as to access its funding), see Scott (1995: 69–86).
5. The *indígenas* were a group composed by the majority of native Africans, whereas the *não indígenas* were an elite composed of the great majority of Afro-Portuguese and native Africans who had been educated in the Portuguese Catholic missions. As such, the latter were in a better position to develop the consciousness that would later materialise in the formation of the nationalist movements.

6. Signed in 1994 by the MPLA and the UNITA representatives, the Lusaka Agreement proposed the formation of a coalition government, the GURN (Governo de Unidade e Reconciliação Nacional) [Government of National Unity and Reconciliation] in which power would be shared by the two parties. Nevertheless, this coalition would only be made possible on the condition that UNITA would disarm and its military forces would be integrated into the national army, which, of course, was controlled by the MPLA government. Given that none of the parties demonstrated the will to respect the conditions imposed, the agreement was unsuccessful (Messiant 2001: 102–03).
7. On the nature of the Eduardo dos Santos Foundation (FESA) and the context of its emergence in the year 1996, as part of a strategic plan devised by both the president and the MPLA to minimise popular discontent, see Messiant (2001).
8. Tripp (2015: 128) argues that 'The Family Code recognised common-law marriage, introduced protections for children born out of wedlock, and encouraged an equal division of labour within the home. It also encouraged debate on customary marriage, abortion, and other controversial topics'.
9. Mama (2001: 63–73) focuses on the examples of Zaire and Zimbabwe to show how the authoritarian Mobutu and Mugabe governments, respectively, made use of international gender discourses to secure external funds and, simultaneously, reinforce their hold on power.

CONCLUSION

Rethinking National Identity through Gender

> Identity is all about power and resistance, subjection and citizenship, action and reaction.
> I would suggest that *rather than simply passing over identity*
> *in order to rethink power,*
> we need to profoundly *rethink* identity
> *if we are to begin to comprehend the meaning of power.*
>
> Amina Mama

This study sought to promote the critical analysis of literary works written in Portuguese by female African writers in an attempt to enlarge the field of literary research, from a postcolonial theoretical perspective, inside the Portuguese-speaking world. It aimed to formulate a new and timely approach to the marginalised female voices that emerge from within these countries with a view to furthering the understanding of how the authors build their postcolonial nations culturally, from a female-focalised point of view, and how they represent the women of these nations in interaction with the transcultural contexts that pertain to each country. This was done through the comparative analysis of a corpus from Cape Verde, Mozambique and Angola, with a specific focus on the literary production of the female authors Dina Salústio (1941–), Paulina Chiziane (1955–) and Rosária da Silva (1959–).

The works developed by all three authors demonstrate the importance of considering nationalism and national identity from a gender perspective, gender being the foundation on which these cultural constructions are built. At the same time, they highlight the potential of suitably located and contextualised gender analyses for the understanding of the power networks that maintain hegemonic national narratives; the various intersecting marginal subjectivities that emerge from these discourses; and consequently, the practices of resistance put forward to oppose them. In order to think about nationalism and national identity through this particular literary corpus, the study has departed from the global approaches of specific postcolonial theorists whose works analyse and deconstruct hegemonic discourses of identity. By engaging with and assessing the feasibility and limitation of the application of these theories to the gender-related issues emerging from the specific postcolonial contexts under analysis, as represented by the female authors, this study amplified those theories.

The point of departure was a discussion of Anderson's understanding of the nation as an 'imagined community' and the limitations of its applicability to the contexts of Cape Verde, Mozambique and Angola (1991). This is an understanding which not only highlights the invented nature of the aforementioned conceptualisation (and, thus, its openness and flexibility), but which also reveals the potential for communion of marginal discourses. This perspective was explored alongside Bhabha's theorisation of the dynamics of national discourse, the instability of which comes from its pedagogical dimension being constantly disturbed and subverted by the performative one (1990: 291–322). Again, marginality emerged as an empowered place of renegotiation and reconstruction, which took us to Edward Said's reflections on exile. Said (2001a) defends that the condition of exile represents an irrecoverable displacement of the human being as regards their own homeland, which makes them struggle constantly in order to build strategies and mechanisms that will enable them to attempt to somehow recapture a sense of continuity in relation to their origins. This experience, which normally entails a geographical displacement, acquires a whole new dimension when observed within the geographical limits of the nation. Andrea O'Reilly Herrera uses the term *insílio* to refer to this specific condition, claiming that it is a psychological and emotional state that precedes the actual physical exile, and manifests itself through feelings of alienation (2001: xvii–xxxiii).

These reflections on the awareness and subsequent active involvement of the displaced in the discussion of the discourses of nationhood were also at the core of Mary Louise Pratt's theorisation of contact zones, autoethnography and transculturation (1991). Pratt advances the term 'contact zone' with reference 'to social spaces where cultures meet, clash, and grapple with each other, often in contexts of highly asymmetrical relations of power, such as colonialism, slavery, or their aftermaths as they are lived out in many parts of the world today' (1991:1). Regardless of being positive or negative, Pratt continues, these 'contact zones' always disrupt the continuity of instituted models of community. Hence, Pratt defends that autoethnographic texts have an unquestionably relevant role in the production of negative contact zones (such as colonial environments). This is due to their ability to propose alternative representations in dialogue with established ethnographic texts. The dialogue results in a phenomenon that the Cuban sociologist Fernando Ortiz called transculturation, which stands for the capacity demonstrated by marginal groups to select and appropriate certain features of the dominant culture (and vice versa), thus continuously renegotiating the conceptualisation of the community (1991: 2). This emphasis on the disruptive potential of autoethnography was recaptured in Graham Huggan's study of the Post-Colonial Exotic, as he observed the possibilities that emerge from what he called 'celebratory autoethnography' (2001: 34–57). Huggan advances the term 'the anthropological exotic' to refer to a general tendency to make Africa and African literature more attractive to Western audiences, simultaneously highlighting the emergence of 'ethnographic counter-discourse[s]' in contemporary African literary production that respond[s] to this phenomenon (2001: 37–40). 'Celebratory autoethnography' is, therefore, a strategy of resistance that keeps dismantling predefined representations, as well as reopening and adding to the debate on nationhood (2001: 43).

However, considering that the above-mentioned approaches largely exclude gender perspectives, the present study interrogated their premises further by incorporating postcolonial feminist theories as well as feminist theories from sociology. Anne McClintock (1995) and Nira Yuval-Davis (1997) advocate that all nations are based on gender difference. This means that all discourses of nationhood are built upon defined conceptualisations of womanhood and manhood which arise from specific historical, geographical and sociocultural contexts (being those colonial, anti-colonial or postcolonial). McClintock points out that women have historically been labelled as the 'symbolic bearers of the nation', despite not having any real access to national agency. As such, the analysis of nationalism through the lens of a theory of gender power would give access to various experiences of the nation (which change according to gender, class, ethnic group, race, generation, etc.), simultaneously enabling the rethinking of national identities (1995: 354–60). Amina Mama (2001) reinforces this position by affirming that the analysis of identity through gender enables a greater understanding of the intricacies of power structures in operation. In doing so, it simultaneously unveils the best tools to dismantle these structures, with a view to constructing more inclusive and democratic ways of experiencing selfhood and/in nationhood. Hence, localised examinations of women's representations within national discourses, and the contextualised strategies they put forward to force the renegotiation of their identities, emerge as empowering places of resistance and change (2001: 67).

Considering that the three nation states under analysis had one-party socialist regimes immediately after independence, Catherine Scott's study on gender and development theories comes to complement the aforementioned theorisations, in terms of a situated analysis of gender (1995: 105–19). Scott argues that revolutionary discourses influenced by Marxism-Leninism considered modernity (and women's emancipation) to be a revolutionary process that could occur only within the public space. This led to the immediate association of the private sphere — and therefore the household — with obsolete traditionalism and obscurantism. The omission of a space which was historically bound to women and, to a certain extent, of a female historicity is not innocent. Focusing particularly on the cases of Mozambique and Angola, Scott claims that in the years that followed independence, both the Frelimo and the MPLA governments negotiated their hold on power with other social elites by allowing male authority to remain uncontested within the household (1995: 110). As the 'symbolic bearers of the nation', women became simultaneous markers of modernity and tradition, and the female body turned into a place of power struggle where the limits of the nation were defined (McClintock 1995: 354). It is, therefore, not surprising that in these contexts the household setting and its consequent politicisation emerged as women's site of resistance.

As such, the present study provided a series of readings which draw on the above-mentioned theoretical framework, and simultaneously assess the feasibility and limitation of the application of such theories to the gender-related issues which emerge from each specific context under analysis. This was achieved through a detailed exploration of the ways in which each author represented, narrated and mediated the social, linguistic, cultural and anthropological coordinates of the internally differentiated spaces that constitute Cape Verde, Mozambique and Angola. In addition, these readings allowed me to explore the possible existence of points of convergence that link these women's experiences of Portuguese colonialism and the socialist experiment — i.e. to postulate some common postcolonial spaces that reproduce African women's experiences.

What Brings Them Together

Cape Verde, Mozambique and Angola are three young nation states bound by some specific commonalities as well as differences in terms of their Portuguese colonial inheritance and their experiences of liberation wars. Their distinct pre-colonial, colonial and post-colonial histories determined the development of the discussion on national identity that followed independence in the three countries. Although this discussion took place in relation to various areas of public life, it found a special place in literary production. Writers were therefore given the responsibility of creating national literary canons which could reflect the cultural uniqueness of their newly born nations. As such, in the representations of the three contexts, identity is portrayed as a work in progress, an open process which is conceptualised within specific power structures that emerge from particular historical, geographical and circumstantial frameworks. Indeed, literature becomes a privileged place for contemplating national identity and questioning the processes of identity building, as Inocência Mata points out (2006: 17–31).

Despite their different nationalities, backgrounds and ages, Dina Salústio, Paulina Chiziane and Rosária da Silva each share the common achievement of being the first female novel writer to emerge in the context of their own independent countries of origin. As women of their time, all three of them were connected with the three pro-liberation movements that took control of the governments at independence (PAIGC, Frelimo and MPLA, respectively). Hence, they made use of the space created for women in the public realm by the socialist governments, in order to enter the male-dominated literary circles. They subsequently engaged in forms of writing that aimed to shed light on a blind spot in the nation's imaginary: they set out to contemplate the national identity project, in the post-independence period, through women's experience. More than simply putting women on the national map, their expositions of female experience (which had been marginalised up to that point) reveal the complex and multiple layers that make up the construction of identity, as well as the power structures in operation at the moment of its production. Taking these facts into consideration, this study was divided into three sections, each devoted to the analysis of works by each author. This structure enabled a greater understanding of the specificities that particularise each of the distinct contexts and, consequently, the literary production that emerges from them, which facilitated contextualised and situated gender analyses.

Simultaneously, this individualised reading allowed for the emergence of a set of commonalities that transverse the works of the three authors, therefore broadly confirming the existence of a postcolonial space that reproduces African women's experiences, with some modifications.

The three authors' points of departure for thinking about national identity through gender correspond to what Mama (2001: 67) calls 'the politicization of personal experience'. This allows for the examination of how gender identity and subjectivities come to be constructed and maintained by hegemonic ideological discourses. Considering the dialectical relationship between text and context in African literatures (Mata 2006: 17–31), I argue that the three authors portray scenes of everyday female life within specific geographical, historical and political contexts, in order to reveal that the stability that underpins the imagining of the community depends on strict gender representations which, very often, imply a subjugation of feminine subjectivities. Hence, this analysis of female experiences within the collective imaginary exposes the flaws in the discourses of communal cohesion experienced throughout the history of these young nation states — the hegemonic colonial discourse; the unifying ideal of the socialist nation; the discourse of survival throughout the internal conflicts and civil wars, in the specific cases of Mozambique and Angola, respectively; the democratic ideal of the modern nation, mediated by powerful international entities such as the World Bank and the IMF. It simultaneously unveils their patriarchal nature, through identifying not only their unitary and authoritarian character, but also their dependence on the exercise of control over the female body.

At a subsequent stage, I argue that this revelation exposes a set of experiences of the nation that have been continuously marginalised in favour of an imposed unifying national identity. In other words, the process of gender marginalisation is the point of departure for rethinking the complexities of the formation of a national narrative which is able to recognise and incorporate its margins, through historical revision. The historicisation of female experience through the recovery of a genealogical memory allows access to multiple experiences of womanhood that emerge through the intersection of variants such as race, class, ethnicity and place of origin. Through the recuperation of these female genealogical memories it becomes possible to retrieve other marginal experiences of the nation, which are also part of the grand national narrative (Sanches 2007: 133). These experiences force the decentralisation of the hegemonic discourses of nationhood by making the nation confront its own mirrored image of multiplicity, and bring about cartographic and other reconfigurations in the delineation of the national narrative. Hence, by demonstrating that the imagination of the nation is not a shared conceptualisation, these female subjectivities question the imposed cultural construction, ultimately forcing the national discourse to review and rewrite itself. It is, therefore, by rethinking gender identity that these authors set out to rethink the whole conceptualisation of identity, in general, and national identity, specifically. While deconstructing the intrinsic power structures, they simultaneously propose alternatives. These alternative configurations of gender identity assert the limitations of conventional gender identities and, consequently, destabilise the patriarchal, elitist and exclusivist discourses of community which are built upon them. Through their affirmation, these subversive, challenging identities will ultimately put forward new, diverse, decentralised and more inclusive ways of imagining the collective.

What Sets Them Apart

Notwithstanding the existence of these points of convergence made up of shared female preoccupations and strategies, there are also specificities that particularise the experiences of each context. Dina Salústio's proposal of debating nationhood and national identity through gender emphasises the colonial continuities which are still visible in a Cape Verdean post-independence context. Her revision of the cultural material that composes the national identity and defines the national community reveals the historical alienation of women. This is achieved through the maintenance of a patriarchal social structure which, in turn, feeds upon static gender conceptualisations that keep women in subalternity. Hence, Salústio's interventionist attempt to denounce the inconsistencies of the modern discourse of nationhood, from a gender perspective, exposes the ongoing practice of colonial sexual ideals and practices of fertility. In addition, by observing the various intersecting power relations that sustain that discourse, Salústio reflects on how gender, class, race and colour interact with a view to maintaining the colonial conceptualisations of social dynamics in postcoloniality. These choices made by the author, so as to promote the debate on nationalism and gender, become clearer in light of the country's historical trajectory. Cape Verde suffered a very particular type of colonisation under Portuguese rule, which enabled its inhabitants to imagine themselves as part of a consolidated and 'relatively homogenous Creole culture' (E. S. Andrade 2002: 265). This was due to three factors that must be taken into consideration. Firstly, the country did not suffer the impact of an actual anti-colonial war taking place within the geographical limits of its territory. Secondly, after independence PAIGC/PAICV ruled the country's politics uncontested for fifteen years, having been replaced by MpD (Movimento para a Democracia [Movement for Democracy]) in 1990, after the first multiparty elections took place at the archipelago. Finally, socialism acquired a much less orthodox character in this setting, not only due to the social, economic and cultural characteristics of the archipelago, but also due to the fact that the country was historically subject to continuous external influence and dependency (mostly through the action of emigrants). As such, it is possible to affirm that this image of a stable, solid and — above all, dare I say — uninterrupted Creole culture was praised and maintained in order to remain undisturbed as the basis for a unifying discourse of nationhood. In other words, tradition, as representative of a solid cultural identity — along with its intrinsic power structures — was recuperated and recycled so as to serve the purposes of the modern nation, whose long-term success depended on the impact and assimilation of this adaptable national narrative. Although PAIGC/PAICV's one-party political regime in Cape

Verde did not have the impact that Frelimo's or MPLA's had in Mozambique and Angola, respectively, the modern Cape Verdean nation was built upon patriarchal structures of power that expose colonial continuities. Indeed, the promises of what Chabal (2008: 46) calls '"the imagined modernity" [...] turned out to have been a cruel mirage for the immense majority', particularly women. The author's emphasis on the ongoing nature of these interrelationships seems to indicate the need to actively engage in the decolonisation of minds, habits and customs — the culture which is taken for granted. This will enable the open defiance of the stagnant nature of that Creole culture and demonstrate that identity, national identity and nationhood are works in progress.

Given their similar colonial inheritance, orthodox socialist experience and problematic internal negotiation of the nation in the immediate post-independence period, it is possible to generate some important parallels between the Mozambican and the Angolan cases that do not apply to the Cape Verdean one. This became quite visible throughout the analysis of both Chiziane and Da Silva's depictions of their respective countries of origins, stances and treatments of the questions of nationalism and gender. It is true that all three authors set out to indicate new and more challenging ways of undertaking gender struggle in the future, by deconstructing past and present conceptualisations of gender in communal discourses of identity. However, it is very clear that Chiziane and Da Silva do so from within a Marxist-Leninist framework, which was, considering their proximity in generational terms, the ideological system they were formed in as young adults — in contrast to Salústio. Another aspect which is very relevant for the delineation of this parallel is the fact that both Chiziane and Da Silva perceive not only their gender, but also their race, as highly determinant factors to consider with regard to their emergence as novel writers. For these authors, it is a major affirmation to be the first black female novel writer to emerge in the specific contexts of their newly independent countries. On the one hand, it represents a disruption of the male domination of the literary canon. On the other hand, it demonstrates a disturbance of the colonial social tendency to limit people's access to the nation according to their race and colour — which, to a certain extent, legitimises the success of the socialist project.

Focusing on the specific case of Mozambique, Chiziane's proposal presents a critique of Frelimo's socialist ideal of the modern nation and national identity, from a female point of view. Throughout the process, the author reveals its limitations not only as regards women and gender struggle, but also as regards other identities and communal projects that extrapolate the boundaries of its discourse. As such, rethinking nationalism through gender in various intersections is the author's strategy for exposing, dismantling and renegotiating the power structures at work within the socialist and post-socialist modern narratives of the nation. Firstly, it enabled Chiziane to focus on the authoritarian and discriminatory nature of a markedly southern cultural conception of nationhood that did not acknowledge other ethnicities or races, and expected to be fully recognised by a multi-ethnic and multiracial society such as that of Mozambique. Secondly, it provided the author with the tools to demonstrate that that conception of nationhood was markedly male-oriented, as the socialist revolution envisioned women's emancipation primarily in economic terms, thus permitting the propagation of gender inequalities within the private sphere, which was beyond the field of revolutionary action. Thirdly, it gave Chiziane the means to reflect on how gender struggle was sacrificed in order to ensure Frelimo's hold on power, by showing that the survival of the modern nation was negotiated across race, colour, ethnicity and class, and through the female body. The author's deconstruction of the southern male-oriented socialist conceptualisation of the nation is achieved through a process of historicising female genealogies from different ethnic, racial, colour and class backgrounds. This recovery of female micro-histories exposes the colonial continuities which are strategically kept alive in the postcolonial era. Furthermore, it allows the emergence of new and more democratic ways to envision gender struggle in a post-socialist future.

Nonetheless, Chiziane's questioning of the socialist macro-history of the nation from within proves to be a revisionist work. This is something that becomes visible, for example, when the author highlights the problematic areas of socialist thinking and shows how dangerous they can be when strategically used (by a group such as RENAMO, for example). In *Ventos*, the author emphasises how in its eagerness to consolidate its hold on power, Frelimo ended up alienating those who were marginal to its socialist, markedly southern, tendentiously urban and hegemonic conceptualisation of the nation — namely villagers and traditional power representatives — simultaneously resorting to the affirmation of conventional gender identities. Aware of these dynamics, RENAMO used them against Frelimo, by recruiting new members amongst those who were dissatisfied with Frelimo's policies and using women to infiltrate the areas under Frelimo's protection so that they could study the spaces and provide RENAMO with the necessary information in order to attack the villages. Therefore, the strategies that Chiziane puts forward, with a view to building a more inclusive and democratic society, are still very much in consonance with a socialist conceptualisation of community.

Notwithstanding the particularities that individualise each literary project, some of Chiziane's concerns find an echo in Da Silva's problematisation of Angolan national identities and communities. Much like her peer, Chiziane, Da Silva aims to criticise the MPLA's univocal Marxist-Leninist discourse of nationhood from within its limits, simultaneously questioning the grounds on which this legitimisation was achieved. Aware of the existence of more than one discourse of nationhood in Angola, Da Silva moves on to test the limits of MPLA's socialist nation within two distinct territories that the party governed, only to demonstrate the imposing and assimilative nature of its discourse. Furthermore, examining the cultural dynamics in Luanda and Benguela from a female-focalised point of view leads Da Silva to disclose the masculine nature of the modern nation's discourse, in which the private sphere emerges as a blind spot. Just like Chiziane, Da Silva demonstrates that the power tension between traditional and modern that occurred in the cultural arena was balanced by the definition of areas of influence. The modern discourse of nationhood thus emerged empowered within the public sphere, whereas the influence of the traditional sphere was able to remain undisturbed within the private domain. By these means, the author proved that the modern nation that arose out of this negotiation was designed by and for men. The main preoccupation of these negotiations appeared to be the maintenance of a stable and continuous image of revolutionary and successful masculinity, which was achieved at the expense of female identity. In other words, both Chiziane and Da Silva defend the view that the successful cohesion of the socialist revolutionary nation was achieved through the maintenance of gender roles in the private sphere, a blind spot which was strategically left outside the boundaries of the modern discourse of nationhood. Both authors claim that the feasibility of the male revolution as a whole depended on the maintenance of a paradoxical female identity. In this sense, as 'symbolic bearers of the nation', women emerged as simultaneous representatives of a successful male modern nation and of a solid and continuous male cultural tradition (McClintock 1995: 354). As such, this masculinised vicious circle always prevented women from having real access to the nation. According to both Chiziane and Da Silva, this tendency could only be fought through women's self-awareness and active engagement in the renegotiation of the terms of the gender struggle in Mozambique and Angola. This would ultimately enable them to reopen the debate on Mozambican and Angolan national identities, and become empowered in the national narratives.

Conclusion

Taking into consideration the commonalities and differences between the works of Dina Salústio, Paulina Chiziane, and Rosária da Silva framed within the scope of the present study, I believe that it is possible to affirm that the three authors make history out of stories of everyday life. The micro-histories of women's daily lives, emerging from the problematic and forgotten domestic space (the arena which they are constructed to represent) disturb the macro-histories of the nations by exposing their hidden layers of power structures, thus forcing them to assume and rethink themselves in their full complexity. If the microcosms of the family and the household emerge as a metonymy for the official post-independence state and its national discourse, its collapse, as is suggested in the works of the three authors, foretells the rise of a new conception of community and, subsequently, a new conception of women within it. The emphasis that is placed on the recuperation of female genealogies not only sheds light upon the historical silencing of women's stories, but also demonstrates their alienation from a memory of continuity. Hence, the effort to proceed to that recuperation suggests the recovery of a diachronic trajectory able to promote dialogue between present and past, in order to give the future a whole new perspective. In the three authors' works, power, power relations, hegemonies and women's conditions are themes that go beyond a feminist perspective and a local contextualisation, meaning that these female-focalised stories acquire a universal and global dimension. In the end, Salústio, Chiziane and

Da Silva's literary projects of freedom take these localised specificities as a point of departure, with a view to promoting a debate over the human condition and, perhaps, delineating some strategies for conceptualising a better, fairer and more democratic existence.

BIBLIOGRAPHY

Abousema, Mona. 1990. 'Towards a New Strategy for Comparative Literature', in *Os Estudos Literários: (Entre) Ciência e Hermenêutica (Actas do I Congresso da APLC)* Vol. I (Lisbon: Associação Portuguesa de Literatura Comparada), pp. 263–70

Abranches, Henrique. 1980. *Reflexões Sobre a Cultura Nacional* (Lisbon: Edições 70)

Adão, Deolinda. 2007. 'Novos Espaços no Feminino: Uma Leitura de *Ventos do Apocalipse*, de Paulina Chiziane', in *A Mulher em África: Vozes de uma Margem Sempre Presente*, ed. by I. Mata and L. C. Padilha (Lisbon: Edições Colibri), pp. 199–207

Afonso, Maria Manuela. 2002. *Educação e Classes Sociais em Cabo Verde* (Praia: Spleen)

Almada, José Luís Hopffer Cordeiro. 1988. *Mirabílis de Veias ao Sol: Antologia dos Novíssimos Poetas Cabo-Verdianos* (Praia: Instituto Caboverdiano do Livro and Caminho)

—— (ed.) 2008. *O Ano Mágico de 2006: Olhares Retrospectivos Sobre a História e a Cultura Cabo-Verdianas* (Praia: IBNL)

Almeida, Miguel Vale de. 2004. *An Earth-Colored Sea: 'Race', Culture and the Politics of Identity in the Post-Colonial Portuguese-Speaking World* (Oxford and New York: Berghahn)

Althusser, Louis. 1970. 'Ideology and Ideological State Apparatuses (Notes Towards an Investigation)', in *Marxists Internet Archive* <https://www.marxists.org/reference/archive/althusser/1970/ideology.htm#n18> [accessed 22 May 2017]

Amâncio, Iris Maria da Costa (ed.). 2008. *África-Brasil-África: Matrizes, Heranças e Diálogos Contemporâneos* (Minas Gerais: PucMinas)

Amarílis, Orlanda. 1944. 'Acerca da Mulher', *Certeza*, 1 & 2: 6

Anderson, Benedict. 1991. *Imagined Communities: Reflections on the Origin and Spread of Nationalism* (London: Verso)

Andrade, Elisa Silva. 2002. 'Cape Verde', in *A History of Postcolonial Lusophone Africa*, ed. by Patrick Chabal et al. (London: Hurst & Company), pp. 264–90

Andrade, Mário Pinto de. 1976. *Antologia Temática de Poesia Africana: Na Noite Grávida de Punhais* (Lisbon: Sá da Costa Editora)

—— 1979. *Antologia Temática de Poesia Africana: O Canto Armado* (Lisbon: Sá da Costa Editora)

—— 1997. *Origens do Nacionalismo Africano* (Lisbon: Dom Quixote)

Arnfred, Signe. 2005. 'Conceptions of Gender in Colonial and Post-Colonial Discourses: The Case of Mozambique', in *Gender Activism and Studies in Africa*, ed. by Signe Arnfred et al. (Dakar: CODESRIA), pp. 108–28

—— 2011. *Sexuality & Gender Politics in Mozambique: Rethinking Gender in Africa* (Oxford: James Currey)

Arthur, Maria José. 2007. 'Linguagem e Discriminação: As Mulheres Não São de Confiança', in *Memórias do Activismo pelos Direitos Humanos das Mulheres*, ed. by Maria José Arthur (Maputo: WLSA), pp. 203–05

Ashcroft, B., G. Griffiths, and H. Tiffin. (eds) 1995. *The Post-Colonial Studies Reader* (London and New York: Routledge)

—— 1998. *Key Concepts in Post-Colonial Studies* (London and New York: Routledge)

—— 2002. *The Empire Writes Back: Theory and Practice in Post-Colonial Literatures*, 2nd edn (London and New York: Routledge)

BALIBAR, ETIENNE. 1997. 'Globalisation/Civilisation Part 1 Interview: Etienne Balibar, Catherine David, Nadia Tazi, Jean-François Chevrier', in *Politics, Poetics: Documenta X — The Book*, ed. by C. David and J.-F. Chevrier (Ostfildern: Cantz-Verlag), pp. 774–85

BARRY, PETER. 2002. *Beginning Theory: An Introduction to Literary and Cultural Theory* (Manchester and New York: Manchester University Press)

BHABHA, HOMI K. (ed.). 1990. *Nation and Narration* (London: Routledge)

——1994. *The Location of Culture* (London: Routledge)

——2001. 'Disseminação: Tempo, Narrativa e as Margens da Nação Moderna', in *Floresta Encantada: Novos Caminhos da Literatura Comparada*, ed. by Helena Buescu et al. (Lisbon: Publicações Dom Quixote), pp. 533–69

BIRMINGHAM, DAVID. 2002. 'Angola', in *A History of Postcolonial Lusophone Africa*, ed. by Patrick Chabal et al. (London: Hurst & Company), pp. 137–84

——2006. *Empire in Africa: Angola and its Neighbours* (Athens: Ohio University Press)

BOURDIEU, PIERRE. 2010. *Distinction: A Social Critique of the Judgement of Taste*, trans. by Richard Nice [this edn first publ. 1984] (London and New York: Routledge)

BRITO-SEMEDO, MANUEL. 2006. *A Construção da Identidade Nacional: Análise da Imprensa Entre 1877 e 1975* (Praia: IBNL)

BRUGIONI, E. ET AL. (eds). 2010. *Áfricas Contemporâneas/Contemporary Africas* (Famalicão: Húmus)

——2012. 'Contiguidades Ambíguas: Crítica Pós-Colonial e Literaturas Africanas', in *Nação e Narrativa Pós-Colonial I: Angola e Moçambique — Ensaios*, ed. by A. M. Leite et al. (Lisbon: Colibri), pp. 379–92

CABRAL, AMÍLCAR. 2011. 'Libertação Nacional e Cultura', in *Malhas que os Impérios Tecem: Textos Anticoloniais, Contextos Pós-Coloniais*, ed. by Manuela Ribeiro Sanches (Lisbon: Edições 70), pp. 355–75

CALDEIRA, ISABEL. 1993. 'O Afro-Americano e o Cabo-Verdiano: Identidade Étnica e Identidade Nacional', in *Portugal: Um Retrato Singular*, ed. by Boaventura de Sousa Santos (Porto: Edições Afrontamento, Centro de Estudos Sociais), pp. 593–626

CAMERON, ELISABETH L. 1998. 'Potential and Fulfilled Woman: Initiations, Sculpture, and Masquerades in Kabompo District, Zambia', in *Chokwe!: Art and Initiation Among Chokwe and Related Peoples*, ed. by Manuel Jordán et al. (Munich; London; New York: Prestel), pp. 77–83

CAMPBELL, HORACE. 2001. *Militarism, Warfare and the Search for Peace in Angola: The Contribution of Angolan Women* (Pretoria: Africa Institute of South Africa)

CAMPOS, SANDRA. 2004. 'Corporeal Identity: Representations of Female Sexuality and the Body in the Novels of Paulina Chiziane', in *Sexual/Textual Empires: Gender and Marginality in Lusophone African Literature*, ed. by H. Owen and P. Rothwell, *Lusophone Studies*, 2 (Bristol: HIPLAS), pp. 137–54

CARDOSO, HUMBERTO. 1993. *O Partido Único em Cabo Verde: Um Assalto à Esperança* (Praia: INCV)

CARVALHO, MARISA. 2010. *A Participação da Mulher na Vida de Cabo Verde* (Ermesinde: Edições Ecopy)

CASIMIRO, ISABEL MARIA. 2005. 'Samora Machel e as Relações de Género', *Estudos Moçambicanos*, 21: 55–84

——and X. ANDRADE. 2005. 'Investigação Sobre Mulher e Género no Centro de Estudos Africanos', *Estudos Moçambicanos*, 21: 7–27

——and X. ANDRADE. 2007. 'Feminismo e Direitos Humanos das Mulheres', in *Memórias do Activismo pelos Direitos Humanos das Mulheres*, ed. by Maria José Arthur (Maputo: WLSA), pp. 223–27

CASTELO, CLÁUDIA. 1999. *O Modo Português de Estar no Mundo: O Luso-tropicalismo e a Ideologia Colonial Portuguesa (1933–1961)* (Porto: Edições Afrontamento)

——2007. *Passagens para África: O Povoamento de Angola e Moçambique com Naturais da Metrópole (1920–1974)* (Porto: Edições Afrontamento)

CAVACAS, FERNANDA. 1995. 'A Mulher nas Literaturas Africanas de Expressão Portuguesa', in *O Rosto Feminino da Expansão Portuguesa — Actas II* (Lisbon: Comissão para a Igualdade e para os Direitos das Mulheres), pp. 267–74

CHABAL, PATRICK. 1994. *Vozes Moçambicanas: Literatura e Nacionalidade* (Lisbon: Vega)

——1996. 'Introduction', in *The Post-Colonial Literature of Lusophone Africa*, ed. by Patrick Chabal et al. (London: Hurst & Company), pp. 1–28

——et al. (eds) 2002. *A History of Postcolonial Lusophone Africa* (London: Hurst & Company)

——. 2007. 'Introduction — E Pluribus Unum: Transitions in Angola', in *Angola: The Weight of History*, ed. by P. Chabal and N. Vidal (London: Hurst & Company), pp. 1–18

——. 2008. 'Imagined Modernities: Community, Nation, and State in Postcolonial Africa', in *Comunidades Imaginadas: Nação e Nacionalismos em África*, ed. by Fernando Tavares Pimenta et al. (Coimbra: Imprensa da Universidade de Coimbra)

CHATTERJEE, PARTHA. 1993. *The Nation and its Fragments: Colonial and Postcolonial Histories* (Princeton, NJ: Princeton University Press)

CHAVES, RITA. 2005. *Angola e Moçambique: Experiência Colonial e Territórios Literários* (São Paulo: Ateliê Editora)

——, and T. MACÊDO (eds). 2003. *Literaturas em Movimento: Hibridismo Cultural e Exercício Crítico* (São Paulo: Arte e Ciência Editora)

——, and T. MACÊDO (eds). 2006. *Marcas da Diferença: As Literaturas Africanas de Língua Portuguesa* (São Paulo: Alameda)

——, T. MACÊDO, and R. VECCHIA (eds). 2007. *A Kinda e a Missanga: Encontros Brasileiros com a Literatura Angolana* (São Paulo and Luanda: Editorial Nzila and Cultura Académica Editora)

CHEVRIER, JAQUES. 1989. 'Les Littératures africaines dans le champ de la recherche comparatiste', in *Précis de Littérature Comparée*, ed. by P. Brunel and Y. Chevrel (Paris: P.U.F.)

CHIZIANE, PAULINA. 1990. 'O Futebol é sempre a mesma coisa!', *Tempo*, 1033, July, p. 46

——1993. 'A Paz', *Tempo*, 1195, October, p. 34

——1994. 'Eu, Mulher...Por uma Nova Visão do Mundo', in *Eu Mulher em Moçambique* (Maputo: Comissão Nacional para a UNESCO em Moçambique e Associação dos Escritores Moçambicanos), pp. 12–18

——1999. *Ventos do Apocalipse* [first edn 1996] (Lisbon: Caminho)

——2000. *O Sétimo Juramento* (Lisbon: Caminho)

——2002. *Niketche: Uma História de Poligamia* (Lisbon: Caminho)

——2003. *Balada de Amor ao Vento* [first edn 1990] (Lisbon: Caminho)

——2008. *O Alegre Canto da Perdiz* (Lisbon: Caminho)

——2009. *As Andorinhas* (Maputo: Índico)

——, and R. PITA. 2013A. *Por Quem Vibram os Tambores do Além?* (Maputo: Índico)

——, and M. C. DA SILVA. 2013B. *Na Mão de Deus* (Maputo: Carmo Editora)

——, and M. MARTINS. 2015. *Ngoma Yethu. O Curandeiro e o Novo Testamento* (Maputo: Matiko Editora)

——2016. *The First Wife: A Tale of Polygamy*, trans. by David Brookshaw (Brooklyn, NY: Archipelago Books)

CORREIA, FÁTIMA CRISTINA. 2004. 'Marcas da Insularidade no Romance Cabo-Verdiano *A Louca de Serrano*, de Dina Salústio' (unpublished master's thesis, Faculdade de Ciências Sociais e Humanas da Universidade Nova de Lisboa)

COSTA, NORBERTO. 2012. '*Totonya* a mulher das sete vidas', in *Jornal de Angola Online* <http://jornaldeangola.sapo.ao/cultura/totonya_a_mulher_das_sete_vidas> [accessed 3 May 2017]

COUTINHO, EDUARDO F. 2001. 'Reconfigurando Identidades: Literatura Comparada em Tempos Pós-Coloniais na América Latina', in *Floresta Encantada: Novos Caminhos da Literatura Comparada*, ed. by Helena Buescu et al. (Lisbon: Dom Quixote)

CUNHA, LUÍS. 2001. *A Nação nas Malhas da sua Identidade: O Estado Novo e a Construção da Identidade Nacional* (Porto: Edições Afrontamento)

DARCH, COLIN. 2010. 'Centros de Reeducação, 1974–', *Mozambique History Net*, Dossier MZ-0318 <http://www.mozambiquehistory.net/reeducation.php> [accessed 14 July 2017]

DAVIDSON, BASIL. 1972. *In the Eye of the Storm: Angola's People* (Harmondsworth: Penguin Books)

—— 1989. *The Fortunate Isles: A Study in African Transformation* (Trenton, NJ: Africa World Press)

DUCADOS, HENDA. 2004. 'Angolan Women in the Aftermath of Conflict', *Accord*, 15, 58–61 <http://www.c-r.org/our-work/accord/angola/women-conflict.php> [accessed 21 March 2017]

DUTRA, ROBSON. 2007. '*Niketche* e os Vários Passos da Dança', in *A Mulher em África: Vozes de uma Margem Sempre Presente*, ed. by I. Mata and L. C. Padilha (Lisbon: Edições Colibri), pp. 309–15

ENLOE, CYNTHIA. 1989. 'Nationalism and Masculinity', in *Bananas, Beaches and Bases: Making Feminist Sense of International Politics* (Berkeley: University of California Press), pp. 42–64

FEIJOÓ K., J. A. S. LOPITO. 1988. *No Caminho Doloroso das Coisas: Antologia Panorâmica de Jovens Poetas Angolanos* (Luanda: UEA)

FERNANDES, GABRIEL. 2006. *Em Busca da Nação: Notas para uma Reinterpretação do Cabo Verde Crioulo* (Florianópolis; Praia: Editora da UFSC; IBNL)

FERREIRA, MANUEL. 1973. *A Aventura Crioula* (Lisbon: Plátano Editora)

—— 1997. *No Reino de Caliban: Antologia Panorâmica da Poesia Africana de Expressão Portuguesa*, 3 vols (Lisbon: Plátano Editora)

FILHO, JOÃO LOPES. 1995. *Cabo Verde: Retalhos do Quotidiano* (Lisbon: Caminho)

—— 1996. *Ilha de S. Nicolau. Cabo Verde. Formação da Sociedade e Mudança Cultural*, 2 vols (Lisbon: Editorial do Ministério da Educação)

FILIPE, GIL. 2008. 'Hasteámos a bandeira e parámos de discutir o projecto de nação — Alerta Paulina Chiziane, que convida moçambicanos para um debate afogado... pelo tempo', in *Carmo Editora* <http://carmoeditora.blogspot.de/p/paulina-chiziane-em-noticias-2.html> [accessed 26 April 2017]

FONSECA, MARIA NAZARETH. 2003. 'Campos de Guerra com Mulher ao Fundo no Romance *Ventos do Apocalipse*', *SCRIPTA*, 7: 302–13

—— 2007. 'Mulher-Poeta e Poetisas em Antologias Africanas de Língua Portuguesa: O Feminino Como Exceção', in *A Mulher em África: Vozes de uma Margem Sempre Presente*, ed. by I. Mata and L. C. Padilha (Lisbon: Edições Colibri), pp. 489–518

FOY, COLM. 1988. *Cape Verde: Politics, Economics and Society* (London and New York: Pinter)

FREYRE, GILBERTO. 1961. *The Portuguese and the Tropics: Suggestions Inspired by the Portuguese Methods of Integrating Autocthonous Peoples and Cultures Differing From the European in a New, or Luso-Tropical Complex of Civilisation*, trans. by H. M. D'O. Matthew and F. de Mello Moser (Lisbon: Executive Committee for the Commemoration of the Vth Centenary of the Death of Prince Henry the Navigator)

—— 1983. *Casa-Grande e Senzala: Formação da Família Brasileira sob Regime de Economia Patriarcal* (Lisbon: Livros do Brasil)

—— 1986. *The Masters and the Slaves: A Study in the Development of Brazilian Civilization*, trans. by Samuel Putnam (Berkeley: University of California Press)

FUNDAÇÃO AMÍLCAR CABRAL. 1998. *Que Estados, Que Nações em Construção nos Cinco?* (Praia: Fundação Amílcar Cabral)

GALLO, MAYRANT. 2009. 'Guerreira das Letras Africanas: Entrevista com a Escritora Isabel Ferreira', *Tabuleiro de Letras*, 2.1 <http://www.tabuleirodeletras.uneb.br/secun/numero_02/pdf/entrevista_isabel_ferreira.pdf> [accessed 21 March 2017]

GANHO, ANA SOFIA. 2004. 'Sex in the Shadows of the Nation: Angola in the Voices of Lopito Feijó and Paula Tavares', in *Sexual/Textual Empires: Gender and Marginality in Lusophone African Literature*, ed. by H. Owen and P. Rothwell, Lusophone Studies, 2 (Bristol: HIPLAS), pp. 155–75

GEFFRAY, C. 1990. *La Cause des Armes au Mozambique: Anthropologie d'une Guerre Civile* (Paris: Éditions Karthala)

GEFFRAY, C., and M. PEDERSON. 1986. 'Sobre a Guerra na Província de Nampula: Elementos de Análise e Hipóteses Sobre as Determinações e Consequências Sócio-Económicas Locais', *Revista Internacional de Estudos Africanos* 4/5, pp. 303–18

GENTILI, ANNA MARIA. 1999. *O Leão e o Caçador: Uma História da África Sub-Saariana* (Maputo: Arquivo Histórico de Moçambique)

GOMES, SIMONE CAPUTO. 1995. 'Cabo Verde: Rosto e Trabalho Femininos na Evolução da Cultura e da Literatura', in *O Rosto Feminino da Expansão Portuguesa — Actas II* (Lisbon: Comissão para a Igualdade e para os Direitos das Mulheres), pp. 275–84

——2000A. 'Mulher Com Paisagem ao Fundo: *Dina Salústio Apresenta Cabo Verde*', in *África & Brasil: Letras e Laços*, ed. by M. C. Sepúlveda and M. T. Salgado (São Paulo: Atlântica Editora), pp. 113–32

——2000B. 'A Mulher Lê a Realidade: Escritura Feminina em Cabo Verde', Biblioteca Virtual CLACSO <http://bibliotecavirtual.clacso.org.ar/ar/libros/aladaa/caputo.rtf> [accessed 21 March 2017]

——2003. 'Echoes of Cape Verdean Identity: Literature and Music in the Archipelago', *Portuguese Literary & Cultural Studies*, 8: 265–85

——2007. 'O Texto Literário de Autoria Feminina Escreve e Inscreve a Mulher e(m) Cabo Verde', in *A Mulher em África: Vozes de uma Margem Sempre Presente*, ed. by I. Mata and L. C. Padilha (Lisbon: Edições Colibri), pp. 535–58

——, A. A. MANTOVANI, and E. A. PEREIRA (eds.). 2015. *Literatura Cabo Verdiana: Leituras Universitárias* (Cáceres: Ed. UNEMAT). Ebook

GORDON, MARIA DA CONCEIÇÃO LOPES. 2009. 'The (Un)Holy Trinity: Women's Protagonism in *O Testamento do Sr. Napumoceno da Silva Araújo*', *Portuguese Studies*, 25.1: 65–79

GRASSI, M., and I. ÉVORA (eds). 2007. *Género e Migrações Cabo-Verdianas* (Lisbon: ICS)

GUERREIRO, MANUELA SOUSA. 1999. 'Paulina Chiziane: a Escrita no Feminino', *Revista Moçambique — Câmara de Comércio Portugal Moçambique*, 23 <http://www.ccpm.pt/paulina.htm> [accessed 21 March 2011]

GUIBERNAU, MONSERRAT. 1996. *Nationalisms: The Nation-State and Nationalism in the Twentieth Century* (Cambridge: Polity Press)

HAMILTON, RUSSELL G. 1975. *Voices From an Empire: A History of Afro-Portuguese Literature* (Wisconsin: University of Minnesota Press)

——2000. 'Uma Reconfiguração Pós-Colonial de Realidades e Ficções: *Totonya*, o Primeiro Romance Angolano Escrito por uma Mulher', *Ellipsis*, 2: 60–70

——2003. 'A Feminist Dance of Love, Eroticism, and Life: Paulina Chiziane's Novelistic Recreation of Tradition and Language in Postcolonial Mozambique', *Portuguese Literary & Cultural Studies*, 10: 153–67

——2007. '*Niketche* — a Dança de Amor, Erotismo e Vida: Uma Recriação Novelística de Tradições e Linguagem por Paulina Chiziane', in *A Mulher em África: Vozes de uma Margem Sempre Presente*, ed. by I. Mata and L. C. Padilha (Lisbon: Edições Colibri), pp. 317–30

Herrera, Andrea O'Reilly. 2001. *Remembering Cuba: Legacy of a Diaspora* (Austin: University of Texas Press)

Huggan, Graham. 2001. *The Post-Colonial Exotic: Marketing the Margins* (London and New York: Routledge)

ICIEG. 2007. *Cabo Verde e a CEDAW: Relatório à Convenção Sobre a Eliminação de Todas as Formas de Discriminação Contra as Mulheres e Documentos Conexos* (Praia: ICIEG)

Isaacman, A., and B. Isaacman. 1983. *Mozambique: From Colonialism to Revolution, 1900–1982* (Boulder, CO: Westview Press)

Isaacman, B., and J. Stefhan. 1984. *A Mulher Moçambicana no Processo de Libertação* (Maputo: INLD)

Jordán, Manuel. 1998. 'Engaging the Ancestors: *Makishi* Masquerades and the Transmission of Knowledge Among Chokwe and Related People', in *Chokwe!: Art and Initiation Among Chokwe and Related Peoples*, ed. by Manuel Jordán et al. (Munich; London; New York: Prestel), pp. 67–75

Jorge, Sílvio Renato. 2008. 'Entre Guerras e Narrativas: Percursos da Escrita de Paulina Chiziane e Lília Momplé', in *Moçambique: Das Palavras Escritas*, ed. by M. C. Ribeiro and P. Meneses (Porto: Afrontamento), pp. 177–86

Kandjimbo, Luis. 2001. 'Para uma Breve História da Ficção Narrativa Angolana nos Últimos 50 Anos', *Revista de Filologia Românica*, 2: 161–84

Kasembe, D., and P. Chiziane (eds). 2009. *O Livro da Paz da Mulher Angolana: As Heroínas sem Nome* (Luanda: Nzila)

Khan, Sheila. 2008. 'Velhas Margens, Novos Centros: A Língua do Exílio em *Ventos do Apocalipse*, de Paulina Chiziane', *Teia Literária*, 1: 119–32

Klobucka, Anna. 2011. 'Lusotropicalism, Race, and Ethnicity', in *A Historical Companion to Postcolonial Literatures: Continental Europe and its Empires*, ed. by Prem Poddar et al. (Edinburgh: Edinburgh University Press), pp. 471–76

Laban, Michel. 1991. *Angola: Encontro com Escritores*, 2 vols (Porto: Fundação Engenheiro António de Almeida)

——1992. *Cabo Verde: Encontro com Escritores*, 2 vols (Porto: Fundação Engenheiro António de Almeida)

——1998. *Moçambique: Encontro com Escritores*, 3 vols (Porto: Fundação Engenheiro António de Almeida)

Laranjeira, Pires. 1992. *De Letra em Riste: Identidade, Autonomia e Outras Questões na Literatura de Angola, Cabo Verde, Moçambique e S. Tomé e Príncipe* (Porto: Afrontamento)

——with I. Mata and E. R. dos Santos. 1995. *Literaturas Africanas de Expressão Portuguesa* (Lisbon: Universidade Aberta)

——2007. 'O Feminino da Escrita: Espinhoso Marfim', in *A Mulher em África: Vozes de uma Margem Sempre Presente*, ed. by I. Mata and L. C. Padilha (Lisbon: Edições Colibri), pp. 527–34

——2008. 'Paulina Chiziane: Ficção Ensaística', *Jornal de Letras*, 8, 21 October, p. 25

——(ed.) 2015. *Revista de Estudos Literários — Literaturas Africanas de Língua Portuguesa*, 5

Leite, Ana Mafalda. 1996. 'Angola', in *The Post-Colonial Literature of Lusophone Africa*, ed. by Patrick Chabal et al. (London: Hurst & Company), pp. 103–64

——(ed.) 2002. *Portuguese Literary & Cultural Studies — Cape Verde: Language, Literature & Music*, 8 (University of Massachusetts–Dartmouth)

——2003a. 'Pauline Chiziane: Romance de Costumes, Histórias Morais', in *Literaturas Africanas e Formulações Pós-Coloniais* (Lisbon: Edições Colibri), pp. 75–87

——2003b. 'Em torno de Modelos no Romance Moçambicano', *Portuguese Literary & Cultural Studies — Reevaluating Mozambique*, 10 (University of Massachusetts–Dartmouth): 185–99

——2007. 'Cenografias Pós-Coloniais nas Literaturas Africanas', in *Postcolonial Theory and Lusophone Literatures*, ed. by Paulo de Medeiros (Utrecht: Portuguese Studies Center), pp. 99–107

——et al. 2012a. *Nação e Narrativa Pós-Colonial I: Angola e Moçambique — Ensaios* (Lisbon: Colibri)

——et al. 2012b. *Nação e Narrativa Pós-Colonial II: Angola e Moçambique — Entrevistas* (Lisbon: Colibri)

——et al. (eds). 2014a. *Narrating the Postcolonial Nation: Mapping Angola and Mozambique* (Oxford; New York: Peter Lang)

——et al. (eds). 2014b. *Speaking the Postcolonial Nation: Interviews with Writers from Angola and Mozambique* (Oxford: Peter Lang)

——2015. 'Perspectivas Teóricas e Críticas nas Literaturas Africanas', *Revista de Estudos Literários*, 5: 129–42

Loforte, Ana Maria. 1998. 'Género e Direitos Reprodutivos', in *Relações de Género em Moçambique: Educação, Trabalho e Saúde*, ed. by A. M. Loforte and M. J. Arthur (Maputo: Imprensa Universitária), pp. 55–63

——2007a. 'Mulher, Poder e Tradição em Moçambique', in *Memórias do Activismo pelos Direitos Humanos das Mulheres*, ed. by Maria José Arthur (Maputo: WLSA), pp. 207–12

——2007b. 'Políticas e Estratégias para a Igualdade de Género: Constrangimentos e Ambiguidades', in *Memórias do Activismo pelos Direitos Humanos das Mulheres*, ed. by Maria José Arthur (Maputo: WLSA), pp. 229–37

Lopes, Baltasar. 1956. *Cabo Verde Visto por Gilberto Freyre: Apontamentos Lidos ao Microfone de Rádio Barlavento* (Praia: INCV)

Lopes, José Vicente. 2002. *Cabo Verde: Os Bastidores da Independência* (Praia: Spleen)

Machel, Samora. 1981. *Mozambique: Sowing the Seeds of Revolution* (Harare: Zimbabwe Publ. House)

Madeira, João Paulo Carvalho e Branco. 2015. 'Nação e Identidade: A Singularidade de Cabo Verde' (unpublished PhD thesis, Instituto Superior de Ciências Sociais e Políticas da Universidade de Lisboa)

Maimona, João. 2000. 'Literatura Angolana: Situação Actual e Perspectivas', *Vértice*, 97: 39–40

Maio, Marcos Chor. 2001. 'The UNESCO Project: Social Sciences and Race Studies in Brazil in the 1950s', *Portuguese Literary & Cultural Studies*, 4/5: 51–63

Mama, Amina. 2001. 'Challenging Subjects: Gender and Power in African Contexts', *African Sociological Review*, 5.2: 63–73

Manghezi, Nadja. 1999. *O Meu Coração Está nas Mãos de um Negro: Uma História da Vida de Janet Mondlane* (Maputo: UEM and Imprensa Universitária)

Manjate, Rogério (ed.). 2000. *Colectânea Breve de Literatura Moçambicana* (Porto: GESTO)

Mariano, Gabriel. 1991. *Cultura Caboverdeana: Ensaios* (Lisbon: Veja)

Martinho, Ana Maria Mão-de-Ferro (ed.). 1994. *Contos de África Escritos Por Mulheres* (Évora: Pendor Editorial)

——1995. 'Mulheres Escritoras na África Lusófona', in *O Rosto Feminino da Expansão Portuguesa — Actas II* (Lisbon: Comissão para a Igualdade e para os Direitos das Mulheres), pp. 259–65

——1999. *A Mulher Escritora em África e na América Latina* (Évora: Editorial NUM)

——2000. 'Escritoras Africanas: Permanência, Descontinuidades, Exílios', in *Faces de Eva: Estudos Sobre a Mulher*, 3 (Lisbon: Edições Colibri / UNL), pp. 121–34

Martins, Ana Margarida. 2006a. Unpublished interview with Paulina Chiziane (Minneapolis)

——2006b. 'The Whip of Love: Decolonising the Imposition of Authority in Paulina Chiziane's *Niketche: Uma História de Poligamia*', *The Journal of Pan-African Studies*, 3.1: 69–85

——2012. *Magic Stones and Flying Snakes: Gender and the 'Postcolonial Exotic' in the Work of Paulina Chiziane and Lídia Jorge* (Oxford: Peter Lang)

MATA, INOCÊNCIA. 1995. 'As Vozes Femininas na Literatura Africana: Passado e Presente — Representações das Mulheres na Produção Literária de Mulheres', in *O Rosto Feminino da Expansão Portuguesa — Actas II* (Lisbon: Comissão para a Igualdade e para os Direitos das Mulheres), pp. 251–58

——2000. 'Paulina Chiziane: Uma Colectora de *Memórias Imaginadas*', *Metamorfoses*, 1: 135–42

——2006. *Laços de Memórias & Outros Ensaios sobre Literatura Angolana* (Luanda: União dos Escritores Angolanos)

——2007A. 'Mulheres de África no Espaço da Escrita: A Inscrição da Mulher na sua Diferença', in *A Mulher em África: Vozes de uma Margem Sempre Presente*, ed. by I. Mata and L. C. Padilha (Lisbon: Edições Colibri), pp. 421–40

——AND L. C. PADILHA (eds). 2007b. *A Mulher em África: Vozes de uma Margem Sempre Presente* (Lisbon: Edições Colibri)

MATOS, PATRÍCIA FERRAZ DE. 2006. *As Côres do Império: Representações Raciais no Império Colonial Português* (Lisbon: Imprensa de Ciências Sociais)

MATUSSE, GILBERTO. 1998. *A Construção da Imagem de Moçambicanidade em José Craveirinha, Mia Couto e Ungulani Ba Ka Khosa* (Maputo: Livraria Universitária)

MCCLINTOCK, ANNE. 1995. *Imperial Leather: Race, Gender and Sexuality in the Colonial Contest* (London; New York: Routledge)

——1997. '"No Longer in a Future Heaven": Gender, Race and Nationalism', in *Dangerous Liaisons: Gender, Nations, and Postcolonial Perspectives*, ed. by Anne McClintock et al. (London and Minneapolis: University of Minnesota Press), pp. 89–112

MEDEIROS, P. DE, and A. P. FERREIRA (eds). 1999. *Ellipsis — Special Issue on Engendering the Nation*, 1 (Journal of the American Portuguese Studies Association)

——2006A. 'Apontamentos para Conceptualizar uma Europa Pós-Colonial', in *Portugal não é um País Pequeno: Contar o 'Império' na Pós-Colonialidade*, ed. by Manuela Ribeiro Sanches (Lisbon: Cotovia), pp. 339–56

——2006B. 'Voiding the Centre: Notes Towards a Reconfiguration of Postcolonial Studies', in *Towards a Portuguese Postcolonialism*, ed. by Anthony Soares, *Lusophone Studies*, 4 (Bristol: University of Bristol), pp. 27–46

——2007. 'Turning Points: An Introduction to Postcolonial Theory and Lusophone Studies', in *Postcolonial Theory and Lusophone Literatures*, ed. by Paulo de Medeiros (Utrecht: Portuguese Studies Center), pp. 1–7

——2011. 'Shifting Borders', *Journal of Romance Studies*, 11.1: 103–16

——2012. '7 Passos (Para Pensar uma Europa Pós-Imperial)', in *Nação e Narrativa Pós-Colonial I: Angola e Moçambique — Ensaios*, ed. by A. M. Leite et al. (Lisbon: Colibri), pp. 323–38

MELO, ROSA. 2007. *Homem é Homem, Mulher é Sapo: Género e Identidade entre os Handa no Sul de Angola* (Lisbon: Edições Colibri)

MENDONÇA, F., and N. SAÚTE. 1989. *Antologia da Nova Poesia Moçambicana, 1975–1988* (Maputo: AEMO)

MENESES, MARIA PAULA. 2008. 'Mundos Locais, Mundos Globais: a Diferença da História', in *Comunicação Intercultural: Perspectivas, Dilemas e Desafios*, ed. by R. Cabecinhas and L. Cunha (Porto: Campo das Letras)

——2012. 'Nação e Narrativas Pós-Coloniais: Interrogações em Torno dos Processos Identitários em Moçambique', in *Nação e Narrativa Pós-Colonial I: Angola e Moçambique — Ensaios*, ed. by A. M. Leite et al. (Lisbon: Colibri), pp. 311–22

MESSIANT, CHRISTINE. 2001. 'The Eduardo dos Santos Foundation: or How Angola's Regime is Taking Over Civil Society', *African Affairs*, 100: 287–309

——2007. 'The Mutation of Hegemonic Domination: Multiparty Politics Without Democracy', in *Angola: The Weight of History*, ed. by P. Chabal and N. Vidal (London: Hurst & Company), pp. 93–123

MIRANDA, M. G DE, and C. L. T. SECCO (eds). 2014. *Paulina Chiziane: Vozes e Rostos Femininos de Moçambique* (Curitiba: Appris)

MONDLANE, EDUARDO. 1983. *The Struggle for Mozambique* (London: Zed Press)

MONTEIRO, EURÍDICE FURTADO. 2009. *Mulheres, Democracia e Desafios Pós-Coloniais: Uma Análise da Participação Política das Mulheres em Cabo Verde* (Praia: INCV)

MONTEIRO, FERNANDO. 1989. 'Literatura e Línguas em Cabo Verde e em África', *Tribuna*, 18, June, pp. 21–22

MOREIRA, JOSÉ. 1997. *Os Assimilados, João Albasini e as Eleições, 1900–1922* (Maputo: Arquivo Histórico de Moçambique)

MOSCA, JOÃO. 2005. *Economia de Moçambique: Século XX* (Lisbon: Instituto Piaget)

MUNSLOW, BARRY (ed.). 1985. *Samora Machel: An African Revolutionary* (London: Zed Books)

NETO, AGOSTINHO. 1985. *...Ainda o Meu Sonho (Discursos Sobre a Cultura Nacional)* (Luanda: UEA)

NEUBAUER, J., and H. GEYER-RYAN. 2000. 'Introduction — Gender, Memory, Literature', in *Gendered Memories*, ed. by J. Neubauer and H. Geyer-Ryan (Amsterdam: Editions Rodopi), pp. 5–8

NEWITT, MALYN. 1995. *A History of Mozambique* (London: Hurst & Company)

——2002. 'Mozambique', in *A History of Postcolonial Lusophone Africa*, ed. by Patrick Chabal et al. (London: Hurst & Company), pp. 185–235

——2007. 'Angola in Historical Context', in *Angola: The Weight of History*, ed. by P. Chabal and N. Vidal (London: Hurst & Company), pp. 19–92

NGOMANE, NATANIEL. 2008. 'Posfácio', in *O Alegre Canto da Perdiz*, by Paulina Chiziane (Lisbon: Caminho), pp. 339–42

NHANTUMBO, S., and M. P. MENESES. 2005. 'Inventário das Actividades com abordagem de Género em Cursos Realizados na UEM nos últimos 25 Anos', *Estudos Moçambicanos*, 21: 105–29

NOA, FRANCISCO. 1998. 'A Dimensão Escatológica da Ficção Moçambicana: Ungulani Ba Ka Khosa e Mia Couto', in *A Escrita Infinita* (Maputo: Livraria Universitária), pp. 11–19

——2002. *Império, Mito e Miopia: Moçambique como Invenção Literária* (Lisbon: Caminho)

NORDSTROM, CAROLYN. 1997. *A Different Kind of War Story* (Philadelphia: University of Pennsylvania Press)

ORGANIZATION OF ANGOLAN WOMEN. 1984. *Angolan Women Building the Future: From National Liberation to Women's Emancipation*, trans. by Marga Holness (London: Zed Books)

OSÓRIO, CONCEIÇÃO. 1998. 'Escola e Família: Diferenças e Complementaridades', in *Relações de Género em Moçambique: Educação, Trabalho e Saúde*, ed. by A. M. Loforte and M. J. Arthur (Maputo: Imprensa Universitária), pp. 65–74

——2007A. 'Mulheres, Poder e Democracia', in *Memórias do Activismo pelos Direitos Humanos das Mulheres*, ed. by Maria José Arthur (Maputo: WLSA), pp. 239–45

——2007B. 'Sociedade Matrilinear em Nampula: Estamos a Falar do Passado?', in *Memórias do Activismo pelos Direitos Humanos das Mulheres*, ed. by Maria José Arthur (Maputo: WLSA), pp. 247–53

——2007C. 'Sexualidade: Uma História Masculina', in *Memórias do Activismo pelos Direitos Humanos das Mulheres*, ed. by Maria José Arthur (Maputo: WLSA), pp. 315–25

——2007D. 'Identidades Sociais/Identidades Sexuais: Uma Análise de Género', in *Memórias do Activismo pelos Direitos Humanos das Mulheres*, ed. by Maria José Arthur (Maputo: WLSA), pp. 327–39

OWEN, HILARY. 2003. 'The Serpent's Tongue Gendering Autoethnography in Paulina Chiziane's *Balada de Amor ao Vento*', *Portuguese Literary & Cultural Studies*, 10: 169–84

——, and P. ROTHWELL (eds). 2004. *Sexual/Textual Empires: Gender and Marginality in Lusophone African Literature, Lusophone Studies*, 2 (Bristol: University of Bristol)

——2007A. 'Ironic Nations and the Women's State in Paulina Chiziane's *Niketche. Uma História de Poligamia*', in *Postcolonial Theory and Lusophone Literatures*, ed. by Paulo de Medeiros (Utrecht: Portuguese Studies Center), pp. 109–18

——2007B. *Mother Africa, Father Marx: Women's Writing of Mozambique, 1948–2002* (Lewisburg, PN: Bucknell University Press)

——2008A. 'A Língua da Serpente — A Auto-Etnografia no Feminino em *Balada de Amor ao Vento*, de Paulina Chiziane', in *Moçambique: Das Palavras Escritas*, ed. by M. C. Ribeiro and P. Meneses (Porto: Afrontamento), pp. 161–75

——2008B. 'Women's Histories', in *A Historical Companion to Postcolonial Literatures: Continental Europe and its Empires*, ed. by Prem Poddar et al. (Edinburgh: Edinburgh University Press), pp. 498–502

——2014A. 'Women on the Edge of a Nervous Empire in Paulina Chiziane and Ungulani Ba Ka Khosa', in *Narrating the Postcolonial Nation: Mapping Angola and Mozambique*, ed. by A. M. Leite et al. (Oxford; New York: Peter Lang), pp. 199–211

——, and A. M. KLOBUCKA (eds). 2014b. *Gender, Empire, and Postcolony: Luso-Afro-Brazilian Intersections* (New York: Palgrave)

PADILHA, LAURA CAVALCANTE. 2002. *Novos Pactos, Outras Ficções: Ensaios sobre Literaturas Afro-Luso-Brasileiras* (Lisbon: Novo Imbondeiro)

——2004. 'Bordejando a Margem (Escrita Feminina, Cânone Africano e Encenação de Diferenças)', *SCRIPTA*, 8: 253–66

——2005. *Entre Voz e Letra: A Ancestralidade na Literatura Angolana* (Lisbon: Novo Imbondeiro)

——, and M. C. RIBEIRO (eds). 2008. *Lendo Angola* (Porto: Afrontamento)

PAIGC. 1974. *História: A Guiné e as Ilhas de Cabo Verde* (Porto: Afrontamento)

PANGUANA, M., and J. D'OLIVEIRA. 1999. *Fazedores da Alma* (Maputo: Edição de Autor)

PASSOS, JOANA. 2003. *Micro-Universes and Situated Critical Theory: Postcolonial and Feminist Dialogues in a Comparative Study of Indo-English and Lusophone Women Writers* (Utrecht: Universiteit Utrecht)

PEIXEIRA, LUÍS MANUEL DE SOUSA. 2003. *Da Mestiçagem à Caboverdianidade: Registos de uma Sociocultura* (Lisbon: Edições Colibri)

PEREIRA, ALINE. 2005. 'Desenvolvimento de Políticas Públicas para a Inserção da Mulher Angolana no Mercado de Trabalho', *Codesria 11th General Assembly*, 1–17 <http://www.info-angola.ao/images/documentos/pdf/pereira.pdf > [accessed 21 March 2017]

PERES, PHYLLIS. 1997. *Transculturation and Resistance in Lusophone African Narrative* (Gainesville: University Press of Florida)

PITCHER, A., and S. KLOECK-JENSON. 2001. 'Homens, Mulheres, Memória e Direitos aos Recursos Naturais na Província da Zambézia', in *Estratégias das Mulheres, Proveito dos Homens: Género, Terra e Recursos Naturais em Diferentes Contextos Rurais em Moçambique*, ed. by R. Waterhouse and C. Vijfhuizen (Maputo: Imprensa Universitária), pp. 147–79

PRATT, MARY LOUISE. 1991. 'Arts of the Contact Zone', *Profession*, 91: 33–40 <http://www.jstor.org/stable/25595469 > [accessed 21 March 2017]

——1992. *Imperial Eyes: Travel Writing and Transculturation* (London; New York: Routledge)

RAINHO, P., and S. SILVA. 2007. 'A Escrita no Feminino e a Escrita Feminista em *Balada de Amor ao Vento* e *Niketche, Uma História de Poligamia*', in *A Mulher em África: Vozes de uma Margem Sempre Presente*, ed. by I. Mata and L. C. Padilha (Lisbon: Edições Colibri), pp. 519–25

RAMALHO, CHRISTINA, 'Balada de Amor ao Vento: Representações do Universo Familiar Moçambicano', in *Biblioteca Virtual CLACSO* <bibliotecavirtual.clacso.org.ar/ar/libros/aladaa/ramal.rtf> [accessed 21 March 2017]

REIS, CARLOS. 1995. *Discursos: Estudos de Língua Portuguesa e Cultura Portuguesa*, 9 (Lisbon: Universidade Aberta)

RIBEIRO, M. C., and P. MENESES (eds). 2008. *Moçambique: Das Palavras Escritas* (Porto: Afrontamento)

ROSÁRIO, LOURENÇO DO. 1996. *Singularidades: Estudos Africanos* (Lisbon: Edições Universitárias Lusófonas)

——2007. *Singularidades II* (Maputo: Texto Editores)

ROTHWELL, PHILLIP (ed.). 2003. *Reevaluating Mozambique*, Portuguese Literary & Cultural Studies, 10 (University of Massachusetts–Dartmouth)

——2004. *A Postmodern Nationalist: Truth, Orality and Gender in the Work of Mia Couto* (Lewisburg, PN: Bucknell University Press)

SAID, EDWARD. 2001A. 'Reflections on Exile', in *Reflections on Exile and Other Literary and Cultural Essays* (London: Granta Books), pp. 173–86

——2001B. 'Traveling Theory Reconsidered', in *Reflections on Exile and Other Literary and Cultural Essays* (London: Granta Books), pp. 436–52

——2003. *Reflexões Sobre o Exílio e Outros Ensaios* (São Paulo: Companhia das Letras)

——2005. 'Reconsiderando a Teoria Itinerante', in *Deslocalizar a Europa: Antropologia, Arte, Literatura e História na Pós-Colonialidade*, ed. by Manuela Ribeiro Sanches (Lisbon: Livros Cotovia), pp. 25–42

SALGADO, MARIA TERESA. 2004. 'Um Olhar em Direcção à Narrativa Contemporânea Moçambicana', *SCRIPTA*, 8: 297–308

SALÚSTIO, DINA. 1986. 'No Feminino', *Tribuna*, 22, April, p. 1; p. 8

—— 1990. 'Um Caso de Amor', *Tribuna*, 56, December, p. 21

—— 1991. 'Chuva Amor', *Pré-Textos*, October, p. 12

—— 1993. 'Cantar...ou chorar apenas', *Revue Noire*, 10.25: 25

—— 1998A. *A Louca de Serrano* (São Vicente: Spleen Edições)

—— 1998B. *A Estrelinha Tlim Tlim* (Praia and Mindelo: IC/CCP)

—— 1999A. *Mornas eram as Noites* [1st edn 1994] (Lisbon: Instituto Camões)

—— 1999B. *Violência Contra as Mulheres* (Praia: ICF)

——2003. 'Introdução: Cabo Verde, o Mar e os Selos', in *O Mar nos Selos Postais da República de Cabo Verde*, by Tiago Estrela (Praia: Instituto da Biblioteca Nacional e do Livro), pp. 9–12

——2009. *Filhas do Vento* (Praia: IBNL)

SANCHES, MANUELA RIBEIRO (ed.). 2006a. *Portugal não é um País Pequeno: Contar o 'Império' na Pós-Colonialidade* (Lisbon: Cotovia)

——2006B. 'Where is the Post-Colonial? In-Betweenness, Identity and "Lusophonia" in Trans/National Contexts', in *New Hibridities: Societies and Cultures in Transition*, ed. by A. Toro and F. Heidemann (Leipzig: Olms), pp. 115–45

——2007. 'Reading the Postcolonial: History, Anthropology, Literature and Art in a "Lusophone" Context', in *Postcolonial Theory and Lusophone Literatures*, ed. by Paulo de Medeiros (Utrecht: Portuguese Studies Center), pp. 129–47

——2011. 'Viagens da Teoria Antes do Pós-Colonial', in *Malhas que os Impérios Tecem: Textos Anticoloniais, Contextos Pós-Coloniais*, ed. by Manuela Ribeiro Sanches (Lisbon: Edições 70), pp. 9–43

——2012. 'Tráfico de Teorias: Subalternidade, Estado-Nação e Heterogeneidades', in *Nação e Narrativa Pós-Colonial I: Angola e Moçambique — Ensaios*, ed. by A. M. Leite et al. (Lisbon: Colibri), pp. 291–310

SANTILLI, MARIA APARECIDA. 1985. *Estórias Africanas: História e Antologia* (São Paulo: Editora Ática)
——2003. *Paralelas e Tangentes entre Literaturas de Língua Portuguesa* (São Paulo: Via Atlântica)
SANTOS, BOAVENTURA DE SOUSA. 2002. 'Para uma Sociologia das Ausências e uma Sociologia das Emergências', *Revista Crítica de Ciências Sociais*, 63: 237–80
——, and T. CRUZ E SILVA (eds). 2004. 'Moçambique e a Reinvenção da Emancipação Social', in *Moçambique e a Reinvenção da Emancipação Social*, ed. by B. S. Santos and T. Cruz e Silva (Maputo: Centro de Formação Jurídica e Judiciária), pp. 19–47
——, and M. P. MENESES (eds). 2009. *Epistemologias do Sul* (Coimbra: Almedina)
SANTOS, NAIOLE COHEN DOS. 2000. *Para além das Desigualdades: A Mulher em Angola* (Luanda and Harare: ADRA/ DW/ SARDC)
SANTOS, SÔNIA MARIA. 2009. 'Experiências Femininas no Quotidiano Crioulo', in *UEA Ensaios* <http://www.ueangola.com/index.php/criticas-e-ensaios/item/221-experi%C3%AAncias-femininas-no-quotidiano-crioulo.html> [accessed 25 July 2017]
SAPEGA, ELLEN W. 2002. 'Notes on the Historical Context of Claridade', *Portuguese Literary & Cultural Studies*, 8: 159–70
SARAMAGO, JOSÉ. 1998. 'Caboverdiando', *Jornal de Letras*, 731, 14 October, pp. 28–29
SARMENTO, CLARA (ed.). 2008. *Condição Feminina no Império Colonial Português* (Porto: FIPP)
SAÚTE, NELSON. 1998. *Os Habitantes da Memória: Entrevistas com Escritores Moçambicanos* (Praia: CCP)
——(ed.) 2000. *As Mãos dos Pretos* (Lisbon: Dom Quixote)
——(ed.) 2004. *Nunca Mais é Sábado: Antologia de Poesia Moçambicana* (Lisbon: D. Quixote)
SCOTT, CATHERINE V. 1995. *Gender and Development: Rethinking Modernization and Dependency Theory* (Boulder, CO, and London: Lynne Rienner)
SECCO, CARMEN LUCIA TINDÓ. 2003. *A Magia das Letras Africanas: Ensaios Escolhidos sobre as Literaturas de Angola e Moçambique e Alguns Outros Diálogos* (Rio de Janeiro: UFRJ)
SEPÚLVEDA, M. C., and M. T. SALGADO (eds). 2000. *África & Brasil: Letras em Laços* (São Paulo: Atlântica Editora)
——(eds) 2006. *África & Brasil: Letras em Laços* (São Paulo: Yendis Editora)
SERRA, CARLOS. 1997. *Combates pela Mentalidade Sociológica* (Maputo: Universidade Eduardo Mondlane)
——(ed.) 1998. *Identidade, Moçambicanidade, Moçambicanização* (Maputo: Livraria Universitária)
——(ed.) 2000. *Racismo, Etnicidade e Poder: Um Estudo em Cinco Cidades de Moçambique* (Maputo: Universidade Eduardo Mondlane)
SHARP, JOANNE P. 2009. *Geographies of Postcolonialism: Spaces of Power and Representation* (London: SAGE)
SHELDON, KATHLEEN E. 2002. *Pounders of Grain: A History of Women, Work, and Politics in Mozambique* (Portsmouth, NH: Heinemann)
SHOHAT, ELLA. 1992. 'Notes on the «Post-Colonial»', *Social Text*, 31/32: 99–113
SILVA, JOSÉ MONTEIRO DA. 1994. 'Uma Abordagem ao Fenómeno da Insularidade', *Discursos*, 10: 21–52
SILVA, ROSÁRIA DA. 1988A. 'Boas Entradas', *Jornal de Angola*, 8 January, p. 12
——. 1988B. 'Feliz Aniversário', *Jornal de Angola*, 8 February, p. 10
——. 2005. *Totonya* [1st edn 1998] (Luanda: Brigada Jovem de Literatura de Angola)
SILVA, T. V. DA (ed.). 2002. *Antologia da Ficção Cabo-Verdiana: Vol. III — Pós-Claridosos* (Praia: AEC-Editora)
SILVA, T. DA, X. ANDRADE, L. MAXIMIANO, B. LEVI, and M. J. ARTHUR. 2007. 'Porque

é que a Poligamia é Inaceitável na Lei de Família, à Luz dos Direitos Humanos', in *Memórias do Activismo pelos Direitos Humanos das Mulheres*, ed. by Maria José Arthur (Maputo: WLSA), pp. 111–15

SOUTO, A. N. DE, and T. CRUZ E SILVA (eds). 1999. *Estudos Moçambicanos*, 16 (Maputo: CEA, UM)

TAVARES, ANA PAULA. 2004. *A Cabeça de Salomé* (Lisbon: Caminho)

TAVARES, M., and A. M. MARTINS. 2008. Unpublished interview with Paulina Chiziane (Maputo)

——2008. 'Resituando as Margens e o Centro: Uma Leitura de *Mornas Eram as Noites*, de Dina Salústio', *Teia Literária*, 2: 105–20

——2009. Unpublished interview with Dina Salústio (Praia)

——2014. 'Das Margens e dos Centros: Uma Leitura d'*A Louca de Serrano* de Dina Salústio', in *O Feminino nas Literaturas Africanas em Língua Portuguesa*, ed. by Fabio Mario da Silva (Lisbon: Centro de Literaturas e Culturas Lusófonas e Europeias, Faculdade de Letras da Universidade de Lisboa), pp. 67–100

TOMÁS, ANTÓNIO. 2007. *O Fazedor de Utopias: Uma Biografia de Amílcar Cabral* (Lisbon: Tinta da China)

TRIGO, SALVATO. 1986. *Ensaios de Literatura Comparada Afro-Luso-Brasileira* (Lisbon: Vega)

——1990. 'A Importância do Comparatismo nas Literaturas de Língua Portuguesa", in *Os Estudos Literários: (entre) Ciência e Hermenêutica (Actas do I Congresso da APLC)*, 2 vols (Lisbon: Associação Portuguesa de Literatura Comparada)

TRIPP, AILI MARI. 2015. 'Angola: The Limits of Postconflict Gender Policy Reform', in *Women and Power in Post-Conflict Africa* (Cambridge: Cambridge University Press), pp. 114–42

UEA. 2015. 'Rosária da Silva', in *União de Escritores Angolanos* <http://www.ueangola.com/bio-quem/item/41-rosária-da-silva> [accessed 19 July 2017]

UNESCO. 2008. 'Chopi Timbila', in *Intangible Cultural Heritage* <https://ich.unesco.org/en/RL/chopi-timbila-00133> [accessed 25 May 2017]

URDANG, STEPHANIE. 1984. 'Women in National Liberation Movements', in *African Women South of the Sahara*, ed. by M. J. Hay and S. Stichter (London: Longman), pp. 156–69

——1989. *And Still They Dance: Women, War, and the Struggle for Change in Mozambique* (London: Earthscan)

VALE, FERNANDO. 1999. 'A Situação das Mulheres Escritoras de Livros para Crianças e Jovens nos Países de Língua Portuguesa', in *A Mulher Escritora em África e na América Latina*, ed. by Ana Maria Mão-de-Ferro Martinho (Évora: Editorial NUM), pp. 59–70

VALENTIM, JORGE. 2007. 'Do Conto ao Canto: As Mornas Cabo-Verdianas na Voz Feminina de Dina Salústio', in *A Mulher em África: Vozes de uma Margem sempre Presente*, ed. by I. Mata and L. C. Padilha (Lisbon: Edições Colibri), pp. 253–68

VEIGA, MANUEL (ed.). 1998. *Cabo Verde: Insularidade e Literatura* (Éditions Karthala: Paris)

——1989. 'Insularidade Fecunda', *Colóquio Luso-Francófono de Literatura e Ciência Humana*, 3

VICTORINO, SHIRLEI CAMPOS. 2007. 'A Geografia da Guerra em *Ventos do Apocalipse* de Paulina Chiziane', in *A Mulher em África: Vozes de uma Margem Sempre Presente*, ed. by I. Mata and L. C. Padilha (Lisbon: Edições Colibri), pp. 351–64

VIDAL, NUNO. 2007A. 'The Angolan Regime and the Move to Multiparty Politics', in *Angola: The Weight of History*, ed. by P. Chabal and N. Vidal (London: Hurst & Company), pp. 124–74

——2007B. 'Social Neglect and the Emergence of Civil Society in Angola', in *Angola: The Weight of History*, ed. by P. Chabal and N. Vidal (London: Hurst & Company), pp. 200–35

WAYLEN, GEORGINA. 1996. *Gender in Third World Politics* (Buckingham: Open University Press)

WHEELER, D., and R. PÉLISSIER. 2009. *História de Angola* (Lisbon: Tinta da China)

WIEVIORKA, MICHEL. 2000. 'A Nova Era do Racismo', in *Racismo, Etnicidade e Poder: Um Estudo em Cinco Cidades de Moçambique*, ed. by Carlos Serra (Maputo: Universidade Eduardo Mondlane), pp. 169–208

WOLFERS, M., and J. BERGEROL. 1983. *Angola in the Frontline* (London: Zed Press)

Women and Law in South Africa (WLSA) <http://www.wlsa.org.mz> [accessed 22 March 2017]

YUVAL-DAVIS, NIRA. 1997. *Gender and Nation* (London: Sage)

——, and F. ANTHIAS. 1989. 'Introduction', in *Women-Nation-State*, ed. by N. Yuval-Davis and F. Anthias (London: Macmillan), pp. 1–15

ZAWANGONI, SALVADOR ANDRÉ. 2007. *A Frelimo e a Formação do Homem Novo (1964–1974 e 1975–1982)* (Maputo: CIEDIMA)

INDEX

www.ingramcontent.com/pod-product-compliance
Lightning Source LLC
LaVergne TN
LVHW081259100826
845148LV00005B/916

* 9 7 8 1 7 8 1 8 8 5 3 4 5 *